A TIME FOR CHOOSING

A TIME FOR CHOOSING

The Rise of Modern American Conservatism

———

Jonathan M. Schoenwald

OXFORD
UNIVERSITY PRESS

2001

OXFORD
UNIVERSITY PRESS

Oxford   New York
Athens   Auckland   Bangkok   Bogotá   Buenos Aires   Cape Town
Chennai   Dar es Salaam   Delhi   Florence   Hong Kong   Istanbul   Karachi
Kolkata   Kuala Lumpur   Madrid   Melbourne   Mexico City   Mumbai   Nairobi
Paris   São Paulo   Shanghai   Singapore   Taipei   Tokyo   Toronto   Warsaw

and associated companies in
Berlin   Ibadan

Copyright © 2001 by Jonathan M. Schoenwald

Published by Oxford University Press, Inc.
198 Madison Avenue, New York, New York 10016

Oxford is a registered trademark of Oxford University Press

Library of Congress Cataloging-in-Publication Data
Schoenwald, Jonathan M., 1964-
A time for choosing : the rise of modern American conservatism
/ Jonathan M. Schoenwald.
p.   cm.
Includes bibliographical references (p.) and index.
ISBN 0-19-513473-7
1. United States—Politics and government—1945–1989.   2. Conservatism—United
States—History—20th century.   3. Radicalism—United States—History—20th century.
4. Right and left (Political science)—History—20th century.   I. Title.
E839.5 .S333   2001
320.52'0973'09045—dc21   00-047824

1 3 5 7 9 8 6 4 2

Printed in the United States of America
on acid-free paper

For my parents

ACKNOWLEDGMENTS

In the course of writing this book I incurred debts to a number of institutions and individuals, and it is my pleasure to acknowledge them here. Archivists at the Library of Congress, Yale's Sterling Library, Brown's John Hay Library, the University of Oregon's Division of Special Collections and University Archives, the Arizona Historical Foundation in Tempe, Stanford University's Department of Special Collections, the Bancroft Library at the University of California at Berkeley, the John F. Kennedy Presidential Library, and the Lyndon Baines Johnson Presidential Library all generously offered assistance and helped me make sense of literally dozens of collections of documents, many of which had never been examined. Special thanks go to the staff of the Hoover Institution Archives, without whom this book could not have been written. Their unflappable nature and indefatigable efforts at retrieving hundreds of boxes of documents helped my work proceed smoothly; in the process they helped me unearth a cast of characters who otherwise might have remained anonymous. The staffs of the history departments at Stanford and the College of Wooster helped me clear hurdles both as a graduate student and as a faculty member.

I received financial assistance from the Lyndon B. Johnson Foundation, the Mellon Foundation, and a number of sources at Stanford University, all of which made research and writing a far easier process. Edwin Meese III granted me permission to examine the Reagan Gubernatorial Papers at the Hoover Institution. William F. Buckley, Jr., gave me access to his papers at Yale. William Rusher not only opened his papers at the Library of Congress to me but also met with me on several occasions to discuss the conservative movement. The estate of Lawrence Spivak allowed me to examine the files of "Meet the Press."

When I was a graduate student at Stanford, Barton Bernstein always offered a critical eye and forced me to rethink arguments and my use of evidence. Gordon Chang, Karen Sawislak, Jack Rakove, and Albert Camarillo offered their consistent encouragement and treated me like a colleague rather than a student. Richard Roberts shared a passion for teaching and helped me find a balance among the classroom, research, and writing. My greatest thanks, however, go to my adviser, David M. Kennedy. He challenged me to think broadly and precisely and forced me to consider arguments and ideas I might have otherwise dismissed. I grew to rely on his judgment and learned that his advice would steer me down the right path. If imitation is the most sincere form of flattery, I hope that one day I will be able to advise students similarly and emulate his hard work, generosity, and dedication. I cannot thank him enough.

A number of friends deserve credit for reading drafts, giving advice, making me laugh, and offering a couch on research trips. They include Michael Alvarez, Mark Brilliant, Josh and Kristine Collins, Bud Cox, Holly Holmquist, Maura Keefe, Tamara Lave, Tony Michels, Steve Pitti, Nancy Reynolds, Michael Schoenwald, Nancy Stearns, and Sarah Stein. Jana Bruns has been an intellectual and emotional partner without peer; this book, and my life, are far better for having met her. At Oxford, Susan Ferber's keen editorial insight improved my writing and thinking, and her enthusiasm for the project never wavered.

Finally, this book is for my parents, Audrey and Richard Schoenwald. My mother's ability to ask the right questions helped me traverse difficult sections, and her constant support has been invaluable. My father taught me to think deeply, acknowledge beauty, and live an inspired life. While he did not live to see this project completed, I know he has been beside me at every critical juncture, every disappointment, and every triumph.

CONTENTS

A TIME FOR CHOOSING

INTRODUCTION

Stamping their feet and rubbing their hands to keep warm, the crowds patiently waited in line to enter the Dallas Memorial Auditorium. The night was unusually cold, with temperatures well below freezing. Yet the attendance was impressive, especially for southerners not used to the frigid air. Almost 6,000 Texans had turned up on that December evening in 1961 to hear one of America's most controversial figures. They would not leave disappointed.

As the applause erupted, Major General Edwin A. Walker strode to the middle of the stage, took his place at the podium, and turned to face his audience. Standing ramrod straight, Walker looked every part the general—except for his clothes. Coat and tie had replaced a chest full of medals accumulated since World War II. When the applause died down, Walker began to speak. Having spent thirty-four of his fifty-one years in the military, he knew how to command an audience. After some brief opening remarks—including a poetic homage to Texas and its soldiers—Walker began his sermon:

> Tonight I stand alone before you as Edwin A. Walker. I have been charged with nothing. I have been found guilty of nothing. I have been punished for nothing. . . . I welcome the opportunity to stand before you as the symbol of the capability to co-ordinate the inspired and unchallengeable power of the people with the strength of our military forces. Such unity of purpose and spirit would cause an immediate capitulation of Reds and Pinks from Dallas to Moscow to Peking.[1]

Walker's audience knew to what he referred: he had been admonished by President John F. Kennedy for indoctrinating his troops with anticommunist literature and, in response, had quit the corps he had loyally served most of his life. Nodding their heads in agreement, the members of the Dallas audience frequently interrupted Walker with applause. Television cameras relayed the speech to those who could not attend. After listening to an hour-long indictment of the Kennedy administration, liberalism, and the United Nations, the crowd erupted in a thunderous ninety-second ovation after which, invigorated, it filed out into the chilly Texas night.

In late 1961 Edwin Walker represented not just the apparent capitulation of American liberalism to the enemy but also the birth of a new kind of far-right conservatism, which the press, moderates, and liberals labeled "extremism." Extremism scared many Americans. Periodicals contained articles on such topics as "Military Control: Can It Happen Here?" and "Crackpots: How They Help Communism."[2] Walker even graced the cover of *Newsweek* with the warning, "Thunder on the Right."[3]

At the same time, however, Walker represented a dilemma for a burgeoning conservative movement. Those on the far Right demanded action and were willing to work for it. "Responsible" conservatives, however, wanted the Walker affair to disappear as quickly as possible. The threat to the Republican party was considerable, because if it became linked to Walker and others on the far Right, moderates and liberals within the party might flee to the Democrats. But conservative activists often were loyal, hard-working party members, a constituency crucial to any winning political operation. The conundrum that had developed by 1961, then, was whether a movement composed of the fraternal twins of responsible and extremist conservatism could remain intact and capture a presidential nomination. Not surprisingly, like modern American conservatism itself, extremists such as Walker were products of the postwar world.

Shortly after the end of World War II American conservatives launched a crusade to reverse the liberal political and social order prevalent since Franklin D. Roosevelt's inauguration in 1933. By the 1950s a handful of conservative intellectuals had delineated a tripartite ideology, out of which activists soon began forging the backbone of a political movement. In 1964 the Republican nominee, Barry Goldwater, was an avowed conservative who espoused ideology pioneered during the previous decade. In 1966 former actor and Democrat-turned-conservative-Republican Ronald Reagan became governor of the most populous state in the nation. And by 1968 enough Americans identified themselves as conservative to elect Richard Nixon as president.

Between 1957 and 1972 conservatives engineered their own revolution. Dissatisfied with what they perceived as a liberal Republican party, yet knowing they needed that same powerful vehicle to deliver their beliefs to the nation, conservatives built a movement from the ground up, intent on capturing the GOP. Just as liberalism comprised a wide range of ideas, organizations, and individuals, conservatism was also anything but monolithic.[4] Confronting the New Deal Coalition in the mid-1960s—at the height of its renaissance as the Great Society—the conservative coalition included individuals and organizations that espoused ideas that ranged from outright reaction to pure libertarianism. Though some observers have argued that it was not until the 1970s that conservative critiques of liberalism became "the basis of an effective political movement by creating . . . a network of publications, think tanks, and political action committees that have come to rival and often outperform their powerful liberal counterparts," conservatives clearly demonstrated otherwise.[5]

Out of the conservative ideological categories of traditionalism, libertarianism, and anticommunism, two broad branches of organized conservatism were conceived in the decade after World War II, and they challenged each other for control of what would eventually be a political and social movement. Mainstream or electoral conservatism relied on the Republican party as its vehicle in the two-party system and depended on time-tested methods for assessing, developing, and entrenching power. The GOP served as a top-down conduit of information, regulations, and strategies. Lifting postwar conservative ideology directly from its creators, these activists initially altered it only slightly to appeal to voters.

Extremist conservatives, however, borrowed more heavily and energetically from anticommunism. Hoping to end (or at least circumvent) the "eastern Establishment's" dominance of the Republican party, extremists sought to widen participation in the electoral process. The Republicans in power, they knew, would not be converted easily, since the upshot effectively meant dislodging the power structures that had for so long determined who could and could not guide America.[6]

Not all extremists were conspiracy theorists, and not all electoral conservatives believed in the power of the GOP. But each camp understood the importance of guiding conservatism in its battle against the ideology and practitioners of the New Deal Coalition. Franklin Roosevelt, through the accidents and opportunities created by the Great Depression, helped to create one of the most powerful and seemingly impregnable voting blocs in American history.[7] Though Dwight Eisenhower had broken the two-decade–long Democratic lock on the White House, neither electoral nor extremist conservatives thought him conservative. Unable to challenge the New Deal Coalition, Eisenhower perpetuated the welfare state.[8] Conservatives of both persuasions needed an alternative, although few existed prior to the early 1960s. Robert A. Taft had all the right credentials, although he had limited appeal to the middle of the party, but then he died young. Joseph McCarthy was too embroiled in controversy to mean more than he was—a lightning rod and symbol for the increasing frustrations of many conservatives across the country. Richard Nixon was almost the opposite: more politician than man, a chameleon eager to please. Not until Barry Goldwater would the two branches of the movement agree on a candidate. But then extremism reared its ugly head and forced the "responsible" or electoral conservatives to wonder what they had wrought. Still, Goldwater helped fuse the two movements into one, and his symbolic power enlivened the grassroots as well as the party proper. In effect, January 1965 marked two inaugurals: one for Lyndon Johnson's first full term as president and the other for the conservative movement, recently defeated but pulsing with vitality.

Political movements are not easily defined. At a minimum they must possess a group consciousness, with members identifying with each other and with common political aims.[9] Typically, members categorize themselves in a specific social stratum, preferring their own group and disdaining outsiders. Dissatisfaction with the group's status, power, or material resources is frequently blamed on either specific individuals or the inequities of the social or political system.[10] Taken together these components signify the birth of a movement, or that moment when participants refuse to continue accepting their lot and begin working together to correct perceived wrongs. Given the relatively weak political position of conservatives between 1932 and 1960, it is not surprising that many self-professed conservatives in the late 1950s and 1960s acquired some or all of these belief components.

Political movements, however, are continually evolving. Democratically based movements, or movement cultures, often pass through four stages. First an independent institution is created in the form of a political party, organization, or other group to provide a context for new, oppositional interpretations. Next members formulate a tactical approach to recruit adherents. The institution then generates new explanations, which previously had held no legitimate place in society. Finally the group's ideas, now solidly in place, are made public with the aim of expanding the movement beyond its initial constituents.[11] The self-respect and confidence gained by members of a political movement—the ability to believe in themselves and their cause—is crucial, since they realize that their world can, in fact, change. Of course such a concept might be seen as inherently contradictory in describing conservatives. But when considering the political circumstances in America since the mid-1930s, conservatives could imagine themselves to be as beleaguered as any ideological minority in the twentieth century.

The conservative movement attained each stage of the sequence, and its participants gained confidence in their ability to alter the American landscape. The conservative movement, however, was also different from other democratic movements in that it relied on elites to provide an intellectual backbone and an organizational structure. Yet despite its top-down framework, the movement was supple enough so that the rank and file could enter and influence the nature and direction of the undertaking. Moreover the groundswell relied as much on impulse as official membership in any sanctioned organization. In other words since people believed they belonged to a movement, they did, thus adding to its political and social power. Much like a self-fulfilling prophecy, this increased momentum not only convinced activists they were succeeding but also helped draw in hesitant participants.

This book argues that in the 1950s conservatives initially created two distinct but overlapping movement cultures.[12] One advocated the development of party and electoral solutions to the problem of liberalism, while the other looked to private organizations to initiate the changes its members thought necessary to reform America. The latter, furthermore, relied heavily on the work of extremists, who believed it imperative to use not only electoral politics but also methods that invited confrontation with the "enemy." This split in conservatism deepened in the early 1960s and reached its nadir in 1964 at the Republican National Convention, when Barry Goldwater threw down the gauntlet and challenged moderate Republicans to confront his wing of the party.

The division gave rise to two sets of strategies, tactics, and personalities. Still the divide was permeable, with cross-fertilization giving rise to new strategic and tactical strains. More important, in the wake of Goldwater's defeat, the Republican party reaped an unexpected dividend—the perception of ideological objectivity. As extremism was pushed out of the conservative equation, moderate Republicans who had backed Lyndon Johnson began to reassess their old party. Since extremism had been so intimately connected with conservatism, the *absence* of extremism meant that conservatism gained newfound legitimacy. In other words the lack of extremist influences signified that the GOP's stances were not tainted, so their policies were not only more "purely" conservative, they were also perceived as more balanced, responsible, and acceptable to larger numbers of voters.

Although the Republicans lost the election in 1964 in large part due to extremism, they learned to deal with the fringe elements that threatened their party far earlier and more effectively than did the Democrats. Republicans marginalized extremists in favor of the solid middle of the party, while simultaneously calculating how to retain extremists' loyalty. In this way the GOP learned how to act like a broker state or the informal regulatory system adopted during Franklin Roosevelt's administrations when competing interests fought for attention, favor, and the chance to influence the federal government. The GOP forced extremists to take their place alongside other conservative interest groups, which were also fighting for resources and supporters in their attempts to influence the party. Unable to continue circumventing the process obeyed by all other conservative bands, extremists found themselves unable to slip the noose—tied and adjusted by their conservative comrades—which slowly began to tighten. The best option left to the extremists, then, was acting like the other organizations that had contributed to the ideological solidification of the single movement. Extremists hoped that they would retain a proportional share of the influence (for example, if there were ten adjunct groups, extremists would wield one-tenth of the power), although party leaders felt differently.

The factionalism and internecine warfare among conservatives gave little indication that a robust and relatively united movement would emerge by the end of the 1960s. The individuals who shaped the contours of the rise of conservatism were a mixed lot; some were well known, while others labored in obscurity. How these people and the events they created and to which they reacted shaped the emergence of a vital conservative political force is the story of this book.

The history of this transformation has only been told in decidedly limited ways and has relied heavily on electoral politics and the most public of actors. Such approaches do a disservice not only to the events, ideas, and individuals of the time but also to the determination of the consequences of the era. The perennial underdog in national politics, prior to 1960 American conservatism had been an ideology accorded little respect by intellectuals. By 1968 everything was different. No longer did liberals set the agenda and force conservatives to react. Conservative ideology fused with political action and created opportunities for dissatisfied Americans to express their disgust. Although conservative ideology was not created during the 1960s, its political components were, and the conservatism of the 1970s, 1980s, and 1990s is its direct descendant. To understand this period in the American political arena, it is crucial that the processes that created the progenitor and its offspring be unraveled.

As conservative theorist Richard Weaver notes, "ideas have consequences," a bon mot that rings especially true when charting the course of the modern American conservative movement. In the first decade after World War II, such intellectuals as Russell Kirk, Friedrich A. Hayek, William F. Buckley, Jr., and Whittaker Chambers weighed in with important works that outlined the three powerful strands of conservatism: traditionalism, libertarianism, and anticommunism. These general categories remained flexible, and their lack of definition permitted widespread contradictions. By the early 1950s the three strands, anchored by anticommunism, began to be absorbed by a self-selected population. A number of speakers and writers on lecture circuits started contacting Americans who already held conservative beliefs and began to convey what the "new" conservatism looked like. In perhaps the boldest challenge during the first half of the 1950s, foreign-policy specialist James Burnham attacked the theory of containment and proposed a more aggressive strategy to win the Cold War, which set off debates in the Pentagon and raised questions about national security. As the second half of the decade began, conservative ideology, while still limited in its exposure to the general population, had made a strong showing around the country.

In the second half of the decade a series of events helped catalyze the conservative enterprise in America. Three Supreme Court decisions handed down on the same day in 1957 elicited howls of protest about the dangers of communist infiltration in the United States. Soviet Premier Nikita Khrushchev's visit in 1959 prompted some Americans to wonder if Eisenhower was simply capitulating to the enemy. FBI Director J. Edgar Hoover's book *Masters of Deceit* detailed a communist plot to overthrow the country from within. As part of Eisenhower's attempt to thaw relations between the two superpowers, the United States displayed art in the American National Exhibition in Moscow in 1959. When the House Un-American Activities Committee (HUAC) suspected that some of the artists had communist ties, the show became a conservative cause célèbre. Finally as HUAC continued its investigations into education, entertainment, and other areas of American life, in 1960 liberals challenged the committee's very existence. After HUAC hearings in San Francisco disintegrated into a melee, conservatives in Congress and elsewhere produced a film that defended the committee, which renewed concerns over whether the country, now led by John F. Kennedy, would end up in the hands of the enemy. As the 1950s ended, conservatives saw the need for political solutions to social and cultural problems. Some thought that independent organizations would offer the best answers, while others believed that the two-party system had to be hijacked and the GOP used to engineer a political revolution. Activists, however, tapped the reserves of conservative discontent first and gave birth to a number of independent factions.

To create groups populated by non-intellectuals, conservative ideology had to move from unproved theory to social and political action, where average Americans could be exposed to and understand what conservatism meant. Recently inspired Americans searched for places to manifest their newfound excitement. Filling the vacuum in the early 1960s were a number of extremist organizations, heretofore ignored or belittled by most chroniclers of the era. Led by Robert H. W. Welch, Jr.'s John Birch Society (JBS), far rightists turned to conspiracy theories to explain how the nation was aiding its own demise. Welch created a national organization to sell his particular brand of conservatism and in the process attracted almost 100,000 members and the attention of the Kennedy administration and the Republican party. Typically dismissed as a collection of "kooks," the JBS performed much like a third party: it forced the GOP, the Democrats, and conservatives of all types to respond to its agenda. Moreover the complex organizational hierarchy helped create a new kind of conservative activism. In neighborhoods and towns scattered across the country, small groups of Americans comprised the beginnings of what became a national protest movement, challenging the status quo and refusing to compromise. The JBS helped develop a conservative movement culture, or those components critical to a political movement or campaign that might not be expressly political. Rallies, letter drives, social events, and a variety of local projects all helped Birchers hone their skills, spread the word of conservatism, and become more deeply invested in American politics. For some members the society was an end unto itself, while for others it was a starting point, an introduction that led to much more.

As the number of Americans who turned to organizations such as the JBS swelled, episodes like the 1961 case of General Edwin A. Walker justified fears of anticommunism and conservatism gone amok. After being relieved of his army command in West Germany for indoctrinating his troops with anticommunist literature, Walker became an instant conservative symbol. Taking a stand on his actions could be interpreted as supporting the radical Right or acquiescing to the liberal establishment. Trying to rally around the general without alienating more moderate or liberal Republicans, conservatives appeared to support Walker wholeheartedly. In fact public solidarity masked private discontent among conservatives and camouflaged divisions within the movement. Moreover the Republican party's reluctance to criticize Walker or to purge extremists came back to haunt it three years later when leaders refused to oust extremists in the belief that the "big tent" could stand the strain. A window onto the conservative movement just before Barry Goldwater took the country by storm, the Walker incident illustrated the Right's essential dilemma: should conservatives of all stripes stick together, or should extremists who could alienate the center of the GOP be purged in order to win political power?

As action took precedence over ideology, a grassroots constituency emerged, which backed local and national candidates, created new circles in which to socialize, and developed a cultural component necessary to sustain the political apparatus. At the same time, however, extremists forced the responsible Right to react. Non-extremists faced a press and federal government made hostile by their brethren, but they also understood that to kowtow to the liberals meant, in effect, joining them. Events based on both liberal and conservative circumstances helped solidify conservatism's grip on a growing number of Americans, and in late 1961 a small number of political operatives realized that their chance to capture the GOP and perhaps the White House had arrived.

A full three years before the 1964 election, a group of well-placed conservative Republicans decided that they would nominate a "true" conservative and if that meant sacrificing the election in order to gain the party, so be it. Barry Goldwater, a senator from Arizona with rock-solid libertarian, anticommunist, and traditionalist credentials, became the rallying point for the nascent conservative movement. Grassroots efforts, including a number of extremist factions, sprang up to support the senator. Deciding that the party should suffer the kooks, Republican leaders decided not to purge those supporters on the far Right and hoped that the moderates and liberals would tolerate the newcomers in order to gain the White House. A combination of a badly run campaign, too much faith in ideology as a political product, and a candidate who eschewed pressing the flesh created a referendum on Goldwater, which helped Lyndon Johnson win an apparent mandate and truly inaugurated the Great Society.

Conservatives, however, did achieve a number of crucial goals with this campaign. They seized the party and legitimized the movement. Thousands of Americans were introduced to campaigning and politics, a commitment many sustained after 1964, and a vibrant political culture emerged. Conservatives pioneered new fundraising techniques, which solicited small contributions from millions of Americans, mirroring the shift from a GOP dominated by easterners to one that was beginning to penetrate the South and the Sunbelt. The Goldwaterites lost, but lessons were learned from the experience. Moderates and liberals could not be ignored were the party to form a powerful enough coalition to win. Something would have to be done about the radical Right. Ideology could only take a campaign so far. In short while the GOP had been pried open to include millions of new conservatives, it still needed charismatic salespeople to spread the gospel. Drafting Barry Goldwater was not, as it turned out, a conservative panacea. It did, however, expose problems the movement had to confront, namely what to do with extremists; how to recruit, coordinate, and satisfy volunteers; and how to sell an ideology to enough Americans to win a national contest.

It did not take long for conservatives to regroup from their devastating loss. Nationally publicized elections in New York City and California taught them how to manage campaigns that would attract moderate and liberal Republicans or conservative Democrats, without ostracizing the hardcore of the movement. Soon a test case presented itself to the conservative wing of the GOP: William F. Buckley, Jr.'s candidacy for the mayor of New York City in 1965. Conceived as a defensive maneuver to prevent liberal Republican John V. Lindsay from defiling the GOP, Buckley ran as much to test other Republicans as to apply the lessons of 1964. Like Goldwater, Buckley knew he had little chance of winning. Yet he never wavered from his stringent conservative stances, bringing a number of issues, such as race, education, employment, and the role of the government, to light for millions. Buckley was also the first conservative to take a solid stand against extremist support, which created a template other candidates would use in the future. Hoping to prove the vitality of conservative Republicanism, Buckley ran one of the most fascinating campaigns of the 1960s. Moreover he confirmed what 1964 had shown: that conservatives still had work to do, that the big tent was not yet erected, and that ideology had its political limits. But he also told Americans, millions of whom followed the campaign, that conservatism was not an overnight political tactic but a philosophy, which had developed over years and was unlikely to disappear because of one or two defeats. The conservative revival had begun.

The Goldwater debacle had served to open the party up to political novices, particularly in the South and West, allowing newly-made activist Americans to play a part in the democratic process. It was in California, with Ronald Reagan's 1966 gubernatorial campaign, that the tide turned for electoral conservatism in the post-Goldwater era. Here party and movement first merged smoothly; extremism was dealt with effectively (so effectively, in fact, that responsible conservatives accelerated its rapid demise); and factionalism was overcome. Reagan's candidacy was not without its difficulties: his acting career, lack of government service, connection to various extremists, and a seemingly superficial understanding of the issues could have left the California GOP hamstrung. Instead Reagan and his handlers mounted a brilliant campaign, defeating incumbent Edmund G. "Pat" Brown and confirming the state as a leader of political trends. Reagan's "Eleventh Commandment," which forbade one Republican to speak ill of another, papered over private and public differences. Moreover Reagan's agenda shored up those factions that suddenly found themselves co-opted by a reinvigorated party and helped them carry conservatism into the next decade. With Reagan's landslide victory, conservatism was reborn stronger than in 1964 and determined to emerge victorious before the end of the decade, a goal achieved a mere two years later.

By the late 1960s conservatives, still in control of the GOP, had managed to consolidate their efforts behind Richard Nixon, a man few conservatives fully trusted, although most realized he was their best hope to capture the White House. A number of citizen groups—vestiges of the Goldwater campaign—maintained the momentum from one decade to the next and solidified the bond between party and movement. Four of these splinter groups in particular helped to carry the conservative agenda into the next decade. Americans for Constitutional Action, the Free Society Association, the American Conservative Union, and Young Americans for Freedom all worked to refine an ideological and programmatic agenda, raise money for candidates, and mount issue-based campaigns. Far more sophisticated than their forebears from the Goldwater campaign, these groups also provided an outlet for dispossessed extremists. Facing internal and external hostility, the John Birch Society and other far-right organizations shrank. The four main splinters, however, redirected some of that extremist energy into more constructive applications and, in the case of Young Americans for Freedom, even trained a new generation of conservative activists.

By 1980 the revolution was complete. With a true conservative as the party's nominee, conservative Republicans and Democrats threw their support behind Ronald Reagan without hesitation. Whether or not they knew that his policies had their roots in 1940s and 1950s ideology, they understood that they liked the man as much or more than what he represented.

Innumerable social and political movements were born—and died—in the 1960s. How many of those achieved their goals or even survived past infancy is debatable. It is only recently that some of the light shone upon the decade is striking actors on the Right. And yet, perhaps more than any other postwar political crusade, modern American conservatism, which experienced its formative years during the sixties, represents a successful pursuit of an ideological and programmatic agenda. Though the ideology proved to have its limitations, the enterprise never ventured far from belief systems rooted in a response to postwar society. Traditionalism, libertarianism, and anticommunism all offered something for those inclined to believe that the country needed to change, that the programs wrought by the New Deal hurt rather than helped. With a movement culture and a political culture supporting electoral efforts, such endeavors helped to attract millions of formerly politically apathetic Americans.

But if a conservative birth was inevitable, its growth into maturity and eventual triumph were not. Liberal failures alone did not ensure conservative success; conservatives themselves did and only after many failures of their own. Hazily defined and with too few activists in the 1950s, conservatism, which was never fully united, nonetheless split; its two main factions developed their own agendas, heroes, and villains. Joined behind Barry Goldwater, electoral and extremist conservatives tolerated each other as they hoped that the senator from Arizona would be the balm to heal their wounds. The party succumbed, but not the White House. In the election's aftermath the division between extremist and electoral conservatives helped chart the movement's direction, often forcing it to tack an indirect path to its final destination. Reevaluating what it would take to win the White House, mainstream conservatives realized that only with a cleansed party did they stand a chance. At the 1960 Republican National Convention, Goldwater had told his fellow conservatives to "grow up."[13] This is the story of how the movement did just that.

THE BIRTH OF

POSTWAR CONSERVATISM

In 1950 the literary and cultural critic Lionel Trilling said out loud what many American intellectuals silently believed about their country's political and social heritage: liberalism prevailed so completely that conservatism might be seen forever as illegitimate. "In the United States at this time liberalism is not only the dominant but even the sole intellectual tradition. For it is the plain fact that nowadays there are no conservative or reactionary ideas in general circulation."[1] After guiding America through almost two decades of difficult times, liberal leadership had proved, Trilling believed, that not only was the country better off politically but that society—particularly the culture—had progressed, which demonstrated the superiority of such a system. Moreover whatever conservative notions did exist were not worthy of discussion. They were "impulses" rather than "ideas": "the conservative impulse and the reactionary impulse do not, with some isolated and ecclesiastical exceptions, express themselves in ideas but only in actions or in irritable mental gestures which seem to resemble ideas."

During the first half of the 1950s a host of observers, including historians Louis Hartz and Richard Hofstadter; sociologists Daniel Bell, Seymour Martin Lipset, Nathan Glazer, and David Riesman; and popular commentators writing in such journals as the *Nation*, the *New Republic*, and the *Atlantic*, seconded Trilling's opinion. Even with Senator Joseph McCarthy's notorious Wheeling, West Virginia, speech on February 8, 1950, which opened an era that outlived its namesake, conservatism appeared destined to remain little more than a whining voice in the wilderness. McCarthyism seemed merely to add to liberal critiques of conservatism; the witch hunters were conservatives in their death throes, blindly lashing out in feeble attempts to hold onto some semblance of power. Moreover even though such respectable conservatives as Senator Robert A. Taft had stridently opposed communism before McCarthy's mudslinging began, the association with the junior senator from Wisconsin made the job of anticommunist liberals even easier.[2] All that remained, said Trilling and the others, were the last rites.

In 1955 a volume edited by Daniel Bell neatly summed up how many academics felt about the vestigial residues of postwar conservatism. In *The New American Right*, Bell and his colleagues assembled what they believed was a careful and multidisciplinary critique of what Trilling had called conservative "impulses." Not so immediately dismissive as Trilling, the authors acknowledged that some Americans *believed* in conservatism and took issue with the ideology's core beliefs. In perhaps the most famous essay of the seven, historian Richard Hofstadter examined the growing discontent with liberalism and the legacies of the New Deal and pronounced the reaction "pseudo-conservatism."[3] Besides delivering the ultimate insult to such conservative theorists as Russell Kirk and William F. Buckley, Jr., Hofstadter sought to fortify what Trilling and others felt: that pseudoconservatives perceived themselves as victims of a changing world.[4] Hofstadter acknowledged that there was good reason to fear international communism. Both Republicans and Democrats, in fact, denounced the American Communist party.[5] But why, he asked, would some Americans blame their own government for the growth of communism? The answer lay in "the rootlessness and heterogeneity of American life, and above all, . . . its peculiar scramble for status and its peculiar search for secure identity."[6] In times of prosperity, Hofstadter said, "status politics" dominated the public's attitudes toward politics. Discontent was voiced more often in "vindictiveness, in sour memories, in the search for scapegoats, than in realistic proposals for positive action."[7] Two groups were most susceptible to experiencing status anxiety: the old Yankee Protestant Americans, who felt crowded by the nouveau riche, and the recent immigrants, who had something to prove about their loyalty to their newly adopted country. To relieve their anxiety, these groups practiced a kind of "hyper-patriotism" and "hyperconformity," values that Hofstadter also saw in prejudiced Americans. Focusing their hatred on the Dean Achesons, Alger Hisses, and Franklin Roosevelts of the country, the pseudoconservatives attempted to boost their status and ensure order between classes, which they hoped would guarantee their own place in the nation's hierarchy.

According to Hofstadter pseudoconservatism had not appeared until the 1950s for four reasons. First the disappearance of the "automatic built-in status elevator" meant that one's child might not be the next Horatio Alger. In the uncertainty of the postwar world, the expectation that a child would surpass his or her parents in level of education, type of employment, and material comfort was disappearing rapidly. (It is unclear, however, how Hofstadter reached the conclusion that social mobility was decreasing during an era of nearly unparalleled economic growth.) Second mass communication enabled average Americans to participate in politics in ways previously unthinkable, injecting their "private emotions and personal problems" into the mix. Third the long reign of liberalism gave rise to the increased frustration of those who felt disenfranchised by increased government activism and promoted more open combat between businessmen and supporters of the New Deal. Finally pseudoconservatives were frustrated by the continued but confusing war footing on which the country had remained after World War II. Instead of returning to a time when individuals could focus on themselves and their families, Americans were forced—by their own government, many thought—to remain prepared for an unknown future. Although Hofstadter trusted that pseudoconservatism would not spread, Bell and the others feared that conservatives and pseudoconservatives were in desperate straits, and desperate people do desperate things.

To a degree the liberals—both academic and otherwise—were correct. Conservatives had not climbed out of the hole they had dug during the New Deal and in their isolationism prior to World War II. After fifteen years of government intervention in the economy, business was booming, and the United States was the world leader in manufacturing and consumption. After Roosevelt's charismatic leadership and Harry Truman's surprisingly inspired guidance, America, while not preventing Eastern Europe or China from falling into communist hands, had set the tone in world diplomacy. Most important, after a decade of economic uncertainty and the costliest foreign war in American history, most citizens were ready to return to predictable, stable lives in which government helped them when they needed it but otherwise remained invisible. Yet even in the wild success of the American war experience and its aftermath, there were rumblings of discontent that, shielded by their hubris, liberals either failed to hear or to take seriously. Moreover liberals' willingness to dismiss conservatism as a psychological phenomenon instead of recognizing it as a young but legitimate political and social ideology did the Left a disservice in the decades to come. They failed to anticipate the drastic changes that were to take place in the coming years.

Two years after Trilling's eulogy for what he claimed was a stillborn political philosophy, one of the men responsible for helping inspire a new liberal generation during the New Deal spoke to a group of Republican precinct workers in Cleveland. Raymond Moley, a professor at Columbia and one of the brain trusters brought to Washington by FDR to combat the depression, had had a change of faith and had become a Republican. By the late 1940s he had a reputation as an astute political and social analyst, penned a column for *Newsweek*, and frequently spoke to conservatives across the country. Trying to rally the troops for the 1952 election, Moley hammered home the idea that Republicans had lost since 1932 for one simple reason: they were outnumbered. In 1948, said Moley, 42 million eligible voters failed to go to the polls. These were the people who could help swing the country from the Left to the Right. He named the people for whom precinct workers should keep an eye out:

> They are the people who have some property, who have some savings of their own, insurance policies, government bonds, and bank accounts. They are the people who are struggling to get on in the world, to educate their children and to live decent, respectable lives.[8]

Although Moley's Americans sounded suspiciously similar to the cast of a Frank Capra movie, he urged his audience not to view these people as a class or group but instead as a limitless constituency that, as the years passed, would welcome new members with each liberal misstep and new communist advance.

Over the next two decades the people Moley described—the targets of those Republican canvassers—would be responsible for creating and staffing the conservative movement in America. Yet prior to 1955 most conservative intellectuals concerned themselves with defining different types of conservatism and, if possible, offering prescriptions for changing the country to conform more closely to their visions. As one historian of the intellectual movement described it, "There is probably no better proof of the isolation of the conservative intellectual movement from American politics in the 1950s than its estrangement from the immensely popular President Eisenhower."[9] Operating in a vacuum that effectively shut out popular opinion, conservative intellectuals debated issues that Moley's audience (and its target constituents) considered esoteric. Yet they *did* transmit the issues to the populace, albeit slowly at first. The challenge to the liberal status quo, which came from both the intellectuals and the novice activists, help set the stage for a conservative revolution during the next two decades.

Between 1948 and 1955 conservatives formulated working definitions of their belief system, while simultaneously the nascent ideology invited participation by Americans searching for ways to halt what they perceived as increasingly dangerous trends: an overly strong central government, restricted individual rights, and a weakened presence abroad. While little progress was made that resulted in conservatives being elected or organizations being formed, during these seven years they confronted necessary dilemmas, including defining a common language, figuring out how to ford the ideological moats that isolated conservative camps, and deciding how to take the first tentative steps toward becoming an activist movement. The tenets intellectuals provided helped adherents identify each other more readily whereas before, when asked how to identify a fellow conservative, practitioners were often left wondering exactly what made a person "belong."[10] Yet even with tangible gains in a variety of arenas, including the Republican capture of the White House, conservatives in 1955 remained amateurs compared to liberals. For activists to emerge, rally, and recruit, they would need a coherent belief system around which to organize. Intent on formulating an assertive rather than reactionary ideology, conservative theorists searched for ways to integrate philosophical truisms with politically viable axioms. Intellectuals and practitioners who set their minds to the task, however, faced a formidable challenge. It would not be until the appearance of a handful of thinkers and provocateurs in the 1950s that conservatism began to take a discernible shape.

Russell Kirk and Postwar Conservatism

Conservatism after the war eventually meant something completely different than it had before 1945. Not the least difference was its lack of organization. Before and shortly after the war, such individuals as John T. Flynn and Albert Jay Nock wrote volumes of eloquent attacks on the government and its growing power, and politicians like Gerald Nye, Robert Taft, and John Bricker had substantial followings. But these individuals remained lone operators, and they rarely attempted to cross boundaries or form coalitions. What was missing was a definable ideology or, as one writer explained it, "the descriptive vocabulary of day-to-day existence, through which people make rough sense of the social reality that they live and create from day to day."[11] Perhaps some of the aforementioned individuals could have described the vocabulary that they themselves used. But beyond this small coterie, most Americans were not familiar with a conservative lingua franca, and in the mid-1950s few Americans were investing themselves in determining what constituted conservatism.

One of the reasons that conservatism gained traction only hesitantly at first was the postwar variant's lack of a single definition. Conservatism is based on a set of core beliefs, most frequently identified with the writings of Edmund Burke. Here, human nature is "unchanging and unalterable," and there is "an objective moral order, independent of man's knowledge or perception of it."[12] These core ideas often manifest themselves in everyday life in a number of ways. For example, although freedom is an inalienable right, the same forces that demand one's freedom also require that authority be exercised to regulate society so that an individual can, in fact, be free. Moreover since humans are essentially unchanging, the government—or any institution—oversteps its bounds by attempting such social engineering as welfare. Thus tradition—whether of limited government, responsibility for one's self and one's community, or a strong defense—is essential for a civil society. And yet, since humans are fallible, these traditions must be subject to change. One of the best attempts at distilling these core ideas into a single definition came in 1962 from M. Stanton Evans, who wrote, "The conservative believes ours is a God-centered, and therefore an ordered, universe; that man's purpose is to shape his life to the patterns of order proceeding from the Divine center of life; and that, in seeking this objective, man is hampered by a fallible intellect and vagrant will."[13] Still, since such an explication allows for a wide range of interpretation in practical terms, a great deal of ideological diversity (within limits) has appeared in the conservative community.

Conservatism's lack of a single definition was in part responsible for the rampant factionalism that brought it to its political nadir in the first half of the 1960s. At the same time that flexibility also allowed political operatives to capitalize on a growing constituency that, if handled correctly, could provide enormous electoral dividends. Most immediately, however, the failure to agree on a single, universal definition resulted in the advent of several distinct though sometimes converging streams of conservatism.

Three main groups of conservatives eventually appeared from the intersection of postwar events and ideas: traditionalists, libertarians, and anticommunists. Traditionalism and libertarianism focused on preventing the state from meddling in an individual's affairs, while simultaneously they promoted a belief system that adhered to a universal moral code. American anticommunism, sanctioned by the federal government, emerged as a belief system at the end of World War II and the beginning of the Cold War. Adopted by conservatives as a bulwark against America's newest enemy, anticommunism also bridged conservatism of the prewar and postwar eras. Since communism represented the antithesis of Burkean conservatism, anticommunism served not only to defend America and the West against its encroachment but also to promote conservative values at home. Although in the first few years after the war political leaders often focused only on containing communism abroad, conservative theorists quickly found anticommunism could help them promote traditionalism and libertarianism at home. American postwar conservatism, then, adapted prewar ideas to peculiar domestic circumstances and created a new ideology that nevertheless contained readily identifiable roots. This did not mean, however, that such foundations translated easily to the world of practical politics.

Beginning in the early 1950s and lasting for about a decade conservative intellectuals debated, often raucously, the interwoven problems of defining what made a person conservative and, if such a definition could be created, how the general population could eventually assimilate those beliefs, thus generating an ideology. Of the major conservative intellectuals in the immediate postwar era, Russell Kirk weighed in most dramatically as he defined the parameters of the debate and forever placed the conservative movement in a more easily recognizable context.[14] Born in 1918 in Michigan, Kirk left his working-class background behind (his father was a railroad engineer) in favor of studying the theories of Edmund Burke and others.[15] After a stint in the army during the war, Kirk received a doctorate at St. Andrews University in Scotland, where he honed his ideas about civilization and the roles of the individual and government in society. An open admirer of agrarianism, elites, and nonprogressive methods of education, Kirk swam against the tide of political philosophy in the late 1940s and early 1950s. In 1953 he published his groundbreaking work, *The Conservative Mind*, soon cited by all major American conservative thinkers as one of the most influential books in their lives.

In *The Conservative Mind*, Kirk outlined six truisms that guided conservative philosophy. The first, that a "divine intent rules society as well as conscience" and that "political problems, at bottom, are religious and moral problems," explained what would repeatedly confuse many liberals: although conservatives believed in the sanctity of the Constitution, total separation of church and state would always be impossible.[16] To acknowledge that God affected politics meant that politicians should consider "divine intent" when making decisions and that morality, while difficult to legislate, was present in legislation nonetheless. Second Kirk declared that conservatives had an "affection for the proliferating variety and mystery of traditional life, as distinguished from the narrowing uniformity and equalitarianism and utilitarian aims of most radical systems." Here Kirk railed against totalitarianism in any guise and declared that life was not lived best when, as later conservatives would call it, engineered. But although Kirk declared that humans should respect the "variety and mystery of traditional life," conservatives in the 1950s and after decided that "traditional" would supersede either "variety" or "mystery" when determining what lifestyles were acceptable. Third, said Kirk, "civilized society requires orders and classes," and further "society longs for leadership." Here Kirk began to get at one of the most vexing dilemmas for conservatives: the apparent contradiction between freedom and order. How society can achieve a balance between the two poles remains a problem for each new generation of conservatives. Fourth Kirk reminded readers that "property and freedom are inseparably connected, and that economic leveling is not economic progress." Borrowing from the Founding Fathers as well as from English conservative thinkers, Kirk demonstrated that economic opportunity created freedom. But opportunity was very different from equalization, a utopian value that realists knew was impossible to attain. Fifth an individual must "put a control upon his will and his appetite"; it was only through "tradition and sound prejudice" that people would control their "anarchic impulses." This desire to revert to a simple life spoke to the same concerns as Kirk's third point, where the rhythms of the agrarian world had defined honesty, and similar environmental and internal restraints would ground the twentieth century in timeless values. Finally Kirk noted that conservatives needed to recognize "that change and reform are not identical." For example, when liberals tried to level society economically or politically, they failed to comprehend that such change could never improve the whole as they hoped. Rather humans would become more dependent on one another, in effect violating the first, second, and fourth tenets of Kirk's canon, and thus never achieve the independence of thought and action (aided by God and the distrust of too much freedom) that defined the apotheosis of a civilized society. Society could never—nor should it ever—be perfect. But following Kirk's guidelines Americans could perhaps move the country in that direction.[17]

Appearing at a time when he could bridge the gap between prewar and postwar conservatism, Kirk laid the foundation for the next generation of conservative intellectuals—and politicians. Kirk did not remain embedded in the beliefs of the prewar old Right but instead chose to shine a new light on American political philosophy. Just as the aforementioned events affected millions of

Americans by showing them that the world had changed drastically, Kirk understood that the world was entering a new era, which required a reinvigorated set of guidelines. Moreover Kirk was also one of the first to show conservatives that one could remain an intellectual while still acting and thinking constructively about practical politics. In the years following the debut of *The Conservative Mind*, Kirk wrote a syndicated column about American politics, contributed a column called "From the Academy" to *National Review*, and served as an adviser to a number of politicians.[18] Forty years after *The Conservative Mind*, one historian of the intellectual movement went so far as to say, "Above all, it stimulated the development of a self-conscious conservative intellectual movement in the early years of the Cold War. It is not too much to say that without this book we, the conservative intellectual community, would not exist today."[19] Kirk helped provide the intellectual content for conservative popularizers to disseminate, which eventually proved that Americans could understand and adopt ideas formerly considered too esoteric and formal to enter the political mainstream.

The Conservative Mind influenced generations of conservatives, sparked a wave of interest among intellectuals, and led a number of new works that same year. Leo Strauss's *Natural Right and History*, Robert Nisbet's *The Quest for Community*, and Whittaker Chambers's *Witness* were all released in 1953, creating an instant required reading list for aspiring or committed conservatives.[20] Moreover these works showed conservatives that they could respond to liberals like Trilling and later Hofstadter. And yet, even with the declaration of canons by the most pedigreed conservative theorists in the country, most Americans did not know what conservatism was in 1955. The political philosophy was essentially new, and for all of Kirk's and others' implied permanence of their canons, in practical terms much of conservatism in the mid-1950s was defined by its opposition to liberalism. Nevertheless, with each argument created to counter liberal ideas, conservatives moved one step closer to more practical and applicable definitions of their ideology. Rather than simply accepting, for example, Kirk's definition of conservatism and then moving on, conservatives continued to search for methods by which they could apply his and others' theories. The fact that conservatives refused to accept a single interpretation of their philosophy meant that not only was it a dynamic and creative time to be a part of the intellectual and later the political forces, but it also served notice to those liberals who bothered to listen, giving them fair warning that here was a power with which they would someday have to reckon. Still no network linked the three strands of conservatism, and this lack of infrastructure appeared most obvious in the disjuncture between those who generated the theory and those who practiced it.

Unlike liberals, conservative intellectuals and political operatives did not work shoulder-to-shoulder. Among liberals, of course, Roosevelt had pioneered the brain trust, drawing professors from Harvard and Columbia to Washington where they advised him on New Deal policies, which began a Democratic tradition that lasted for decades. But what intellectuals were publicly identified with, for example, Robert Taft? There is no single story of how conservative intellectuals and politicians began collaborating, although three discrete steps greatly contributed to the process. First the postwar events that signaled such a drastic change made an impact on intellectuals and politicians alike. Next such men as Kirk, Taft, Buckley, and William Rusher learned to traverse between areas traditionally reserved for either theoretical or political writing and action. Finally a small but growing number of individuals who made their living lecturing to and writing for a mass audience began to study and adopt the ideas of conservative intellectuals. These popularizers played a key role in disseminating information to audiences, whose members then helped spread the word even further. But as the events took place, it was left to Kirk, Buckley, and others to show that they were cognizant of immediate developments and had something to say about them. Conservatism was beginning to descend from the ivory tower.

Conservative Challenge to Containment

The decade between 1945 and 1955 was a pastiche of events that, when seen by conservatives, comprised a bleak picture: American influence abroad seemed to crumble before policymakers' eyes, and at home "un-American" activities and troubles multiplied with each new controversy. With the end of World War II and the beginning of the Cold War most Americans hoped to regain stability and predictability in their lives. For the previous sixteen years normalcy had been rare, upstaged by the depression, a new activist government that created a welfare state, and finally entry into World War II, ending a twenty-year period of unwavering isolationism. When the less-than-mythical Harry S. Truman replaced Franklin D. Roosevelt in 1945, Americans came to realize that the postwar world would not be joined seamlessly to what had come before. Truman's dealings with the Soviets at Potsdam and his use of the atomic bomb three weeks later gave reason for optimism: shrugging off prewar isolationism, the United States, finally taking its proper place in world affairs, would lead the postwar world.

Little, however, seemed to go right. America "lost" China when the communist revolution led by Mao Tse-tung ended with the U.S. decision to curtail military aid to Chiang Kai-shek. Not only had the Democrats failed to live up to their purported vision of a democratic world, but they had let the planet's largest country fall victim to that vision's antithesis. Although Truman had issued in 1947 his Truman Doctrine, which stated that communism would be opposed on all fronts by using economic and military aid, hot spots still flared and real wars broke out. When North Korea invaded South Korea on June 24, 1950, the

United States became involved under the aegis of the United Nations, a strategy designed to avoid a direct confrontation with the Soviets.

Fears of communism manifested themselves in nearly all parts of society, trickling down to average citizens, who came to expect episodes like the Hiss trial or the Rosenberg case to present themselves on a somewhat regular basis. Politicians, most famously Joseph McCarthy, had exploited these fears, which led some observers to decry the "irresponsible" conservatives. But even responsible conservatives like Robert Taft were, as one friend recalled, "rabid on the subject of communism. Just the word would make him furious about it."[21] Yet anticommunism was a confused patchwork of opinions, sometimes contradictory or formed without an obvious rationale. By 1954 only 5% of Americans believed that communists could practice communism and remain loyal Americans.[22] Conversely, less than 1% of those surveyed worried about the internal communist threat enough to mention it when describing what kinds of things worried them in their day-to-day lives.[23] And 87% of Americans felt they had never known anyone who was or who they suspected to be a communist.[24] Still Americans did not need to act rationally in order to justify their fears, and although most conservatives did not deliberately hope to increase paranoia surrounding communism, they took advantage of the anxiety nonetheless.

Perhaps the most important predicament that creators of postwar conservatism had to confront was how to reconcile so many different definitions of what outsiders thought was a single belief system. In other words, what was "conservatism," and what might it look like in ten years? These questions mattered since most scholars—and many political operatives—believed that in the early 1950s conservatism was being *created*, whereas liberalism simply existed as (liberals believed) a combination of American heritage and the product of decades of Democratic rule. This "invention" of conservatism gave conservatives themselves a chance to figure out what they believed, and it was not long before a range of ideas found their place in the conservative pantheon. One opportunity to define the ideology more explicitly presented itself in 1950, when a relatively little known conservative challenged one of the luminaries of liberal foreign policy, George Kennan.

When the Cold War began at the end of World War II the question that dominated U.S. foreign policy was how to preserve American interests abroad and help free-market democracies expand across the globe while not pushing the Soviets too far. By 1947 the Truman administration seemed to have its answer: containment. First coined by State Department official George F. Kennan in his "long telegram" from Moscow and then in a *Foreign Affairs* article, "The Sources of Soviet Conduct" (which Kennan signed "X," giving rise to its more common title, "The X Article"), containment was predicated on the belief that communism carried the seeds of its own destruction. If democracies around the world could prevent its spread and restrict the ideology to those areas already possessed by the Soviets (and later Chinese), soon the red dominion would crumble under its own weight. Kennan became the darling of the liberals; not only was his analysis perceptive because it elegantly articulated what many State Department and foreign policy analysts had already been thinking, but it was also a strategy that did not seem to require America to go to war in order to oppose and eventually defeat communism. Many conservatives, however, believed that waiting was akin to appeasement, a comparison that invariably triggered memories of the 1938 Munich Conference, where the British and French acceded to Hitler's demands, which exposed their weaknesses and ensured the invasion of Poland.

The burden of the conservative response to containment fell on a young philosophy professor at New York University named James Burnham. Like some others who composed the intellectual Right in the early 1950s, Burnham had begun his political career as a member of the far Left during the 1930s. Born in 1905 and educated at Princeton and Oxford, Burnham worked with communist unions in Detroit and eventually became a hardcore Trotskyite. Toward the end of the 1930s, however, Burnham became disillusioned with Stalin's rule in the Soviet Union and simply could not accept Trotsky's explanation that the autocratic leader and the conditions he imposed were an "aberration."[25] The Hitler-Stalin Pact and the Soviet war with Finland both helped assure Burnham that he had assumed correctly, and his conversion from leftist to rightist continued for the rest of the decade. By the late 1940s he was satisfied that the ruthless communists would stop at nothing to achieve their goals, and by the early 1950s he was decidedly in the conservative camp.[26]

In many ways Burnham was like Kirk: a transitional figure between the old and new Right. Decidedly not a libertarian, Burnham opposed military demobilization after the war and believed that conscription was necessary if the country were to resist the communists seriously. The government had a crucial role to play, decided Burnham, and if that meant impinging upon some people's rights in order to guarantee safety for the vast majority, then so be it. In his 1947 book, *The Struggle for the World*, Burnham urged the government to outlaw the American Communist party.[27] When Burnham turned his sights on Kennan's policy of containment, he continued moving in a direction that signaled increased reliance on concerted government power and a faith in leaders to make the right decisions. Burnham's refusal to join with the postwar isolationists and his willingness to apply the country's resources energetically meant that his ideas emerged as a viable alternative to Kennan or to what many conservatives thought of as an updated *sitzkrieg*.

The Coming Defeat of Communism spelled out Burnham's convictions about not only the present world political and military situations but also what needed to be done in the future to guarantee the survival of Western democracy. Now that the war was over the world was at a crucial juncture: the United States was the only power left that could oppose the Soviets and Chinese. Germany, Japan, Great Britain, and France were all vanquished in one respect or another.[28] Since the war American foreign policy had avoided the absolute worst but had gained nothing for its caution. With the democracies of Europe in such a weakened state, could the United States really afford to maintain a defensive posture? Since containment was "a variant of the defensive," and the "communist war for world control is not limited by formal declarations, but is continuous," it was clear that a static strategy like containment could only mean disaster once the communists had started to overwhelm Europe.[29] America could not rely on Europe to defend itself; not only was it battered from the war, but in some cases it was questionable whether those democracies *wanted* to survive. A postwar openness toward fascism and communism in some countries forced Burnham to wonder how waiting for the Soviets to collapse—even as they used subversion to undermine neighboring countries' governments and attitudes toward democracy—would be effective.

As an alternative to containment, Burnham suggested that the first acts of engagement be "untraditional" insurgency, using Soviet methods to beat them at their own game. Propaganda should be integrated into foreign policy as an essential element. In Soviet spheres like Poland and Czechoslovakia America should begin training and supplying guerrillas and recruiting refugees, exiles, and dissidents to spread unrest.[30] "Yielding, compromise, conciliation, always and invariably result in increased communist boldness, increased demands, further aggressions," wrote Burnham.[31] Although the "net trend" between 1946 and 1949 favored democracy, it remained to be seen what would happen next. It was America's choice: "Does the United States *choose* to win? Can it make the necessary *decision*? Is it going to have, at the required tension, the *will* to survive?" Like much of the rest of his book, Burnham concluded on a hopeful note: "The defeat of communism, probable on the facts, is also *inevitable*, because there are enough determined men in the world—and their number grows daily— who have so resolved."[32] The implication, however, was clear: if the government did not change its strategy and instead kept those "determined men" hamstrung by the policy of containment, it would not matter how committed they actually were.

Although Burnham did not attempt to construct an ideological bridge between divisions of conservatism, the conservative and general community received his work favorably. In popular journals Burnham's book created a stir. The *New York Times* devoted an interview to Burnham and two book reviews, including the front page of the Sunday *Book Review*. Most important, perhaps, was the work's impact in the intellectual and foreign policy circles in Washington and New York. The *Washington Post* led off the debate with an editorial entitled "Burnham vs. Kennan." Outlining Burnham's argument, the editors praised his "incisive logic."

Five months later the *Post* followed up with another editorial, this time detailing the split that had developed within the Departments of Defense and State between followers of Burnham and followers of Kennan. Francis P. Matthews, secretary of the navy, was a "Burnhamite," while Dean Acheson, secretary of state, was an avowed "Kennanite." At a speech in Boston Matthews reiterated Burnham's theory of "preventative war" when he stated that the United States must be willing to pay "even the price of instituting a war to compel cooperation for peace."[33] With the outbreak of war in Korea, said the editors, the Burnhamites must have felt that their argument had taken on new gravity. But the war did not change the editors' opinions; it only served to strengthen their support for containment. Military actions should serve political ends, not the other way around, they said. But that was not what Burnham was really saying. He never claimed that diplomacy should be secondary to outright action. Rather if diplomacy failed or the enemy failed to heed warnings then action would have to be taken.

Not long after Burnham's book was released in February 1950, the National Security Council drafted Document 68, which laid out the government's Cold War aims and the solutions its authors thought would work best. NSC-68 called for a dramatic increase in the military budget and the provision of political and economic aid to free countries threatened by Soviet expansionism. The invasion of South Korea by North Korea seemed to validate the new plans, and soon the military budget began to skyrocket. By the fall of 1950 observers noticed that a new tone could be heard in the hallways of the Pentagon and in congressional offices. One of the first reports of such a change came in the *Wall Street Journal*, where the reporters seemed to have gotten wind of NSC-68 and the impact of Burnham's theories on the NSC and other high-level decisionmakers. For many, the article implied, the Korean War had demonstrated that "it's clear to us the Kremlin won't hesitate to start a whole series of similar local fights. That could keep us on a war footing for decades. We've got to start pushing the iron curtain back, not just holding it steady."[34]

What worried policymakers most was the possibility of a protracted struggle that would cost Americans untold billions. In an unofficial Department of Defense study entitled "The Inadequacy of Containment," the authors argued that containment relied too heavily on time and money, neither of which was a limitless commodity possessed by the West. The alternative was "aggressive containment," which, when linked to an arms buildup, would possibly push the Soviets to economic and military crisis sooner rather than later. The Marshall Plan and the North Atlantic Treaty Organization (NATO) were both based on Kennan's theory of containment, argued the *Journal*, and now a new wave of officials looked to Burnham's *Coming Defeat of Communism* as a potential solution to what could be a stalemate. Still Burnham's theory contained one troubling aspect: his idea of preventative war was tough to defend, since no one could suggest publicly that starting a war in order to prevent one was rational. Nevertheless Burnham had achieved his goal; his ideas had made it into the inner sanctum of military and political policy circles and finally had given conservatives an alternative to the liberalism of Kennan and containment.

Burnham's influence on the conservative community in the early 1950s is difficult to overestimate. His confidence in his ideas and his ability to tackle the symbol of the apotheosis of liberal foreign policy meant that nothing was out of reach. Senator Robert A. Taft echoed many of Burnham's ideas in his treatise on foreign policy published a year later, *A Foreign Policy for Americans*.[35] William Rusher, a young conservative who in the mid-1950s was about to embark on a long career as publisher of *National Review*, recalled that Burnham's book *The Web of Subversion*, published four years after *The Coming Defeat of Communism*, had a profound impact on him since it "put the facts of important Communist penetration of American life beyond serious doubt, regardless of one's opinion of Joseph McCarthy."[36] Throughout the early 1950s Burnham continued to influence policymakers, lecturing at the National War College, the Air War College, the Naval War College, and Johns Hopkins's School for Advanced International Studies. Burnham might also have worked for the Central Intelligence Agency; he at least served as a consultant for the agency, and he continued to write books and articles for such journals as the *American Mercury* and the *Freeman*.[37] And when Buckley decided to heed the advice of Kirk, Burnham, and others and begin a magazine to, in Burnham's words, reach "opinion-makers all over the country every week," Burnham was recruited as a senior editor of *National Review* with a regular column on foreign affairs, appropriately entitled "The Third World War."[38] By 1964, after Barry Goldwater's rise and electoral fall, Burnham could look back on the previous ten years and realize that an "idea in a few hundred heads" in the early 1950s now had millions of supporters.[39]

Two Popularizers: Albert Wedemeyer and Raymond Moley

The first half of the 1950s was crucial to the formation of conservative attitudes toward the state, liberals, and the communist enemy. Although conservatives did not create a new activist agenda and formed few significant organizations designed to influence the Republican party, they did start building a system based on public gatherings built around a combination of intellectual exercises and shared knowledge of the ambient popular culture, creating, in effect, a nascent conservative political culture. Conservatives began stepping up their activities, hoping to bring their message to voters who perhaps had had enough of the New Deal and Truman. Some wrote for such periodicals as the *Freeman*, a libertarian magazine published by the Foundation for Economic Education (FEE), and *Human Events*, originally published by isolationists beginning in 1944. Neither, however, had large followings outside of a small group of intellectuals, but those who read either magazine were likely to be politically active. The constituency the postwar conservatives needed to reach consisted of those Republicans frustrated with the party's weaknesses who also realized that acting independently was futile or those Republicans who were minimally involved in the party yet felt that something was just not right about the country. Conservatives who wanted to change America could not target either postwar isolationists or libertarians; not only were both groups on the fringe of mainstream politics, but each was minuscule compared to the main body of potential conservatives. The question remained, then, how to energize dormant activists who could help usher in an era of politics the likes of which had not been seen for at least two decades.

To spread the word traditionalist conservatives turned to a method that had not only served them well for the past two centuries at least but also provided the face-to-face contact often necessary in the early stages of a political or social movement: they gave speeches. While talks were often keyed to a recent publication by a notable author or some other promotional gimmick, these conservatives took their jobs as town criers seriously. Speakers followed a circuit around the country; stopped in major cities, smaller towns, and college campuses; and addressed largely sympathetic audiences. The lecturers served to tie together percolating ideas while also reinforcing the notion that the listeners were on the right track. Anticommunism was the common bond among the speakers, cinching together events and theories that otherwise might have seemed disparate. There were exceptions, of course, but these political circuit riders knew they were on safe ground if they used communism as a common enemy.

In early 1952 Lieutenant General Albert C. Wedemeyer (U.S. Army, ret.) spoke to students of the University of Utah and Brigham Young University on the 102d anniversary of the creation of the University of Utah by Brigham Young. Wedemeyer, who was now serving as a vice president of a large corporation, had become familiar with virtually every important official in the U.S. government during his long and distinguished military career.[40] While Wedemeyer was still active in advising the military on matters like Korea, in public he had shifted his focus to examining the relationship between individual morality and political and social systems and what could be done to correct what he believed was a dangerous movement toward adopting ignoble positions vis-à-vis social relations and foreign policy. Not only was the enemy a threat, but so was the state. Here Wedemeyer faced the same dilemma conservative intellectuals did: how much power should be granted to the state, and how could it best be applied?

"The curse of our time," declared Wedemeyer, "is Caesarism—the usurpation by the State of the things belonging to the People."[41] Incredibly Wedemeyer lashed out at his own government: "We must make our Government more responsive to the will of the people. We have suffered and sacrificed far too much under secret diplomacy and Government bureaucracy. All citizens must participate fully in all the processes of government, from the precinct to the White House and Congress."[42] Much of Wedemeyer's vitriol, obviously, was aimed at the Democrats and the Truman administration—a thinly veiled call for Republicans to begin administering the country. Still, to hear such open criticism from a man who owed his career to serving a civilian government must have been surprising.

Wedemeyer's philosophy was revealing in a number of ways. First and foremost his perception of the role of the federal government reflected how conservatives at this time balanced libertarianism and traditionalism in crude yet pragmatic ways. On domestic issues and the role of the military, the government was meant to stay out of the peoples' way, letting citizens act as the check on "Caesarism." But in terms of internal security and foreign policy, the government needed to remain strong and let its enemies know that it would not buckle under when challenged. The duality of libertarianism, or classical liberalism, and traditionalism demonstrated an uneasy coexistence with speakers like Wedemeyer trying to define where each belief system should be applied and under what circumstances. If anticommunism served as the glue joining the two types of conservatism, the bond held fast in some places, was tenuous in others, and was separating in others still. Yet, even though no one had told Wedemeyer to define conservatism, this speech—and many others like it—advanced the process a step or two. It would be up to other commentators to refine the relationships among traditionalism, anticommunism, and libertarianism, and often those pundits had, like Whittaker Chambers and Frank Meyer, traversed the range of political persuasions. Raymond Moley was one of those ideologues.

Following the publication of his book *How to Keep Our Liberty*, Moley embarked on a promotional tour, which coincided with the 1952 election.[43] As a professor of public law at Columbia in 1932, Moley was recruited by Franklin D. Roosevelt first to write campaign speeches and then to head up the brain trust, which set to work trying to solve the depression. In 1933 FDR appointed him as assistant secretary of state, a position he held for less than one year. Moley continued to assist FDR informally until 1936, writing speeches and advising the administration. Soon, however, Moley began to question the degree to which the government was trying to engineer society by controlling the economy, law, and social relations. The president, Moley realized, had concluded that in order to win reelection he would have to pander to urban voters and jettison the traditional rural constituency. But Moley must have known that American demographics were shifting; the 1920 census had registered the first urban majority ever, and interest groups such as African Americans and labor were increasingly demanding recognition and bargaining power. Equally important was the growth of the northern urban ethnic constituency during the 1920s and 1930s, when the children of nonvoting immigrants deepened the New Deal Coalition. Still in 1936 Moley made a decision that changed the rest of his life: "The sudden shift in Roosevelt's policies and strategy in the 1935–1936 period meant to me the repudiation of Democratic Party principles of the past. Since I believed in supporting one of the two parties, I accepted the Republican Party as an alternative."[44] Moley returned to his position at Columbia and also became a columnist and contributing editor for *Newsweek*, a post that gained him a substantial following.

Moley railed against "planning," or trying to control the economy (and thus other aspects of society) by impinging upon the "natural" relations among businesses, employers, and employees and in the area of supply and demand. The temptation to control the economy often led to the "narcotic of authority," a delusion that Moley thought had captured Roosevelt and Truman and that led to the dangerous phenomenon of a loss of contrasting opinions within the White House. When a leader perceived himself to be without peer when making decisions, Moley believed, the propensity for "statism" increased but usually in the benign garb of welfare programs, controls on trade, and aid to interest groups (particularly unions), all of which guaranteed continued electoral support. Such corruption bred moral decay and contempt for authority, causing, obviously, a need to increase yet again the leader's control over the people. Moley believed that only a conservative response could challenge the increasingly powerful liberal ideology.

One month after Dwight Eisenhower's 1952 victory, Moley spoke to the National Coffee Association convention in Boca Raton, Florida, about "The New Conservatism."[45] Never one to mince words, Moley believed that not only were the Democrats driving the country into the ground, but that instead of economic downturns periodically endemic in a capitalist economy, the free-market system would be replaced by socialism, resulting not in immediate failure but in gradual and possibly permanent decay. Now that the Democrats had been ousted, however, what would help ensure the country's continued success and vitality? It was here that Moley invoked his "new conservatism."

According to Moley new conservatism meant "applying the best of the past," refusing alliances with minority factions, and realizing that it was in the best interest of conservatives to consolidate themselves into a single, powerful group. Leaving his audience with a series of observations about how conservatives could consolidate their power in the Republican party, Moley recommended that they look to President Eisenhower for leadership on all issues. Returning to the question his recent book posed, Moley asked conservatives how they expected to retain their liberty. Democracy entails some degree of risk, Moley reminded his audience, since "the very nature of liberty precludes a determination of exactly what will happen in the future," and while individuals may set goals for themselves, it was folly for a free society to try to achieve success by coercion. "The primary concern of conservatism—the old as well as the new conservatism—is to preserve human liberty that may be overlooked in our common use of the

term." Liberty—as differentiated from freedom—has an intrinsic value separate from materialistic concerns. Without liberty, Moley advised, life itself has
no value.

Although they could not know it, Moley's audience had been treated to a
forward-looking synopsis of much of conservatism's direction over the next half
decade or so. While Moley could not have predicted the events that coincided
with the changes taking place on the right of the political spectrum (most immediately in response to the 1954 *Brown v. Board of Education* decision), in
broad, sweeping strokes he offered an outline of postwar conservative ideology
in its infancy.[46] Like Wedemeyer, Moley had not been asked by anyone to attempt to define conservatism, yet he did just that. Both men not only suggested
the range of popular conservative opinions circa 1952 but also analyzed which
opinions did and did not jibe. The traditionalism the speakers articulated involved
far more than just preserving the past and questioning the future. Its adaptation
of libertarianism meant that even as the government was growing more complicated from the responsibilities it had assumed since the beginning of the welfare state in the 1930s, some Americans were rebelling against the trend of
administrative growth that matched economic and demographic growth. The
American experience in World War II had forever changed the country; the war
alone cost twice as much as all government spending combined between 1789
and 1940. For the first time in its history the United States ran a deliberate deficit so that by the end of the war the government owed $258 billion.[47] Conserva-
tives questioned such Keynesian spending, however, and the Democrats' willingness to continue what seemed like almost assured economic folly further
strengthened their resolve to combat liberalism.

Conservatives' fiscal restraint combined with a growing wariness toward the
ever-increasing power of the state helped begin the process of integrating traditionalism and libertarianism, in which the individual remained the most important commodity.[48] Conservatives would have to prevail against encroachments
by liberals, who hoped to continue expanding the reach of the government. And
yet such invocations raised practical problems for the conservative community.
How were they to oppose liberalism when they were far from united in their
basic beliefs? Anticommunism could only take them so far before policies not
involving internal or external security forced leaders to make decisions that would
expose their various conservative leanings. The fact remained that in the early
1950s conservatism was not a political ideology with a number of equally legitimate interpretations, but it did possess a tiny grassroots base of support independent of that generated by the Republican party. Moreover the very act of
Wedemeyer and Moley speaking to audiences symbolized the one-way, top-down
nature of decisionmaking within conservative ranks. This is not to say, of course,
that there *should* have been a grassroots conservative element at this time. That
would signal a more united movement, something that did not yet exist. For all

intents and purposes conservatism at this time was an exercise reserved for politicians and intellectuals.

Wedemeyer and Moley, however, tested, applied, and revised conservative ideology, and they were surrounded by an array of intellectuals who kept them supplied with theories that could then be configured to sell to the mainstream public. But unlike other eras when intellectuals and activists conspired (either deliberately or by chance) to influence the masses, the circumstances of the Cold War reshaped both intellectuals' ideas and activists' implementation of those ideas. Sometimes the Cold War acted as a gatekeeper, limiting the public's exposure to certain ideas. At other times the standoff distorted circumstances, changing them to suit the needs of an administration or political party. In any case postwar conservatives continued to assemble the tools they needed to compete politically and socially with liberals, and as they gained confidence their dreams became more sweeping while their plans became more pragmatic.

Forced to grapple with such issues as how a conservative would be self-identified, what would define the differences among the various factions, and how they would create a movement to challenge liberals, conservatives took what had been older ideas, put them in relatively new packages, and tested them, preparing themselves for the struggles ahead. Liberals, on the other hand, did not face the equivalent challenges for another fifteen years. During the Eisenhower years they managed to make conservatives feel like illegitimate children, observers who merely commented on the action taking place in the main arena, which liberals controlled. As challengers, conservatives would need to define the terms of a new debate, something that could demonstrate how different the two ideologies really were. When such chances began appearing regularly in the late 1950s and early 1960s, conservatives started seeking them out until, by the mid-1960s, they could choose their battles. In the early 1950s, however, opportunities were still rare.

Toward a Definition of Conservatism

A decade after the publication of *The Coming Defeat of Communism,* James Burnham took a blank sheet of paper and literally sketched out a contemporary political spectrum, diagramming where the country stood at the brink of a new decade. In the drawing's center, or "the Establishment," was Lyndon Johnson. To his immediate right was Eisenhower, and to his immediate left was Adlai Stevenson. Much farther to the left was John F. Kennedy, then Hubert Humphrey, after which Burnham grouped the socialists, communists, nihilists, and leftist anarchists. On the right, the equivalents were Harry F. Byrd and Barry Goldwater, followed by authoritarianism, fascism, racists, and finally, rightist anarchists.[49] Trying to define conservatism, Burnham then made lists: "conservative (in the full and conscious sense) persons," "conservative journals, newspapers, magazines, and books," and finally a set of "litmus propositions for Liberal-Conservative test." While most of the people and publications named were predictable, Burnham's litmus test was more interesting. Posing a series of true–false questions, Burnham hoped to clarify who was a liberal and who was a conservative by contemplating quandaries that indicated how one viewed the world. Such statements as "All forms of racial segregation and discrimination are wrong," "Any interference with free speech and free assembly is wrong," "There should be no interference with academic freedom," "Everyone has the right to equal pay for equal work," and "In deciding who is to be admitted to schools and universities, any quota system based on color, religion, family or similar factors is wrong" all attempted to define how people decided how society worked best. In Burnham's opinion, "A full-blown Liberal will mark ever[y] one of these thirty-three sentences True. A consistent Conservative will mark many of them, probably a majority and possibly even all of them, False."[50] Like his contemporaries, Burnham was still hard at work trying to define a set of beliefs that would allow conservatives to identify themselves and others, thus closing the political and cultural gap with liberals.

In their small circle Burnham and his colleagues had brought the battle lines into high relief. Not only were they refining what they believed, but they were beginning to agree with each other on a number of universalities and, perhaps most important, were looking for examples in America to justify their ideas. The gap between theory and reality was shrinking with each new addition to the canon. Moreover while many of the postwar conservative tenets remained consistent from year to year after their initial definitions, their authors and agents refused to let them stagnate, applying and reapplying them to situations everyday Americans confronted in their lives. Although circumstances did not conspire to provide optimal conditions until the late 1950s and early 1960s, conservatives were not deterred and continued to search for ways to demonstrate that their ideas had consequences. Burnham's views of foreign policy were perhaps the most obvious examples of postwar conservatism and how it could revamp the way America responded to a changing world order. By the end of the 1950s conservatives were applying similar beliefs to domestic policy, and although their voices were quiet at first, within a few years the handful of advocates had garnered millions of adherents. While such conversions were still a relatively long way off in the early to mid-1950s the first steps had been taken, perhaps the most important being the willingness of the Establishment to take conservative ideas seriously. That Burnham became a contender against Kennan, Kirk against Louis Hartz, Buckley against Lionel Trilling (eventually), Chambers against Alger Hiss, and Moley against Arthur Schlesinger, Jr., meant that these alternatives to the status quo were beginning to be seen as *legitimate* alternatives.

Anticommunism sparked the birth of the postwar conservative movement. While the New Deal Democrats had run rampant over Republican challengers for more years than any conservative cared to remember, without the pressure of communism threatening their way of life, conservatives could have continued living their quiet, isolated existences under Democratic rule. First in the early and mid-1950s and later again periodically events came in series, where their combined impact created a kind of synergy, which helped the parts add up to much more than the whole. Taken alone, any one of the occurrences was probably not enough to cause great alarm. But when one episode was followed within weeks or months by another, some Americans questioned the veracity of their leaders. In this intersection of policy, individual values, intellectual maturation, and the appearance of new leaders, conservatives began to understand that the waiting had to end and the action had to begin.

Ideologues set the stage in the first half of the 1950s. As their ideas became accepted by those who followed politics and were conservative, the fact that liberals gave battle to the pioneers meant that if average Americans decided to follow, they would not be seen as crackpots on the fringe. But what would activate those individuals about whom the intellectuals thought and wrote? While speeches and articles helped, they would never convince voters to do more than simply accept party politics. For a real conservative change to occur, something (or some things) would have to transform those voters from passive to active, would have to encourage them to demand a new agenda for a new America. While leaders for this movement were not quick to appear, the events that would help spark such a transformation were just around the corner.

THE COLD WAR

HITS HOME

One September day in 1959 William Rusher, publisher of the upstart conservative journal *National Review*, was strolling up Fifth Avenue in New York City. What he saw stopped him dead in his tracks:

> Looking westward along Fifty-ninth Street, I saw flying grandly over the Coliseum a huge flag I had never seen there before—or anywhere else in America, as far as I could remember. It was, of course, the Hammer and Sickle—the flag of the USSR, its bright red folds flapping briskly against the brilliant blue of the New York sky.[1]

Hoisted to honor the presence of Soviet Premier Nikita Khrushchev, the Soviet standard, although celebrated by some Americans as a sign that tensions between the two superpowers were easing, represented capitulation to Rusher and millions like him.

At the end of the 1950s the nature of anticommunism and the state of conservatism were called into question. Developments between 1957 and 1961 convinced some Americans that not only were communists and liberals making gains but that American institutions often aided and abetted (albeit sometimes unwittingly) the enemy's cause. It was in such an explosive atmosphere that the Supreme Court and Khrushchev acted as flint and tinder, igniting a political brush fire that resisted repeated dousings, which grew until the entire nation took note.

"Red Monday" at the Supreme Court

In 1940 Congress passed the Alien Registration Act, more commonly known as the Smith Act, which prohibited teaching or advocating "the forceful overthrow of any government in the United States, or . . . join[ing] any organization bent on such a course."[2] For anticommunists the Smith Act was a blank check, a twentieth-century version of the eighteenth-century Alien and Sedition laws. Until the courts began narrowing its meaning, congressional committees like the House Committee on Un-American Activities (HUAC) could investigate any group or individual on the grounds that they threatened the government. In 1951 the Supreme Court limited the vague law slightly, although its main intent remained prohibiting "a number of persons from advocating under certain circumstances violent overthrow of the government."[3]

In the mid-1950s, however, Attorney General Herbert Brownell, Jr., continued to prosecute Americans suspected of being members of the Communist party. In the lower courts these cases almost always returned guilty verdicts, which the defendants then appealed. By 1956 three Smith Act cases had made their way to the Supreme Court, which, with the appointment of Earl Warren in late 1953, had taken a decidedly liberal turn. Compared to Courts that had been at the behest of big business or government, conservatives often termed the Warren Court as "freewheeling" and Warren himself as "Ike's worst appointment."[5] In essence what most conservatives found upsetting about the new trend in Supreme Court decisions was the tendency to enlarge the role of the federal government at the expense of the states and to favor individual rights instead of protecting the entire society. In cases involving private business and the free market, they saw the Court using a double standard in which the rights of businesses run by individuals were not equivalent to the rights of practitioners of communism or socialism. Conservatives were especially bitter that Eisenhower's four appointees did not consistently vote to uphold laws like the Smith Act.

The June 29, 1957, issue of *National Review* led off its articles with a discussion of recent Supreme Court decisions. No conservative reader needed to be reminded about what the Court had concluded twelve days earlier, but *National Review* hammered it home anyway:

> The Supreme Court struts on in its drive to subvert American political institutions. Of the three decisions last week, the boldest, the most impudent, and the most anarchical was that calling for the reversal of the contempt citation against John Watkins. The meaning of that decision is stupefying, for it sets up the Supreme Court as arbiter of the intentions of Congress.[6]

The magazine was referring to three decisions handed down by the Court on June 17, 1957, a day that came to be known as "Red Monday" by anticommunists and conservatives around the nation. In *Watkins v. United States, Yates v. United States*, and *Sweezy v. New Hampshire*, the Court ordered an about-face in how Americans accused of communist connections could be treated. A former official of the Farm Equipment Workers Union and the United Auto Workers, John T. Watkins had freely provided the names of already known communists in his testimony before HUAC in 1954, yet he had balked when told to divulge the names of alleged party members.[7] Warren and the Court decided that Watkins had not been given "a fair opportunity to determine whether he was within his rights in refusing to answer, and his conviction is necessarily invalid under the Due Process Clause of the Fifth Amendment."[8]

In *Yates v. United States*, which considered the convictions of fourteen alleged communists on the West Coast under the Smith Act, Justice John Harlan's decision drew a distinction between discussing communism as a theoretical system and working for an outcome illegal under the Smith Act.[9] *Yates* threw out the convictions of five of the accused and called for retrials for the others.[10]

Finally, in *Sweezy v. New Hampshire*, Warren himself wrote the opinion that reversed Professor Paul Sweezy's contempt conviction for refusing to answer questions from the New Hampshire attorney general about his past political activities. Striking a nerve among many conservatives as he defended academic freedom, Warren wrote, "Mere unorthodoxy or dissent from the prevailing mores is not to be condemned: The absence of such voices would be a symptom of grave illness."[11] Furthermore the Court limited the attorney general's investigations to more germane issues and individuals, thus offering even greater protection from similar inquiries.

Taken separately any one of these cases might have stirred Americans' fears of encroaching liberalism in government, although none would have had the impact of, say, a *Brown* or *Miranda v. Arizona* (1966). Together, however, they signaled a drastic shift. The three decisions were not likely to affect large numbers of people—certainly not like *Brown*. But their symbolism extended far beyond such facts. A typical illustration could be found in the cartoons of Burris Jenkins, Jr. In one scene he depicted the nine justices, all tottering precariously on their left feet, ascending the steps to a leftward-leaning Supreme Court.[12]

More than any other mainstream publication, *U.S. News and World Report* registered shock and disgust over the Court's recent decisions. A moderately conservative periodical, *U.S. News* saw the Warren Court as an agitator that was upsetting the delicate balance among the three branches of government and that was immune to attempts to rein it in. After the June 17 decisions *U.S. News* lashed out, claiming, "The Court's historic ruling on school segregation in 1954 was only the beginning. Since then, a Court majority under Chief Justice Warren has steadily limited the power of the States and of Congress, while broadening the rights of individuals."[13] The editors' two main complaints were that the Court had overstepped its boundaries, intruding upon Congress's turf, and that by applying such broad interpretive powers the Court had helped throw Washington into chaos. The combination of rulings over the previous three years and the uncertainty over future decisions left lawmakers scratching their heads and wondering what would remain on the books. It was not clear, the editors thought, just what the decisions of June 17 would mean in the long run. The government would surely have a tougher time prosecuting communists and subversives, and Congress would plainly have to rethink its approach to committee hearings and investigations. Most of all, however, *U.S. News* saw the Court's decrees as adding to a disturbing drift overtaking the federal government: confusion and a resulting inefficiency threatened to paralyze Washington at a time when Soviet might blustered, the economy was turning downward, and social relations—specifically race relations—were ready to ignite.

While it would be wrong to describe the conservative community before 1957 as a "movement," there were more and more signs that political commentators, writers, analysts, and ordinary citizens realized that a critical mass was beginning to form. In addition to those speakers and writers mentioned previously, perhaps the most important development during this time was the creation of *National Review* in 1955. Begun by William F. Buckley, Jr., and William S. Schlamm, a conservative writer, the journal quickly became a theoretical and later a practical conservative switchboard, which plugged the famous and the ordinary into the same conversation. Still the existence of a journal did not signify the existence of a full-fledged movement. That would have to wait at least another three or four years. Nevertheless Buckley's and Schlamm's efforts represented a huge leap forward, and in the case of Red Monday, *National Review* showed individual conservatives that they did not stand alone.

Conservatives refused to see the Court's pronouncements as isolated cases, and their response was far more condemnatory than anyone could have expected. *National Review* led the assault, running short articles immediately after the decisions, and in the July 6 issue journalist Forrest Davis wrote that the Court's recent decisions, unlike previous times, indicated a pattern that was cause for great concern. Not only were Warren and his fellow liberals reaching far beyond precedent, but Congress was letting them get away with it. Furthermore Warren's leadership had "precipitated a constitutional crisis long in the making which, should Congress defend its prerogatives, will give rise to a struggle for power reminiscent of the quarrels between King and Commons in Stuart and Hanoverian England."[14] This showdown, similar to the one predicted by *U.S. News*, threatened not just to produce an impotent court system but might also expose a weakness to the enemy that, if exploited, could help them gain new ideological, political, and economic ground.

Confronting why the Court would go to such lengths to protect individuals obviously dangerous to America, Davis offered a diagnosis that a wide range of conservatives adopted. Since there was no good reason to defend communists, Davis argued, the reason must be almost absurdly simple:

> The Warren-Black-Douglas axis on which the Court lies, in my judgment, [is] under the nihilistic blight of fashionable Liberalism. Intellectually inadequate, the Justices of the childish Left mistake the liberty of the citizen for the franchise of the Soviet subversionist. It pains me to say this, but I fear that we have a dumb core of the Court and a timid fringe.[15]

Other explanations simply did not fit.

The *American Mercury*, a conservative monthly started in 1923, was prepared to go further. Writing in August 1958 Harold Lord Varney went beyond Davis's theory that Warren had changed his mind for some unknown reason. Sifting back through Warren's career in public life, Varney stopped at the 1952 Republican National Convention in Chicago. There the Eisenhower forces did not have enough nominating votes to put their man over the top, since challenger Robert Taft still held key delegations like Texas and Louisiana. Only a Credentials Committee report could authorize the votes for Ike and, to approve the tainted report, moderates needed the support of the California delegation, which was commanded by Governor Earl Warren. Eisenhower's handlers promised a cabinet post in exchange for his votes. Warren upped the ante, demanding the first Supreme Court vacancy. The deal was sealed: Eisenhower's rules got the go-ahead, and Taft, the true conservative, was finished.[16]

Shortly after the June 17 decisions, *National Review* ran an unsigned column that posed the question "Has Congress Abdicated?" Prior to the twentieth century, the editors claimed, it was Congress "that had been given the duty of making the country's laws; and it was not for the Court to tell it how that duty was to be performed."[17] Because Congress was not doing its job, the Court had been able to extend its power beyond its traditional boundaries, claiming new ground with each unprecedented decision. As the editors said so succinctly, "[The Court] is sitting no longer as a judicial bench but as the nation's supreme legislature, unmaking *and making* the nation's laws, often in arrogant disregard of the explicit words and recorded intentions of the constitutionally designated legislative body." There was but one choice to exert control over a part of government that had run amok: the people, through the institution of Congress, had to exercise their legal authority over the nine men who threatened the balance of power among lawmakers.

Within two weeks of Red Monday, congressmen were churning out bills designed to limit the Court's power. In *Jencks v. United States*, a June 3 ruling, the Court had decided that Clinton Jencks should have been allowed to examine the FBI files on his loyalty/security case. In response the House and Senate Judiciary committees introduced bills to safeguard such files.[18] Southerners concentrated on reversing the Warren Court's rulings on civil rights. A bill proposed by Herman Talmadge (D-Ga.) hoped to remove the public schools from the jurisdiction of federal courts. Others wanted to make the states the exclusive executors of policy relating to education, health, and morale.[19] Talmadge also wanted the Court to hear oral arguments for any case it accepted, a tactic that, while on its face guaranteeing a citizen's civil liberties, also assured a colossal slowdown in the number of decisions rendered annually.

Many congressmen went further, however, proposing bills aimed directly at the justices themselves. Congressman D. R. Matthews (D-Fla.) offered a bill that would prevent a justice from becoming a political candidate within two years of his resignation or retirement. Senator Russell Long (D-La.) wanted a constitutional amendment requiring reconfirmation of the justices every twelve years. Senators Olin E. Johnston (D-S.C.) and James O. Eastland (D-Miss.) wanted this exercise every four years. Other lawmakers wanted to rescind lifetime tenure or require a fixed amount of judicial experience before appointment to the highest court.[20]

After 1957 conservatives kept a constant watch on the Court, publicizing rulings they supported and opposed. The Constitution, they agreed, should not be a document tossed about by political winds—particularly liberal winds. Moreover the rulings in the late 1950s, like those a decade later, convinced many conservatives that to prevent any more rewriting of the Constitution, they needed to be in a position to determine who would make those decisions. Even though the last Smith Act prosecutions were overturned in 1964, the act had helped destroy the American Communist party, as well as stifle behavior that could be interpreted as threatening the government.[21] Yet internal security, the communist threat, and unilaterally rewriting the nation's laws were only a few worries among many for these critics. Within two years the enemy was literally arriving at America's doorstep.

Khrushchev in America

By the end of the 1950s the Cold War confrontation between American and Soviet diplomacy had reached new heights, with the rivalry extending to cultural, scientific, and economic arenas. After the Korean War, fought by Americans under the aegis of the United Nations and without any official participation by the Soviets, the superpowers used their proxies to clash at regular intervals. In 1956 the Soviets put down the Hungarian uprising, outraging much of the free world. In 1957 the Soviets launched Sputnik, initiating a scientific competition that lasted for the next thirty years.

But these landmarks, though symbolic of the tense standoff, did not occur in rapid succession, which left most Americans with the feeling that the Cold War would simply be an ongoing, relatively unchanging fact of life. Though episodes like the 1956 battle over Hungarian sovereignty represented a swelling Soviet menace, the threat was still distant, not like Sputnik, which literally flew over Americans' heads. Of course those Americans who counted themselves among the growing number of conservatives watched these developments with outrage. But for other citizens 1959 marked a moment when, for the first time since Sputnik, the Cold War became "real." Early that year Fidel Castro took over Cuba, ousting dictator Fulgencio Batista, and months later Soviet Premier Nikita Khrushchev and Vice President Richard Nixon argued over the merits of Soviet and American houses in the famous "kitchen debate." By that summer the Cold

War was a revitalized part of the political and cultural *zeitgeist*, with Eisenhower and Khrushchev holding the fate of the world in their hands. There had been, however, moves by both sides to ease tensions so that negotiations might take place on some fronts. What had devolved into the farcical debate between Nixon and Khrushchev had started out as a friendly exchange during Nixon's visit to Moscow. Soon after Nixon's return, in the spirit of continuing negotiations between the superpowers, Eisenhower invited Khrushchev to visit America for a summit and to meet its people up close. Khrushchev accepted, giving conservatives and many moderates reason to pause in disbelief, a feeling that soon turned to anger at the thought of hosting the "Butcher of Budapest."

National Review set itself the task of trying to either stop the summit or at least expose it for what its writers and editors thought it was: a revisit to the 1938 Munich Conference. In the first issue after the summit was announced, *National Review* loosed a salvo against the Eisenhower administration, condemning it for not only receiving Khrushchev but also for legitimizing an illegitimate regime. Incredulous that the president did not understand what his actions meant, the editors drew comparisons to Roosevelt inviting Hitler to the White House, which they illustrated by taking a *New York Times* editorial on the summit and substituting Roosevelt's and Hitler's names.[22] Khrushchev's invasion into the very heart of the government was a Soviet diplomatic and public relations coup, since he would become linked to the White House and its famous inhabitants: "This is the guest who will be welcomed to the White House—the most cherished home of our national tradition and honor; who will walk the floors trod by Washington and Jefferson, and sleep in Lincoln's bed." Conservatives' sense of outrage, however, only grew as their fears turned into realities, and as the visit grew nearer, *National Review* increased its activities on all fronts, hoping to force a showdown before the Soviet leader's actual arrival.[23]

In the weeks leading up to the visit, *National Review* railed, "The United States . . . has nothing to gain from, no intelligible political motive for, the Eisenhower-Khrushchev visit."[24] Besides adding credibility to an outlaw government, the visit would also serve to drive a wedge between the United States and its NATO allies, since they lucidly understood what the visit meant to their security. As details of Khrushchev's schedule were released to the press, *National Review* took each point as a separate affront to American dignity and pride. The plan to display the hammer-and-sickle flag next to the Stars and Stripes along the road from National Airport to the White House elicited a howl of protest. *National Review* began selling stickers reading, "Khrushchev Not Welcome Here," and urged its readers to place them anywhere they would not want to see the Russian visitor.[25] At twenty-five cents each, the stickers were an easy way for readers to let their neighbors know how they felt. Readers of *National Review* quickly registered their disgust over the decision. "The invitation to Khrushchev to accept our hospitality . . . sickens those of us who believe in freedom," wrote one reader.

"I have put my United States flag at half mast—to mark the death in so many souls of the God-given devotion to *freedom*," wrote another.[26]

Citizens' groups began organizing, taking out advertisements in newspapers, collecting signatures on petitions, and encouraging their members to come up with creative ways to draw attention to the scandalous visit.[27] Senators Styles Bridges, Thomas Dodd, and Paul Douglas and Congressman Walter Judd formed the Committee for Freedom of All Peoples, called for a time of national mourning, and suggested that communities respond by holding religious services when Khrushchev visited their town or city.[28] The committee took out a full-page advertisement in the *New York Times*, which told readers, "In ordinary times . . . we, the undersigned, may differ profoundly, but when Nikita Khrushchev comes to America, we unite on this . . . a call for national mourning."[29] Continuing to lead the charge, *National Review* organized a protest rally at Carnegie Hall and invited such speakers as Clarence Manion, radio commentator and former dean of the Notre Dame Law School; the Reverend Daniel Poling, editor of the *Christian Herald*; L. Brent Bozell, a *National Review* editor and columnist; and, of course, Buckley.[30] Never above a little showmanship, Buckley at a pre-rally press conference displayed the same bravado found in the journal; the editor threatened to dye the Hudson River red, so that the dictator would enter New York on a "river of blood."[31] Twenty-five hundred protesters filled the hall, having purchased their tickets that same morning when they went on sale.

Even before Khrushchev arrived, spontaneous demonstrations broke out across the nation. A small group led by a former Polish freedom fighter started a hunger strike in front of the White House. The Foundation for Religious Action in the Social and Civil Order organized a national moment of silence. A Hungarian freedom fighter blindfolded the Statue of Liberty, remarking, "She shouldn't gaze at a murderer." An industrialist in Hartford stopped his machinery for three minutes of silent prayer. The Catholic Church of St. Joseph's in Buffalo and a citizens' group in Minneapolis worked together to coordinate the flying of their flags upside down, an international sign of distress.[32]

On September 15, the day Khrushchev arrived in Washington, a skywriter, hired by a group of anticommunist Christians, traced a cross in the dazzling blue sky over the White House.[33] Some citizens translated phrases into Russian to make placards that the Soviet leader could not avoid understanding. Milder maxims included "Scoundrel," "Down with Red Colonialism," and "Instigator of a New World War."[34] A Brooklyn newspaper urged its readers to attend Khrushchev's entrance to New York and "turn your back and say a prayer."[35] Vandals in New York threw red paint on the sidewalk in front of Averell Harriman's home, where the diplomat had hosted a party for the Soviet leader. Finally the Committee for Freedom of All Peoples continued its work by mailing 500 black armbands a day to citizens across the country, organizing a continuous presence in front of the White House, and setting up branch committees where interest demanded more local action.[36]

Coverage of the visit in mainstream publications ranged from cordial to op-positional. *Time* saw the positive side of Khrushchev's travels as he visited cities from San Jose, California, where he toured an IBM plant, to Coon Rapids, Iowa, where he visited a high-tech farm.[37] *U.S. News and World Report*, normally conservative on foreign affairs and relations with the Soviets, took a mostly favorable view of his time in America, pointing out that although the dictator threatened the destruction of noncommunist countries if they did not participate in friendly competition with their communist rivals, he also advocated a relaxation of relations between the rivals, encouraging coexistence instead of elimination through war.[38] Most interesting, however, was *Newsweek*'s coverage. Comparing Khrushchev to a "latter-day Paul Revere, alerting the nation to its clear and present—and total—danger," the magazine took the offensive and noted that perhaps such a visit, as abhorrent as many found it, would serve a useful purpose.[39] Americans had become complacent about those basic qualities that had given them so much: freedom, innovation, and the ability to work together. Khrushchev's visit should serve as a reminder to Americans that, given the chance, the Soviets *would* bury them.

Newsweek's tone was much like that found in *National Review*: tough, surprised that Khrushchev was so complacently accepted by most of America, but hopeful that the visit would serve to reawaken the American spirit. Curiously *Newsweek*'s survey of Americans revealed that they supported the visit overwhelmingly but that they did not trust him.[40] Unlike *National Review* conservatives, however, *Newsweek* readers did trust Eisenhower to stand up to the challenges such a visit posed. Businessmen saw the exchange as a sign that not only was the world opening up but also that America needed to prepare for future markets and competitors like the Russians, a factor that, up to this point, had been considered usually as theory and not as an actual possibility.

But for all of Khrushchev's diplomacy—visiting the IBM plant or the high-tech farm or watching the filming of a scene from *Can-Can* in Hollywood—the trust that liberals thought the visit might foster did not materialize.[41] Each meeting between Soviet and American officials was a showdown in which the sides faced off to see who would get the better of whom.

When the visit ended, conservative analysts registered what they believed was the utter failure of American diplomats to stand up to the communist challenge. To them Khrushchev's presence on American soil marked the nadir of American diplomacy, where all of government, from the president and his advisers down to the policeman walking his beat in New York, paid homage to the enemy's leader. That American leaders had acquiesced to communist demands did not bode well, conservatives wrote. Although free people might not lie down in the face of advancing communist forces, they would allow the enemy to set the terms of engagement—whether diplomatic or military. Once the country became accustomed to viewing the issues from a communist perspective, a "surrender potential" might well be realized as the Orwellian dialogue slowly wore down the nation's defenses.[42] It was little wonder, then, thought conservatives, that most Americans believed Khrushchev's visit had been "a good thing."[43]

The gullibility of the American people was not surprising, said conservative critics, since their leaders refused to get tough with the enemy. For example, when Khrushchev spoke to the UN about disarming the two countries, many Americans (especially liberals) were taken in by the gambit. What they did not realize, conservatives fumed, was that the arms race was doing more to damage the Soviet Union than almost any program the United States might design. The Soviet economy, never very strong, was pushed to its limits in trying to keep pace with U.S. arms production. The arms race would certainly help bring the Soviet empire to the brink of economic disaster, and therefore there was no need to halt a strategy that was clearly working.[44]

Even for those Americans who did not follow politics closely, Khrushchev's visit was impossible to ignore. Although it gave liberals hope that the Cold War could thaw, for conservatives the Khrushchev visit climaxed two years of decreasing American prestige accompanied by a lack of concern on the part of American leaders. In addition some conservatives understood that such a dramatic event might force moderates to align themselves with the Left or the Right. Conservative responses to these events have usually been categorized by historians in arenas typically political, such as congressional inquiries, debates, conservatives' opposition to Eisenhower, and attempts to push the GOP to the right. Far less explored, however, have been the conservative cultural responses to the political events of the late 1950s.[45] Answers to social and political issues came in the form of cultural and political actions, and between the late 1950s and early 1970s American conservatives used trial and error to develop powerful algorithms, which they constantly adapted to a changing landscape. Examining cultural answers in addition to political responses reveals two things: how politics and culture intersected and especially how politicians perceived culture and the uses of culture; and second how conservative political organizers moved from prewar political strategy and tactics to more "modern" political culture. The late 1950s was a time when the culture of two groups of conservatives were at play in the same arena: conservatives familiar with older styles of politicking coexisted with conservatives of a new era, in which new mediums and methods had the potential to produce exciting results. By the mid-1960s the latter were quickly replacing the former in a wide range of areas but particularly in those requiring communication between conservative elites and average voters. By examining conservative cultural responses to the belief that America was indeed in decline, an entirely new facet of American political culture—both liberal and conservative—is revealed.

Hoover's *Masters of Deceit*

In 1958 three books appeared that defined the conservative perception of the events taking place across the United States and around the world. J. Edgar Hoover's *Masters of Deceit*, Rosalie M. Gordon's *Nine Men against America*, and W. Cleon Skousen's *The Naked Communist* all addressed the same basic question: what was going wrong with America, and how could it be stopped? Between them the audience they reached spanned nearly the entire conservative spectrum, and they also served to recruit nonconservatives into the fold. Of the three Hoover's book was most widely read. Entering the *New York Times* bestseller list at the number five position on March 30, a month later it had made its way up to number one, a spot it would hold for six weeks.[46] Gordon's book was heavily advertised in conservative periodicals like *National Review* and the *American Mercury*, and it attracted the already converted. Skousen's book became a guide for serious anticommunists, particularly those likely to join an organization, and became part of a trend among Americans to reinvigorate the process of educating themselves about and taking action against the ever-present communist menace. Taken together these works represent one facet of the cultural response by conservatives and nonconservatives to the problems facing their country.[47]

Most Americans acknowledged Hoover, director of the Federal Bureau of Investigation from 1924 to 1972, to be the country's foremost authority on communism. In a poll taken in mid-1954 asking whose opinion they respected most concerning how to handle communists in the country, more people picked Hoover than Eisenhower or McCarthy.[48] An enigma studied by dozens of scholars, Hoover's word defined law enforcement.[49] He had taken a little-respected government agency and made it feared by criminals and praised by law-abiding citizens, essentially creating the "G-Man." By the time *Masters of Deceit* appeared, Hoover, while not exuding the paternalism of Eisenhower, commanded the respect of nearly all Americans; his was a cult of personality stronger than anyone else in the government.[50] As the FBI gained political strength, its investigations delved deeper into internal security, singling out groups it deemed subversive for a blacklist and secretly observing suspicious citizens for years. The combination of adoration and fear made Hoover a celebrity, a status he exploited for his agency and himself.

Hoover chose a propitious time to publish his book; efforts to discredit communism reached new heights in the mid-1950s. Although the Smith Act began to weaken in 1955, it had done its job thoroughly, helping to reduce membership in the Communist Party of the United States (CPUSA) to around 20,000 members, down from a high of 80,000 during World War II. In early 1956 Khrushchev denounced Stalin's crimes, further weakening the American movement. Later that year Soviet tanks rolled into Budapest, putting down the Hungarian pro-democracy movement. Such events cast the CPUSA into internal turmoil and engendered the belief that the movement was dying. Not content with what seemed like an imminent death, in 1956 Hoover authorized the Counter Intelligence Program (COINTELPRO) to hammer the final nail in the party's coffin.[51] In the late 1950s the program's sole purpose was to discredit the CPUSA, and it did so using a variety of "dirty tricks," including having informants raise embarrassing questions at party meetings, starting feuds within cells, making anonymous phone calls to members, and framing a loyal party member as an FBI informant to discredit him with his comrades.[52] By the end of 1956 the party's membership had dropped to between 4,000 and 6,000, and a year later it sat at only 3,474.[53]

The irony that the FBI and the Smith Act had possibly done their jobs so well as to end the agency's pursuit of subversives was not lost on Hoover. In one sense he had reason to be suspicious of a weakened CPUSA: during the Justice Department's assault on the American Communist party in 1919 and 1920, many thought the CPUSA was all but extinct, yet it had rebounded dramatically over the next twenty years. In another sense Hoover knew that he had to fortify the FBI against liberal assaults on its budget, and fighting communists at home was one task with which most Americans sympathized.[54] Hoover thought that he should take his message directly to the American people and what better way than to produce a book outlining his beliefs on communism and morality in the United States. The result was *Masters of Deceit*, ghostwritten by a team of FBI writers and edited by Hoover, who made sure that whatever was in it reflected his program for eliminating communists and ensuring that the country steered the proper course.[55] The book went through 250,000 hardback and 2 million paperback copies between 1958 and 1970.[56] Thus not only did the book help justify the existence of the bureau's anticommunist units when such a threat seemed nearly nonexistent, but it helped Hoover broadcast his vision of what America should be like to millions of readers during troubled times, an exercise that, in all likelihood, was more important to Hoover than fighting the few thousand communists left in the country.

In a book densely packed with information and anecdotes, Hoover and his ghostwriters emphasized a handful of themes to convince the reader that not only did the communist menace still exist but also that the FBI played a vital role in defending America against its aggressors. Communism threatened the major American institutions, which traditionalists like Hoover believed were the mortar holding together the country's diverse population. The nation's defense,

the burgeoning scientific industry, a powerful economy that depended on innovation and rapid production of goods, and national interests abroad were all
potential targets for an internal and external enemy. Most threatened, however,
were the family and religion, two institutions that stood as a bulwark against
communist inroads. In Hoover's world communism was not only the antithesis
of Americanism, but its agents actively sought to replace one set of values with
another, in effect disarming America from the inside out. No one took the
threat of subversion more seriously than Hoover; although there were few
"card-carrying members" of the CPUSA, other Americans lived under communist "thought control," including "concealed Party members," "Fellow Travelers," "Opportunists," and "Dupes."[57] Added together this covert group multiplied the CPUSA's power far beyond its 4,000 or so open members, and this
cloaked threat was highly dangerous since it could be unleashed at any time.

Hoover and his writers missed no opportunity to emphasize how communists
planned to break down the family structure taken for granted by most Americans. No longer would such priorities as a comfortable, neat household, food on
the table, and parents who doted upon their children be the norm. Loyalty to
one another and mutual respect were not values in the communist family; rather,
loyalty to the party and materialistic ideology came first. If, for example, a communist organizer was needed in another city or was compelled to go underground
to protect the party, his children were told that he was dead. If the family were
forced into poverty through the long hours and low pay that came with working
for the communist cause, the wife was to get a job; if the wife refused to work
because she wanted to "keep house," the husband should think about getting a
divorce, since she was "selfish [and] self-centered . . . she doesn't understand
the movement."[58] Hoover's real-life examples emphasized how an entity as strong
as the CPUSA could put the very bedrock of America at risk, threaten the family, upset the "natural" balance between men and women in the household, and
transmit the resulting chaos to the children, innocent victims of their parents'
ideological adventures.

Religion was the other institutional pillar crucial to the perpetuation of whole-
some American values, which were under attack. The relationship between religion and communism was cyclical, Hoover believed. If a man or woman somehow began losing faith in God, communism—"the false religion"—was there to
take his place. The absence of spiritual values resulted in a misguided search for
the truth, and inevitably communism provided answers although never the right
ones. Unless this downward spiral was checked by a reinvigorated belief in God,
that individual would be lost to the Communist party. Such a scenario was increasingly likely in modern America, where strict adherence to the separation
of church and state made it probable that more and more young people would
not understand the "deep religious roots" of their "Western civilization." Hoover's
conviction that democracy was "rooted in a belief in a Supreme Being" led him

to outline six points he believed ensured a strong defense of democracy and the defeat of communism. The sanctity of the individual, the need for mutual responsibility among Americans, a life transcending materialism, one's responsibility to future generations, that humans and not political parties should establish moral values, and that love would triumph over hate were all part of a larger value system that guided the thoughts and actions of upstanding, moral Americans.[59] Were this value system to be swallowed up by communist ideology not only would the armor plating fall away from the country's ideological shield, but the qualities that made American democracy so appealing would disappear, making communism seem much more inviting.

Hoover's descriptions of communism, the party, and his utopian vision of America appealed to Americans of all political beliefs but particularly to conservatives. Echoing postwar conservatism's blend of anticommunism, traditionalism, and libertarianism, Hoover promoted the values with which each group could identify. Conservatives of all types read the book, and it received on the whole fabulous reviews in a variety of publications, ranging from conservative to mainstream. One review in the *New York Times* called it "the most authoritative book ever written on communism in America."[60] Although the book's style was simplistic, the anecdotes perhaps more likely to be found in pulp magazines, and the depiction of what was truly American probably offensive to some readers, the public adopted the book as an anticommunist and conservative Bible.

Much of the book's popularity among conservatives was due to Hoover telling conservatives what they thought they already knew: that the country was threatened by an internal and external enemy and that now was the time for all Americans to join together in defense of their country. That defense would rely on vigilance, reinvigorated fundamental values, and the defeat or replacement of politicians and institutional leaders who were soft on communism. While such actions were not easily accomplished, they were achievable, particularly when Americans who felt they had been living in a time of political and social turmoil were offered the chance through newly founded conservative organizations. Moreover Hoover's book was not the only cultural representation to emerge out of this period. Conservatives were bombarded with similar messages; they just needed to know where to look.

A New Battleground: Cold War Art

In 1959 President Eisenhower became an art critic. Asked by the press to comment on art chosen to be displayed at that summer's American National Exhibition in Sokolniki Park in Moscow, Eisenhower called Jack Levine's 1946 painting *Welcome Home*, which depicts a group of cavorting generals, "a lampoon more than art as far as I am concerned."[61] While Eisenhower did consider himself an amateur artist (he enjoyed painting-by-numbers), he admittedly had no expertise in the field. But somehow the esoteric subject of modern art had become a presidential priority.

With Khrushchev's denunciation in 1956 of some of Stalin's crimes, cultural exchanges began, albeit hesitantly, between the United States and the Soviet Union. In 1958 U.S. Information Agency officials started planning for the American National Exhibition, which was designed to show Russians what it was like to live in America. A small but important part of the exhibition was the art display, where the works of sixty-seven artists offered a taste of American culture. While most Americans understood that the show was thinly veiled propaganda, others wondered what kind of propaganda the government intended to disperse.

While art did not directly affect Americans' daily lives, some observers saw it as a weapon on the new battleground, part of the Cold War's momentum not bound by physical borders.[62] In a war of symbols and rhetoric, art could be as powerful as a battalion of soldiers or a legion of spies; its subversion was just below the surface, and it did not need to be smuggled into a hostile land. The key to art's political power was the combination of public appreciation and desire to understand it and the potentially subversive messages embedded within it. Moreover if the Cold War were not to be a shooting war, then its battles, fought in the economic, psychological, and cultural trenches, might be missed by Americans who were concerned with day-to-day life. With paintings and sculptures being the armaments of this nonshooting war, conservatives saw every reason to investigate and regulate the artists responsible for defending the country's cultural national security.

On May 31, 1959, the U.S. Information Agency made public the list of artists whose work would be sent to July's American National Exhibition. Four days later Francis Walter, Democratic congressman from Pennsylvania and chairman of the House Un-American Activities Committee, raised the issue on the House floor, starting a debate that raged in conservative circles for months. After an initial investigation by his staff, Walter claimed that nearly half of the sixty-seven artists had some sort of communist connection, and of those twenty-two were significantly involved in front activities. Walter went on to enumerate their various subversive connections, from Max Weber's CPUSA membership to Ben Shahn's affiliations "with over two dozen Communist fronts and causes."[63] At issue was not freedom of expression or what the artists themselves thought best represented America. Art was a quantifiable commodity with judgments based on aesthetic sensibilities and not politics. That argument, the congressman flatly stated, was plain liberal "poppycock."[64] At issue was the question of what America stood for, and how it would be represented. Would real Americans allow communists to lay claim to their country? If Americans forfeited the cultural arena, what would come next? Walter vowed that he would not be party to such surrender, and he threw himself into the cultural wars with a vigor no one could match.

Following in HUAC's founder Martin Dies's footsteps, Walter had gained a reputation for showing suspected subversives no mercy, and he produced results for the House and his constituents.[65] Although conservative publications like *Human Events* and the *American Mercury* picked up the story, Walter was not satisfied and immediately convened a hearing of HUAC to consider some larger questions about the exhibition.[66] On July 1, 1959, about one month before the exhibition was to open, Walter conducted a one-day HUAC hearing on modern art and communism. While Walter must have known that the CPUSA was reeling from attacks by the FBI and his own committee, he had two good reasons to pursue the inquiry. First he sincerely believed that the actual number of communists did not matter. Agreeing with Hoover, he felt that between Communist party agents, fellow travelers, dupes, and others, the enemy was deceptively strong. Second, like Hoover and the FBI, with the CPUSA becoming less of an obvious menace, HUAC was threatened with having helped to achieve its own obsolescence. More and more Americans were questioning whether the monetary expense and societal discord the committee generated were actually worth the price. Knowing he had to make as big a splash as possible, Walter began the hearings with his star witness, Wheeler Williams.

One of the most outspoken critics of modern art, Williams, a sculptor, was also president of the American Artists Professional League, an organization dedicated to promoting classical art and demystifying modern art. In early 1959 Williams had taken time out from sculpting a likeness of Robert A. Taft to trace the history of modern art. Williams argued that it came from "mediocre artists, seeking an audience, employing shock treatment methods of deformity, color discord, and other tricks to attract attention, however loaded with ridicule or scorn the reaction might be."[67] In his view such inferior art became popular when dealers, facing a shortage of old masterpieces, began capitalizing on these new artists and created a market where none had existed a few years before. But, Williams argued, the art had little redeeming value, and virtually anyone could be an artist with no training whatever: "Since there are no standards, anything can be called a masterpiece." He was further convinced that some museum curators and dealers were Communist agents, who reserved a percentage of their wall space or profits for the party.

The U.S. Information Agency, said Williams, simply did not understand the battle being waged between the simultaneous exhibits in Moscow and New York. The Soviets, Williams understood, would be overjoyed with the American contributions, since they would see how much of the American art world they controlled. The evidence was in the art. Instead of sending a work like Jackson Pollock's *Cathedral*, which Williams called "the worst doodle that you could imagine on a telephone pad," Williams believed artists like Winslow Homer or Frederick Remington would make a better impression on the Soviets and accu-

rately portray a United States that anyone could understand.[68] Joining the rep-
artee, Richard Arens, staff director for HUAC, asked Williams:

> If I took this bottle of ink and splashed it on this piece of paper here in a
> haphazard manner and then smeared the ink around and handed you that
> and asked you, on the basis of your extensive background and experience,
> to compare the ink blob with what you see before you, what would be your
> honest reaction as to the comparative artistic merits of the ink blob?[69]

Williams replied, "The ink blob accidentally might be better."

Although Williams pushed for a reinvigoration of classic styles, for him, like
Walter, what mattered most was not *how* something was depicted but *what* was
depicted. The two men were concerned with which version of America the
Soviets saw. Would they see the grandeur of the West in a Frederick Remington
painting or sculpture? a pastoral by a Hudson River painter? a portrait of Samuel
Adams by John Singleton Copley? No. Rather they would see Philip Evergood's
painting *Street Corner*, which Williams described as a crudely drawn "street scene
of a curious bunch of characters out in front of a drug store or bar or something
or a barbershop. . . . It is another example of 'social protest' art."[70] Walter wanted
to know if *Street Corner* showed a slum, would the Soviets think that all Americans lived in slums? Williams affirmed this, saying the painting's purpose was
"to show the fact that we have slums and give them the impression that that is
all we have."

After hearing from another opponent of modern art, Walter used the afternoon to listen to artists themselves, specifically two who had been accused of
having communist backgrounds. Ben Shahn, a painter involved in the New York
avant-garde between the 1930s and 1950s, and Philip Evergood, who was responsible for *Street Corner*, both testified in front of HUAC. When each was
questioned by Richard Arens a curious phenomenon emerged. After a few in-
formational questions, Arens asked each if he had ever been a member of the
CPUSA. First Shahn and then Evergood soon were answering every question
with a variation of "My refusal to answer this question propounded is on the
ground that the Congress and this committee must exercise its powers subject
to the limitations placed by the Constitution of the United States on governmental action and more particularly in the context of this question, the relevant
limitations of the Bill of Rights."[71] Arens fired question after question as he tried
to link the artists with the CPUSA or a front organization. Both Shahn and
Evergood refused to answer any of the questions; their scorn eventually seemed
like an admission of guilt.

Arens avoided asking them about their art—how they conceived their ideas,
how they painted, what they saw as the meanings within the works, and what
audience they aimed to reach. Shahn and Evergood never had a chance to de-

fend themselves against Walter, Williams, and the others. Placed on the defensive from the beginning, they were forced to answer questions to which the committee knew they would plead the Fifth Amendment. That the committee ensured that the hearings favored their side of the argument was not surprising. What was surprising, however, was how the focus shifted from the content to the artists' uses of their works, in effect paralyzing the artists, since they were critiqued on subjective grounds and then questioned on historical grounds, an approach that the committee must have known would leave them little room in which to maneuver.

Although Walter's speeches and the HUAC hearings did not succeed in having the paintings at the American National Exhibition removed, conservatives did succeed in bringing the issue into a national spotlight, briefly illustrating how subversion and the decaying of American values had extended to areas previously thought to be immune from the Cold War. The concept of Cold War as Total War was reinvigorated in the late 1950s and early 1960s as competition on every level—from kitchen appliances to art to long-range missiles—indicated who was "winning." For Americans who believed that their prestige and security were slipping away—now more rapidly than ever—such skirmishes were crucial. As Wheeler Williams had testified, "If they can destroy our faith in God and our faith in the beauty and wonders of our cultural heritage, including the arts and literature and music and so forth, they can take us over without a hydrogen bomb. They can take us over with popguns."[72] Moreover, in the Eisenhower climate, which emphasized compatibility instead of conflict, observers who liked to think of themselves as informed about politics and the Soviet menace noticed that incidents like the American National Exhibition were becoming more frequent. The Eisenhower complacency, conservatives believed, gave liberals the chance to rekindle their efforts as they initiated new programs that would eventually benefit the enemy. But the word was getting out to conservative publications and fledgling organizations, and although the news was not good, the tocsin helped trigger a vigorous effort to strengthen the conservative cause, the likes of which had not been seen since 1952.

"Operation Abolition": Attack and Counterattack

On September 21, 1957, a small, almost unnoticeable piece appeared in the *New York Times* entitled "Leftists Open Drive to End House Group." Following on the heels of the *Watkins* decision, the Emergency Civil Liberties Committee, founded in 1951, had held a rally at Carnegie Hall to kick off a campaign to abolish HUAC. There was no report of how many supporters turned out, but a "stench bomb was released in the rear of the main floor at 9:15 p.m."[73] This inauspicious beginning marked a series of events that, stretching over the next four years, came to epitomize the desperate struggle between, as conservatives saw it, appeasers and defenders of America. The debate over whether HUAC should continue in its traditional form or might instead be subsumed by another House committee spoke not only to the deep divisions between liberals and conservatives but also to the fears many conservatives had over America holding its own against the Soviet empire.

Three years after the Emergency Civil Liberties Committee's first meeting, HUAC was threatened on two fronts. First many critics called it obsolete, pointing out that the number of communists in America had dropped to its lowest level since the 1930s. Second liberals in the new administration and those who believed that the two superpowers should draw closer together demanded its end out of purely political motives. Forced to prove their worth, committee chairman Walter and his colleagues investigated incidents like the American National Exhibition or reported on subversive groups that could end up on the attorney general's blacklist. The campaign to abolish HUAC rang a warning bell for conservatives; the communist threat was still very real, and yet here was a constituency not only willing to lower America's guard but calling for a permanent end to a long-held vigilance. The upshot was obvious to anyone: liberals charged that the work that upstanding Americans had done and were doing was worthless, and those same critics were willing to surrender their country to an enemy who was alive and well and living among them.

By 1959 the attacks on HUAC had prompted Walter and his colleagues to take the offensive through both the uses of their committee and its duties. Walter proposed that HUAC assume jurisdiction over immigration and passport legislation, claiming that those areas were most germane to internal security. At the same time, however, California congressman James Roosevelt proposed a resolution to kill the committee outright and transfer all of its jurisdiction to the Judiciary Committee. Roosevelt became an unlikely crusader, leading the fight against HUAC while standing up to withering attacks by his colleagues on both sides of the aisle. Although Speaker Sam Rayburn declared Roosevelt's plan dead before it reached a vote, the issue did not go away.[74]

The year 1960 turned out to be crucial for both HUAC and conservatives. Months before the disheartening election of John F. Kennedy, the committee and its supporters again took the offensive, scheduling hearings in San Francisco for May. Unlike the investigations into the American National Exhibition one year earlier, these hearings hoped to expose the fact that communists and subversives still threatened internal security and that the campaign opposing HUAC was making headway among naive Americans. Moreover the lineage of Operation Abolition was traceable directly back to the Emergency Civil Liberties Committee meeting in September 1957. Now, though, other groups like the American Civil Liberties Union and Americans for Democratic Action and liberal politicians joined in the calls for eradicating the long-standing body. But what might have been just another series of questions to defendants pleading

the Fifth Amendment became a cause célèbre among conservatives, reinvigorating their moribund struggle against the enemy.

The San Francisco hearings of May 1960 had first been scheduled for June
1959, but they were delayed until September, then October, and then finally
until May.[75] Originally meant to investigate un-American activities among school-
teachers in California, HUAC also subpoenaed union organizers and others with
potential communist ties. After the September delay, the California Teachers
Association suggested to the committee that they simply hand over their files to
local school boards, which could then investigate their own teachers in private.
Walter agreed to the suggestion, and eventually a few teachers lost their jobs as
a result.[76] But in handing over the files, HUAC had suddenly changed the rules
by which it played. By providing authorities who had hiring and firing power
with inflammatory data, it was in effect acting as an omniscient authority with
no legislative, judicial, or executive body to check its power, a fact that outraged
liberals and civil libertarians in California and the rest of the country.

Two weeks before the hearings began, students in the San Francisco Bay area
began organizing ad hoc committees to oppose the proceedings. Inspired but
frustrated by their failed protests over Caryl Chessman's execution on May 2,
1960 (Chessman had been found guilty in 1948 of kidnapping, although the
state's evidence was highly suspicious), as well as the southern sit-ins, which
had moved north (in which African-American and white students sat-in at
Woolworth's and other lunch counters, demanding their desegregation), students
were primed for acting on an issue that affected both their own communities
and the nation as a whole.[77] The hearings provided a perfect opportunity to
challenge what seemed like conservatism—and anticommunist liberalism—
gone amok. Centered primarily at the University of California at Berkeley but
also including students from San Francisco State College and a handful from
Stanford, leaders planned to pack the hearing room and staff a picket line outside of City Hall. The signatures of 165 professors from San Francisco State
College and 300 from Berkeley appeared on statements protesting HUAC's
presence.[78] Petitions were passed, and one day before the hearings began 1,000
people attended a rally in the city's Union Square.

HUAC appropriated the supervisors' chambers in City Hall, a room seating
approximately 400. Defendants and their lawyers received passes with only a
limited number of seats held open for students and other observers . The committee's decision to restrict the number of students in the hearing room backfired, however, since it "provided the protestors with a real cause and an effective rallying cry."[79] On the morning of May 13, the second day of the hearings,
200 students lined up to enter the hearing room, and soon those who gained
admission began jeering the committee, hissing the questioners, and laughing
in the faces of their antagonists. After the noon recess those who had been subpoenaed began chanting, "Open the doors! Open the doors!" in an effort to get

more students into the room. A squad of police removed the protesters and restored some semblance of order so that the hearings could proceed. The next day, however, the protesters were back in force. Although the same number were admitted to the proceedings room students took up positions outside of the doors and began singing and chanting. Eventually the noise became too much for the committee, which called in the police to clear the demonstrators out of the building. When it became clear that the students would not move, fire hoses were turned on them, and many were either washed or dragged by police officers down the long, slick marble staircase.[80] Outside, nearly 2,000 people watched as students came tumbling out of the building. On the last day of hearings the crowd remained noisy but restrained, and the committee wrapped up its questioning and quickly slipped out of City Hall.

The demonstrations convinced conservative observers that not only were subversives still active in the United States but that contemplating shutting down the one legislative body committed to their annihilation was nothing less than preposterous. May 13, or "Black Friday" as some conservatives labeled it, convinced them that playing defensively would not win the game. While they might make use of what seemed like a defensive posture by the committee against the students, they needed to advertise aggressively what had gone on and what might happen next. Furthermore, although the HUAC budget had been rubber-stamped in the past, with a new administration controlling Washington and incidents like the one in San Francisco producing uncontrolled and ugly publicity, the committee realized it had to preempt criticism by forcefully telling its side of the story.

The result was *Operation Abolition*, a forty-five-minute documentary about the San Francisco hearings produced by HUAC. Assembled from subpoenaed news footage from local television stations, the film combined protest scenes with talking heads from the committee and Congress. After a brief introduction by Fulton Lewis III, a well-known anticommunist and former HUAC staff member, Chairman Walter set the stage for the rest of the film:

> "Operation Abolition": This is what the Communists call their current drive to destroy the House Committee on Un-American Activities, weaken the Federal Bureau of Investigation, to discredit its great director, J. Edgar Hoover, and to render sterile the security laws of our Government. The Communist Party has given top priority to "Operation Abolition" and has assigned agents trained in propaganda and agitation to this project.[81]

Walter realized that to guarantee HUAC's survival, he had to link Operation Abolition to a better-known agency and individual, and invoking Hoover's name achieved that goal perfectly, a tactic endorsed by Hoover. By Walter's reckoning the Operation Abolition campaign—which he was convinced was CPUSA-organized and -funded and used gullible students to carry out the dirty work—

was extremely ambitious; the possibility that it reflected nothing more than an effort by left-leaning (or civil libertarian) Americans with no ties to the Kremlin was never even entertained. This was the unveiling of the new anti-anticommunism, Walter said, with loyal Americans suddenly labeled traitors for not tolerating unruly mobs, which were whipped into frenzies by professional communist agitators.

The body of the film documented the committee's attempts to preside over orderly hearings juxtaposed against the student demonstrators inside and out-side of the meeting room. Always the emphasis was on the fact that the CPUSA had professional agitators in the mob egging on the students who, left to their own devices, would not have been nearly so unruly. In many ways this is what troubled conservatives most: that American youth were as susceptible to com-munist influences as youth from other countries. In later remarks to the House Walter quoted from an editorial supporting the film, which echoed his exact thoughts:

> "Operation Abolition" produces documentary evidence that the same thing that happened in Tokyo and in Caracas and other Central and South Ameri-can countries can happen here and did happen here in San Francisco.[82]

Although such connections were difficult to prove, they were also difficult to disprove, and HUAC was certain to exploit any fears such comparisons might raise. How much Walter and his companions believed in the linkages is difficult to ascertain; in terms of self-propagation, however, it was in their best interest to ensure that the audience understood that America faced the same threat as the rest of the world. Moreover, in claiming that the students themselves had been duped by professional communist agitators, HUAC could argue that the students' actions were not wholly their own, thus allowing them to renounce their deluded ways and return to the fold.

HUAC contracted Washington Video Productions to print hundreds of cop-ies of the film, which were then sent out across the country to both public and private organizations. Eventually some 2,000 prints of the film were in circula-tion, and by mid-1961 one estimate placed the total number of viewers at 15 million, a number rivaling or surpassing many contemporary major Hollywood releases.[83] HUAC made the film part of its official report on the disturbances, and soon some officers in the armed forces began showing the film to their troops.[84] The riots had aided Walter and his colleagues more than they could have hoped; not only did they have concrete proof that the problems caused by communist agitators were not over, but their film served the dual purpose of publicizing the threat and convincing people of the need to sustain HUAC's funding. Yet even with the film's overwhelmingly positive reception by the con-servative community, the committee was hardly prepared for the controversy that erupted once it began public screenings.

Debate over the film began almost as soon as it was released, although surprisingly the film received relatively little coverage in the press. In the House,
however, congressmen discussed the film at length, knowing that a vote on the
committee's budget appropriations would follow. Leading critics of the film
included James Roosevelt and William Fitts Ryan, a Democrat from New York.
A son of FDR, Roosevelt was an old opponent of HUAC; he had been the one
to suggest its abolition in early 1959, which had earned him the wrath of anticommunists across the country. On a visit to Houston in 1960, for example,
Roosevelt found himself hanged in effigy by a group of self-described conservatives.[85] Roosevelt and Ryan protested the film by diligently entering into the
Congressional Record critical editorials and articles their staffs clipped from
newspapers in their home states.[86] Although Ryan was a supportive comrade-
in-arms for Roosevelt, it was really Roosevelt who took up the fight, standing as
the most outspoken opponent of the committee. Roosevelt's strategy consisted
of questioning the committee's depiction of truth in the film—and thus by default the premises on which HUAC was based.

Rather than using every instance to attack HUAC directly, however, Roosevelt
played it safe, remarking that he was trying to ensure that the committee's reports were "free of error." Unlike his colleague Ryan from New York, Roosevelt
dodged the main issues: that HUAC violated citizens' civil liberties, that it was
obsolete, and that the only purpose it could possibly serve was self-propagation.
Roosevelt was more reluctant than Ryan to challenge the committee directly
because he had become the symbol for anti-anticommunism, and his political
career was in jeopardy because of it. The situation was not aided by Roosevelt's
sacrificial lamb status, a fact his party understood clearly, and a major reason
why Roosevelt hedged his bets when attacking HUAC. For example, Roosevelt
decided not to introduce a resolution to abolish HUAC outright since the initiative's lopsided defeat would "mislead the public into thinking that this Committee really has the backing of this House."[87] Unfortunately for Roosevelt, his
fears were true—at least politically.[88]

Although most of the country remained staunchly anticommunist in 1961,
ideological skirmishes with the enemy no longer garnered the same attention,
which gave some the impression that the populace was not only less vigilant about
subversion but perhaps even more accepting of the formerly taboo beliefs. Such
events as the Supreme Court rulings over the previous four years and Khrushchev's visit had shocked many Americans and renewed the fires that had been
kindled earlier in that decade. Yet a year or two after the Soviet leader's visit,
the nation had experienced a presidential election, the Bay of Pigs, and how the
space race was progressing. What mattered most to people personally—their
jobs, their standard of living, and providing for their children—was once again
solidly entrenched as their number one priority. In early 1961, for example, most
Americans wanted newly elected President Kennedy to "follow a middle-of-the-

road policy." By midyear, after heeding their advice, the president had won approval ratings of 83%.[89] The series of events of the late 1950s had activated some Americans, but the impact was limited to those who prided themselves on their vigilance as anticommunists and conservatives. Later many of these individuals became standard-bearers in the grassroots conservative movement and rallied their communities to become bastions of conservative activity.

The year 1961 was, for many future conservative activists, a time when they realized they were not only on their own, but that their government was not on the "right" side. This understanding led many to contemplate what would later be termed "conspiracy theories," and a great number converted their ideas into action, joining groups to help to rekindle a conservative blaze. Another group of conservatives, however, looked not to conspiracy theories but to politics; they focused on the Republican party and mainstream ideas and carefully avoided what they saw as farfetched speculation. Both groups of conservatives independently coalesced between 1957 and 1961, yet few in either circle pondered the possibility that they would eventually challenge each other for leadership of a movement.

Operation Abolition helped commence that new era for both liberals and conservatives. Students in the Bay Area and across the country used the protests and then HUAC's official response as a clarion call to action. In September 1960 the Bay Area Student Committee for the Abolition of the House Committee on Un-American Activities began moving off the campuses to inform the public about HUAC's misinformation and systematized injustice. After the release of the film, it purchased a copy and sent students who had been at the protests to other campuses to point out falsifications made by the committee. In 1962 the student committee sent its chairman on a two-month speaking tour of college campuses to drum up anti-HUAC sentiment, and the ACLU and other liberal groups followed suit.[90] Furthermore whenever conservatives showed the film, it sparked debates over its accuracy and the nature of the investigations. For many students the injustices depicted by the film and its invention of a communist-controlled riot led them to question their government for the first time. And unlike such incidents as the Chessman execution, where students in the Bay Area had been activated to save one man's life, *Operation Abolition* could be shown night after night, letting each viewer decide for himself or herself what the "truth" really was. The film's replication benefited its supporters, too, as seen by the staggering estimates for viewers in 1961. One could not be neutral about *Operation Abolition*, and for those who looked upon the events or their depiction with disdain, this remained one of the seminal events of the 1960s.[91] Moreover, with the government film acting as a call to arms for liberals as well as conservatives, many moribund organizations received vital transfusions of new blood, helping to replace the old Left with the first wave of the new Left.

On the other hand, conservatives looked to HUAC to support their allegations against the unexpectedly spirited liberal response. In reply the committee
published *The Truth about the Film "Operation Abolition,"* a two-part study of
the accusations made by the film's opponents. Pointing out that "to the best of
the committee's knowledge, this was the first time in history that a moving picture was made a part of an official report of any committee to the House of
Representatives," the members focused on the film's purposes particularly "the
need for stricter laws governing the conduct of spectators and witnesses at congressional hearings."[92] Law and order were concepts that any citizen watching
the film could comprehend. Moreover most of the study centered on proving
that the riots had been communist-inspired and -led. These two purposes worked
hand in hand since, "as part of its over-all campaign to subvert the United States,
the Communist Party is attempting to promote contempt for law and order
among the American people and to sabotage the operations of the Congress."[93]
To break down American social structure, the communists employed tactics that,
while seeming trivial, worked surreptitiously to achieve their goal. The protest
song "We Shall Not Be Moved" sung by the demonstrators, for example, came
from a communist songbook.[94] Any lies or intentionally misleading segments,
which liberals claimed the filmmakers created by splicing together sequences
out of order, amounted to minor "errors," or were simply not part of the film.[95]

The committee had rebuffed its critics by using the same techniques that the
film employed—convincing for those who already believed in HUAC's purpose
and its righteousness but ineffective at converting hardcore liberals. Nevertheless conservatives watching the film saw riots that were clearly not staged and
would not have happened had the students and their leaders stayed away. Liberals might tolerate such blatant disrespect for law and order, but conservatives
saw only opposition to the moral imperative that laws were necessary for individuals to live together in society. If some people decided they were above the
law, it was society's duty to reel them back in. This social conservatism would
grow in scope over the coming years, but for many, watching the film of the San
Francisco protests was a nightmare come true.

Meanwhile some conservatives had begun looking for political solutions to
these problems. These new ideologues—many of them connected to the *National Review* circle of conservative intellectuals—looked for answers to solve
the problems embodied by JFK and increasingly active liberal interest groups.
They understood that through politics they could achieve not only their goal of
reinvigorating anticommunism as a belief system but also they might crack the
New Deal Coalition and use conservative ideology to reach an entirely new
audience. While these conservatives did not want to give up the successes they
had seen (or been a part of) in the 1950s, many believed that new strategies and
tactics were necessary to spread their ideology and then win the White House.

Though they certainly did not want to alienate HUAC and its supporters, this new generation of conservatives saw politics as the key to ensuring that America's position included ideas and policies that countered the New Deal and the New Frontier.

Also arising from this denouement of late 1950s events and the HUAC battle was a group of conservatives who saw the government abdicating its responsibility to protect the national interests from domestic subversion. Odder still was the fact that the government almost seemed to be encouraging subversives to make headway in the United States. After years of doing battle with communists and other threatening peoples, the great protector was giving up. While not all conservatives in this category bought into conspiracy theories, many saw few explanations for what was happening on a daily basis. By mid-1961 more and more of them had been tallying the bad events for four years. Some had been activated and had begun participating in groups formed to fight communism and subversion. Others, however, held back, hoping the government would realize its mistake and crack down on the students, communist agitators, and civil rights demonstrators. Still others waited, knowing that the events within and without America indicated that nothing was going to change unless they made an effort.

From these seeds the modern conservative movement was born. Each loosely defined group turned to nongovernmental organizations to do their political and social legwork, yet the category dominated by a new generation of conservatives relied on party politics first, using organizations to enforce their ideas about what those politics should do for conservatives. The other group used organizations as ends in themselves, realizing that they could not wait any longer nor use any more energy to change the political system. Instead they would have to replace the government agencies that liberals (and many Eisenhower Republicans) had emasculated. This shift, from public to private enforcement of American morals, values, and ideology, came at the expense of some established politicians, some political strategies, and some conservatives, who failed to recognize the institutional changes all around them. But the changes were not all negative; with the government's abdication of its responsibility to enforce anticommunism and prevent the growth of subversive movements, the opportunities for private organizations to conduct such affairs exactly how they wanted became realities. The damage liberals had done to institutional conservatism ensconced in the government was severe, but at the same time those liberals had opened the door for new initiatives by conservatives, which would eventually restructure conservatism in America.

After more than four years of assaults on conservative ideology in America, optimistic individuals became keystones and leaders in a burgeoning movement. They had seen the signs for years, yet getting others to pay attention had been difficult and expensive. Without steady financial backing no grassroots political initiative could be expected to do more than appear briefly before disappearing forever. These new conservatives, however, wanted to make a lasting impact on the political and social systems, and they needed adequate funding to make those goals a reality. As important as the money were the people themselves. Without a new influx of ideas, workers, and enthusiasm, conservatism would be in the shadow of the New Frontier for perhaps eight long years. Moreover, unless they acted now, the next time a series of events akin to those between 1957 and 1961 occurred, the public would probably accept them as the new norm; under liberalism such events were *supposed* to occur. Both groups of conservatives, then, looked to untapped pools of Americans who were upset with the last four years of events but had had nowhere to turn except inward. Conservative organizers wanted to bring those individuals into contact with each other and channel their frustrations and anxieties into politically and socially useful projects and directions. The startling reversal that conservatism underwent between 1957 and 1964 was not accidental. Organizers worked long and hard to harness what had been building over time, and within a few years had achieved many of their goals, the most important of which was placing conservatism on the map. The road to get there, however, would be a treacherous one, and not all who set off on it returned as heroes of the cause.

A NEW KIND OF CONSERVATISM

THE JOHN BIRCH SOCIETY

On December 8, 1958, eleven men arrived at a brick Tudor house in a quiet Indianapolis neighborhood to discuss the fate of the United States and the free world. That Monday these workingmen temporarily left their jobs and families after receiving invitations from a fellow National Association of Manufacturers (NAM) member that urged them—without providing many details—to attend. One of the invitees was T. Coleman Andrews, a long-time resident of Richmond, Virginia, and holder of offices on both the state and federal levels.[1] The letter's sense of urgency—and secrecy—made Andrews feel as though the world's destiny lay upon his shoulders:

> Would you be able and willing to meet with about ten other men, all from different parts of the nation, in Indianapolis on Monday, December 8 and Tuesday, December 9?

> Except for myself, they are all men of well recognized stature, unshakable integrity, proved ability, and fervent patriotism. The meeting will be completely "off the record." . . . And since there is no way I can tell you of the ideas which I hope to see thoroughly discussed there, without writing volumes, you will have to take for granted that I would not ask such busy men to give up two whole days in this way unless I thought it would be worthwhile.[2]

Andrews accepted.

Stepping into the house on the bitter, blustery morning, Andrews and the others hung their coats in the closet and gratefully accepted the first of many cups of coffee from Marguerite Dice, who had volunteered her house for the meeting. Repairing to the living room, the men took seats in a semicircle, surrounding an empty chair. Soon a tall, balding man entered the room, greeted each of the men, and arranged a sheaf of notes. Robert H. W. Welch, Jr., candy manufacturer, sometime politician, and virulent anticommunist, prepared to begin a talk that would change not only his life but the lives of tens of thousands of Americans. Thus was born the John Birch Society (JBS), the premier example of right-wing activism in the early 1960s.

At precisely nine in the morning Welch began speaking. With just a brief break for lunch, he spoke for almost seven hours straight. The eleven men sat transfixed, took notes, and let the facts sink in. The next day's session was almost as long, with Welch speaking for nearly six hours. Welch's notes for the meeting—which he read verbatim—became *The Blue Book*, the main text for all JBS members, and illustrate what resonated with him and his fellow conservatives.[3] Beginning with the depth of communist infiltration, Andrews recorded in his notes, there had been an "800% expansion of Communist membership in [the] last 20 years" and that "'wastefulness' [was] a primary element of the Communist conspiracy, with complete devaluation of the dollar the immediate aim and economic collapse and political and social chaos the ultimate objective."[4] Welch's statements hit these fiscal conservatives particularly hard, and Welch laid it on thick as he adapted ideas from Oswald Spengler's *Decline of the West* to tell his listeners that "civilizations die of the cause of collectivism by destroying the usefulness of the individual to society."[5] Instead of fighting communism using American principles of warfare, Welch believed that they would have to "fight dirty" and reduce themselves to the level of their enemy in order to understand what made him tick.

Using his experience as an expert salesman, Welch marched the men down a path that dead-ended with an obvious question: what next? At the end of the second day Welch answered it, proposing the founding of the John Birch Society. Asking for "no other title than that of its Founder," he made no attempt to hide the fact that the organization would be monolithic.[6] Welch warned that a body based on a republican form of government "lends itself too readily to infiltration, distortion, and disruption" and that a democracy "is merely a deceptive phrase, a weapon of demagoguery, and a perennial fraud."[7]

From this meeting Welch recruited ten of the eleven men as the first members of the John Birch Society. Nine of them ended up on the JBS Council, where they gave pro forma approval to Welch's various projects and ideas. Perhaps most remarkable is the level of agreement among Welch and his recruits. T. Coleman Andrews never seemed to question Welch's ideas nor the thought process from which the John Birch Society emerged; neither did any of the other attendees.

Less than a year later the meeting's official transcript, *The Blue Book*, was making the rounds among conservatives and anticommunists of all types, and Robert Welch was on his way to becoming a household name. Few were neutral about Welch; he and his plan were either admired or despised. One conservative from Arkansas wrote Welch to thank him for his inspiration:

> Last night when I finished reading it [*The Blue Book*] I took flight into the wonderful World of Hope, after a considerable absence. This morning I tossed my hat in the air with a "Yipee!"

> The John Birch Society is a God-send. Your plan is Divinely inspired.
> And you, Robert Welch—you have become the key to one of mankind's
> greatest opportunities. The need was for inspired leadership; and we didn't
> have it.[8]

Within two years Welch's vision grew into a full-fledged national organization
with membership estimates ranging between 20,000 and 100,000.[9]

Not everyone was as enthusiastic as the gentleman from Arkansas, however,
and some were discomfited by a phenomenon they feared was growing out of
control. In 1963, after observing three years of the society's dizzying growth,
Myer Feldman, an assistant to President John F. Kennedy, reported:

> Estimates of its membership strength vary from 20,000 to 100,000, but its
> impact derives from the energy, dedication, and devotion to the Society
> and to founder Welch of the members. They have 124 full-time paid em-
> ployees, including 40 full-time paid organizers. There are some 200 sec-
> tion leaders scattered around the country who are paid only expenses. They
> publish a monthly magazine, called "American Opinion," and members
> are given instructions each month on tasks to be carried out via the Society's
> "Bulletin."
>   Last year they had an income, according to a report filed by the Massa-
> chusetts Attorney General's office, of $737,000. This is a 40 percent in-
> crease over 1961. Next year they hope to double their field staff, triple
> their libraries, and launch a full-scale public relations program.[10]

Kennedy's advisers had good reason to worry about the right wing. By this time
not only was the JBS more visible than ever before, but its potential to wield
political power was untested. Clearly some conservatives—namely the extremists—had entered a new era, and liberals were only now finding out what they
were up against.

Beginnings: Robert H. W. Welch, Jr.

The John Birch Society was but one faction within the conservative movement
between the late 1950s and 1960s. After the raucous events of the late 1950s
those who held conservative beliefs began looking for organizations into which
they could pour their energy. They sought each other out, and perhaps more
than any other service it provided, the JBS acted as a kind of matchmaker, where
lone individuals with broad visions could join each other and help turn an ideology into a movement.

This far-right group had an impact on conservatives of all hues and on American political culture as a whole. Far rightists, like more moderate conservatives,
forced the Republican party—and the Democratic party too—to adjust its

agenda. The GOP, of course, did not simply accept what the JBS and other extremists ordered. Nevertheless politicians were compelled to consider what demands were made, why they were made, about whom or what they were made, and who the Americans who issued the calls were. As much as Robert Welch despised democracy, it was through the mechanisms of this same system that conservatives succeeded in changing American political culture. Acting in much the same way as a third party, the JBS brought to the forefront of the GOP a number of issues that it might otherwise have ignored.[11] It helped to move ideas once considered on the fringes of conservative ideology into mainstream politics. Although the JBS had a few members elected to office, its strength did not come from influencing voters at the ballot box but rather in its revelatory effect on its members, who came to realize that not all was right with America.

To understand the JBS one must understand Welch, and to understand Welch it is necessary to delve briefly into his life before the JBS. Born on December 1, 1899, in rural North Carolina, Welch was raised by a father who worked the land and a mother who, as a former grade school teacher, tutored Welch at home instead of sending him to public school. Raised as a fundamentalist Baptist, Welch immersed himself in the Bible, becoming somewhat of an expert while still a youngster. Welch, however, later rejected some of the main tenets of his fundamentalist beliefs, so that by 1958 he could tell fellow conservatives that instead of trusting solely in religion to save America, there was "a broader and more encompassing faith to which we can all subscribe, without any of us doing the slightest violation to the more specific doctrines of his own creed or altars of his own devotion."[12] By any measurement Welch was a prodigy; he entered the University of North Carolina when he was twelve and graduated with the class of 1916. Hoping for a career in the navy, Welch entered Annapolis but left after two years since the war had ended and his enthusiasm for the military had rapidly dropped off. Welch then entered Harvard Law School but droped out halfway through his final year. Hoping to become a successful businessman, Welch started the Oxford Candy Company in Cambridge, Massachusetts. Fairly successful until early in the depression, Welch struggled to balance the business and a new marriage while still in his mid-twenties. During the depression Welch had to work for his brother's candy firm, the James O. Welch Company. Here Robert learned what it took to be a successful salesman, eventually authoring *The Road to Salesmanship*, the first of many short books.

Welch eventually found success in the candy business: in 1926 he began marketing a candy he called the "Papa Sucker"—later known to millions as the "Sugar Daddy"—and by 1949 had established his name in the world of mass-marketed confectioneries.[13] His ability to round up volunteer workers and make supporting speeches led Massachusetts politicians to turn to him for endorsements. Late that year he decided to make a run for the lieutenant governor's position in Massachusetts. Alarmed that "everything which has made America envied by the rest of the world we are now throwing away for a phony 'security' and a creeping collectivism," Welch declared, "To do my part to my own satisfaction, as a crusader on one small front of this battle, I have to go into politics."[14] Welch's old Right conservatism sans conspiracy theories was evident in his belief in time-tested values, which he felt were superior to competing systems; in his feeling that only a small percentage of the population favored these competing systems of socialism or state-condoned welfarism; in his rejection of the New Deal and the Fair Deal; and in his desire to return to individual responsibility.

Welch lost the primary by nearly a three-to-one margin. Even though the defeat was an unmistakable rejection of Welch and perhaps his ideas, his candidacy taught him valuable lessons about politics and spread his reputation among conservatives. Although Welch made no further personal forays into politics, he was from this point on known as a conservative, one to whom others turned for his opinions, advice, and support.

In 1952 he campaigned heartily for Robert Taft, purchasing radio time with his own money and traveling around Massachusetts to drum up support. When Eisenhower instead got the Republican nomination, Welch later reflected:

> But for the dirtiest deal in American political history, participated in if not actually engineered by Richard Nixon in order to make himself vice-president (and to put Warren on the Supreme Court as part of that deal), Taft would have been nominated in Chicago in 1952. It is almost certain that Taft would then have been elected President by a far greater plurality than was Eisenhower, that a grand rout of the Communists in our government and in our midst would have been started, that McCarthy would be alive today, and that we wouldn't even be in this mess that we are supposed to look to Nixon to lead us out of.[15]

Taft's loss and Eisenhower's actions as president showed Welch that America was more vulnerable to communist corruption than most people believed. Welch had started down the road to saving America; now there was no turning back.

Welch's next major political endeavor was the publication and promotion of a speech that he eventually turned into a thirty-thousand-word letter and released as *May God Forgive Us*. He circulated a draft around Boston, where it accumulated a following of conservatives, some of whom privately published additional copies to distribute themselves. By late 1951, although still supervising the sales force of the James O. Welch Company, Welch realized that the letter could have an even wider impact. He wrote to Henry Regnery, one of the few self-avowed conservative publishers, who had recently produced young William F. Buckley's *God and Man at Yale*. Revealing an understanding for marketing that he would later use in the founding of the JBS, Welch decided that it was more important to have a known publisher's seal of approval on the tract than to self-publish:

> I have no interest in anything that could remotely be classified as "vanity publishing" either in whole or in part. So I should like to have you consider the proposal strictly as a regular publishing venture, as I am sure you will. But it does seem worth pointing out, nevertheless, that one friend of mine, a prominent lawyer in New York City, has flatly offered to stand all the expense of duplicating and mailing this letter to the seventeen thousand members of the National Association of Manufacturers—of which I have the honor to be on the board of directors.[16]

Welch offered to put up the initial costs of duplication, sell at least 17,000 copies, and pay Regnery a percentage of the profit, all without Regnery risking a cent. Regnery agreed and eventually sold or gave away almost 200,000 copies of the pamphlet. Welch also involved himself in distribution, establishing the Welch Letter Mailing Committee, a group of five conservative young men from Massachusetts who sent out letters soliciting sales of May God Forgive Us. Enlisting these helpers was a stroke of political genius; by bypassing typical distribution channels, Welch made the pamphlet's contents seem that much more revelatory.[17] Welch's willingness to rely on friends, workers from his 1950 campaign, and even employees in the candy company showed him that a semigrassroots effort could take the place of a more established company and that dedication and a little self-sacrifice could substitute for money or status.[18]

Welch's successful foray into political commentary helped establish a lifelong pattern of linking political ideology (either his own or beliefs he admired) to a top-down grassroots promotional and organizational effort. Welch became known to publishers like Regnery as an author who wrote clearly for the common American about topics of the utmost importance. Building on his impressive track record in business, Welch soon became a player among conservatives in politics, publishing, and commerce.

In 1954 Welch published The Life of John Birch, a biography of a Baptist missionary in China who was killed by the Chinese communists ten days after the end of World War II.[19] Birch was an interesting subject for Welch to have settled on; not only were the two of similar family backgrounds, but Birch also had a history of refusing to believe that others' opinions might be as valid as his own. In 1939, long before McCarthy or Welch, Birch helped engineer a heresy trial at Mercer College in Macon, Georgia, in which he led twelve students in charging five teachers with accusations ranging from teaching evolution to speculating about salvation for nonbelievers. The trial was big news in fundamentalist Georgia and attracted press attention from around the South. According to a Mercer student, "There was something fanatical in John Birch's dedication, something messianic in his confidence in his mission to save souls."[20] Welch always claimed that he named the society after Birch because the soldier was an unknown yet dedicated anticommunist who deserved recognition. Just as likely, however, was Welch's identification with Birch's unbending personality, his refusal to admit defeat or wrongdoing, and his belief that he was the only one who could do what was necessary, whether fighting the communists or teaching men how to sell candy.

Throughout the mid-1950s Welch continued to make a name for himself among conservative politicians, businessmen, and commentators. Welch was a member of the National Association of Manufacturers, which functioned, for his purposes, as a kind of fraternity of conservative businessmen. Flourishing in leadership roles, Welch served on the NAM Board of Directors from 1950 to 1957, was a NAM regional vice president for three years, and chaired the NAM Educational Committee.[21] He gave speeches, wrote articles, developed his contacts and ideas, and tried to awaken the American people to the tragedy unfolding before their eyes. In 1956 Welch delivered a speech before the Economic Club of Detroit entitled "What Is Happening to America Abroad?"[22] His analysis of American foreign policy reveals that his reasoning, while not fully developed, was inspired as much by what was *not* happening as what was. Welch's organizing question focused on why, in the ten years after the end of the war, had so many countries fallen to communism. After surveying nations from Asia to Latin America, Welch concluded, "Our defensive strength in proportion to the force of a known enemy, our moral leadership throughout the world, and our very security itself have toppled from great heights into a sticky morass where the footing grows less solid every day."[23] American leaders had resigned themselves to eventual defeat. Equal to communist advances were American retreats—"betrayals"—that further aided the enemy's cause. He blamed the actions of the U.S. government; the people, he felt confident, would never consciously choose to aid an enemy. Welch examined Korea, China, and, presciently, Vietnam, and in all cases found that politicians had accepted defeat before the final battle.[24]

Perhaps most perplexing about Welch's vision, however, were its similarities to nonconspiracy theories, which sought to explain the same political trends. Paralleling the critics of the Right in the 1960s who used liberal middle-class democracy as their norm, Welch developed a paradigm that labeled middle-class democracy (or noncommunism) as the standard for the entire world. Countries that did not conform to such a model were deviant. He believed that deviancy most certainly was not chosen by citizens, since nonpoliticians should have been the least corruptible. Countries "lost" to the communists must have had help; resisting the advances of Moscow was tough but not impossible. Thus, he argued, America had played a crucial role either by its actions or inactions.

Welch's demands were also little different from those of many in the government. In the years between Woodrow Wilson's administration and the early 1960s presidents and their aides believed that American middle-class democracy was the pinnacle to which all societies should aspire. These leaders balanced their ideologies with the knowledge that imperialism was antithetical to such a system, thus tying their hands—albeit sometimes loosely—when a country chose a competing form of government. And yet the government did get involved in fighting communist influences abroad. Eisenhower aided the French in Indochina, although he drew the line in 1954 at Dien Bien Phu. The CIA engineered coups in Iran in 1953, Guatemala in 1954, and Vietnam in 1963, just to name a few. Even though much of this activity was public knowledge Welch could not believe that America had actually attempted to help countries that had succumbed to the "red tide." Welch took the pervasive American ideology one step further: not only did all countries *want* to be like us, they *should* be like us, and if they were not, it was our fault. Though Welch's ideology was an affront to those who believed that America was doing its best and that it had no place in doing more, for others he spelled out their exact thoughts. And the number of Americans sympathetic to his and others' conservative ideology was growing.

Welch's influence among conservatives mounted throughout the 1950s. While *National Review* eventually helped unify conservatives as it provided an alternative to left-leaning periodicals, founder William F. Buckley initially found it tough going. In 1955 when he launched his magazine (first called *National Weekly*) he solicited investments from wealthy conservatives who believed such a publication would help fortify the conservative community. One of the wealthy conservatives who responded was Robert Welch. After receiving a letter in which Welch pledged $1,000 to purchase Buckley's privately issued stock, Buckley responded glowingly:

> Two-thirds of the capital are now pledged, and we are working quite hopefully on the last third—so hopefully, in fact, that we expect to start publication this Fall. If we do, I'm afraid we shall have to count on the literary contributions of Robert H. W. Welch, Jr., the author of two of the finest pamphlets this country has read in a decade. One of the great promises of National Weekly is precisely that we now shall be able to synchronize these desperately isolated voices and make the country at last listen to a growing unisono.[25]

At this point in their careers, Welch and Buckley seemed to be in total agreement in regard to what direction the movement should go. Both realized that to guard against the liberal press, conservatives would need clearer and more self-regulated lines of communication. Two years later Welch again responded to

Buckley's need for funds, pledging another $1,000.[26] By the mid-1950s, long before the creation of the John Birch Society, Welch was undeniably one of the best known—and well-respected—conservatives in the United States. The fact that the 1950s conservative community embraced Welch so warmly makes his later ostracization that much more telling. Moreover Welch's acceptance and expulsion is, in some ways, a metaphor for the entire conservative movement from the late 1950s to the early 1970s.

The year 1954 was a watershed politically for Welch. In addition to his revelations about Birch, he turned the Republican loss of eighteen congressional seats to his own political advantage.[27] After initially blaming the loss on Eisenhower's refusal to support conservative candidates, Welch came to a realization about the turn of political affairs during the previous nine years. After a discussion with some prominent friends in the NAM, Welch penned his thoughts in a long letter, which he distributed by carbon copy to others. The enthusiastic recipients spread it further to like-minded businessmen, lawyers, doctors, and industrialists. From 1954 to 1959 Welch continued to expand the letter, eventually producing more than 300 pages of text, which he bound in a black cover with a black plastic link binding. This document came to be known as *The Black Book* and later as *The Politician*.[28]

Though *The Politician* did not make headlines across the country until 1960, some conservatives read and responded to the manuscript before Welch was a household name.[29] Reactions to the work provide a window onto the burgeoning movement in a number of ways. First their range helps gauge the degree of cohesion among those conservatives surrounding Welch. Second Welch's responses to his fellow conservatives help clarify why he persevered when the society later came under heavy attack by the press and liberal and conservative groups. Finally the various individuals to whom Welch sent copies outlines a loose network of conservatives. Welch's letter quickly became a critical document and its public debut a decisive event for all conservatives and liberals. In the same way that James Burnham's 1960 litmus test distinguished liberals from conservatives, *The Politician* served, according to observers, to separate a radical from a responsible Right.

The early reactions to Welch's vision of America controlled by a communist conspiracy ranged from wholehearted acceptance to mild skepticism to outright disbelief. Welch displayed little response to disbelievers; he rarely leveled criticism at anyone and maintained a surprising degree of congeniality even with his most outspoken enemies. Welch played the politician and tried not to alienate anyone he thought might help the cause; in essence he advocated a limited version of "popular front" conservatism, where there is always more room under the tent for those willing to subscribe to conservative beliefs. Welch's ideas, however, forced his conservative friends and colleagues to reevaluate their own beliefs and to figure out whether to side with him or with Buckley and other traditionalists or to strike out on a wholly different path. For most, however, these decisions did not come until after 1961.

Welch's close friend Alfred Kohlberg was one of the first to respond to a new printing of *The Politician*, which Welch sent out in the late summer of 1958. Kohlberg, a leading industrialist who had devoted his life to fighting communists, was unique among Welch's correspondents in that he was Jewish. Kohlberg had organized and was chairman of the American Jewish League against Communism and had tried doggedly to break down walls between conservative Jews and conservative gentiles. Kohlberg had offered his services to Welch in the early 1950s, helped with the editing and publishing of *May God Forgive Us*, and acted as a sounding board for Welch until his death in 1960. Kohlberg and Welch were close friends, and Kohlberg did not hesitate to tell Welch what he thought about his work, particularly his accusations about the communist conspiracy, that Eisenhower was a communist agent, and that his brother Milton was actually running the government:

> As to the book itself, you do not prove your case except by implication, which is not good enough in so serious a matter. All your material added together could prove an entirely different case by implication, just as well as what you seem to make it prove. It could prove that Ike is a smart cookie when it comes to ingratiating himself with people, but that he is essentially ignorant, uninformed, and lazy as to homework, and therefore easily taken in by people who get on the right side of him.[30]

Although Ike's intentions were questionable, Kohlberg agreed that the evidence Welch collected was indeed difficult to dispute and recommended: "Why not let the facts speak for themselves and let your readers form his [*sic*] own opinion, which is exactly what he will do in any case? If you don't want to do this, why not state the facts and then ask the questions as Joe McCarthy used to do and as he did with his book on General Marshall?"[31]

Welch's reply to Kohlberg illustrates perfectly the difference between his own world view and that of most others, who failed to see the grand conspiracy. In words that became significant in 1961 when controversy about the manuscript threatened to overwhelm the JBS, Welch explained why he did not simply let the reader decide what to make of the facts:

> If this had been a "book", [*sic*] intended for publication, or even for wide distribution, your comments in the last paragraph of your letter would certainly be one hundred percent correct. And perhaps I should have left in this version the few paragraphs, in the earlier one, which explained how the whole thing came about. At any rate, this manuscript, which began as a letter, was written and intended for a specific purpose: Simply to tell a quite limited number of patriotic friends of mine what I personally believed

about the present situation, why I believed it, and what I personally was trying to do about it as just one patriotic American who was greatly concerned. I did not really intend to try to *prove* anything, but to give my reasons for believing what I did, and my opinions for whatever they might be worth. And I thoroughly agree with you that my approach to the public, which is through my speeches and the magazine [*American Opinion*], has to be entirely different.[32]

Welch's defense that the manuscript was a private letter produced for a few close friends was attacked repeatedly beginning in 1960. The mere existence of *The Politician* helped frighten people away from the JBS. When Welch appeared on NBC's "Meet the Press" on May 21, 1961, the show's creator and producer, Lawrence Spivak, posed the question "Do you think . . . you were justified, for example, in saying, 'But my firm belief that Dwight Eisenhower is a dedicated, conscious agent of the Communist conspiracy is based on an accumulation of detailed evidence so extensive and so palpable that it seems to me to put this conviction beyond any reasonable doubt'?" Instead of directly disavowing Spivak's claims, Welch used the same defense he had given to Kohlberg almost three years earlier:

> This was a private letter written in the fall of 1954, added to as I made additional copies to send to friends. . . . Not a copy was ever sold, it was sent out with a flyleaf saying, This is not a book; it is not intended for publication, this is a private letter on loan to you in confidence for your eyes only and will you please try to tell us what is wrong with it and what the errors are, and I don't believe anybody who ever wrote a history before . . . was held responsible for what he said in a first draft of a document that might someday be published.[33]

Welch's defense appeared to be a kind of damage-control device; he realized that once the secret was out, he had to find an excuse for it. But comparing Welch's "Meet the Press" explanation—seen by millions—with the explanation he gave to Kohlberg *before* the John Birch Society existed, gains Welch a bit of credibility. In either case Welch believed that there was an obvious difference in what he said in a letter versus what he said in a published book, and he hoped that many Americans would agree with his reasoning.

Responses to the manuscript also encouraged Welch in his beliefs. Lucille Cardin Crain, editor of the *Educational Reviewer*, wrote to Welch, "Via the grapevine I had heard of a book or monograph you distributed privately which deals with our President. Would you trust me with a copy?"[34] Welch forwarded a copy to Crain, who became a dedicated JBS member. Other conservatives responded similarly. Writing to his friend B. E. Hutchinson, a banker in Detroit, about Welch's manuscript, J. W. Clise, a close associate of a number of conservatives, demonstrated how word was passed among interested individuals, which often culminated in increased membership for the fledgling JBS. Hutchinson had asked Welch to send Clise a copy of the manuscript, and Clise wrote back to "Hutch" to thank him: "I have read the introduction and first chapter and agree completely. The facts and conclusions are not new to me, but I am extremely grateful to have them actually written where they don't get lost and blurred."[35] Adding another link to the chain Clise offered to show the manuscript to trusted, loyal friends. Clise's comments were not unusual. Many anticommunists felt that they knew what was happening all around them, but they could not marshal all of the facts and ideas into a coherent picture. Welch's vision, arriving through their mailboxes, often sparked epiphanies, changing people from liberals, even Communist party members, to anticommunists who dedicated their lives to saving America.[36] While such revelations were extremely personal in nature, they also provided a connection to fellow conservatives who had experienced similar awakenings. Thus the conservative movement grew from intensely personal thoughts and actions to universally recognized beliefs and reactions. And Crain's and Clise's use of the grapevine was not uncommon among the informal network of conservatives. Not only did they see it as an extension of the social and business world, but most participants realized that they would be more effective if they acted deliberately and did not wait until they were forced to respond to a situation.

Those who disagreed with Welch usually took issue with, as Kohlberg had put it, Welch's "drawing conclusions" about Ike's intentions. These readers felt that Eisenhower, while doing almost anything except fighting communism, was not willfully aiding the enemy. In a letter in early 1959 Howard Kershner, a newspaper editor and businessman from Dodge City, Kansas, wrote to Welch:

> Four of us here have read your Eisenhower book. Generally speaking, the facts are not new to us but you have certainly marshaled them very effectively. We agree that Eisenhower has served the Communist cause, that he is a New Deal Democrat, and has kept the old gang in power, but we are not convinced that he is a member of the Communists deliberately seeking to betray our country.[37]

Kershner and his fellow readers, however, actually ended up drawing similar conclusions to Welch: "We would say it is more inertia and ignorance than intentional wrongdoing. Other people who intend wrong are making his decisions for him and, of course, the effect of that is about as bad as if he were making them himself."[38] For both parties Eisenhower's actions—whether initiating the wrongdoing or not preventing it—were tantamount to treason.

Conservative commentator and retired General A. C. Wedemeyer tried to explain to Welch that while he did not "question your sincerity of purpose or motives, . . . I do question your judgment."[39] Wedemeyer wondered how Welch

thought a manuscript sent to hundreds of people could remain secret, and he
also believed Welch had stretched the truth in his retelling of the story of John
Birch, who had served under his command in China.[40] Welch responded to
Wedemeyer with a six-page letter, explaining that *The Politician* had credibility
among 95% of its readers, including "plenty of retired high-ranking officers from
the Army, Navy, and Air Force."[41] If Welch had hoped to use peer pressure on
Wedemeyer, it did not work. Instead Wedemeyer remained steadfast in his refusal to support the JBS or Welch, even going so far as to be placed on a mailing
list of conservatives who might serve on a Voluntary Commission of Inquiry to
investigate the JBS.[42]

The last conservative criticism of Welch prior to the founding of the JBS came
from none other than William F. Buckley. Buckley's response to reading a draft
of *The Politician* foreshadowed their face-off throughout the next decade:

> I for one disavow your hypotheses. I do not even find them plausible. I
> find them—curiously—almost pathetically optimistic. . . . In my view things
> will get not better but very possibly worse when Eisenhower leaves the
> White House. And the reason for this is that virtually the entire nation is
> diseased as a result of the collapse of our faith. We suffer, as Richard
> Weaver so persuasively concludes, from anomie, from which we are not
> likely to emerge with our whole skins, barring a miracle.[43]

Instead of a communist plot, Buckley saw a national deterioration of standards
that stemmed from a weakening of faith—religious, political, and moral. But after
these harsh words, Buckley concluded in a different tone, perhaps because of
Welch's contributions to *National Review* or because of Welch's connections
among conservatives: "Improbable though I believe your reading of events to
be, it is really no less improbable than my own. That is to say, statistically speaking a good guess can be made to say that it is less probable that our leaders of
the past few years have been active Communists, than it is to conclude that our
entire society is bent on suicide."[44]

Instead of delivering one of his usual courteous replies in which he offered
his opinion but never insisted that his reader was incorrect, Welch attempted to
explain exactly how he had arrived at the idea that a conspiracy was the only
possible explanation for the events after World War II. He countered by accusing Buckley of not understanding the full depth of his characterization of
Eisenhower. Welch agreed that once Eisenhower left office the situation would
surely get worse, but not because Eisenhower had been a key figure. The next
president would be just as susceptible, contended Welch, since he would be
similarly motivated—"either for the sake of the increasing prestige and power
thus to be gained, or because he personally is devoted to the same ends as the
conspiracy which he serves"—and because "of what his bosses and manipula-
tors have been able to accomplish while he was there."[45] Welch believed that

Buckley needed to look at the big picture; until he saw the conspiracy unmasked, each individual's actions and each incident would appear as isolated, thus disguising the awful truth.

Welch insisted that the two of them should continue fighting the good fight, since "our chance is damn small anyway." Lastly Welch raised the question of whether Buckley's opinions were in the minority or majority of those who had read the manuscript. Although this was unlikely to change Buckley's mind, Welch's response shows how he himself gained confidence through readers' comments:

> But honestly, Bill, and truly, at least ninety-five percent of those who have read the manuscript—and they do comprise some extremely influential and well informed men throughout the United States—completely *agree* with one or the other of my two conclusions, and invariably state that it makes no difference, so far as the tragic results are concerned, as to which is right.[46]

Welch and Buckley remained on friendly terms until 1961, and even in the following years Welch continued to recommend *National Review* to members of the JBS. But their differences of opinion over why America had struggled so after the war did not change, and chances for reconciliation dimmed with each new statement Welch issued.

Filling a Need: The John Birch Society

Prior to 1958 Welch had considered starting an organization to translate his thoughts into action. His short-lived Welch Letter Mailing Committee taught him a few lessons about organizing citizens without going through the traditional channels. Welch proposed a third-party effort while attending the National States Rights Conference in Memphis in 1956 after both the Democrats and Republicans had been captured by the left wing.[47] Though rejected by the majority, Welch's enthusiasm for a third party never totally died out. Curiously Welch's ultimate decision to stick with the GOP as a vehicle for fashioning a conservative movement based on his own ideology, while attracting far greater numbers into the JBS, would pose serious problems for the party itself since, unlike more radical fringe groups, which made no attempt to systematically influence electoral politics, the JBS made periodic—though cloaked—forays into formal politics.

Although Welch envisioned the society fighting evils within and without the American political and social landscape, he seemed reluctant to realize that potential recruits might already be working on similar issues, which made their expectations of the society different from Welch's. For instance, after being asked to join the JBS, T. Coleman Andrews wrote to Welch to explain some of the reasons that he had to consider dealing with events in more immediate contexts. Foremost on his mind was the civil rights movement, already a hot issue in Richmond, Virginia, in early 1959. Believing "that blood is going to flow before the integration question is settled," Andrews was concerned about being "a party, even unwittingly, to anything that would be done in the name of a man who would have been unalterably opposed to violence of the sort that I fear that we are apt to face sooner or later."[48] Andrews realized that the specter of anticommunism could supersede common sense and that modern-day radicals who wanted sweeping changes in the South, such as Paul Douglas, Democratic senator from Illinois, and Jacob Javits, Republican of New York, were the only ones who could prevent such violence from accompanying the inevitable change. By invoking Birch's name, Andrews told Welch, there might come a time when the JBS would be forced to oppose such radicals, but a man like Birch would never condone such a standoff. Like Andrews, each of the founding members and later each of the rank-and-file members would have comparable situations in their lives, which would compel them to join, or perhaps think twice about joining, the JBS.

The 1958 inaugural meeting set the tone of the society's subsequent history. Ten of the eleven attendees kept in close touch with Welch. Welch sent out a memorandum, "Confidential Report No. 1," which detailed the actions taken by the JBS in the ten days since its founding. Besides setting up its first "front" (the Committee to Protest the Firing of Medford Evans, a conservative professor), Welch informed the men of scheduled meetings similar to the one in Indianapolis, where he could continue to spread the word.[49] Targeting each of the men to head a specific project or committee, Welch hoped that Andrews would agree to lead one of the most controversial of all Birch activities. "There is one major project among those proposed which I have been hoping you would be willing to head up with all of your enthusiasm, experience, and executive ability. This is the one which I think we should call the MOVEMENT TO IMPEACH EARL WARREN."[50] Andrews begged off of running the committee, but Welch, unshaken, forged ahead with JBS activities.

Why did the John Birch Society and not some other manifestation of anticommunist feeling emerge as the preeminent participatory extremist group? While there were a number of anticommunist organizations in existence in 1959, the JBS was unique for a few reasons. First and most important were Robert Welch's idiosyncratic ideas and methods. Unlike such competing anticommunist groups as Fred Schwarz's Christian Anti-Communism Crusade or Kent and Phoebe Courtney's Conservative Society of America, Welch's ideas grew out of a set of circumstances that set the JBS apart from similar organizations. Welch's life experiences, including his childhood precociousness, building a semi-successful business, becoming a driven salesman, and entering the circles of top executives from around the country in the NAM, all helped him realize that for the JBS to succeed, just like any business, it needed to be run in a top-down fashion.

Welch was convinced that a citizen group organized around democratic or republican principles was simply a clever way to avoid saying that such a group would be far less effective and would have a high probability of failure. Welch did not mean to imply that the rank-and-file members of the JBS were unimportant; he knew that without substantial numbers to support his projects and ideas he could do little else besides publishing his monthly journal, *American Opinion*. And since average members of the JBS were never told that their ideas were less important than Welch's or those within the top echelons of the organization, they saw themselves as crucial links between the American public and the JBS. To fulfill such a role, they proposed projects, taking Welch's word at face value. Soon citizens who had rarely been active in politics began discovering the power of the grassroots.

The JBS also took advantage of the events of the late 1950s and early 1960s. Welch, more than most anticommunist leaders, made the effort to establish a context for his ideas, in effect making the founding of the JBS a natural reaction to the events of the previous fifteen or so years. Welch tapped into the suspicion that some citizens had had about the federal government since the end of the war. Although suspicion of the government would become even more widespread in the 1960s, the Right had a virtual monopoly on such feelings at this time, and the JBS directly accessed this reservoir of distrust. Even though the Left's fears of the federal government in the 1960s stemmed from such events as the assassination of President Kennedy, the prosecution of the Vietnam War, the hesitant support of the civil rights movement, and the cultural changes among young people, those on the Right interpreted those same events as an indication that the federal government was not only going easy on liberals but was actually aiding and abetting the enemy's actions.

The JBS filled a void between the end of McCarthyism and the beginning of accelerated events, which indicted the U.S. government as an accessory to the crime of communist domination. Just as McCarthy understood what Americans feared and played a role that took advantage of those fears, Robert Welch realized that he was not alone in his thoughts and that there were plenty of Americans who felt similarly and wanted to do something before it was too late. Welch and his cohorts set out to establish an organization that, in Welch's words, would "last for hundreds of years, and exert an increasing influence on the temporal good and the spiritual ennoblement of mankind throughout those centuries."[51]

Selling an Ideology

Although Welch was the solitary leader of the JBS, he kept groups of advisers closely informed of his actions and used them as sounding boards for new projects and proposed solutions for difficult situations. The JBS Council, made up of between twenty and twenty-five men, served as liaisons to local paid coordina-

tors, who in turn worked with unpaid chapter leaders and ground-level members. Welch detailed the council's purposes in a letter to a prospective member:

> (1) To show the caliber of the men who are supporting and helping to run
> the John Birch Society; (2) to give me the benefit of the experience and
> advice of members of the COUNCIL in determining the policies of the Soci-
> ety, with regard to both substantive and administrative decisions; and (3)
> to select, with complete and final authority, the SUCCESSOR to myself as head
> of The John Birch Society, if and when anything happens to me to make
> such a choice necessary.[52]

Like much of the JBS, the council was ornamental, designed to impress
through its collection of powerful Americans united behind Welch's beliefs.
While most council members often served as yes-men for Welch, some eventually challenged his ability to lead the JBS and commented on the detrimental
effects of the publicity surrounding *The Politician*. Usually, though, the council
reinforced Welch's moves, seconded him, and encouraged his plans, no matter
how farfetched. Some seemed slightly frightened of Welch. For example, just
after the Indianapolis meeting, T. Coleman Andrews responded to Welch's request for comments on his pamphlet *The Life of John Birch* as a recruiting tool.
While Welch never obviously gave council members any reason not to tell the
truth, Andrews seemed cowed: "I hesitate to express anything but satisfaction
with the memorandum answering my question as to the identity of John Birch
and the use of his name in designating the society that you proposed in Indianapolis." Some of Andrews's and other council members' reluctance to criticize
Welch may have been due to Welch's tendency to depict himself not just as an
expert but as the only expert who could weave together so many theories about
communism and the conspiracy to produce a simple yet elegant design. Although
Welch deferred to specialists on specific issues, he often simply used them to
add legitimacy to his own ideas.

On average Welch convened the council once a month. Members gave reports on various projects or topics relevant to the anticommunist struggle. Though
Welch often asked for advice on everything from what to publish in the John
Birch Society *Bulletin* to how a chapter meeting should be run, one gets the
impression that both Welch and those on the council realized that no matter
what they said, Welch would run the society in a manner that would keep himself at the center of all decisionmaking. The council members, however, seemed
untroubled, since they frequently worried that their involvement would damage their business reputations. The arrangement satisfied both parties, and it
continued throughout the controversies that raged within both the council and
the society at large.[53]

Realizing that a high percentage of small businesses failed within their first
three years, Welch focused on creating an infrastructure on which the JBS could

rely well into the future. Selling a product was one skill; selling an ideology was another. Luckily Welch understood that while he could convert some nonbelievers to join the society, most of those who would join had already reached similar conclusions before hearing about the JBS. Welch saw his job as letting these comrades know that there was an alternative to lying down and waiting for the Soviet tanks to roll down Main Street. The JBS's most appealing ideological point was that it connected all of the disparate pieces into a coherent whole and helped the average American make sense out of a jumble of facts and opinions. Welch needed to transmit this ideology to Americans, and he needed to do so without regard to location or individual characteristics, such as occupation, religion, or income. In a nod to his experience as a traveling salesman and as a trainer of salesmen, Welch structured the JBS around maximizing face-to-face contact whenever possible. When there were not enough people to support a chapter in an area, individuals became members of the Home Chapter, just like salesmen reported to their home office. As soon as a region accumulated five or ten members, the Belmont office (and later the West Coast office in San Marino, California) recruited one of the more active members to serve as the chapter leader, and another enclave was born.

The JBS business aspects showed in nearly all facets of the group. It generated an extraordinarily high income through its bookstores, publications, and membership fees. In 1962 the reported income of the JBS exceeded $1 million.[54] As the membership grew, the Belmont office expanded to accommodate the correspondence of thousands of people, who felt compelled to communicate with either Robert Welch or the Home Office in general. Welch encouraged members to write in with their thoughts and suggestions, and he and his assistants soon institutionalized this practice in what they called "Member's Monthly Messages," or MMMs. Each monthly *Bulletin* contained a page that could be ripped out and sent to Belmont. Soon an entire department was created to handle the MMMs, and, like nearly everything that the society undertook, a set of guidelines was formulated for answering the mountains of correspondence delivered to Belmont each week.

Although the MMM Department might be seen simply as one spoke in a wheel that cared little about what it rolled over, Welch's efforts to satisfy his followers must be addressed with more scrutiny. Furthermore the discussion of what defines a grassroots movement is particularly relevant to the JBS. How "grassroots" is an organization that becomes so well run that it devises a formula that can handle a multitude of individuals without giving them the impression that they are just anonymous members? Successful businesses figure out how to treat thousands or millions of customers as if each individual were the most important person to that business; Welch and his coworkers figured out a similar formula for the JBS. To a large degree the JBS successfully stimulated exchanges among its members, its Home Office, and its regional organizers. Being a JBS member was not like being a member of the ACLU or the ADA; those liberal groups did not expect their members to do much more than contribute money and perhaps periodically write to a senator or representative. Joining the JBS was entirely different; although some people merely renewed their memberships annually, the majority was active on one level, if not several. One of the most popular ways of contributing to the fight was to send in an MMM each month. Representing the gray area between organized political activity and grassroots citizen movement, which much of the JBS occupied, MMMs served one purpose for JBS members and another purpose for the Home Office.[55]

Besides encouraging a cult of personality, the MMM Department seemed to impose its own vision of what the JBS should be onto its members. Although Welch wrote in *The Blue Book* and told the council that he desired opinions on his ideas and actions, the MMM Department promoted the idea that JBS members should think alike:

> Two of the main qualities of the John Birch Society which set us apart from any other organization are that:
> a) We are a tightly-knit group, which acts as a body and thinks as one concerning the conspiracy and the items on the agenda of our bulletin.
> b) We are an action group with a main emphasis on educating and recruiting . . . an army fighting with facts.
>
> It is this department's job to maintain this cohesiveness by realizing that each member who writes in is important and deserves the best we can give him, if only by typing out his bonus envelope or label correctly.[56]

Staff who answered MMMs were told not to formulate their own opinions and that politics had no place in their jobs. They were simply to convey what the society believed about an issue.

As the MMMs became an entrenched part of JBS culture, the society laid out more explicit guidelines to explain exactly why MMMs were so crucial to its sound operation. While their appearance did not change, the primary purposes of MMMs were to "stimulate the sales of A.O. [*American Opinion*] and JBS material" and to "receive necessary contributions vital to the progress of the Society."[57] Although fundraising took on an increasingly important role, MMMs were not promoted solely to raise money. The staff realized that the simple act of exchanging information between members and the Home Office would not only help stimulate members to take action but also that the quality of the correspondence—including grammar, spelling, punctuation, and neatness—would color relations between Birchers and non-Birchers.

MMMs usually offered suggestions to Welch and the Belmont office for improving the society, although some members simply praised or, less frequently, criticized it. Some proposals included making bumper stickers to read "Let's Give

Red China Our Seat [in the UN]," offering discounted subscriptions to conservative periodicals (imitating a liberal practice), and assembling lists of communist fronts so members knew instantly whether they were being duped.[58] Members praised the society for providing the inspiration to get involved with politics or other organizations. One man wrote that his sixteen-year-old son joined the JBS and promptly organized a teenage Republican club with more than fifty members, who worked "with more zeal toward the election of conservative republicans [*sic*] than most of the adults."[59] Welch believed that if members and nonmembers realized that the JBS was composed of good people, they would see that slanders and smears insinuating that the society wanted to take over the country were inventions of bad people, like the communists.

Between the Home Office in Belmont and the individual members writing MMMs were JBS coordinators, salaried men who served as liaisons between Welch and chapter leaders, spokespeople for the small groups that dotted the country.[60] Coordinators handled geographically defined regions and oversaw the continued growth of the society's membership. Like a traveling salesman the coordinator spent hours shuttling from meeting to meeting, making phone calls to chapter leaders, giving speeches, observing Birchers who were moving up through the ranks, and, of course, recruiting new members. The coordinator was on an ideological crusade in which one measured progress by how many chapters one created, how many new members one recruited, or how many letters to the editor one could generate out of local Birchers. Welch recognized that the task was thankless; while rarely fun or rewarding, it was unfortunately the most effective way to get the job done. Coordinators came from two sources: those who stood out in their chapters or regions as hard workers and dedicated believers and new members from other careers whose skills served the society's needs. Welch's willingness to take in inexperienced ideologues and train them to help run the society sometimes had surprising benefits, but the strategy also resulted in periodic misunderstandings and disappointments. While no two coordinators were the same, examining their common responsibilities illuminates what life was like as a JBS employee.

Bryton Barron took the job of coordinator for the Commonwealth of Virginia. Barron, who had worked in the State Department for nearly thirty years, had independently reached the same conclusions as Welch regarding a conspiracy within the American government, so when the JBS came to his attention, he plunged in with gusto. Although he was sixty-two years old when he started, Barron relished the chance to help create an organization that would bring more bodies into the fight. Much in the same way that conservative groups recruited former communists to testify that it was possible to see the light after being submerged in darkness, Barron's former State Department status provided similar legitimacy for the JBS, demonstrating that one who had been on the inside was now not only talking about its dangers but actively organizing against it.[61] While

Barron was a more public figure than most coordinators, his daily logs for 1960–1961 provide a window onto a coordinator's life.

Barron's role was as much that of a cheerleader as a political organizer or strategist. He attended meetings, encouraged chapter leaders to take more initiative and handle increasing responsibilities, and delivered speeches about foreign policy and the State Department. A typical day for Barron consisted of phone calls to various chapter leaders, urging them to forge ahead with their efforts:

> Called Mrs. Sam Jones—will call me back later in week—told her I was counting on her and said time is short—she had heard JBS is extreme but said she saw no evidence of that in what I handed her.
>
> Called Mrs. Nash—she suggested I contact Mrs. Basten who might get groups together—Mrs. N. would give me material to take to Mr. Welch.
>
> Mrs. Troyak called—change mtg. date to Nov. 9—talk about Mrs. Harris as leader, but I urge her to stick.
>
> Called Mrs. Basten—she will arrange to get groups together after election for afternoon mtg.
>
> Called Mrs. Philip Siling—she will call me back, when husband returns to arrange for me to answer their questions.[62]

Besides Barron's hands-on approach to guiding the chapters under his aegis, perhaps the most interesting fact is the number of women serving as Barron's lead contacts. In many regions—Barron's included—women made up a majority of chapter leaders and members. Although few women were ever in the upper echelons of the society, they comprised many of the hardest working and most dedicated volunteers. Coordinators frequently nudged women, typically housewives, into assuming greater leadership roles than they might have had either in the home or in women's groups. The confidence some gained is palpable in their correspondence with both the Home Office and their regional coordinator.

One of the chapter leaders to whom Barron was closest, Leslie Zodun, showed how his attention and faith in her as an effective activist helped her blossom into a far more independent thinker. On November 9, 1960, for example, Barron wrote, "Mrs. Zodun calls—I return call—we discuss role of new members brought in result [sic] recent drive—she was worried about effort her group—I said we would try get new chapter going there soon—she asked re. purpose of next mtg., felt it should be preparatory for work in Bulletin." Two months later Barron visited one of Zodun's chapter meetings. Barron evaluated the meeting as "good," high praise from a coordinator who sometimes depicted meetings as "unsatisfactory" or disappointing.[63] In April 1961 Zodun forwarded to Barron a report for March in which she described herself as "working especially hard this month to obtain new members, and have obtained promises from a number of people to attend our April meeting." Zodun went on to make suggestions for Barron to pass to Welch on how to handle the recent wave of bad publicity.[64] Through Barron's encouragement Zodun and other women took on more leadership; the nature of the work, the organization's reliance on citizens instead of professionals, and its willingness to cultivate women as leaders all helped these women enter the realm of political organizing in the early 1960s. While some conservative women did not get involved until Goldwater's nomination in 1964, others, specifically those Birchers who had gone beyond the duties of simply being members, were primed for political activism, and it took little to get them caught up in grassroots party politics. For some women in the 1960s, therefore, the JBS acted as a liberating agent, helping them to realize not only where their political priorities lay but also their potential as contributors to a cause.[65]

Barron's diaries also reveal one of the biggest problems faced by the JBS: the potential for chapters to drift away from the prescribed agenda and focus instead on local projects, which Belmont had trouble evaluating and regulating. Due in part to Welch's obsession with control, he believed local projects usually resulted in more harm than good. Not only did they weaken a national project by redirecting the energy of valuable letter writers, protesters, or recruiters, but they also encouraged chapters to ignore directives issued by Belmont. Barron and his colleagues in the field were responsible for making sure that chapters did not break away from the JBS and that members did not usurp their leaders' power. The coordinator's job was not easy; he had to walk a fine line between teaching Birchers to think for themselves and making sure they remained in accordance with the beliefs in *The Blue Book* and directives from Belmont. Barron understood the dilemma faced by himself and other Birchers; while each member should come to his or her own conclusions about the conspiracy or other issues, the conclusions they reached were supposed to parallel those of Welch. How, then, was a coordinator to inculcate such beliefs without eliminating competing theories on any given topic? Barron never solved this vexing problem. He was called up to Belmont and given a three-hour lecture by Welch and eventually parted ways with the society after a nasty battle over whether he had the right to appear in the press or if the only public spokesman would be Welch.

The reluctance of the Home Office to permit local projects calls into question the grassroots nature of the JBS. If Belmont issued directives, which trickled down to local chapters through coordinators, chapter leaders, and the John Birch Society *Bulletin*, the society was little different than a large business, a well-established political party, or, for that matter, the Communist party. Critics of the society claimed just that: Welch ran the body with absolute control, purging anyone who appeared to challenge his authority. Welch made sure that protocols were established for virtually every aspect of the day-to-day operations of the organization. There were instructions on how to establish either brand-new chapters or chapters that had split off from other chapters, as well as how to close down chapters ("There is no point in trying to carry with us any dead weight. This tightening of the belt, so to speak, will generate and improve the 'esprit de corps' that is necessary in our undertaking").[66] There were lessons on giving presentations ("The battle for saving our Republic could well be won or lost in our living rooms") and suggested discussion questions for meetings such as "Should Communist teachers be allowed to hide behind the doctrine of academic freedom?"[67]

But to argue that the JBS was not a grassroots organization fails to consider how much members, both close to and far away from Belmont, reacted to such instructions. If each chapter and each member took Welch's words at face value, the society would not have differed significantly from the communists. While many members never challenged—or had reason to challenge—Welch's ideas, others used the society to further their own ideas and projects. Their beliefs sometimes ran counter to official policies and other times pushed Belmont's limit of how much it would tolerate. It is tempting to categorize Birchers as following orders blindly, never defying Welch or other supervisors, and never thinking too much about what they were doing. Yet the rank and file did challenge decisions handed down from Belmont and fully believed that they were helping to control the direction in which the society was heading. So the question of whether the JBS helped foster grassroots activity among conservatives is not easily answered. In order to delve deeper it is necessary to turn to the rank-and-file members themselves.

Birchers

Birchers distinguished themselves from the rest of the population in many ways, not least by their choice to join an organization that ardently and aggressively criticized the government. Unlike membership in a political party, which could involve little personal commitment, joining the JBS involved risks that jeopardized some individuals' standing in their communities and among friends. Making their political beliefs public (or at least semi-public) meant that they would be forced to defend ideas not only unpopular among the general populace but also considered by some to be dangerously un-American.

In 1966 Belmont published a recruiting pamphlet entitled "Why Join the John Birch Society?"[68] Although a few of the twelve reasons focused on the projects and issues that the JBS emphasized, other motives appealed to a certain stratum of society. Belmont's first argument, "You will be proud of your membership," hinted that those who joined the JBS would join a group of people like themselves:

> We seek to have associated with us only men and women of good character, good conscience, *and* religious ideals, as well as fervent patriotism.

Simply being anti-Communist is not enough. We are a growing body of citizens, with a deep sense of responsibility, who are dedicated to saving for our children and their children as much as possible of the glorious country and humane civilization which we ourselves inherited.

The society was not composed of professionals, experts, nor those simply interested in politics, even if the primary purpose was to vanquish the communists. Instead the society wanted solid members of the community. If one removes the sentence "Simply being anti-Communist is not enough," the description could be of the Chamber of Commerce, the Rotary Club, the PTA, or any similar fraternal or community organization. Welch understood that to save civilization, each American needed to start at home, and placing less emphasis on strident anticommunism made the JBS more like a booster club for "real" Americans. Who would not want to consider himself or herself a person of good character, conscience, and religious values?

In 1965 an academic researcher used surveys by 650 Birchers to sketch a portrait that, although perhaps slightly overrepresenting the better-educated and higher-status members, presented one perspective of the core JBS membership.[69] The study's typical Bircher was a forty-one-year-old white male. He was more likely than the average American to live in a less densely populated state and in a smaller community; had nearly a 50% chance of practicing a form of liberal Protestant Christianity and was much more likely than his neighbors actually to attend church; and was perhaps a college graduate, although if he were (like one-third surveyed), he probably had majored in either engineering or some other practical study and had received his training at a lesser-quality college or university.[70] A Bircher's social class and income registered far above average, and not surprisingly he was probably a Republican.[71]

The study differentiated between Birchers who simply attended meetings and paid their dues and those who wanted to play a part in a larger drama, arguing that the division would be bridged only by a common belief in conspiracy. But while observers of the society noted that members participated in projects that rarely had successful outcomes, they failed to acknowledge that these same members worked on issues with which Belmont had no involvement. Most members considered themselves part of two JBS communities: local and national. To be sure these areas overlapped; sometimes local projects would start as offshoots of sanctioned national projects. Furthermore this dual citizenship helped members deal with any cognitive dissonance that might have arisen from such a conflict. Instead of feeling guilty for not completing one or the other project, Birchers could defer to the official directives from Belmont, which urged them to remember, "We are neither a study group nor a discussion group. We are an action group and our meetings should reflect this fact at all times."[72] What constituted "action," however, was flexible enough to include anything from reading the *Bulletin* to working on a political campaign, thus satisfying the greatest number of members.

Besides their stance on political and social issues, Birchers *were* different from members of other citizen-based political groups. Unlike such groups as the ADA or the ACLU, which demanded little more than paying one's monetary dues, the JBS, at least on the surface, demanded that its members participate in the daily and monthly rituals that separated it from its rivals, both liberal and conservative. While it was unlikely that chapter leaders or regional coordinators would take seriously the statement "There is no room in the John Birch Society for dreamers, drifters, or deadwood," it was unusual for a group reliant on its membership rolls for political power to threaten to kick out stragglers.[73] Belmont listed four basic responsibilities for members to measure their usefulness to the society and America:

1. Participation in national projects suggested from Belmont.
2. The number of new members brought in.
3. Attendance at chapter meetings.
4. Completion of Member's Monthly Message envelopes.[74]

The most difficult responsibility, participating in national projects, was also the toughest to evaluate. Unlike the other three duties, which could be enumerated, participation might mean anything from acting as the lead organizer to gathering petition signatures to telling a friend about the project. Chapter leaders, therefore, were encouraged not to drop anyone from the rolls completely but to instead recommend to seemingly inactive members that they join the Home Chapter, where one simply paid dues, read publications, and sent a monthly message. Those members who wanted to be active leaders in the fight against America's enemies were afforded ample opportunities. Those patriots who wished to remain in the background, no matter how much they were urged to join the battle, were also accommodated, although the society never lost faith that someday they would understand the importance of participation.

Instead of forbidding local projects and thus almost assuredly restricting the growth of the society, Belmont fashioned a policy that placed most of the decisionmaking power about local projects in the hands of its local paid and unpaid officers. In its recruiting pamphlet Belmont stated, "Membership increases but does not limit your patriotic labors." National projects took first priority, but members could use the criteria of whether the work "appeal[ed] to his own judgment and conscience."[75] Although such flexibility probably served as an effective recruitment device, it sometimes set Belmont's agenda against the plans of a local group. Instead of writing letters to impeach Earl Warren, for example, chapters might focus on boycotting a local media outlet that had failed

to provide conservative responses to what was perceived to be outrageously liberal perspectives. Or a local chapter might focus on flooding a school board with
Birchers, thereby ensuring a majority—or at least a blocking vote—in the crucial
arena of education. In short, local projects could prove beneficial, since they
"provide our members with an opportunity to see the tangible results of their
efforts which can be a powerful factor in keeping the morale and esprit de corps
of the chapters at a high pitch."[76]

In some cases these local efforts took on a tenor that worried even those at
the Home Office. Because Welch had pledged to "fight dirty," unsanctioned
projects had a tendency to combine the tactics of moralistic polarization with
symbols of deadly combat, which created a sense of urgency that came to distinguish the JBS from rival groups. A practice adopted by leftists in the later part
of the 1960s, grabbing the moral high ground and then using confrontational
tactics, could often be used to win concessions from targets who simply wanted
to be out of the spotlight. These campaigns, directed at local businesses, individuals, or governmental policies, came to personify the JBS style and choice of
issues. Journalists in particular focused on local activities, often characterizing
the entire society based on a local group's actions. For instance the JBS was
behind such local actions as "card parties," where Birchers fanned out to retail
stores and dropped off cards reading, "Always buy your Communist products
at _____," in effect terrorizing merchants suspected of un-American activities.[77] Moreover Belmont did little to prevent such actions from taking place,
reasoning only that national projects should be tackled first since local issues
would not matter anyway if the country fell to the communists:

> It is pointless to worry about compulsory fluoridation of our water supply
> if, by so doing, we syphon off effort and money from the far more serious
> and immediate threat of being completely swallowed up in a one-world
> Socialist-Communist government . . . *non-fluoridated water and all!*[78]

However, Belmont understood that although it advertised the JBS as an
action-oriented group, much of that action was based on goals that often seemed
unattainable or difficult to grasp. To retain a national focus the society then had
to come up with projects, some of which were to last only a few weeks, others a
year or more, in order to concentrate attention on a particular issue and to keep
members active and motivated. It might be possible to hurt the communists
where they lived, but without national campaigns attracting political and media
attention, the society would never evolve into an institution with which to be
reckoned. Perhaps the best example of an effort to tie together the needs of the
society with the need to fight the enemy was the movement to impeach Earl
Warren.

Although in retrospect such a campaign might strike one as exceedingly ab-
surd, the possibility of impeaching Earl Warren generated an unexpectedly in-

tense reaction, as Congress and state legislatures were flooded with thousands and thousands of postcards and letters.[79] Welch grounded the impeachment campaign on the pattern of the Warren Court's decisions since the former California governor was appointed chief justice. He proposed the idea to his friend T. Coleman Andrews:

> The approach should be as dignified, as well reasoned, and as carefully based on constitutional grounds and the principles of Anglo-American jurisprudence, and as completely devoid of any apparent tinge of emotionalism, as possible. . . . I think we should approach this job, therefore, on the carefully explained basis, in legalistic as well as in everyday terms, that Warren has definitely violated the oath of office which he took when he became Chief Justice, and should be impeached on that basis and for that reason—rather than the fact that we or the signers of the petitions disagree with the decisions or the results.[80]

Welch, however, knew that most Birchers would critique Warren's decisions rather than allege that he violated the oath of office. Welch also knew it would be a long process, as did his associates. In 1961 Andrews wrote to Welch that "one of the most prominent men in Virginia" had told him that while they might find some congressmen who would support a resolution to impeach Warren, it would be difficult to get initial sponsors.[81] Since no congressman ever did put forth the resolution, it is unlikely that the movement ever went beyond an elaborate publicity campaign.

The improbability of actually ever getting the political wheels to turn for such an effort did not diminish Welch's enthusiasm. In 1961 he sent a letter to "one of our country's ablest and most conservative Congressmen," stating, "The Liberals have not been able simply to laugh off, as they had obviously expected at first, our long-range campaign to get Chief Justice Earl Warren impeached. As has become increasingly clear in our monthly bulletins, we did not intend this drive as a flash-in-the-pan effort, and we were well aware of the magnitude of the task set for ourselves."[82] Welch understood that Birchers and non-Birchers alike, although questioning their own patriotism for attempting to impeach the chief justice of the United States, deeply doubted Warren's rulings and realized that the latter trumped the former in importance. Warren's decisions regularly supplied the JBS with fresh ideological and political ammunition. In 1963, for example, the Court struck down prayer in school, which prompted the society to declare, "Although the Supreme Court decision, forbidding the reading of the Bible or the recital of the Lord's Prayer in the schools, had been anticipated, it still seems almost unbelievable. It is obvious that the Warren-led Court intends, step-by-step, to declare the whole Constitution of the United States *unconstitutional*." In response, Welch took to advertising "Warren Impeachment Packets," comprised of Impeach Earl Warren stickers, a form to petition

Congress for Warren's removal, Rosalie Gordon's *Nine Men against America*, his own *Republics and Democracies*, and numerous pamphlets concerning the Court.[83]

Of course few non-Birchers ever seriously considered impeaching Warren, but this did not discourage society members. Even Welch himself was realistic enough to know that their chances of success were infinitesimal. In the same letter in which he asked Andrews to head up the movement, Welch confessed:

> Frankly, with the Left Wing control now so strong, insidious, and ubiquitous in Washington, I am not deceiving myself that we have very much chance of really bringing about the impeachment of Earl Warren. Although we might. But I don't think that is really as important as dramatizing to the whole country where he stands, where the Supreme Court as now constituted under him stands, and how important it is to face the facts about the road we are now traveling so fast.[84]

Here was a rare occasion when Welch admitted that a project was designed to stir up publicity and controversy rather than to achieve its apparent goal. If it took a Pyrrhic campaign to show Americans what was happening around them, the sacrifice was worth it.

Another national campaign with a more immediate impact on Americans was designed to expose the civil rights movement as a communist-directed Trojan Horse, which would eventually draw the country into the chaos of race wars and economic destruction. Unlike the movement to impeach Earl Warren, the society's attempts to oppose racial advances in the South and North used much more subtle approaches. Opposition to the civil rights movement began as an effort to protest the federal government's usurpation of what had been state-controlled powers. In "A Letter to the South on Segregation," one of his first attempts to clarify how the civil rights movement fit into a larger communist conspiracy, Welch directed most of his anger at the Supreme Court rather than at any common citizens.[85] He attacked the civil rights movement as emanating from a Court decision that was nothing less than "judicial fiat," since instead of letting the people petition for an amendment, the Court simply reversed the traditional hegemonic relationship between the Tenth and Fourteenth amendments, which allowed the equal protection clause to take precedence over states' rights.[86] Welch blamed the Court for establishing "the doctrine that the meaning of our laws and of our constitution itself changes—without any new legislation being needed for that purpose—with changes in psychological and sociological theories, and according to the preferences for particular theories on the part of the current justices." He argued that those theories—offered by liberal sociologists and psychologists such as E. Franklin Frazer, Gunnar Myrdal, and others—were tinged with communism. Thus the real trouble came not from blacks but from manipulative communists who used the blacks as tools against

America. Communists, cried Welch, "do not have the slightest real interest in the welfare of either the colored people or the white people of the South. It is not desegregation as an end in which they are interested, but the bitterness, strife, and terrors of mob action which can be instigated while that end is supposedly being sought."

What should Americans do? First, said Welch, whites must not blame blacks. Welch declared to his white audience:

> Do not blame your neighbors, the colored people of the South. They had nothing to do with the Supreme Court decision, did not seek it, and as a class have not been the ones to bring the racial issue to a boil. Most of them would be just as embarrassed as you would at *forced* integration, and are just as opposed to the whole idea.

Welch was a native-born southerner, and his vision was that of the white patrician who knew what was best for blacks. Welch relieved the guilt of whites— both northern and southern—by claiming that blacks, given the opportunity to take advantage of government-mandated integration, would probably look down, grin, and shake their heads at the absurdity of such a solution. Blacks were smarter than communists, implied Welch; blacks were Americans, but like many Americans they "can easily be misled by clever agitators, as you would be if you were in their position." Believing that no American in his or her right mind would actually ever pursue court-ordered integration, Welch thought that communist deception aimed to blind people to the real purposes of the so-called civil rights movement.

Welch applied similar logic to any situation in the United States in which his conservative vision of the country's natural order was upset. Americans could not have been so reckless as to have wanted Eisenhower instead of Taft; there must have been a larger plot at work. Why would citizens protest against the Vietnam War? Certainly not because they knew the truth—that the communists planned the war to spark dissent in the United States and to set off tremors that might add up to a larger shock wave and perhaps collapse the country's infrastructure. Although most Americans dismissed Welch's logic and his reading of recent history, tens of thousands agreed.

Welch would not always have this attitude, a cross between believing in the innocence of Americans and the deviousness of communists. In 1967 the JBS produced a film called *Anarchy—U.S.A.*, which documented the links between various communist revolutions around the world and the civil rights movement, which by that time had spread from the South to the North and other parts of the country. Because conditions had only worsened during the ten years since Welch wrote his letter to the South, he assigned blame more widely, not just to the Supreme Court but also to the federal government as a whole. The film attacked the 1965 Voting Rights Act, which authorized the attorney general to appoint voting registrars, on the grounds that it effectively bypassed the traditional constitutional doctrine reserving such powers for the states. John Fall, a JBS Home Office coordinator, concluded, "In a word, it is another usurpation of rights reserved to the States and a step closer to to[t]al government which is tyranny."[87] For many Birchers then the civil rights movement was the equivalent of a political Rube Goldberg mechanism, intricately transferring power from honest people in the states to corrupt politicians in Washington.[88]

Such national projects as the movement to impeach Earl Warren or the effort to expose the true purposes of the civil rights movement helped clarify for the public, for better or for worse, the JBS's positions. The campaigns virtually guaranteed an audience for the organization, since the media often needed an oppositional body to set against a variety of protagonists. The society conducted organized efforts that focused on issues from fighting the citizen initiative to subject police to civilian review boards to tax reform, Vietnam, and in the 1970s the Panama Canal.[89] Many of these amounted to little more than complicated publicity efforts for the society. Others, like the effort to block civilian review boards for local police, garnered a surprising amount of support.[90] It was in the area of party politics, however, that the JBS presented its truly unpredictable side. Although at first the society rarely undertook formal campaigns to influence elections, pending legislation, or executive decisions at the local, state, or federal level, it was forced, by virtue of its ideological position, to take informal political stances, which often created controversy inside and outside of the ranks.[91] But as the civility of the dialogue about social and political conditions in America continued to disintegrate throughout the 1960s, the organization became more willing to back, either openly or surreptitiously, candidates it thought might forward its unswerving agenda. In any case for the JBS to claim nonpartisanship—as it repeatedly did—caused as much or more trouble as openly declaring its support for candidates; instead of recognizing such a declaration as an exemption, politicians used the JBS as much or more than the JBS used them.

Since one of the tenets of the society included an inherent distrust of the political system, during elections or at times of crucial votes the JBS often found itself in an uncomfortable position. By 1962 it had become by default the most quoted (and perhaps respected) of all the so-called extremist groups. The membership itself clamored for advice on what to do in the various political realms. One way the society avoided publicly endorsing or denouncing a candidate or party was by commenting solely on a politician's or party's policies. For example in March 1962 Welch issued a press release from the council that stated that it "deplore[d] the continued failure of the Kennedy Administration to enforce the Monroe Doctrine in the Cuban situation." Rather than attacking the policies of Democrats or Kennedy himself, Welch focused on why the policy made sense:

The Monroe Doctrine is not concerned merely with the presence of troops and armaments. It is aimed at preventing control of territory in the Western Hemisphere by any foreign government, particularly by one founded on principles hostile to basic American ideals of freedom.[92]

Here Welch linked the doctrine only to the struggle between communism and Americanism; what mattered was not which party the policymakers were from but their actions. This determination to focus on principles instead of party or the political process was well received by Birchers; the practice elevated them above the petty partisan bickering. Always a body of action, they knew what was right and what was wrong.

Whenever possible, Welch steered the society down a political path that avoided taking sides. Although most Birchers were Republicans (except in the South), Welch used the group's nonpartisanship to his advantage and tried to teach members to think about principle instead of party loyalty.[93] Of course this did not prevent both parties from reacting with fear that the JBS was trying to capture their organizations. Moreover in some states (notably California) branches of the JBS attempted just that, sometimes with moderate success. Just as the JBS had flooded local school boards with members, the society applied similar tactics to capture community GOP leadership positions. Overall though the society saw its political involvement as another project with expectations and strategies similar to its other undertakings. To do so Welch continually tried to woo politicians as well as those who had political connections to join the council or advisory board of the JBS. In August 1963 Welch asked each member of the council to write five letters: one to Ezra Taft Benson, former secretary of agriculture under Eisenhower and a leader in the Church of Latter-Day Saints; one to Eddie Rickenbacker, president of Eastern Airlines; one to Strom Thurmond, senator from South Carolina; one to Charles Edison, former governor of New Jersey; and one to David O. McKay, head of the Church of Latter-Day Saints. Each letter seconded Welch's invitation to join the JBS. Making their qualifications and stature known, writers would impress upon the recipients their own commitment to the cause.[94] Although these letters were not successful, a few politicians became members, usually after concluding their public service, but their joining garnered a public relations coup for the society nevertheless. One of the society's most popular organizers and spokesmen, John Rousselot, had been a congressman from the Twenty-fifth District in California.

It was not always so easy, however, to avoid direct commentary on a current political situation. Just after the midterm elections in 1962 Welch issued a hurried memorandum that urged coordinators to capitalize on widespread Democratic victories. Welch called for a renewed educational effort, urging, "The public . . . must be brought to see and understand the real facts—not the halfway, glossed over facts now presented by too many even of the 'Conservative' publications—about the methods, progress, and personalities of the encroaching tyranny."[95] Furthermore Welch knew all too well that in grim times, membership jumped:

> But the development [the election results] does offer quite a recruiting opportunity to the John Birch Society. For at long last it is going to be easier to make a lot of good Conservatives believe what we have been trying to tell them ever since the Society was founded: That the job of saving our country depends on educational rather than political effort.[96]

However, as the tantalizing prospect of what many considered to be a truly conservative candidate became closer to a reality, Welch was compelled to comment on Barry Goldwater.

The rapid rise of Goldwater in 1963 forced Welch to take a position relatively early; many Birchers were getting active in the draft Goldwater movement, and most, before they had joined the society, had held him in high esteem. A year before Goldwater was even nominated, Welch issued a statement to all members of the society, clarifying his thoughts on Goldwater and the political process. Welch urged members to look at the whole man and noted that while he disagreed with some of Goldwater's positions, in sum, "I personally think that Barry Goldwater is a very patriotic American and a very able politician, who is determined to use his political skills to do all he can towards saving our country from the dangers now closing in from every side."[97] But he warned Birchers not to lose their focus: "Senator Goldwater himself obviously and honestly feels that 'direct political action' is the most important part of any total program for saving our country from either the menace of Communist terror and tyranny, or the more gradual disaster of the Socialist situation. We disagree." Welch again hammered home the importance of education, since only after enough people found the truth would politics be purged of the disingenuous and misguided. For at heart politicians were susceptible to the same corrupting experiences, no matter what their political alignment, and Goldwater was no exception: "I think that, under the circumstances which actually prevail today, Barry Goldwater would be a far smarter politician if he were less of a politician."[98] In any case Welch knew that he could not order individual members to refrain from taking political action. If anything, Birchers were more likely to take political action. Not only were they predisposed to carry out their beliefs, but the society had taught them that organizing for a cause, no matter how large or small, was both noble and never too far out of reach for average Americans.[99]

The Leviathan Investigates

By 1963, only five years after Robert Welch started the society in a living room in Indianapolis, it had already made an impact on citizens from suburbia to the

White House. The Federal Bureau of Investigation received thousands of inquiries about the purposes of the organization, asking if it was an acceptable choice for Americans who wished to serve their country by ridding it of the communist menace. Typical of such inquiries, one American wrote to J. Edgar Hoover, "Can you advise if the John Birch Society is a subversive organization? The Attorney General's letter was not explicit in regards to our question. Hoping you can help me."[100] Correspondents sought Hoover's personal approval; though they felt compelled to join, they wanted to be sure that they were helping and not hurting their country. Politicians might not tell the truth, but Hoover surely would. As another writer inquired:

> I am a member of the City Council, the local school board, the official board of my church, and I attempt to be a good citizen. I do not want to be involved with any organization that is not 100% American and above board. I have a very great respect for you and the organization which you have built; your opinion will be greatly appreciated.
>
> Keep up the good work. Americans appreciate the tremendous job you and the F.B.I. are doing for us.[101]

The bureau's responses ranged from ambivalence ("In response to your request, I would like to point out that information in our files must be maintained as confidential pursuant to regulations of the Department of Justice and is available for official use only") to a limited endorsement ("It is important that our citizens educate themselves concerning the true nature of this insidious philosophy [communism] in order that they will be able to resist its eroding influence") to outright condemnation:

> I have stated that I have little respect for the leader of that organization in view of the statements he made linking former President Dwight D. Eisenhower, former Secretary of State John Foster Dulles and former CIA Director Allen Dulles with communism. You may wish to know, however, that the FBI has never investigated the John Birch Society.[102]

The FBI, however, did investigate the JBS. Every JBS member who wrote to Hoover declaring his or her affiliation was noted in the bureau files. If a JBS chapter opened a bookstore or library, conducted a project that attracted a fair amount of attention, or had members who got their names in the press on a regular basis, the FBI documented the activities. One example of the FBI's surveillance is a 1965 report from a special agent in Buffalo, New York, to Hoover, describing the proprietor and the operations of the American Opinion Bookstore in Buffalo. The manager, John W. Hines, had gotten in touch with the local FBI office in an effort to gather anticommunist literature he could use for study meetings at the library. As the field report stated:

Hines was contacted on 4/13/65 by SA [deleted] of this office who visited the American Opinion Library at 1232 Hertel Avenue, under the pretext that the Agent wished to acknowledge his letter to the Buffalo FBI Office and to explain to him that the FBI did not distribute literature to private enterprises.

At the time of the contact with Hines, the Agent observed a late model Volkswagen painted white with the legends "American Opinion Library" and "Book Store on Wheels" parked at the curb which had New York license SR-7796. For information of the Bureau, it was determined from the Buffalo Police Department that this license is registered to [deleted] who is mentioned in referenced Buffalo letter to the Bureau, 11/30/64.[103]

The agent went on to discuss the American Opinion Library in Rochester and concluded with the caveat, "No investigation is being conducted concerning the Buffalo or Rochester American Opinion Libraries, and the above is being submitted for the information of the Bureau."

The fact that agents devoted time to the JBS—whether by mail or in personal investigations—belies the disinterested tone of its responses to most citizens. The FBI not only conducted low-level investigations, but it also gladly received information it thought pertinent to understanding the society. For example, the bureau office in Kansas City forwarded a collection of index cards found by someone who noticed that one of the names listed referred to Chapter "QABF" of the society.[104] Descriptions like "not dangerous at this time. Probably never will be" and "6'1", crescent shaped scar left cheek, blond crewcut hair, blue eyes, dresses neat in blue or grey suits. Karate black belt. Excellent shot, good with knife" sounded more like Walter Mitty's fantasies of a midwestern James Bond than any real organized threat to the nation.[105] Even the radio commentator Walter Winchell forwarded to Hoover a friend's letter, which described the JBS-sponsored Rally for God, Family and Country in Boston in July 1965. Remarking, "I am sure your good friend J. Edgar Hoover would like to know of this scum," Winchell's friend told of rally participants who celebrated an explosion at a Harvard physics lab since, he said, "Harvard is a communist college."[106]

Although the FBI's response to the JBS was nothing like its response to left-wing groups such as the Black Panthers, Students for a Democratic Society, and the Weathermen in the latter half of the decade, it still paid fairly close attention to the society's activities and never passed up an opportunity to gain information. The CIA, while supposedly restricted from any domestic activities, also kept a small information file on the JBS. In 1962 the deputy director of the CIA forwarded a memo to J. Edgar Hoover that discussed a "rascist [sic] leaflet purporting to be from the John Birch Society." The leaflet, a copy of which was attached to the memo, railed against blacks and Jews and celebrated the use of nuclear weapons against communists in Asia and Africa.[107] In 1965 a brief in-formational memo was compiled for the director's benefit, although its details included nothing that was not available from the society itself.

The Kennedy administration, while only publicly responding to the far Right a few times, was quite concerned with what it saw as both a political and moral threat to the nation.[108] Between 1961 and 1963 various officials produced memoranda that dealt with offsetting the gains made by the Right and perhaps even using them to their political advantage. Often focusing on the simple task of gathering information and assessing what kind of threat the Right actually posed, a typical memo was written by Kennedy's aide Myer Feldman to the president in August 1963. After summarizing the Right's financial resources, outlook, and political philosophy, Feldman assessed the Right's immediate political impact and made recommendations for further inquiries. Noting that openly right-wing candidates were relatively rare, Feldman nevertheless pointed out, "While none of the 4 candidates for Congress who were avowed Birchites were elected in 1962, each ran a surprisingly strong race and polled about 45 percent of the vote cast. . . . They raised and spent almost a quarter of a million dollars."[109] Feldman urged the president to further investigate groups like the JBS and individuals like H. L. Hunt, the Texas multimillionaire who openly advocated ending income taxes and any form of state assistance. Feldman also suggested some avenues that might work to stifle right-wing growth such as inquiring into the "irresponsibility of much of the material used on the radio" or halting the post office from subsidizing right-wing literature.[110] Feldman concluded by noting that while the administration was learning a lot about nationally based groups, it knew virtually nothing about local groups that might threaten local institutions. In the conclusion of his memo to Kennedy, Feldman summarized, "I would say, from what I have seen, that the radical right-wing constitutes a formidable force in American life today."

Along with his own memorandum Feldman forwarded to the president a similar assessment from Wyoming Senator Gale McGee, a strident opponent of the JBS and similar groups, who never passed up a chance to expose them as frauds. McGee tried to figure out why the West was more receptive to right-wing activity than other areas of the country:

> There is a reservoir of public opinion susceptible to their ideas. This is made up of pre–World War II isolationism and the remnants of a 19th Century rugged individualism. In fact, it would be fair to say that segments of our population in the West already believed the extreme right-wing line before the current group of extremists invented it.[111]

Rather than attributing the upsurge in popularity on the Right to shifting status anxieties, McGee saw such individualistic attitudes as pervasive, affecting nearly everyone in the West. McGee went on to point out that since the West was less populated than other parts of the country, "the right gets a 'bigger bang for a

buck' out of the low population states of the West." Inseparable from such demographics was the power of the mass media for spreading right-wing information,
as well as the nearly immediate impact such media had on people's ideas, particularly where there were few opposing viewpoints. McGee, however,
jumped to the conclusion that westerners were more predisposed to accepting
Congressman John Rousselot's Birchite arguments, for example, because of
nineteenth-century individualism and prewar isolationism.

Most interesting of McGee's ruminations on the Right, however, was his
conclusion. After acknowledging their threat and their close ties to the conservative wing of the Republican party, McGee made an astute observation:

> But one word of caution, it seems to me, is in order. It revolves around
> the question of timing. A wide open investigation in the Congress of the
> right-wing groups now might have the effect of killing them dead before
> next fall. I am personally convinced that the issue is such a good one that
> we need to keep the villain alive and kicking for a year from now. . . . I
> may be overly optimistic on how long it may take to blow these fellows out
> of the water, but I suspect that a disclosure of their financial operations
> and their tactics on a nation-wide scale would be more devastating than
> the scattered assaults upon them at the present time.[112]

McGee saw the usefulness of the Right for JFK's purposes; not only would it
help him get reelected, but the contrast would highlight the benefits of, as McGee
put it, "the liberal American cause." If McGee's hubris is not surprising, his lack
of understanding of his constituents and their reasons for joining the JBS and
other groups is. McGee somehow believed that if Americans knew how the Right
was financed and the lengths to which it would go to fight communism, they
would quickly disavow any connection to such terroristic and authoritarian organizations. However, small contributions from people like McGee's constituents represented a major source of funding for these groups, and many accepted
or rationalized the extreme tactics by reminding themselves who the enemy was.
At the end of the memo, McGee penciled in "Mike: A final plea for the fireside
chat." Believing that JFK could adopt FDR's tactic to swing Birchers into the
New Deal Coalition, McGee failed to understand that those Americans attracted
to the JBS would not listen to JFK's advice. Moreover if the federal government
actively pursued the Right and fought anticommunism, it would only appear that
a communist alliance had been forged at the highest levels of government.

The John Birch Society forced the government to reconsider what was
acceptable political behavior on the Right as well as on the Left. That the Kennedy
administration at least considered using the JBS and other right-wing groups as
a political tool to help carry the 1964 election reflects not only the government's
willingness to portray the far Right as a moral peril but also the fact that the far
Right had become legitimate enough to force the government to respond.

Advancing the Movement

By the early 1960s conservatives were forced, no matter what their opinions, to take positions on the JBS's role in American society and politics. Often dismissed as a fringe group composed of conspiracy theorists who, to paraphrase a California state attorney general, were likely to be little old ladies in tennis shoes, the JBS was far more complex, played a historically understated role as a faction in the conservative movement, and helped to chart the course of postwar conservatism in America. Acting much like a third party, the JBS forced the Republican party to address a number of issues that it might have otherwise ignored. In turn the GOP learned from the society and adjusted its agenda—particularly in 1964—to attract those on the fringes of the party. Furthermore the JBS provided one of the first opportunities for conservatives to join a grassroots movement. Finally the society was a protest movement, which challenged the status quo through its demands to revise foreign and domestic policy. While not a political kingmaker, it did organize citizens committed to seeing conservatives emerge victorious in elections and to seeing conservative legislation gain the signature of a governor or president, all in an effort to wrench America right.

Just as important, as a force in and of itself, the JBS acted as a buffer for the responsible Right, deflecting criticism that might have otherwise focused on the hardcore of the GOP. Constant scrutiny of the JBS in the press gave conservative Republicans extra latitude with which to work; instead of remaining the singular focus of the press and the White House, conservatives within the party pursued new avenues of power and billed themselves as effective and sane alternatives to the JBS. While Republicans were troubled by the society and did not learn to deal with it effectively until Reagan's 1966 gubernatorial campaign, for American citizens the existence of the society on the right of the conservative wing of the GOP automatically shifted the Republican party one notch toward the center. Thus conservative Republicans subtly used the JBS to move the party right and made the case that their methods would always be more effective and acceptable than those of the society.

Although the JBS lost influence after 1964, it remained a haven for Americans who believed that action—any kind of action—was needed to check the backsliding caused by the liberal establishment. Was the JBS a grassroots organization? From the point of view of its founder, no. Welch designed the operation to follow his lead, and he declared which issues were worthy of the rank and file's attention. But from the members' point of view, the society personified grassroots activism, where groups of ten or fifteen people pursued agendas to bring change to their communities and country. In the end then the JBS did succeed in part of its mission; it challenged the complacency of the American people and government, and it participated in the reconfiguration of the GOP. The JBS was not all things to all people; most of America looked upon it with disdain. Yet for tens of thousands it was a refuge and staging point, a place where words and ideas became action and where America's renaissance was always a phone call or postcard away.

Unlike other political groups in the late 1950s and early 1960s the JBS used the means of organization as an end in itself. Robert Welch understood that to foster a tightly knit group that would remain steadfast even when criticized from both Right and Left, the members needed commonality of action as well as purpose. By virtue of its numbers alone the JBS became a political player. While only one name—Welch's—was recognizable, the image that grew up around the group (and that the group fostered) helped perpetuate both fantasy and reality, ensuring that whether or not the JBS could muster its forces on a specific issue, the impression of such a possibility remained. By forcing Democrats and moderate and liberal Republicans to respond to their actions, Birchers proved that they could make an impact, thus permanently altering the political landscape.

The attention the group generated could not be ignored by the media, politicians, or average citizens. Such an organization lent itself perfectly to political and social campaigns, and Birchers began staffing crusades within months of its founding. But between the advent of the JBS and the dawning of the 1964 election, the first true political litmus test for conservatives since the early 1950s, was an event that helped both to spark and to assess the conservative consolidation: the case of General Edwin A. Walker.

THE CASE OF

GENERAL EDWIN A. WALKER

In mid-1961 Robert Welch was the only official spokesman for the John Birch Society. Its most prominent member, however, was the dashing Major General Edwin A. Walker. On June 12, 1961, Walker, a highly decorated combat veteran of World War II and Korea, was officially "admonished" by the commander in chief of the army in Europe, General Bruce C. Clarke, for teaching his strong anticommunist views to his troops.[1] In designing his "Pro-Blue" program for his troops, Walker borrowed elements of Birchite and other extremist ideology and urged soldiers to question the loyalty of politicians and to prepare for the communist onslaught. On one level Walker was defending American interests against a known enemy. On another Walker's conservatism, some thought, followed extremist contours, which made it difficult to agree with the methods he used to achieve those ends. Almost overnight Walker became a symbol not only of American attitudes about the Cold War but also of a policy shift between the 1950s and the 1960s, which left many conservatives reeling when contemplating how best to overcome the forces of communism. Not all conservatives responded similarly to the general: some actively supported him; others only refrained from excoriating him. The Walker case helped some conservatives band together and reinvigorated the ongoing process of defining conservatives according to a taxonomic scheme of liberals, moderates, and extremists.

Five themes connected the John Birch Society to the General Walker case. First Walker's admonition and the subsequent "military-muzzling" congressional hearings forced conservatives to take sides and united those who defended him against (they believed) those who placed politics above principle. Second the Walker case demonstrated that American national security policy was at a point of transition; rather than opposing communism with traditional military methods, some of JFK's advisers—and JFK himself—believed that the new battleground would be partly an economic one, on which the country with the most industry and efficiency would triumph. This shift forced both liberals and conservatives to reformulate their strategies of fighting communism. The convergence of the policy revision and world events brought about a perceptible shift in some Americans' views of the government and what actions might best aid the situation. Third in the same way that the JBS shone a light on the question of internal subversion and what it meant to be a loyal American, the Walker case forced people to consider how best to fight communism and pursue the Cold War. If the army would relieve a general who was simply trying his hardest to fight communism, what could be expected to happen to an average citizen? The Walker case was about much more than whether or not the general actually accused people like Eleanor Roosevelt, John Foster Dulles, and Milton Eisenhower of being communists or collaborators. It was also about a kind of cognitive dissonance that many conservatives seemed to be experiencing. After the disappointment of Eisenhower's relatively liberal presidency, conservatives expected JFK's tenure to be even worse. But no one believed their government would go so far as to discharge anticommunist generals whose job was fighting communism. Fourth, unlike the JBS, which eventually learned to use the media as a tool, General Walker and his supporters never figured out how to position their beliefs in a wholly favorable light. Moreover the general had almost no idea about how to develop a constituency to support his cause. Walker never worried about the intricacies of recruiting supporters; other conservatives did the job for him. Many conservatives, especially those who had connections with citizen groups like the JBS or who had worked for a politician, eagerly organized on behalf of a conservative symbol. Citizen groups sprang up and wrote letters, sent telegrams, and held demonstrations, always trying to draw attention to what they believed was not only an injustice against an outstanding American but also an indicator of what honest anticommunists had to put up with. Fifth, the Walker case functioned as a heretofore little-acknowledged fission point for conservative factions. Just as Ronald Reagan later labeled 1964, this was "a time for choosing," when conservatives were forced to declare their allegiances. Those who stuck with Walker, even after his testimony before the Senate Armed Services Committee, were branded part of the radical Right. Other conservatives chose to drop their support quietly, explicitly or implicitly siding with more moderate conservatives. Those politicians who tried to give tacit support to Walker but refused to suffer the consequences of being labeled as part of the extremist culture risked losing sustenance from both sides. Combined with Barry Goldwater's later bid for the presidency—which for some activists began as early as 1960—these two events acted like scorecards, not only telling conservatives who among them was most appropriately classified as extremist, moderate, or liberal but informing the American public as well.

Between 1961 and 1964 conservatives divided themselves into more distinct factions yet cooperated to pursue a number of goals, the most important being the election of a conservative to the White House. Those factions that remained adjunct partners of the Republican party strengthened their ties to each other, and by 1968 they had developed a network that surpassed everyone's expectations—except, of course, their own. During these three years conservatives gained increased consciousness that their philosophy was taking root as a political force. The Walker incident helped bridge the gap between political incubation and political activism.

Cold War Military

Although the case of Major General Edwin A. Walker took place over thirteen months, from approximately April 1961 to May 1962, many of the background issues dated to the Korean War and military anticommunist policies of the 1950s. NSC-68, a National Security Council document drafted and approved just before the outbreak of the Korean War in June 1950, helped rewrite American guidelines for waging the Cold War. Partly because of the Korean War the military budget increased from $22.5 billion in 1951 to $44 billion in 1952. Furthermore the directive licensed branches of the military to apply new training methods outside of traditional military protocol. Of course the shock of the Korean conflict made Truman's approval of NSC-68's guidelines, as well as the simultaneous revamping of American national security strategy on a global scale, possible.[2]

By 1958 the policy of containment had been replaced by the Eisenhower-Dulles New Look strategy, and the NSC issued another directive concerning the prosecution of the Cold War. Not satisfied with the effort at thwarting the communists, the NSC recommended that to challenge the communist enemy, all branches of the government should act as a unified team rather than as independent units. The Department of Defense interpreted the directive to mean that troops in the armed services should receive additional education about the communist threat and their own role in America's defense. News of this directive did not reach the public until three years later when, in 1961, Senator J. William Fulbright leaked it to the press. Concerned primarily with a growing practice of right-wing civilians conducting seminars either at military bases or for military personnel off-base, Fulbright challenged the NSC memo, which if interpreted loosely seemed to encourage such gatherings.[3]

NSC-68 and its 1958 revision made clear to commanders like Walker that their job was to do whatever was necessary to prepare their soldiers for battle against the enemy. All of these officers had fought in World War II, and many had fought in Korea. The differences between those two conflicts—in terms of public support, restrictions placed on the soldier in the field, and the demands of fighting as part of the United Nations—taught these senior officers that future conflicts with the communists would demand not only military but also psychological preparation. By 1961, however, civilians like Fulbright hoped to replace battlefield confrontation with economic and educational competition, a fight they believed would result in the triumph of the United States and the breakup of the Soviet bloc. Military officers, however, were not as optimistic. Brush-fire wars seemed to be springing up more quickly than ever. Most important, lessons from the Korean War were still being interpreted, including how to do battle with a communist enemy—a still novel undertaking for Americans, which would come to shape their existence in their bipolar world.

Between mid-1950 and 1953 participation in the Korean War displayed America's willingness to carry the ideological struggle onto the battlefield. It was also one of the recurring tests of the Cold War: where would the United States decide whether or not ideology was worth supporting with action? The settlement of the war not only left America with its first nonvictory in anyone's memory but also caused some Americans to question if the loss of life was truly worth it. For other Americans, however, the real questions revolved around America's "failure." Why did the forces of good not prevail this time? Even more disturbing news came with regard to the Americans taken prisoner by the North Koreans and the Chinese. Unlike POWs from other UN countries, studies found Americans were much more susceptible to brainwashing by the communists. Although psychologists and sociologists posited some explanations about the phenomenon, most observers believed that the root cause was a slackening of cultural values in the upbringing of American young men. Something had happened since World War II, and young men had lost their initiative and their drive to independently pursue problems that confronted an organization.

To understand why officers like Walker and his civilian counterparts felt compelled to take the offensive in the ideological battle against communism, one must turn to the Senate Subcommittee on Armed Services hearings on military Cold War education and speech review policies, which were conducted in March and April 1962 and instigated by Walker's admonishment in 1961. Eisenhower's farewell address had warned of the military-industrial complex, and the Kennedy administration was also seeking new methods with which to deal with its communist enemies. The 1958 revision of NSC-68 had been, for all intents and purposes, repealed by the new administration. Thus the proceedings revealed a group of senators trying to chart a course of action not just for the military but for the country as a whole.[4] Striving to explain the weakening of the American resolve, experts focused on the 1950s as a time of military and social upheaval, the combination of which managed to damage national security to an alarming degree.

Hoping to uncover the connections between the climate in which the soldiers were reared and their willingness to collaborate with their enemy in Korea, senators on the Armed Services Committee called on Lieutenant Colonel William E. Mayer, a doctor who had studied POWs from the Korean War. Mayer testified that the soldiers were "more dependent people, psychologically, upon outside authority, show less initiative, [and] have less inclination to initiate action than was characteristic of our soldiers 15 years ago."[5] Mayer's findings echoed those of sociologists William Whyte and David Riesman: Americans seemed more inclined than ever to conform to standards created by large corporations, universities, and other faceless institutions.[6]

Mayer's testimony distilled the hearings to their essence: what should be taught to Americans to defend themselves against communism, who should teach it, and how should it be taught? Mayer posed the question to the committee:

> Seven thousand Americans were caught in Korea and held by a Communist enemy. This is the first relatively randomly selected group of healthy young adult Americans, who are the inheritors of our cultural heritage, our prejudices, our beliefs, our educational system and our military training, who ever had to live for a prolonged period of time, in groups, under a Communist-controlled state. This is the only time we have ever had a valid chance to see: are we invulnerable or not? Can we be controlled or not?[7]

The failure of the American cultural and social system to prepare its men for the rigors of war and the deceptiveness of communism pointed to a danger for the military and all of society. And it was not just the fault of those tricked by the enemy; a corrupted American cultural heritage and educational system meant that society's elders were not doing their job, and the blame belonged to them as much as their offspring. Mayer acknowledged that a prison camp was not analogous to living in a free society, but he contended that, in other POW situations, Americans had always responded in ways that exploited their educational and cultural advantages. Thus, if other POWs were products of their society and they responded to their predicaments in a manner that reflected the best America had to offer, the Korean experience suggested that America might indeed be subject to psychological control by communist forces.

Much to the chagrin of Fulbright, Mayer recommended that troop education not only continue but also be augmented to compensate for the failures of other social institutions, as well as the deteriorating situation in domestic and foreign affairs. Most witnesses who testified in front of the committee recommended similar actions, although all carefully cautioned against the breakdown of civilian control of the military or the possibility of commanders creating their own set of guidelines for indoctrinating their charges. The irony of Mayer's testimony and recommendations was not lost on the Senate panel; most of what they heard emphasized the need for conscious education rather than simply hoping that the values held by previous generations would be transmitted by osmosis.[8] Officers like Walker knew from experience what Mayer learned from research, and using what they believed was authorization from the 1958 NSC directive and their own initiative, they set out to save America. In their opinion they were not a minute too soon.

Cold Warrior

How did Edwin Walker, one general among the army's many, become so important? Born in 1909 in Center Point, Texas, Walker came from a family of staunchly conservative Texans. He won admission to West Point, distinguished himself on the polo fields, and graduated in 1931. After serving as the commander of a Special Service Force composed of Americans and Canadians that fought at Anzio, Rome, and southern France, Walker continued to climb the army career ladder and received promotions without interruption. Between 1957 and 1959 he commanded the army forces in Arkansas, including federalized National Guard units and the 101st Airborne Division. Ironically Walker's involvement with the 1957 desegregation of the Little Rock schools gave him an element of credibility when he discussed developments in the civil rights movement.[9] Walker always resented this assignment; remaining true to a states' rights doctrine, he felt that local soldiers should take care of local business. In 1959 Walker was transferred to West Germany where he took command of the 24th Infantry Division, one of the units considered most likely to receive the communists' opening salvo. With this in mind, Walker and one of his subordinates, Lieutenant Colonel Archibald Roberts, devised a program that met the guidelines of the 1958 NSC directive. Called Pro-Blue because military maps depicted communist forces in red and free forces in blue, the program suggested a reading list, outlined a series of lectures, exams, and discussions, and eventually recommended to soldiers a list of candidates to vote for in national elections.[10]

Walker made three main mistakes. First he should not have advised his troops on how to cast their votes (he used the Americans for Constitutional Action voter index, a supposedly nonpartisan rating of how congressmen voted on various issues).[11] Second, in a speech to his troops and their wives, reported on by the privately owned tabloid the *Overseas Weekly*, Walker accused certain public figures, including Harry Truman, Eleanor Roosevelt, and Dean Acheson, of being "definitely pink."[12] Here however Walker was also the victim of the media. More sensationalist than accurate, the *Overseas Weekly* went to press without fully investigating the facts of the story while reporting that Walker was psychologically unfit for duty. The *New York Times* and other news outlets quickly repeated the *Weekly*'s charges verbatim, essentially legitimizing the sordid paper. Walker later successfully sued the *Weekly* for slander, but he gained little more than a moral victory.[13] Third Walker included Robert Welch's book *The Life of John Birch* on his list of recommended anticommunist works, which led the press to associate the Pro-Blue program with the JBS *Blue Book*. The irony of the Walker case lies in the fact that had the general not recommended which politicians to vote for and had he not labeled public figures as communists, the Pro-Blue program and the 1958 NSC directive might have stayed in place much longer than they did.

After an inquiry conducted by the army from April to June 1961, the Department of Defense issued a press release on June 12 that finalized its position on political indoctrination within the military. Though the army dismissed any accusations that Walker was disseminating JBS material, he was admonished for making "derogatory remarks of a serious nature about certain prominent Americans, the American Press, and TV industry and certain commentators, which linked the persons and institutions with Communism and Communist influence." Walker also "failed to heed cautions by superior officers to refrain from participating in controversial activities which were contrary to long-standing customs of the military service and beyond the prerogatives of a senior military commander."[14] The Defense Department hoped that the admonishment without further punishment (except Walker's reassignment) would put a damper on the issue of political action within the military. Walker, however, decided that he had "to be free from the power of little men who, in the name of my country, punish loyal service," and he resigned his commission, giving up a hefty pension as well as a career that had not necessarily run its course.[15] Much to the Defense Department's disappointment, the press, politicians, and the public refused to let the case rest.

After Walker resigned and declared his independence from any civilian or government agency, he began a one-man campaign to educate Americans about the dangers of the communist insurgency. A year after he was relieved of his command, Walker testified about his journey from army general to active anticommunist before the Senate Special Preparedness Subcommittee. Walker thus managed to keep his name in print, although his sometimes unbalanced interpretations damaged his reputation more than they helped. After running in the Texas gubernatorial primary and finishing last in a field of six (he received more than 125,000 votes, or about 10% of those cast in the primary), Walker continued to attract attention, first through his opposition to the civil rights movement and later by speaking out about the dangers of communism on the college lecture circuit.[16] In October 1962 Walker was arrested in Oxford, Mississippi, on charges of "inciting rebellion or insurrection" when he led white students against federal marshals at the University of Mississippi.[17] Thereafter he kept up his campaign to rid America of communists and sympathizers, although his actions became more and more unhinged.[18]

More important than the details of Walker's case or even his testimony before the Senate Armed Services Committee, however, were reactions to Walker's predicament from across the American political spectrum. Conservatives registered their opinions of a single event, thus making explicit their attitudes toward the government, liberals, and each other. The window Walker opened afforded some Americans a chance to come to terms with what it meant to be a conservative and to decide whether they fit such a description. In only a few months of intense media coverage, more Americans than ever before had been exposed not just to the radical Right (through Walker and the John Birch Society) but also to such alternatives as the politics of Barry Goldwater, the journalism of *National Review*, and the intellectualism of Russell Kirk, William F. Buckley, and James Burnham. Viable alternatives to liberalism in the form of the JBS and a few other fledgling organizations were publicized, and some responsible conservatives found themselves besieged with eager disciples. A new era was dawning.

Raising the Big Tent

How *did* self-avowed conservatives respond to Walker's predicament? From the far Right to the moderate Right and Republican party, politicians and political activists made decisions to speak out or remain silent about the Walker case. As early as 1961 centrifugal force was already starting to spin different groups to the periphery of the growing movement, while simultaneously producing a clotting effect at the center, which helped create a more effective and tightly knit core. Of course the Walker case was not the only incident that helped determine which conservatives would be part of the movement and which would be cut loose. The incident, however, came at a time in the movement's growth when conservatives with political power were organizationally developed enough that they could respond with loud voices but were not yet mature enough to distance themselves from elements they believed would damage the movement's chances.

Curiously Walker had little to do with promoting his own martyrdom; he was not an effective self-promoter. Whether due to his poor communication skills or simply because he believed that the spotlight should be trained on the issues and not his personality, Walker essentially left it up to conservatives to appropriate his predicament for whatever reasons they saw fit. From the far Right to *National Review* to a smattering of local groups and industrious individuals, conservatives capitalized on the Walker case, using the man and the issues for a variety of purposes. While there was not complete unanimity of judgment about what had happened, what the case meant, and what should be done, differences among the groups never became an issue, a signal that responsible conservatives in 1961–1962 had still not separated out politically detrimental extremists from the coalition being assembled to capture political power. This apparent unity, however, was deceiving in both its breadth and depth. By 1963 conservatives were well along in their plans to draft Goldwater as the Republican nominee. They realized that such indicators as the Walker case seemed to depict bonds that stretched from moderate to the far-right conservatives but in fact were strongest where politically they would hurt the most: among the radical Right.

The JBS was among the more active groups that responded to Walker's plight. Some members urged the Home Office to undertake a letter-writing campaign to convince Walker that he should expose communists or subversives in the government and to urge an investigation of the State Department and other important branches of the government. As one couple from Montana wrote in a Member's Monthly Message in 1961:

> We intend to write General Walker and hope it will be a project of the Society, urging him to come out full force and name names. It would seem that this is his intention altho [*sic*] one reads very little about it in the A. P. Papers. We further hope there will be a consecrated drive on the part of the Society, in the not too distant future, asking (or better yet, demanding) a full-scale investigation of the State Dept. which is long overdue.[19]

Some Birchers struck out on their own and urged friends to write to the Senate Armed Services Committee to demand a hearing about Walker's situation. One friend of a Bircher wrote to another non-Bircher:

> Do you know [name expurgated] of Quakertown, Penn.? She is a John Birch Society member. . . . Today I got a letter from her asking me to write to the chairmen of both the House and Senate Armed Services Committees calling attention to the fact that . . . Major General Edwin A. Walker was accused of indoctrinating his troops with Americanism and [was] summarily removed from his command! She is getting up a letter writing campaign to help General Walker who certainly *deserves better than that from the Country for which he has given so much.*[20]

JBS leaders also considered what action they should take in order to capitalize on the smear directed against Walker. Writing to a fellow council member, Clarence "Pat" Manion, former dean of the Notre Dame Law School, mused, "General Walker has given our side a great opportunity but you may be sure that the enemy will rush in upon him for 'The Kill.'"[21] Welch supported Walker in his monthly publications but, not surprisingly, never acted on the advice of his members.

After Walker was arrested and charged with inciting riots at the University of Mississippi, a new wave of correspondence poured into the Home Office, again urging the society to defend the former general against the trumped-up charges. Responding to one MMM that complained, "The only thing you have printed concerning him was the fact he should never have gone to Mississippi," D. A. Waite, one of Welch's assistants, replied:

> [Welch] wanted me to tell you that when General Walker and Dr. [Billy James] Hargis went on their speaking tour of several weeks in the Spring, not only did the Society officially urge support by our members, right in the Bulletin, but in many cities and parts of the country, it was JBS members who actually took the lead in setting up the arrangements and getting sizable audiences for the team. Before that, when General Walker was

incarcerated in the mental hospital in Missouri, we actually offered to make arrangements with friends to put up the bail, but when the time came, the bail was reduced to $50,000 and General Walker was able and preferred to have that put up by members of his own family.[22]

The society further formalized its support of Walker by publishing in 1963 Earl Lively, Jr.'s *The Invasion of Mississippi*, which described how communists had incited riots, how the actions of federal troops foreshadowed the complete loss of states' rights, and how innocent white students at Ole Miss were the true victims of the messy attempt at integration.[23] But a year or two later, when Walker appeared to have lost touch with reality, the society quietly dropped his name from publications and letters.[24]

Although the JBS remained mildly active in regard to the military muzzling and Walker's case, it did not lead the pack of conservative groups or publications in demanding that something be done about Walker and anticommunist education. Instead two very different periodicals, the *Independent American* and *National Review*, took charge of pushing the Walker case and published a series of articles about Walker and the problem of free speech and anticommunism. In addition a slew of autonomous individuals and groups held Walker up as a symbol for what was wrong with America. Although each cohort stood by a position made unique by its own perspective, to arrive there, they strode across a great deal of common ground.

In 1961–1962 Kent and Phoebe Courtney, heads of the New Orleans–based Conservative Society of America (CSA) and publishers of the *Independent American*, turned the Walker case into their own cottage industry. The Courtneys, outspoken segregationists (the initials of their organization were, not coincidentally, identical to those of the Confederate States of America), saw Walker as both an advocate for states' rights and as the victim of a communist-coordinated campaign to rid America of true patriots. Leaders in the New Orleans JBS chapter, the Courtneys were essentially a two-person front. Although they advertised for memberships in the CSA, other names—in bylines, letters, signed editorials, published books, or press releases—rarely appeared. When the Walker case splashed across the front pages, they wasted little time in reorienting their publications to focus on the general.

Immediately after Walker was relieved of his command in Germany, the Courtneys relied on one of their tried-and-true publishing techniques: quoting verbatim the *Congressional Record* remarks of conservative congressmen to prove that some politicians really *did* think similarly to their readers. In the May 1961 issue the Courtneys quoted California Congressman Edgar Hiestand, a self-admitted Bircher, asking, "Since when, Mr. Speaker, is it proper procedure to relieve a military officer of his command for distributing the information of a patriotic society? Since when is it wrong to advance the cause of Americanism?"[25]

Not surprisingly neither the Courtneys nor any of their readers ever saw any contradiction in relying on a conservative politician's word while frequently bashing the federal government as corrupt and untrustworthy. The fact that Hiestand called for an investigation seemed impressive, and the Courtneys clearly fell victim to the same rationalizations as their readers.

For more than a year the *Independent American* ran at least one article on Walker in nearly every issue. The Courtneys often reprinted articles from conservative, usually southern, newspapers and built up what they hoped would be an unassailable wall of evidence supporting the general. When Walker decided to enter the Texas gubernatorial race in early 1962, the Courtneys endorsed his candidacy. In the April–May 1962 lead story, "Why the Liberals Fear Gen. Walker," Phoebe Courtney argued that liberals feared Walker because "he has the qualifications for leadership in the campaign to restore this nation to Constitutional principles."[26] Only one problem remained: convincing the corrupt politicians that what Walker had charged—that persons in high places in the government were soft on communism—was true and that he should be fully exonerated as a result. Calling for a "mobiliz[ation of] grass roots support in your community demanding that Walker's charges be thoroughly investigated," the editors hoped to repeat the earlier feat of flooding Congress with telegrams and letters, an effort that helped stimulate the original subcommittee hearings.[27]

Periodically the Courtneys expanded upon the ideas they proposed in the *Independent American* by publishing short books on topics ranging from the dangers of disarmament to an annual ACA-style voting index. Produced rapidly to take advantage of any controversy generated by the press, the books were often based on extended quotations from CSA periodicals, the *Congressional Record*, and other "reliable" documents. *The Case of General Edwin A. Walker* reprinted almost ninety pages of evidence culled from the *Congressional Record*, the press—including a special appendix of editorials from the Manchester (N.H.) *Union-Leader*—and the Pro-Blue program itself.[28] As with most of their arguments the Courtneys simply assumed that their insight into the "facts" enabled them to see the "truth," and testimony that might be completely false when interpreted by a liberal source would be rendered reliable and trustworthy through their analytical powers. The Walker case was a godsend for the Courtneys; not only was it a self-contained event that measured the gains the enemy had already made, but it also provided a reference point for future incidents, explaining why, for example, a politician was unwilling to defend the military. For the Courtneys one's courage or timidity in a time of crisis was the truest measurement of one's character. They would not forget, nor would they let their audience forget, who had defended, attacked, or remained silent about Walker.

While the Courtneys represented best how the far Right viewed Walker, the reaction of the staff of *National Review* showed how a more moderate—albeit still staunchly conservative—community saw the event. Two main differences separated the far Right from its more moderate relatives. First, while each saw Walker as a symbol, they disagreed over what exactly he symbolized. Second, in the eight months between April and December 1961, each group's position changed as new developments came to light, which revealed how they attempted to appropriate Walker for their own political purposes.

The first story that *National Review* ran about Walker was actually not a story at all. In the May 6, 1961, issue the editors reprinted a letter sent to them from an officer who served under Walker in the 24th Division in Germany. Introducing the full-page letter as providing "another view of army life under General Walker, recently humiliated for allegedly committing heinous political crimes," the editors thought the officer was privy to reliable and accurate information.[29] After assailing the *Overseas Weekly*'s deceitfulness, the officer described the Pro-Blue program, aghast that investigators would single out *The Life of John Birch*, when it was only one book among many, as cause for shutting down the entire affair. The real issue for the officer and perhaps for the editors as well was "How far can the military go in teaching its soldiers why they fight, who they fight, and when the [Cold] war began?"[30] The officer concluded with a defense of his division and a call to arms:

> If you want to join us in the fight, help start a letter-writing campaign to your congressman, your leaders of opinion in the community, the President, and patriotic groups like the American Legion, backing the Pro-Blue Program—and you might drop General Walker a letter of encouragement.[31]

National Review's decision to publish the letter was likely based on what the editors believed was the salient issue: restraining the military would only harm the nation. But the fact that the magazine ended up defending the JBS, as well as trusting the officer's account simply because he was there, put it in an awkward position. *National Review* had been trying to move away from Robert Welch since the JBS's spate of publicity in 1960, but the editors feared that if the magazine criticized the society, it would lose readership as well as advertising revenue. The editors were faced with the options of not defending Walker, attacking him, or defending him. Attacking Walker was out, since that would align them with the liberals. Failing to defend Walker was also not really an option, since the magazine's readers included not only intellectuals but grassroots conservatives, who *were* writing letters and sending telegrams demanding an investigation into the government's muzzling of officers. So *National Review* was left defending Walker.

Buckley was interested in whether the general *had* accused Eleanor Roosevelt, Truman, and others of being communists. As editor in chief he knew that to distance his journal from Kent and Phoebe Courtney and Robert Welch, he would have to act in a more discriminating manner. Buckley called Walker on June 14, 1961, to ask him about the charges leveled by the *Overseas Weekly* and for more information about the case. Walker wrote to Buckley the next day, although he did not discuss exactly what he had said about personalities like Eleanor Roosevelt and Edward R. Murrow.[32] Two weeks after receiving Walker's reply, Buckley wrote to Walker, and told him that he, as an editor, was hamstrung; without knowing exactly what had happened, *National Review* could not run a full article about the incident:

> I do not know whether you are permitted to divulge what you said, nor whether, assuming you are, you are disposed to. Our position is as we have stated it, that on the basis of what is publicly known you have been treated shabbily; and that the Liberals seem to be seizing the opportunity to degut an orientation program necessary for an enlightened military.[33]

But Buckley cautioned that he could say no more until he had heard—from Walker himself—exactly what he had said. If he found proof that some famous people had tried to muzzle Walker and others, Buckley promised results: "If you *are* disposed to make the facts known, we would go immediately into high gear and produce a major article." Unlike the Courtneys, who reasoned that since Walker was an honest person, he must be telling the truth about Roosevelt, Truman, and the others, Buckley would not resort to such circular logic.

National Review's editors next focused on the Pentagon's and the liberal press's efforts to make Walker "an example" to other officers. Curiously, "Let the Generals Beware" came close to resorting to Courtney-like tactics, emphasizing that "the Liberal community has never grasped the scope of the Communist enterprise" and the fact that it was the responsible officers who decided to respond to lessons from the Korean War.[34] Falling short of accusing officers and civilians in the Pentagon of being communist agents, *National Review* stated that they were not acting responsibly at a time when courage in defending an anticommunist education program was crucial. Since the *New York Times* condoned the Pentagon's use of Walker as a symbol of the problems besetting the military, *National Review* followed suit, simply looking at the case from the opposite perspective—that the Walkers in the military knew the *real* score, while those in the Pentagon sat safe and sound behind their desks. Although it resisted following the Courtneys into a grand conspiracy theory, *National Review* attested that unless those in power realized what lay ahead, the road they were traveling down would surely lead to disaster.

When Walker decided to resign, *National Review* responded with an article clearly articulating its belief not only in Walker as an individual but also in what his predicament should represent. In "Out: Not with a Whimper but a Bang," the editors emphatically urged their readers not to martyr Walker. Such an action would exaggerate the power of the enemy and obfuscate the most important issues: "What we American conservatives, we tough anti-Communists, need these days in America is not martyrs but heroes; not dead-warriors to provide us slogans and battle-cries, but live warriors to provide us leadership and strategy."[35] *National Review* tried to avoid taking a specific stand on Walker's case but sought instead to place the incident in a much larger and more important context. While Walker might have been an upstanding officer, the editors realized that the key issue was what would happen when another "Walker case" came along. Moreover the editors questioned whether politicians should be allowed to foil policies they opposed by using personal attacks, even though definitive consensus positions had yet to be determined. Calling on the president to set the goals for a coherent civilian and military policy, the editors hoped that the commander in chief would take charge and set a path to achieve those ends that hardened anticommunists knew were necessary for survival and victory.

Although one month later *National Review* ran an interview with Walker in which he discussed his future plans and the problems he believed beset the military, for all intents and purposes, the magazine's interest in Walker was exhausted.[36] *National Review*'s use of Walker as a symbol rivaled that of the Courtneys, but some significant differences remained. Rather than urging that Walker assume command of the anticommunist movement as a whole, the editors reminded readers that Walker had been in the military and that he had operated under a different set of rules. When he resigned from the army, the rules changed, and Walker became less interesting since he was no longer a lone voice in the wilderness. Nevertheless the editors used Walker to draw attention to problems in the White House and the Pentagon, conditions they believed were intertwined. The Courtneys saw similar connections, although they believed the links were less due to ideology than to consciously conspiratorial actions. Both publications believed Walker's instincts were correct, although only *National Review* conceded that he was not necessarily the most stable officer in the military. The *Independent American* continued to cover Walker's escapades in Mississippi and elsewhere, while *National Review* emphatically avoided him.

In many ways the differences in coverage between the *Independent American* and *National Review* symbolized the division between the far Right and the comparatively more moderate Right at this moment in the conservative movement. Both factions acknowledged the dire problems that snaked from one institution to another, but they diverged in defining what caused the connections that fomented so much deadly trouble for the United States. The Courtneys saw an out-and-out conspiracy. *National Review* saw an ideology. This difference would help determine which groups remained an integral part of the conservative political movement and which would be unceremoniously drummed out.

Conservative Symbol

The chance that such fanatical anticommunists might have ties deep within the government forced President Kennedy into a difficult situation; he could not allow a subordinate to teach soldiers about an organization that employed tactics running counter to official government policy. At a news conference on April 21, 1961, where the failed Bay of Pigs invasion was the main topic of discussion, Kennedy acknowledged that he had asked Secretary of Defense Robert McNamara to investigate Walker and told reporters that he was most concerned with Walker's indiscriminate naming of communists. When asked for his opinion of the John Birch Society, Kennedy said that he believed the JBS was not "wrestling with the real problems which are created by the Communist advance around the world."[37]

Although the press was reluctant to support Walker as an individual, they supported what he stood for: free speech, a willingness to acknowledge the real dangers of the Cold War, and caution in accepting the word of dubious publications like the *Overseas Weekly*. Some editorials drew analogies between what they saw as the railroading of Walker and McCarthy-like tactics, in which illegitimate sources are accepted as the truth and innocent people are thus coerced into confessions or are blacklisted. The *Saturday Evening Post*, for example, called for distinguishing between "crackpots" and officers who led effective programs on the dangers of the communist threat. Defending these conferences against Senator Fulbright's cautionary memorandum, the *Post* lauded the gatherings as exchanges where military reservists

> discuss with high-level Government officials, writers and industrial executives all phases of the cold war and of American and Soviet military and economic capabilities. They go home to inform their fellow Americans about the Communist threat and how to meet it. Some have got up local seminars with the co-operation of business firms, labor unions, chambers of commerce and universities.[38]

Walker's required seminars were not so different, implied the editorial. Moreover the *Post* feared that Fulbright's suggestions for restraining the political activities of military personnel would also weaken the military's ability to defend the country, both impinging on freedom of speech and hurting the very institution so vital to short- and long-term preparedness.

Life took a similar approach and urged fair treatment of Walker, now a civilian. Acknowledging that he had overstepped boundaries by pinning communist labels on well-known Americans, the magazine believed that when judging Walker, his qualities as an outstanding soldier should take precedence over his tendency to "giv[e] a highly partisan twist to his anticommunist lectures."[39] Two months later, however, *Life* distanced itself from Walker and his supporters, decrying the spread of "superpatriotism." "We don't think the American people are so asleep to the danger of Communism that they need a nationwide posse of Paul Reveres to arouse them. Everybody in his right mind is against Communism," declared the editors.[40] Instead of cultivating fear and suspicion surrounding internal subversion, *Life* recommended that citizens focus on foreign affairs, since: "There's a real [war] in the rest of the world. And to win that, Americans of all shades of rational opinion on domestic issues, from welfare-state liberals to Goldwater conservatives, will need to count on each other's mutual support and common belief in the institutions of freedom."[41]

The editors had shifted their opinion. Before, they believed Americans would benefit from educational seminars on the dangers of communism. Now, however, some individuals like Walker or Dr. Fred Schwarz of the Christian Anti-Communism Crusade were attracting "people who are too superheated to teach or learn anything." Urging that distinctions should be made between seminars conducted by crackpots and those run by legitimate anticommunist educators, the editors seemed to hope that guidelines, such as avoiding "one-man shows" and choosing small groups instead of mass rallies, would foster an atmosphere of restrained education. In the end *Life*'s pronouncements were more prescriptive than descriptive; while many seminar attendees probably read *Life*, they were not likely to be swayed by an editorial that dismissed their own efforts as belonging in the crackpot category.

The public reacted rapidly to the accusations against Walker, his admonishment, and his resignation. Their opinions traced the contours of his journey from a relatively unknown anticommunist to a symbol of the dilemmas inherent in fighting the Cold War. Since the White House had ordered an inquiry into the *Overseas Weekly*'s accusations, much of the public's approval and disapproval was projected onto Kennedy, though at first the White House felt that Walker's immediate army superiors, not the commander in chief, should deal with the situation.[42] These early telegrams and letters reflect a public unable to fathom why a loyal American and dedicated anticommunist would be drummed out of the military, particularly given the source of the incriminating evidence. Two writers from California asked the president:

> Why sacrifice our heroes like General Walker? We should be thankful for men who have the courage and the integrity to fight communism or communist influences of any kind. We strongly oppose the injustice of actions taken against him and ask that careful consideration be given any action that tends to benefit communism.[43]

Most writers argued that not only was an injustice being carried out against Walker as an individual but that achieving the larger goal of defeating communism and spreading democracy was slipping away with every new incident. The other theme emphasized by citizens writing to the president concerned the alleged American reluctance to achieve victory over their enemies. A husband and wife writing from California linked Senator Fulbright's memorandum on the prosecution of the Cold War to the real reasons why Walker was disciplined:

The overwhelming welcome General MacArthur received upon his return from Korea shows beyond doubt that the American people have never seen anything wrong with "Pride in Victory." It is to be hoped that we never will. We view with shame any indication of our Government toward "restraining" our all out resistance to the evil of Communism. We believe it is the duty of our elected officials *not* to *restrain* the American people, but to represent them.[44]

The administration reacted to citizens who appealed to the White House by gently trying to correct misunderstandings about the case, particularly concerning the limits placed on the military by the Constitution. The assistant assigned to handle the bulk of the correspondence, Frederick G. Dutton, emphasized that the Department of Defense understood the importance of educating the public about the dangers of communism, but such duties were simply not its responsibility. In a typical letter Dutton wrote:

I am sure that you will understand that the Department of Defense does not have the authority to influence in any manner the judgment of private citizens concerning the steps which they should take in combating the menace of communism. This, we believe, is a function which, under our democratic system, should be performed by patriotic civic organizations and individual citizens in cooperation with other agencies of government. It is the policy of the Department, therefore, to refrain from participation in any public activities which are not directly connected with its mission and which might give the public the impression that the Department was directly or indirectly sponsoring or indorsing [*sic*] such public indoctrination activities.[45]

Dutton responded to these inquiries without admitting to any privileged information and wrote that "my own personal knowledge about this situation is based entirely on newspaper accounts." Dutton acknowledged that he thought that if Walker's program were based on JBS materials, "I, for one, think that the practice would most certainly be objectionable. There is a fundamental difference between information and propaganda."[46] Whether the president and his advisers wanted to or not, the administration was being forced to respond to extremist conservatives.

The Kennedy administration had been reluctant to pursue the radical Right, and it was not until the assaults became more frequent and concentrated that it investigated the phenomenon further. The most immediate upshot of the administration's decision to take a closer look at the radical Right was the famous—or, for those on the Right, infamous—Reuther Memorandum. In the fall of 1961, after Walker had resigned and the John Birch Society had been revealed, Attorney General Robert F. Kennedy asked labor leaders and Americans

for Democratic Action founders Victor Reuther and Walter Reuther and civil
rights attorney Joseph L. Rauh, Jr., to prepare a memorandum on the problem
of the radical Right. When they finished their final draft in mid-December 1961,
the authors had produced a plan for the Kennedy administration to challenge
the radical Right at the organizational, financial, and political levels. Warning
RFK that *"speeches without action may well only mobilize the radical right instead of mobilizing the democratic forces within our nation"* (italics in original),
the authors outlined the biggest threats to the administration and the nation in
general.[47] Placing the highest priority on dealing with the radical Right's infiltration of the armed forces, they recommended that sure and swift action be taken
against Walker and officers who exhibited similar behavior. Repeatedly emphasizing the same theme, the Reuthers and Rauh urged the administration to "get
off the defensive in the Walker case; it must shift the battleground to an offensive posture supporting the basic American concept of separation of military
personnel from partisan politics."[48] After the administration leaked sections of
it to the press, the Reuther Memorandum became ammunition for the far Right.

The problem the administration faced was that, by singling out supporters of
Walker and organizations like the Christian Anti-Communism Crusade and the
JBS, the government appeared to be persecuting them solely for their beliefs.
The Reuthers and Rauh knew this was a possibility and had cautioned the White
House to focus on how such organizations had violated their tax-exempt statuses
(based on their purported educational missions), as well as on how military officers had overstepped their duties as prescribed by the Constitution. The administration, however, did little more than accept the memo and hope that the problem would go away. In the end, groups and individuals on the far Right used the
memorandum as evidence that the government was intent on stripping their
constitutional rights, and they achieved almost exactly what the authors had
warned against: mobilizing the radical Right instead of mobilizing the democratic
forces within the nation.

False Unity?

In addition to nationally oriented publications and organizations, a wealth of local
groups and independently operated periodicals honed in on the Walker case.
Some followed *National Review*'s example, realizing that Walker was a symbol
and that the issues he raised were indeed germane to much of the debate surrounding foreign and domestic policy. Most, however, followed the Courtneys'
lead, seeing Walker as the flag-bearer for the entire conservative movement and
believing that perhaps this incident would sound the alarm. Much of the strength
of the grassroots movement that sprang up behind Walker came from these
locally operated groups and individuals working with little structural backing.
Signs that America was falling behind in the arms race or its inability to prepare

its fighting men to face the communists should be taken seriously, they said, and the Walker case not only depicted such a breakdown in the training program, it demonstrated literally what would happen if certain political forces had their way with military policy.

After Walker had resigned his commission and was free to speak to conservative gatherings around the country, a number of groups chose Walker as their raison d'être, sponsored an address, and pushed his cause in their publications. In an advertisement for its Seventh Annual National Constitutional Day Convention, We, the People! a national organization based in Chicago, spelled out the problems of the Kennedy administration:

> Under the New Frontier during the last six months—
>
> - Military leaders who have spoken against Communism and Socialism have been relieved of their commands. First, General Walker, then Admiral Burke, and now Capt. Hampton of Glenview Naval Air Base.
> - An attempt has been made to muzzle the press.
> - All F.B.I. agents have been ordered to cease their investigations of Communists.
> - Patriotic groups and military security organizations, such as the Institute for American Strategy, are to be investigated.[49]

More than simply a gathering to listen to such speakers as Billy James Hargis and Robert Welch, the Constitutional Day Convention was an opportunity for patriots to work in their communities and drum up interest in and representatives for the cause. While Walker apparently did not speak at the convention, his admonishment captured top billing for a gathering of people primarily concerned with the traditional conservative values of saving "our personal liberty, private property, and individual freedom."[50]

Acting out of a burning desire to see justice served, individuals instituted a variety of responses to the campaign against the military. First among such efforts was Walker's sometime collaborator, Arch Roberts. A one-man organization, Roberts coordinated a letter-writing and telegram crusade to call for hearings on anticommunist education in the military. Targeting leaders of conservative organizations, Roberts focused on getting participants to the actual hearings in the Old Senate Office Building and generating a flood of letters to the committee that was to decide upon the necessity of an investigation. He did so through a campaign of telegrams, such as this one, sent as the vote on the hearings approached:

> 150,000 Letter Telegrams to Senate Armed Service Committee attest your . . . patriotic effort General Walker case. Committee votes Monday 11 September on Military muzzling. Organized protest by left wing expected.

Urgent need massive American counter action to flood Senator Richard
Russell committee with demands for investigation. Please initiate new
campaign. Success within grasp.[51]

Besides Robert Welch and Priscilla Buckley (an editor at *National Review*),
Roberts targeted publishers or leaders who could communicate with large
numbers of people. Eugene Pullian, head of the Pullian News Service at the
Indiana Star, Calvin Katter of the Christian Crusade against Communism, Mrs.
William D. Leetch of the American Coalition of Patriotic Societies, Edgar C.
Bundy of the Church League of America, and David Lawrence, a syndicated
columnist at *U.S. News and World Report*, all received this telegram and later
updates.

Many expressed their opinion on the Walker case directly to Senator Fulbright, a strident opponent of military education training programs. One writer
called for Fulbright's support for the resolutions proposed by Thurmond and
Hiestand:

> Senator Thurmond has introduced Senate Resolution no. 191 and Con-
> gressman Hiestand has introduced H. Res. 429, both of which propose a
> full investigation of the "Walker Case," and of this whole intimidation pro-
> gram. I urge you to support the proposals in these resolutions and to de-
> mand that this investigation be undertaken at the earliest possible date.[52]

Most letters, however, were not so polite. A writer from Indiana left no doubts
as to where her loyalties lay:

> Who do you think you are and others like you in Washington, who think
> that you can muzzle the voice of freedom? You are not a Hoosier Senator,
> but you are as much beholden to us and the rest of the states as to your
> own. . . . We do not believe that what masquerades as liberalism and a New
> Frontier is progression, but an effort to take us back into Medieval days.[53]

While it is impossible to know if these and the hundreds of other writers were
sparked by Roberts's efforts, their impact was certainly felt on Capitol Hill. The
upshot of Thurmond's resolution was the Senate Armed Services Subcommittee hearings on military Cold War education and speech review policies, although
Roberts and his letter writers did not rejoice over that committee's final recommendations. Nevertheless Roberts's ad hoc organization represented what could
be accomplished using Western Union and the U.S. Postal Service.[54]

The shock waves from the Walker affair eventually reached many Americans
and inspired some to articulate what they had been questioning for some time.
For example, upstate New Yorker James P. Duffy wrote and published his own
investigation into the government's treatment of conservative and anticommunist officers. *Who Is Destroying Our Military?* delved into the history of the

assault on American armed forces since the end of World War II. Writing in 1966 Duffy linked a crippled military with real and imaginary social upheaval in the United States:

> Just imagine what would happen if such a plan [in which the UN deter-mined the size of each country's armed forces] was instituted, and a com-munist controlled organization started street riots, such as those in the Watts area of Los Angeles during 1965. The riots would be carried out to such an extent that the internal force we were allowed to maintain could not handle the situation, and the United Nations would send in one of its infamous peace keeping forces—perhaps African cannibals or Russians—to halt hostilities, and to negotiate a "neutral" government that would be satisfactory to both the legal government and the rioters. This may seem a little farfetched, but it is exactly what the United Nations is doing today, and there would be no power on earth, much less in the United States, that could stop it.[55]

Regardless of his racial prejudice, Duffy managed to link the legacy of Korea (a war fought under UN control) with civil unrest (and by implication the civil rights movement) and the silenced officers, who would have prevented such a trag-edy. What distinguished this scenario from others was that the threat came inter-nally from communist-corrupted Americans rather than directly from the com-munists themselves. Duffy was forecasting not only the demise of the American military but in a sense the American character—the ability to know right from wrong and to defend what was right in the face of overwhelming odds.

However, while calling for a renewed commitment to the military, writers like Duffy ran into a set of contradictions inherent to conservatism. Conserva-tives seeking a Department of Defense budget increase explicitly demanded an expansion of the power of the federal government, but at the same time they also demanded that the federal government reduce its role in citizens' lives, specifically in areas like civil rights. Such bipolar separation, however, did not give rise to a philosophical dilemma; most conservatives believed national secu-rity was a nonnegotiable piece of the federal pie. In fact the Walker case helped a number of ex-military personnel argue in favor of an increased military bud-get and more sovereign power for the armed services in terms of training and education. Civilians knew something about running businesses, they argued, but only soldiers knew how to train their own. The Walker case inspired a number of these former officers to take up pens and sometimes to lend their names to conservative organizations.

Finally politicians from both sides of the aisle appropriated the Walker inci-dent to call for reviews of current military education policy, investigations of the incident's principle characters, or simply to make it known that they had an opinion of the circumstances. The day the *New York Times* broke the news that

Walker had been indoctrinating his troops using JBS literature, Senator William Proxmire used Walker as an example of how exactly a training program
should not be run. Shocked that the general could have conducted a program
for so long without attracting attention, Proxmire agreed with the ends of making soldiers better Americans and fighters for freedom but decried its means:
"Can we permit generals to indoctrinate our soldiers with the ridiculous absurdity that Murrow and Lippman [*sic*] and Sevareid are Communists? What are
we trying to do, instruct our troops that they should defend America against
Walter Lippman?"[56] Beyond demonstrating the extent to which anticommunism
held center stage in American politics, Proxmire's rejoinder against Walker indicted his methods and targets instead of the overall goals of educating the troops
about the enemy they faced. Liberal politicians followed Proxmire's lead, typically avoiding any defamation of Walker's theoretical goals while blasting his
methodology. In actual numbers, however, conservatives defended Walker far
more frequently than liberals attacked his tactics; conservatives never missed a
chance to call for investigations or to remind their colleagues that to relieve an
officer of his command without a full inquiry into the allegations was dictatorial.
In the Senate Thurmond, Goldwater, and Styles Bridges took up Walker's cause,
while in the House Craig Hosmer and Edgar Hiestand of California and Watkins
M. Abbitt of Virginia served as the general's proxies.

The legacy of the Walker incident was fourfold. First, the fear of a renegade
military officer designing and implementing his own programs without any over-
sight led to increased fears about the fragile relationship between civilian and
military rule. Already popularized in such books and films as *Seven Days in May*
and *The Manchurian Candidate*, Americans' fears of a military coup during the
twentieth century were never higher than in 1961–1962. Magazines polled experts about the chances of such an event and usually found enough concerned
pundits to balance out the skeptics. In September 1962, for example, *Look* ran
an article entitled "Military Control: Can It Happen Here?" which reported
enough discontent among officers to support the idea that, unless civilians kept
the military happy, the unthinkable might become possible. "One thing is certain," the authors concluded, "America is already sown with dragon's teeth.
Unwatched, they could take root and create a ruinous upheaval in some distant
year."[57]

Second, Walker and the controversy surrounding military muzzling became
a cause célèbre for the far Right, as well as for a great many closer to the center.
Walker's constitutional rights had been infringed upon, and then liberals had
scrambled to suppress a scandal that reeked of a possible conspiracy. Walker's
admonishment also signaled a shift in administration policy, which these conservatives did not easily comprehend; it seemed as though Kennedy were rewarding those who pandered to the Soviets while punishing those who advocated a strong but educated defense force. Since the public saw little except the

results of the administration's policy meetings, this "black box" foreign policy forced them to judge their leaders on outcomes rather than on their decision-making processes. Walker was another link in the chain that helped convince thousands that postwar liberalism was not working and that change was imminently necessary.

Third, the Walker incident educated conservatives about the value of capitalizing on liberal policies that infuriated the conservative public. Given the black-and-white nature of the "crime" and a set of actors who played dramatic and easily identifiable roles, the Walker case served as a prototype for future organizing efforts. Furthermore the incident provided those on the far Right with a symbol they could appropriate for a variety of purposes, and Walker was preserved as a touchstone for years to come. Conservatives across the spectrum employed Walker to defend and promote their causes, and he became—legitimately or not—a spokesman for segregation, states' rights, a larger military budget, increased anticommunist education, and third-party politics.

Lastly, the Walker case forced politicians to deal with yet another issue that revealed divisions between Left and Right. Except for the South, the Democrat-Republican split increasingly mirrored the division between liberals and conservatives. Clarifying such a divide in 1961–1962 was more troublesome to the Democrats, since they were reluctant to publicly criticize the military or to risk being labeled anti-anticommunists. Republicans had more leeway; they could reprimand renegade officers while still calling for a strong anticommunist educational program.[58] But Republicans who relied on conservative votes that fell outside of the responsible wing were forced to tack between those who saw Walker as a key to larger issues and those who saw the case as partisan politics, which demanded a response. While the number of Republicans in this position were few, Barry Goldwater was one, since he relied upon a base of supporters that included both responsible and irresponsible conservatives. The broad coalition that began assembling behind Goldwater in 1961–1962 did not force him to choose between those factions that were politically viable and those that included conservatives but were potentially damaging to his reputation. Only in 1963–1964, after the conservative movement had built up enough political power to nominate a truly conservative presidential candidate, were the campaign leaders forced to choose sides. They chose a path that, rather than uniting the most powerful elements of the Republican party, expanded cracks formed prior to 1962 and ultimately split the party and its incipient movement into clearly identifiable and separate entities.

The Walker incident, therefore, indicated that while conservative factions did exist, they were reluctant to criticize each other. More interested in gaining power than reconfiguring where and how power was distributed, conservatives accepted their extremist relatives as a trade-off. While not quite a Faustian bargain, in 1961–1962 GOP leaders decided that remaining silent was preferable to drum-

ming out the extremists in an ugly public purge. Furthermore mainstream conservatives' silence created an echo chamber for the utterances of the far Right,
which served to magnify their voices so they appeared much louder and denser
than they actually were. It was not until a year or two later that they realized
their mistake; by then it was too late to close the open arms with which they had
greeted all conservatives. This failure to discriminate cleared a path for extremists to take a leading role in 1964.

The Walker incident gave conservatives the false impression that they *could*
find a common ground on which all factions would remain politically viable, a
vision aided by focusing on attacking the Kennedy administration. What they
did not count on, however, was the dilemma the event came to represent, namely
what to do with extremists who might alienate conservatives within a united front.
Enough conservatives, however, believed that 1964 would be the year when they
not only saved the party but ensured its capture and thus guarantee a conservative ascendancy. They vowed to try.

CREATING CONFLAGRATION

BARRY GOLDWATER AND THE REPUBLICAN PARTY

On July 15, 1964, the day Barry Goldwater was nominated to bear the Republican presidential standard, political pundit Richard Wilson wrote a column summing up the condition of the GOP. In "These Are Strange Bedfellows," Wilson tried to understand how conservatives ranging from Bill Buckley to Kent Courtney could join hands in support of a maverick westerner. Beyond the fact that the men building the infrastructure around Goldwater were virtually unknown in the 1956 and 1960 campaigns, Wilson focused on the unlikely coalition Goldwater brought together. "This is the strange part," he said:

> An intellectual with a keen rationalization of his political position finds himself bedded down with kooks. This is highly embarrassing and hard to explain, especially if you have graduated with honors from the Harvard Law School or have been a respected college professor.[1]

Wilson understood that the kooks and the intellectuals saw very different things in a Goldwater nomination. The kooks wanted a die-hard anticommunist who was willing to up the ante when dealing with the enemy. The intellectuals wanted an economic and social conservative, a politician willing to enforce law and order without trampling on individual freedoms. Each side found its man in Barry Goldwater. Wilson warned liberals and moderates not to "underestimate the calm resignation with which a great many reasonable conservatives permit themselves to suffer the kooky or wild side of the Goldwater movement. They are doing so because they believe in conservative principles which they will continue to support even if it should mean the loss of the Presidential election."

In their pursuit of the presidency and a conservative Republican party, many reasonable conservatives in the GOP *did* suffer the kooks. Their hunt for power helped the big tent bulge with supporters who, in earlier campaigns, would have been shown the nearest exit. But this strategy also caused a problem: Goldwater's reputation as a man of unshakable character came in large part from his unwillingness to lower himself into the morass of politics. Goldwater and his associates, however, were simply trying to seize power by *not* excluding anyone who believed in conservative principles, no matter how kooky, and they hoped that the volatile coalition would stay together through early November.

The strategy further had to contend with a five-year legacy of an independently surging Right, as conservative activists saw Goldwater's nomination not as a time for restraint and perhaps winning the presidency but as a celebration that finally ended their exile and anonymity. By 1963 such incidents as the case surrounding General Edwin A. Walker had led many conservatives to believe that a popular front *did* exist, and that given the right candidate, the entire GOP would unite behind him to promote and—in true conservative fashion—eradicate programs. These conservatives predicated their confidence on a rising tide, which would raise not only the boats of conservatives already in the coalition but the crafts on which liberals and moderates within the GOP navigated the political seas. The ensuing armada would be virtually unstoppable.

But events from the late 1950s and early 1960s, post–World War II conservative ideology, and the vigorous grassroots effort on the part of the radical Right could be interpreted in more than one way. The men who drafted Goldwater saw the signs as pointing to a groundswell that clamored for an unswervingly conservative candidate. They believed that not only was the conservative equivalent of the New Deal Coalition beginning to congeal but that such an alliance would envelop their liberal and moderate cousins in the GOP. That impression was deceptive.

Conservative Conscience

Before 1960, by almost anyone's estimate, Barry Morris Goldwater was an unlikely candidate for president of the United States. Born in Phoenix, Arizona, in 1909 to a Jewish father (originally Goldwasser) and an Episcopalian mother, Goldwater seemed destined to follow his father into the family's department store business. Goldwater attended the University of Arizona at Tempe for a year, but by his own account was an uninspired student. In 1937, when he was only twenty-eight, he was named president of Goldwaters, becoming one of the youngest CEOs in the nation. During World War II Goldwater joined the Army Air Corps and flew transports around the world. After the war Goldwater got involved with Arizona politics, served on the Phoenix City Council, and organized the Arizona Air National Guard. In 1952 he was elected to the U.S. Senate, the first of five terms.[2] Although Goldwater now split his time between Washington and Phoenix, he remained closely attached to his native state. In many ways the archetypal outsider, Goldwater cared most deeply about preserving the beauty of Arizona, ensuring that the Indians of the state received all of the benefits to which they were entitled, and, not least of all, remaining vigilant about national defense and preserving the free-market system.

Raised by an outspoken mother and a quiet but successful father, Goldwater learned to say what he believed rather than what would appease the greatest number of people. Speaking in a folksy, down-to-earth manner came not only from his lack of formal education but also from his sense that people wanted to hear from someone like them. With unshakable conservative ethics, Goldwater embodied the "anti-politician"; his frankness was perceived as an indication of his moral obligation to do good. While more than a few of Goldwater's off-the-cuff remarks got him in trouble during the campaign, this same irreverence endeared him to voters who identified themselves as conservatives as well as those who simply saw him as a true American. This combination of "shooting from the hip" and staunch conservatism catapulted him to the forefront of Republican politics, and by the late 1950s he was serving as the Republican Senatorial Campaign Committee chair. While the position required a great deal of travel, something Goldwater never seemed to relish, it offered him an opportunity to hone his stump speech and increase his contacts within the party. As a *New York Times* profile explained in mid-1961:

> Few positions afford a politician more "exposure" to other politicians throughout the country than this. Day by day, by letter, by telephone and in person, he is in touch with the Governors, state chairmen and other leaders of his party who wield the influence that counts when it come[s] time to write platforms and pick Presidential candidates. If he is a good chairman, as Mr. Goldwater is generally conceded to be, he builds "a line of credit" with party leaders in the key states on which he can draw when the need arises.[3]

In 1960 Goldwater, with a great deal of help from L. Brent Bozell (some say Bozell did all of the writing), published *The Conscience of a Conservative*.[4] This short primer inspired thousands of Americans to join the still-young conservative movement. Goldwater and Bozell did not say anything new; rather they took a handful of ideas, clarified them, and added examples with which a mainstream audience could identify. The book sold 85,000 copies in its first month, 700,000 copies in its first year, and eventually reached the number six spot on the *New York Times*'s nonfiction bestseller list.[6] In early 1960 some observers had already branded Goldwater as the one who would receive Ike's baton. After Kennedy squeezed by Nixon in one of the closest popular votes in history, Goldwater settled in for four years of liberal Democratic rule. Other conservatives, however, refused to accept another four or eight years of Roosevelt New Dealism.

The story of the draft Goldwater movement has been recalled in great detail elsewhere.[7] In short a group of conservatives within the GOP felt that the moderates' hold on the party, personified in the 1960 defeat of Richard Nixon, had to be broken, and Barry Goldwater was the only man in the country who had a chance at succeeding. Beginning with a June 1961 lunch meeting in the Members' Dining Room on Capitol Hill of *National Review* publisher William Rusher and Congressman John Ashbrook of Ohio, one of the most overly ambitious efforts in modern American politics was launched. Both Rusher and Ashbrook had been Young Republican organizers in earlier days, and after a recent YR convention at which a conservative bloc had been cracked by moderates, Rusher realized that if he assembled his former YR colleagues, they would likely comprise the third largest faction within the Republican party.[8] Ashbrook agreed, took Rusher back to his office, and unveiled a filing cabinet with up-to-date records detailing the political activities of many of their old comrades. Rusher returned to New York and contacted conservative political organizer E. Clifton White, a master of delegate gathering and campaign engineering. White also had background files on conservatives, and the three met together in early September 1961 to draw up a list of twenty-six names; nineteen of those people joined them at a secret meeting in Chicago one month later.

The men who met that fall Sunday in Chicago were conservatives through and through. The group included a few politicians, a number of Republican operators, and many businessmen. Goldwater had given no authorization for the group to begin working for his candidacy; he knew nothing of the meeting until one month later when White and a colleague met with him. Even then White did not tell Goldwater they were aiming to nominate him; he merely said they would "concentrate on setting up an organizational vehicle and on finding people within the Republican party around the country who agreed with us that the party should be forged into an effective conservative instrument."[9] Goldwater was enthusiastic about the news and encouraged the men to continue with their efforts.

As the group of twenty-two expanded to some fifty-five in late 1962, four incidents changed the tenor of their efforts to press Goldwater into running. First until this point the media and the public had known nothing of the planners' efforts. At the December 1962 meeting, however, a participant leaked information to the press, and the scheme was unmasked. Second Nelson Rockefeller, governor of New York, had been meeting with Goldwater, by most accounts for the sole purpose of making sure the Arizonan would not run in 1964. Rockefeller did a good job of convincing Goldwater that the governor himself nearly had the nomination sewed up, and when confronted with the doings of White, Rusher, and Ashbrook, Goldwater spurned them, letting them know that he had no intention of running. When an inner circle of the group reconvened in February 1963, the men were discouraged, many ready to abandon their dreams of reworking the GOP. It was at this meeting, however, that the group decided that they had no choice but to *draft* Goldwater. Having made himself the spokesman of American conservatism, Goldwater had an obligation to represent the millions of Americans who looked to his leadership. While he might refuse the plotters' advances, if they drafted him and used the masses to disguise their own goals, Goldwater would have a difficult time refusing.[10]

In May 1963 Richard Nixon announced that he was giving up residence in California to take a job with a New York law firm. Nixon's move virtually guaranteed that he would not run in 1964. Lastly Nelson Rockefeller married the recently divorced Margaretta Murphy, which launched a moral outcry against Rockefeller, since it appeared he had played a key role in the breakup of the Murphy family. The combination of these episodes and Goldwater's growing realization that he indeed was the conservative who could marshal the forces helped him begin his exploratory efforts for 1964.[11]

The draft team, however, was not the only group of political operatives who had high hopes for Goldwater. As early as February 1962 some of Goldwater's friends who were *not* part of the draft had put together a program that outlined some of the steps that would be required before Goldwater could make an informed decision about pursuing the nomination. Of the seven points listed, the first was most important:

> B.M.G. to select an advisory group of not more than 12 persons, all of them to be personal friends of his and . . . in whom he has complete confidence as to their loyalty, ability, and judgment.[12]

Goldwater had always based his professional associations on intuition, and he saw a presidential campaign as no reason to change his ways. Among those Goldwater relied on closely were Phoenix attorney Denison Kitchel; William Baroody, head of the American Enterprise Institute, an early conservative think tank; Dean Burch, another Arizona lawyer; and Richard Kleindienst, a long-time political operator in Arizona. These men eventually became known as the "Arizona Mafia," after they dethroned Clif White and the draft team when Goldwater decided to make his candidacy official.[13]

In late 1962 Kitchel, perhaps with the help of others, laid out scenarios that would help guide Goldwater in the coming years. Most significant among the various points Kitchel raised were the "premises." Beginning on a positive note— "although statistics and traditional pattern[s] militate against your obtaining the 1964 nomination, it is within the realm of reasonable possibility"—Kitchel quickly turned to noting the consequences of Goldwater *not* running. For example, three premises dealt with Rockefeller and the havoc he would wreak if Goldwater did not face him down:

> If Rockefeller receives the nomination in 1964 it is almost certain that he will be renominated in 1968.
>
> If Rockefeller receives the nomination in 1964 without a substantial showing of conservative strength in opposition, the advancing cause of conservatism will sustain a setback from which it might not recover for a generation.

Neither the cause of conservatism nor conservative control of the Republican Party can be allowed to be lost by default.[14]

Kitchel realized that while Goldwater might not stand much of a chance to win a general election, he had to run as an inside spoiler in order to save the party from "modern Republicanism." This notion that Goldwater-the-icon could be used to tie together conservatives from across the country was one of the most consistent themes in both the draft years and 1964. To achieve such fusion, though, organizers would have to create an atmosphere that not only would mobilize the masses behind Goldwater in 1964 but would also help to sustain a conservative movement into 1968.

Conservative Political Culture

Political culture—the events, emotions, and relationships that are intertwined with politics and political campaigns—is present whether under organizers' control or not. Spontaneous or planned, political culture can work to organizers' advantage as participants become more attached to and supportive of their cause or candidate. Conservatives in the 1960s realized that without a psychological attachment to the political ideology, few could sustain the motivation necessary to achieve victory. Culture—meetings, rallies, books, movies, songs, and social organizations—would be the key to their success. The men who decided to draft Goldwater had worked for almost two years behind the scenes before the public knew that the senator already had an infrastructure in place and a sizable number of delegates nailed down nearly a year before the July convention. While the draft group was forced to contend with and rein in independent citizens' movements, by and large they established how the campaign would build momentum among supporters on the road to November. Two examples illustrate their creative insight as well as the limitations they faced: the role they created for women in the campaign and a Goldwater rally on July 4, 1963.

The Republican Women's Committee had long been an instrumental arm of the party, and Clif White realized that he had to tap into Barry Goldwater's ideological and, not surprisingly, physical appeal to women. What convinced White of the potential for women to equal or outstrip men in their dedication, however, was his attendance at the Republican Women's Conference in late April 1963. White's assistant, Rita Bree, along with Ione Harrington and Judy Fernald, organized a hospitality suite at the Sheraton-Park Hotel in Washington, D.C. The three women had invited the chairwomen of all the state delegations, as well as all of the delegates themselves to "stop by for a visit."[15] After working through the night to prepare the suite, they opened the doors at 9 AM to a flood of eager women, who clamored for Goldwater buttons, bumper stickers, petitions, and reprints of articles supporting the senator's candidacy. White, Harrington, Bree, and Fernald understood the power these gatherings had. Primed with "gallons of coffee," the women mingled and planned, taking their enthusiasm home to their husbands, neighbors, and friends. Such receptions were crucial to the Goldwater movement, since face-to-face contact won votes most convincingly. When Goldwater's troops attended one of these receptions, they emerged reinvigorated, ready to work for their candidate. As White reported in a letter to Goldwater after the conference, in three days more than 1,000 women visited the hospitality suite. [16] Such an enthusiastic showing would convince the attendees that they were part of a network extending well beyond their own day-to-day duties.

White contended that Goldwater and those who ran his campaign never understood how much work the women did to secure his nomination. Of course White was not thinking as an early feminist but as a political organizer: he knew that at the 1960 Republican convention 197 women were delegates and 401 were alternates. In 1964 there would surely be more.[17] But the man White worked for was not intrigued by such details of politicking. The fact that they would have to target women specifically or cater to some of the citizens' groups in order to funnel their resources into the official campaign meant little to Goldwater.

Another example of the Draft Committee's instinct for cultivating political and movement culture was their July 4, 1963, Draft Goldwater Rally at the National Guard Armory in Washington, D.C. The armory seated 6,500, a challenge to fill for almost any political purpose, let alone on a national holiday and over one year away from the presidential election. The organizers, including White, "Rally" Don Shafto, a student of political organizer Marvin Liebman, and Peter O'Donnell, Republican state chairman from Texas, committed themselves to the gathering in April, and as July 4th approached they worried that the event could prove to be an embarrassing flop. In a letter to Goldwater, White wrote, "I am certain you have heard of the July 4 Rally which Peter has announced. I am not much of a Rally man myself, but feel now that it is committed, we must make sure that it is a success. I believe that it will be."[18] O'Donnell and the others had to rely on speakers other than Goldwater, since his attendance would be tantamount to announcing his bid for the nomination.

Remarkably the rally drew nearly 9,000 people from forty-four states. New York alone sent forty-two busloads of Goldwater supporters. As biographer and insider Lee Edwards described, the crowd reflected the Goldwater constituency in the summer of 1963, as it would through the primaries and into the final race one year later:

There were little old ladies in tennis shoes, truck drivers with tattoos, professors who read [Ludwig von] Mises rather than Keynes, right-wingers convinced that Wall Street and the Kremlin were conspiring to run the world, Southern whites who had faith in the Cross and the Flag, retired people on Social Security worried about inflation, Westerners tired of catering to Easterners, anticommunists demanding action against Cuba and Khrushchev, small businessmen fighting a losing battle against government rules and regulations, readers of *The Conscience of a Conservative*, high school and college rebels looking for a cause.[19]

Edwards's description is a remarkably accurate picture of the coalition that elevated Goldwater to be the standard-bearer in 1964. Equally remarkable, however, was the adamancy with which Edwards and the campaign managers denied that the kook constituency would play a crucial role in supporting Goldwater as part of the grassroots. Undoubtedly the racists and conspiracy theorists were in the minority of the 27 million who voted for Goldwater the following November. Still those groups, as the John Birch Society had demonstrated so clearly, made more noise than their numbers indicated.

Finally the rally illustrated the kind of coalition upon which Kitchel and his team would come to rely. It was not surprising that the attendees had journeyed from across the country. As Lee Edwards recalled, "Since the city did not have a natural conservative constituency, being 10-to-1 Democratic and 75 percent black, the committee would have to transport people by bus, train, and plane."[20] It was as if conservatives had briefly considered trying to crack the African-American segment of the New Deal Coalition, realized they had no chance, and decided to harvest the disaffected whites who were trying to escape the encroaching civil rights movement. Equally interesting was Edwards's tacit acknowledgment that they did not try to court the capital's Democratic voters. While the admission might seem trivial, estranged Democrats played a major role in conservatives' plans. They hoped that once JFK had gone too far with social engineering, civil rights, or appeasing the communists, these voters would head for the Goldwater camp.

While rallies and hospitality suites worked well for those who had the time and money to get to such meetings, the organizers of the draft needed to employ other tactics to ensure that the national coalition they were assembling would last until November 1964. White and the others, however, faced the task of trying to reach conservatives whose ideas spanned nearly the entire spectrum of conservatism and whose lives also mirrored those differences in regard to class, religion, urban or rural residency, and gender. While all modern political campaigns suffer similar dilemmas, and the Goldwater campaign never had to meet the task of appealing to African Americans (or, for all intents and purposes, to Jews), the Draft Committee and later the Republican National Committee (RNC) had to devise ways to transmit Goldwater's beliefs and goals to a relatively diverse constituency. Although some propaganda had long been in the works, organizers needed to reach not just those willing to read books like *The Conscience of a Conservative* but those who saw politics as a combination of entertainment, education, and a reaffirmation of their own values and ways of life. In the first half of the decade the medium of film was undergoing a revolution: new, lighter-weight equipment, better film stock, and innovative directors all pushed the industry, including those sectors that produced political films, to seek new methods of persuasion. Most political information films circa 1962 were deadly boring to audiences: talking heads who read from teleprompters, few scene changes, and no real drama. The Goldwater organization, however, thought about using film in novel ways to prepare the nation for a live campaign, as well as to follow up on an appearance by Goldwater or other conservatives.

To expand their recruiting and vote-gathering efforts, Marvin Liebman Associates, a conservative public relations firm closely allied with the draft movement, solicited scripts for a film to be entitled "The Conscience of a Conservative." Clif White had commissioned a documentary called *Choice* in 1964 to speak to the issue of moral decay in America, but Goldwater vetoed it just before it was shown on national television, citing its inflammatory nature and potential for carrying a racist label.[21] While "Conscience" never appears to have been produced, the treatments Liebman considered reflect another perspective on what Goldwater meant to a range of Americans.

Perhaps the most interesting treatment for "Conscience" was by Courtney Hafela, one of a stable of public relations men retained by political campaigns. Hafela wanted to produce a film for young people that embodied the conservative principles Bozell drove home in his book. In essence Hafela wanted an art photography film that would "repeatedly say, 'Liberalism has not worked. Welfarism breeds moral decay. Paternalism makes a weak people'."[22] Hafela's central imagery relied on Goldwater acting as a magnet for young people, drawing them to Washington not only to teach them about the virtues of conservatism but also so that they could begin the process of revitalizing America. Hafela's first scene, for example, shows:

> a pair of young masculine hands fastening a "Washington or Bust" sign on the side door of a "well-kept" jalopy.

> In a wider shot we see a fine, young, American college student, tossing his luggage into his car and roaring out of the driveway.

Here Hafela borrowed from Frank Capra's America, where untainted youth flocked to Washington on a mission comprised of education, morality, adventure, and, of course, fun. After Goldwater escorted a group of young people to view various documents and monuments symbolizing limited government and freedom (for example, the Declaration of Independence and Monticello), Hafela inserted a sequence of art photography, which depicted conservative values or, as Hafela labeled them in deference to Goldwater's and Bozell's text, the "Whole Man Idea":

The importance of *Parent-Child relationship*.

The young boy learning to work on a farm.

The child learning discipline.

The older teenager learning thrift, honesty, respect, the ability to survive.
Gaining the roots of Faith and Worship.

Hafela juxtaposed this sequence with a series of shots depicting the "material side":

The comfortable, superficial side of life.

Ersatz materials and gadgets, hand to mouth living.

Young people without confidence in themselves or their past.

The liberal beliefs that satisfying economic need could be equated with progress and that the rate at which society advanced technologically equaled human happiness were both challenged by Hafela as disavowing one's faith in any sort of higher purpose or being.

After a number of scenes in which Goldwater explained the Founding Fathers' original vision of limited government, Hafela offered a shot of state flags, symbolizing states' rights. Goldwater would narrate:

[The states] know that the money comes out of their own pockets, and that it is returned to them minus a broker's fee taken by the federal bureaucracy. They know, too, that the power to decide how that money shall be spent is withdrawn from and excercised [*sic*] by some planning board deep in the caverns of one of the federal agencies.

Hafela kept the story moving by contrasting Goldwater's vision of government with an overreaching liberalism, which threatened everything from farmers' horses to factory workers' paychecks (Hafela intended to show reaction shots of workers opening their paychecks only to realize the massive size of government deductions) to the burden on the family when a wife was forced to go to work. It was only a small step from an encroaching government to widespread dependency on welfare, with socialism the eventual outcome. Dependency on welfare would give rise to "moral breakdown, the skipping father not facing his responsibility," and other telltale signs that society was inching toward dictatorship, socialism, or both.

Although Hafela's treatment glossed over government benefits that conservatives actually valued and managed to lose track of the theme of Goldwater and the youth of America working hand in hand to deliver the country from liberalism, the combination of politics and cultural values the screenplay transmitted accurately reflected the style and mood that Draft Committee hoped to achieve. Liebman was not so sure about Hafela's treatment, however, so he asked his friend William F. Buckley, Jr., for a second opinion. Buckley replied, "I just don't know what to tell you about the Hafela manuscript. Parts of it strike me as sheer corn. Others as rather ingenious."[23] In the end Buckley recommended that they hold off on producing any film, since their financial resources were anything but solid. Still the Hafela treatment was a good indication that although the conservative coalition ranged from Birchers to disaffected Democrats, through some salient cultural images, the Goldwater forces believed they stood a good chance at cementing a united front.

Tens of thousands of Goldwater supporters did not wait for signals from White or Liebman—in any format—to tell them that Goldwater was their man. As early as 1959 a group called Americans for Goldwater reportedly had chapters in thirty-one states.[24] Three years later, in storefronts and dormant campaign offices, Citizens for Goldwater centers sprang up spontaneously around the country. Few of the organizations were headed by people who were experienced political organizers, and it soon became clear that Goldwater, along with the team of men he hired to run his campaign, did not know how to treat the maverick citizen groups. In 1962 Goldwater had gone on record saying that the leaders of the citizen groups were "the same people who caused most of our present party troubles" and that it was "unthinkable that they should be given another opportunity to lead us down the path to political destruction."[25] Unlike Lyndon Johnson, Goldwater never enjoyed the side of politics that involved pressing the flesh, thanking the thousands of volunteers, or making appearances at events for photo opportunities. These citizen groups demanded his time and tribute, and the senator was often loath to give them their due.[26]

Clif White knew these groups existed, and he realized that he would have to marshal their energy so that official and ad hoc groups were not working at cross-purposes. After the Draft Committee went public in mid-1963, White flew to Phoenix to negotiate with the Goldwater for President Committee, a group started by enthusiastic Arizonans gearing up to inaugurate a national chain of clubs. White worried that the Phoenix address would lead people to automatically assume that *they* really were the official committee. Here White also ran head-on into a problem that no organizer ever succeeded in solving: what to do about John Birch Society members working for the senator's election. After explaining to them that "any public identification of the Senator's backers with the Birch Society could do irreparable harm to his candidacy," White left thinking he had achieved very little. Although he recalled that later many of the Birchers did drop out of that group, he also noted, "We were never able to work out a fully cooperative arrangement with him [Jay O'Malley, the head], but his reorganized committee did a good job at the grassroots, particularly in the Western states."[27]

White's approach toward the Phoenix group was similar to that of nearly all the insiders in the Draft Committee and in the RNC after Goldwater declared his candidacy on January 3, 1964. For all of White's skill in mustering delegates, buttonholing state chairs, and thinking two steps ahead, he did not seem to realize that although these conservatives wanted to help the cause, they longed to achieve results they could understand and see. White had a similar experience with a Citizens for Goldwater group from Valley Forge, Pennsylvania. This organization sent out thousands of draft petitions, pamphlets, and other materials and eventually generated a sizable list of supporters. What seemed to trouble the professionals most was the apparent usurpation of their power by amateurs. With a trace of bitterness, White concluded, "I spent an unconscionable amount of time trying to get them to at least accept the Draft Committee's guidance, but with only limited success."[28] After the Republican National Convention in July 1964, White was passed over by Goldwater as head of the Republican National Committee and was instead appointed to head Citizens for Goldwater-Miller. Such an ordination, White must have thought, was no cause for rejoicing.

What exactly did these various citizen groups do? All of them tried to raise money for the senator's bid for the nomination and then the presidency. Before the convention many of the groups reported directly to Clif White with details on delegates from their states. For example, in late April 1964 Maurice Van Nostrand, secretary of Iowans for Goldwater, wrote to White, "Enclosed you will find a list of the 24 delegates who were elected yesterday, their addresses, and how I evaluate their position at the present time."[29] This kind of information was White's bread and butter; when it came time for the roll call at July's convention in San Francisco, he needed to know whose support was solid, whose was wavering, and whose was hopeless. Van Nostrand was hopeful but reserved in his report, telling White that the liberal Republicans were overconfident:

> I can not actually believe that the Lodge and Rockefeller forces can claim a victory, since I defy them to point out to me any one of the 24 elected delegates that they have a better chance with than we do. During the last three weeks I have talked personally with every one of the elected delegates as well as the nominees, and I can flatly state that at this time there is no strong anti-Goldwater sentiment in any of this group.

Van Nostrand was just the kind of organizer White wanted: informative, deferential, and willing to go the extra mile to secure support for Goldwater.

These activists worked long hours for no pay and no immediate satisfaction for two reasons. First for years they had felt excluded from the party machinery, perennially dominated by the hated eastern Republicans. Second, in their search for a politician who understood them and who they themselves could understand, Goldwater stood well above the rest. Realizing that citizen groups could both aid and cripple the campaign, Clif White faced considerable challenges in coordinating the hundreds of groups spread across the country. He had to "smooth the feathers of a hundred county chairmen without dampening the enthusiasm of thousands of volunteers" and control the overenthusiastic.[30] The Goldwater citizens' efforts, however, more than made up for their annoyances. Neither Rockefeller nor Lyndon Johnson could generate the kind of diehard commitment that the Goldwater forces could at almost a moment's notice. In one famous episode during the California primary, 8,000 volunteers canvassed in the Los Angeles and Orange County areas, and in a single day they visited 600,000 homes to secure votes in the most important primary in the country.[31] The heterogeneous collection of radical rightists, libertarians, anticommunists, and party regulars put together one of the most unexpected political drives in American campaigning history. And while they did not see their dream fulfilled that November, they did taste the possibilities.

Problems of Extremism

The events as well as the propaganda materials created for Goldwater had to contend with this wide-ranging self-selected coalition. While White and later Kitchel successfully got conservatives to work for and remain loyal to Goldwater, they never convinced large numbers of Democrats to cross into their camp. Hurt in part by challenging Johnson rather than Kennedy, the Draft Committee seemed to focus more on the goal of consolidating the conservative movement than on winning the election of 1964. This became one of the essential differences between those in the draft group and later the RNC group and the 27 million voters. In his memoirs Goldwater recalled that after Kennedy was killed, he knew, "We'd lose the election but win the party."[32]

While Goldwater and his legions had to surmount a number of obstacles, one loomed largest. From the time when supporters from South Carolina tried to nominate him at the Republican convention in 1960, Goldwater was linked to the extreme Right, including the John Birch Society. This identification became a specter he could not avoid. In late March 1961 Goldwater wrote to Buckley, "Let's keep together on this John Birch thing and I would suggest as of now that we allow it to go along for awhile before we take any other steps."[33] Goldwater and Buckley had discussed what they as "responsible" conservatives should do about Robert Welch's sprawling organization. While neither the editor nor the politician believed in conspiracy theories, each had an interest in not yet disturbing the hornet's nest that the society had become. Welch promoted *National Review* as one of the better conservative publications and urged his tens of thousands of members to subscribe. Goldwater appreciated that such conservatives, when inspired, would work endless hours for a candidate. Moreover Goldwater knew a fair number of Birchers in Phoenix, a fact that got him into trouble later that year when he appeared on "Meet the Press." Asked whether he was worried about extremists, Goldwater replied, "I am far more concerned, frankly, with the extremists to the left than I am with the extremists to the right." When host Lawrence Spivak challenged him about accepting Welch's leadership, Goldwater answered, "I speak—as I have said many, many times—only for one organization [chapter] of the Birch Society, and that is the group I happen to know in my home town of Phoenix, Arizona."[34]

Why did Goldwater not simply distance himself from the JBS? When the senator said that he knew people from his home town who were respectable conservatives and members of the society, he was telling the truth. Goldwater was much more likely to make a decision about someone based on his or her character than by a label hung on that person by the press or other politicians. In much the same way that he ended up choosing his election team on the basis of friendship and faith in their judgment, Goldwater refused to disown any of his friends, who he knew were conservatives of solid character, just because they joined an organization. Distancing himself from them—at any time—for political reasons was a proposition Goldwater found distasteful. In 1961–1962 those who had high hopes for Goldwater realized that something had to be done about the JBS—and not simply to benefit Goldwater. In January 1962 Buckley, Goldwater, Goldwater's "ghost" and adviser Stephen Shadegg, Russell Kirk, William Baroody, and John Hall met for two days in Palm Beach, Florida, to solve the JBS problem.[35]

Not surprisingly Goldwater was reluctant to disassociate himself from the group entirely, citing the presence of balanced, hard-working conservatives as well as the kooks. Buckley and Kirk wanted to drive a wedge between the JBS and other conservatives, since they felt the negativity associated with the name outweighed any value Birchers might add to the movement. In the end the men decided to condemn Welch rather than the entire group and hoped this tactic would unseat him. A month later Buckley used *National Review* to bring the attack into the open. In "The Question of Robert Welch," Buckley and the other editors turned the tables on Welch, took apart his conspiracy theories, and declared, "Woe unto the man who disagrees with Mr. Welch. He is 1) an idiot, or 2) a Comsymp [Welch's label for "communist sympathizer"], or 3) an outright Communist."[36] At the same time that they tore Welch down, they tried to bolster the chapters' sense of purpose beyond listening to and serving their founder:

> There are, as we say, great things that need doing, the winning of a national election, the re-education of the governing class. John Birch chapters can do much to forward those aims, but only as they dissipate the fog of confusion that issues from Mr. Welch's smoking typewriter. Mr. Welch has revived in many men the spirit of patriotism, and that same spirit calls now for rejecting, out of a love of truth and country, his false counsels.[37]

To a degree, the tactic worked. The *Review* story gave conservative credence to the withering media campaign against the JBS, drove some members out, and prevented others from joining. But Welch did not step down, and the overwhelming majority of the members continued to parade Goldwater as *their* hope for American politics.

Had Goldwater unequivocally repudiated the JBS in early 1962, he might have dodged charges of pandering to extremists two years later when the political consequences were much greater. Buckley and others continued trying to take the pressure off of Goldwater, but they had only limited success. Just before Goldwater announced his candidacy, Buckley wrote a piece in his magazine entitled "Goldwater and the John Birch Society." In it he acknowledged that there were some Birchers whose letters demonstrated "the quintessence of intolerance, of a crudeness of spirit, of misanthropy" but that these people did not make up the majority of the society, and liberal Republicans like Jacob Javits had no right to attack the group as a whole.[38] Buckley's defense, though, rang hollow. While he renewed his attack on Welch, the fervency of eighteen months earlier was missing. Instead of controlling the issue of extremism, the Goldwater forces were forced to react to—and defend themselves against—whatever statements the far Right made, no matter how outlandish.

The problem of extremism came to a head in the California primary. California was important not just because of its delegates (and electoral votes) but also because Goldwater had lost in New Hampshire, New Jersey, Pennsylvania, and, in mid-May, Oregon. Goldwater needed to prove he could capture a large and diverse state to put to rest doubts about his ability to attract moderates as well as conservatives. Moreover, even if the victor in the primary came up short at the convention, he would have enough bargaining power to receive an appointment, make a demand about the platform, or perhaps even act as kingmaker by deciding to whom his delegates should go.

By the time of the California primary, extremism was one of the top three or four issues debated (or avoided) by the candidates. Liberal Republican Nelson Rockefeller, the embodiment of everything frustrated conservatives disliked about the GOP, poured money into the state to buy campaign workers, air time, and leaflet distribution (massive infusions of money had won him the Oregon primary only two weeks earlier). Rockefeller's California strategy, according to one of his public relations experts, was "to destroy Barry Goldwater as a member of the human race."[39] Goldwater refused to disavow the Birchers and instead appeared at large rallies and courted such Hollywood stars as John Wayne, Rock Hudson, and Ronald Reagan. The United Republicans of California, a group of hardcore conservatives, distributed Phyllis Schlafly's book on the senator, *A Choice Not an Echo*, to precincts that favored Rockefeller and in a postprimary survey determined that the Goldwater vote had increased by about 20% as compared with nonbook areas.[40] Rockefeller took advantage of a few Goldwater gaffes, most notably a comment about using atomic bombs to defoliate the jungles of Vietnam.[41] And one week before the vote, Eisenhower made a statement to the press concerning the type of man he wished to see as the Republican nominee. Although he did not endorse anyone, the general expressed his wish that the candidate would be committed to "responsible, forward-looking Republicanism," as well as pushing for a logical and humanistic solution to the civil rights situation.[42] Eisenhower did not have to mention Goldwater by name; it was clear he was hoping that a more moderate contender, specifically Rockefeller, would take California.

To counter the assault by liberals and moderates, Goldwater's California campaign mobilized thousands of volunteers and urged them to redouble their efforts as the voting day drew near. Goldwater's campaign manager, William Knowland, sent telegrams to Nixon, Michigan governor George Romney, and Pennsylvania governor William Scranton asking them to respond to rumors that they opposed Goldwater behind his back. Knowland wanted answers to six questions:

1) Are you opposed to Senator Goldwater in the California primary? 2) Do you support Governor Rockefeller's candidacy in the California Republican primary? 3) Do you approve or disapprove of the joining together by other candidates, announced or unannounced, in a "Stop Goldwater" effort in the California Republican Primary? 4) Is it your wish that any California Republican express a preference for one presidential candidate over the other who is listed on the ballot in the California Republican Primary? 5) Does Governor Rockefeller speak for you in the California Republican Primary? 6) Does Governor Rockefeller represent you in the California Republican Primary?[43]

After weeks of conflicting statements and founded and unfounded rumors, Knowland wanted public statements from these Republicans in order to control some of the damage to the campaign. Rumors of a Stop Goldwater coalition were widespread, and the media were fanning the flames. Each of the recipients responded similarly, telling Knowland he was neither supporting nor opposing any candidate.[44]

Goldwater's popularity in California created grave problems for Republicans of the Eisenhower tradition. After watching the step-by-step capture of state GOP organizations, these moderates felt trapped within their own party; their only recourse was to work for Rockefeller and hope that the trend would stop on June 2. Moderate Republicans in the southern part of the state were forced to run a dual campaign against the Democrats and the hardcore conservatives. In combating their relations, they had to make certain that in their quest to oust the conservatives they did not provide the Democrats with ammunition for the general election in November. One such moderate who went to battle was Margaret Meier, a Republican party organizer in Arcadia, near Los Angeles.

Meier's most important task was to act as a clearinghouse and provide Republicans in her community with information about voting records and issues. In her zeal to block Goldwater, Meier collected hundreds of newspaper clippings, magazine articles, and press releases that drew connections among Goldwater, his supporters, and the radical Right. For moderate Republicans like Meier, extremism was *the* issue in California. Taking the offensive Meier set about collecting proof that the far Right was not only stronger than most Republicans imagined but that Goldwater had close ties to some of its major players.

Working with the staff of Senator Thomas Kuchel, a moderate Republican leader in California politics, Meier amassed and redistributed materials to fellow Republicans in her district. For example, in April 1964 she exposed how the JBS planned to gain control of the state party. By running against Democrats—even when they knew they had no chance of winning—the Birchers could exploit the election law that stated that any nominee was automatically a member of the State Central Committee and in addition could appoint three more members.[45] Birchers hoped to use this loophole to capture control of the organization that would run the California campaigns after the July nominating convention. Meier also assembled a list of people in the Los Angeles area who had connections to extremist organizations and the Goldwater campaign. Typical of the entries on her list was the profile of Ralph E. Davis:

> Member, National Council of the John Birch Society, the intimate group of advisers to Birch boss Robert Welch who has called Dwight Eisenhower, Milton Eisenhower, John Foster Dulles, Allan Dulles and a veritable cast of thousands of Republicans in the Eisenhower Administration either Communists or Communist-controlled. Member, exclusive Goldwater Sports Arena Dinner Committee, Los Angeles, March 19, 1964.[46]

Meier planned to accumulate enough irrefutable evidence to convince her fellow Republicans that in nominating Goldwater they would complete the radical capture of the party of Lincoln.

Meier, however, was fighting an uphill battle. She was outnumbered in southern California, and Goldwater supporters were better organized and more deeply committed to their cause.[47] Midway through the primary campaign, the Arcadia Goldwater for President Committee issued a press release representative of their efforts during that May. Enlisting the help of Pat Hillings, a former congressman from Arcadia, the committee responded directly to the charges leveled by Meier and her fellow organizers. Hillings not only accused the moderates of practicing "guilt by association," a favorite Birch tactic, but also of not respecting the American tradition of voting for whomever one wished. Hillings also called for Republican unity: "Although I am supporting Barry Goldwater, I am prepared to campaign enthusiastically for the Republican presidential nominee selected next July in San Francisco; even if that nominee is Nelson Rockefeller."[48]

Knowing that Meier and other moderates would be loath to admit that they would support Goldwater, Hillings and the committee played the role of the conciliator, turning the moderates' ideology on its head so they emerged as the real extremists.

Seventy percent of registered Republicans turned out on June 2. Meier's efforts notwithstanding, Goldwater edged Rockefeller by about 58,000 votes out of slightly more than 2 million cast.[49] Rockefeller captured northern California handily, winning by 100,000 votes, and in places like Santa Clara County, on the peninsula south of San Francisco, Rockefeller won 30% more votes than his conservative rival.[50] With the additional eighty-six delegates (California, unlike some other states, did not split its delegates), Goldwater closed in on securing the nomination on the first ballot. Equally important, however, was the symbolic significance for conservatives and liberals alike. California proved that Goldwater could win a big-state election. The importance of passing such a test could not be underestimated, because it reassured Republican fence sitters outside of the state that Goldwater could carry not just the hardcore conservatives but also enough moderates and liberals.

Most significant, perhaps, was the realization that using a coordinated grassroots effort, the Goldwater campaign had unseated traditional Republicans. The intensity with which the volunteers worked, their resolve when facing slanderous statements from inside and outside of the Republican party, and their unshakable belief in their cause carried them to victory. For some liberal Republicans Goldwater's victory spelled the death of the party as they knew it—particularly those from the eastern wing. After the July convention Russell Kirk, now a syndicated columnist, gloated, "The End of Liberal Republicanism Is Here," and he told his readers that not only had he two years ago predicted Goldwater's triumph but that "the long era of 'me-too' Republicanism is terminated."[51] That was exactly what Goldwater's supporters wanted to hear. Though their coalition still faced a challenge from the moderates and liberals at the convention in San Francisco the next month, the faithful were certain that now nothing could stop Goldwater's march to the White House.

1964 Convention

By the time of the Republican National Convention, the party had grown so far apart that at times its members seemed to be speaking different languages. Conservatives basked in the light of having seen their beliefs carry them through the seven months since Goldwater declared his intentions, while moderates fretted about the future of their party. In addition to the issue of extremism, the dilemma of civil rights illustrated the rift best.

On July 12, 1964, one day before the opening of the convention, civil rights leaders from around the country assembled on Market Street in downtown San

Francisco to march to the city's Civic Center in protest against the impending nomination of Barry Goldwater. James Farmer, head of the Congress of Racial Equality; A. Philip Randolph, legendary head of the Brotherhood of Sleeping Car Porters; John Lewis, head of the Student Nonviolent Coordinating Committee; and Jackie Robinson, the baseball player who had broken the color line, joined 40,000 marchers in San Francisco's largest civil rights rally ever. Each African-American leader in turn questioned Goldwater's nomination, and all called for a renewed effort at nominating an alternative. Lewis expressed the feelings of many when he proclaimed, "No political party can expect to survive that nominates a man like Barry Goldwater for the Presidency of the United States."[52] Randolph compared Goldwater to Jefferson Davis, president of the Confederate States of America, and Robinson, a Republican, called Goldwater a "bigot who will prevent us from moving forward."[53] While African-American leaders told the crowd exactly how they felt about Goldwater, white moderate Republicans in attendance shied away from outright condemnations of the frontrunner. Rockefeller said meekly, "We share your beliefs and aspirations, and we're here to fight to the end," which raised a murmur of discontent from the audience. Henry Cabot Lodge and William Scranton responded in like fashion, opposing the senator yet unwilling to take such a huge political risk.

On the eve of the convention, the Republican party seemed to stand at the brink of an outright split. For African Americans Goldwater threatened to return the country to a time of "home rule," where states had almost complete jurisdiction over civil rights, and the federal government was powerless to enforce the Constitution. He had proved his willingness to take such action when only two weeks after the California primary, Goldwater voted against the 1964 Civil Rights Bill, calling both Title II, which dealt with public accommodations, and Title VII, which concerned fair employment, unconstitutional.

African-American Republicans believed Goldwater's appeal to segregationists was obvious, and his campaign seemed to reinforce the GOP's drift toward an all-white party. Observers at the convention the next day counted no more than twenty-five African-American delegates out of a total of 1,308 and none among the 1,008 alternates.[54] Just as they had not pursued the northeastern or industrial city vote, the Republicans had not pursued the African-American vote. There was a difference, however: if he became president, Goldwater would never be able to ignore the Northeast. African Americans, however, were entrenched in a struggle for their basic rights, which was just now emerging out of the South and into northern cities like Detroit and western cities like Los Angeles. The election of Goldwater might be seen as tacit approval for segregationists to increase their efforts at reversing the tide, possibly dealing the movement a crippling blow.

The convention then was a last chance for moderates to save the party from a conservative capture. After the California primary moderates had abandoned any pretext that the nominee might act even slightly in accord with their relatively liberal beliefs, and now they began a last-minute attempt to revise the platform so that at the end of the week, when Goldwater emerged as the nominee, perhaps some unifying efforts could begin. To the moderates' dismay and the conservatives' pride, there was pitifully little common ground on which to stand.

The story of the 1964 Republican National Convention has been told elsewhere, often by its participants.[55] The week was marked by a number of surprises: a bitter fight over the civil rights plank; Oregon Governor Mark O. Hatfield's keynote address, which condemned extremism; a letter supposedly written by William Scranton denouncing Goldwater's ties to the far Right; Rockefeller's speech against extremism, interrupted time and again by angry conventioneers; and, not least of all, Goldwater's divisive acceptance speech. Of these major events the fights over the civil rights and anti-extremism planks and Goldwater's acceptance speech best reflect the tenor of the primary season, as well as what the Goldwater forces would face over the four months following the convention.

Before the convention began the GOP Platform Committee had met in San Francisco to hash out what the delegates would approve that next week. Scranton, who had declared his candidacy in the aftermath of Goldwater's California primary victory, proposed an amendment that called for "enforcement" of the 1964 Civil Rights Act and stated that the federal government had a "constitutional responsibility" to ensure equality in voting, education, jobs, and public accommodations.[56] At the platform committee hearing Goldwater was challenged by the only African-American delegate on the committee, Robert A. Parker, who questioned whether the candidate would "consistently, conscientiously and in good faith" enforce a law against which he had voted.[57] Goldwater was offended by what he saw as an affront to his character: "When you use that argument, you are questioning my honesty. And I should resent it—but I won't." Explaining that the Civil Rights Act was passed by Congress and was therefore the voice of the majority, Goldwater recalled his efforts to enforce civil rights and desegregate Arizona. Although at the meeting Goldwater called for a platform to unite all Republicans, the following week his legions were less forgiving; they voted down the civil rights proposal and let stand a plank that used only sixty-six words to deal with the issue.[58] Moreover, to counter the plank's meager concessions, the committee added the caveat "to help assure equal opportunity and a good education for all while opposing federally sponsored 'inverse discrimination,' whether by the shifting of jobs, or the abandonment of neighborhood schools for reasons of race."[59]

The convention began with protesters waiting for the delegates, politicians, and media representatives. Confining themselves primarily to picketing outside the Cow Palace, they added to their numbers daily, and by the final two days the crowd had grown to nearly 800 strong. A few times the demonstrators man-

aged to make their way onto the convention floor, where they staged brief protests before being ushered out by security guards.[60] Martin Luther King, Jr.,
spoke for many African Americans—particularly those in the Republican party—
when he said that while Goldwater himself was probably not a racist, he "articu-
lates a philosophy which gives aid and comfort to the racists."[61] Goldwater's nomination forced the party to write off any African-American votes it might have
attracted with a candidate like Rockefeller or Scranton. While some delegates
marched inside the Cow Palace to show their support for the party and their
distaste for Goldwater, others conducted a mock funeral cortege, escorting a
wooden casket around the outside of the convention hall on the next-to-last day
of the proceedings. Protesters used guitars and bongo drums to beat out a dirge,
and in case anyone was unclear as to whose death it was, they hung a sign from
the casket: "Republican Party."[62]

The other major issue of the convention was extremism. Following almost
the same course as the civil rights fight, Scranton asked the Platform Committee for a plank denouncing the John Birch Society by name, although he knew
the motion had little chance of carrying. The second day of the convention,
Oregon Governor Mark O. Hatfield delivered the keynote address in which he
denounced the "bigots in this nation who spew forth their venom of hate. They
parade under hundreds of labels, including the Communist party, the Ku Klux
Klan and the John Birch Society. They must be overcome."[63] The next day,
however, delegates voted down Scranton's amendment in the most dramatic way.
Nelson Rockefeller took the rostrum to use his five minutes to speak in favor of
Scranton's proposal, but as soon as he began, he was interrupted by booing and
hissing from the galleries. Who was responsible for the disruption? Master of
delegates Clif White claimed that when he heard the catcalls begin, he broadcast the order "Cut it!" over his walkie-talkie network, yet nothing could stop
the pandemonium. After dispatching floor leaders to the galleries, White heard
back, "These are not our people." In journalist Theodore White's account of the
events, he drew a distinction between the delegates on the floor—"the Goldwater
organization"—and those in the galleries: "the Goldwater movement":

> The floor itself was comparatively quiet, Goldwater discipline holding firm;
> and here one had the full contrast that plagued all reporters throughout
> the year—the contrast between the Goldwater movement and the Gold-
> water organization. There is not, and was not, anywhere in the entire high
> command, in the brains trust or in the organizational structure of the
> Goldwater campaign, anyone who remotely qualified for the title "kook."
> Nor was there evident any "kook" on the floor. But the "kooks" dominated
> the galleries, hating and screaming and reveling in their own frenzy.[64]

Clif White feared that Americans watching the proceedings on television would
brand Goldwater "and his supporters . . . as extremists, anti–civil rights fanatics

and nuclear warmongers."[65] White probably had tried to do everything in his power to stop the outburst. But these Goldwaterites were not about to give up their chance at paying back one of the men who was trying to destroy Barry.

The issue of extremism came to a head with Goldwater's acceptance speech on July 16 in which he uttered the infamous lines, "I would remind you that extremism in the defense of liberty is no vice! And let me remind you also that moderation in the pursuit of justice is no virtue!" Why did Goldwater include such inflammatory sentences in his address? Harry Jaffa, a professor of political science at Claremont Men's College, wrote the lines after considering how famous political leaders had dealt with similar situations. Although Jaffa claimed that the sentences "originated entirely in my own head, without actually consulting anyone else or any book whatever," at other times he attributed his inspiration to everyone from Thomas Paine to Patrick Henry to Abraham Lincoln to Martin Luther King, Jr.[66] Goldwater and his speechwriters had intended to turn the tables on liberals—both Republicans and Democrats—who for years had hounded him as an extremist. Instead of dousing the fires started by his detractors, Goldwater managed only to fan the flames, engulfing the rest of his speech as well as his entire candidacy.

Goldwater claimed he meant the theme of the address to be "freedom." His defenders seconded this, noted that he mentioned the word *freedom* repeatedly (a total of twenty-five times), and wondered why critics insisted on focusing on Jaffa's two sentences. Goldwater, however, also admitted that he and his speechwriting team were not "in a conciliatory mood."[67] Instead of holding out an olive branch, Goldwater's speech pushed the moderates and conservatives further apart, notifying the losers that they could expect little in the way of compromise over the next four months.

The sentences also served another purpose: they set up a straw man that conservatives could blame for their problems. When the media and nonconservatives attacked the statement, Goldwater's team had a concrete example of the bias inherent not only in the press but now spread openly within their own party. It seems unlikely that the writers failed to consider that using the words *extremism* and *moderation* on the heels of Governor Hatfield's and Rockefeller's addresses on the same topic would inflame much of the party. Goldwater and others claimed that not only did they believe the sentences would not upset anyone, they were confident that had anyone else made a similar statement—JFK, King, FDR, or Eisenhower—there would have been no comparable uproar.[68] Such a defense, however, ignored the rule of politics that ordains that a candidate is wrong if the voters think he is wrong. No matter what explanation he offered, Goldwater would be seen as endorsing extremism.

On separate occasions Goldwater was forced to explain to Nixon and Eisenhower what he *actually* meant. The morning after Goldwater made his address, he and Kitchel paid a visit to Eisenhower at the Mark Hopkins Hotel in San

Francisco. This was not just a courtesy call; without Eisenhower's endorsement, the conservatives would truly be on their own. Eisenhower demanded an explanation of the senator's comments on extremism. After a few futile attempts, neither Goldwater nor Kitchel could make the former president, or his brother Milton, understand just what he had been saying. Just when it looked as though the general would never understand, Goldwater leaned forward in his chair and allegedly said, "General, in June 1944 when you led the Allied forces across the English Channel, you were an 'extremist,' and you did it in defense of liberty." Eisenhower supposedly responded, "By golly, I get it! I see now what you mean. By golly, that makes real sense. That's great, Barry—great, just great. I'm glad you came to see me."[69] Nixon, on the other hand, wrote Goldwater to ask for a clarification of his statement not for himself but for everyone else who still had questions:

> I have assured all of those who have raised this question [regarding the sentences' meanings] with me that you would be the first to reject the use of any illegal or improper methods to achieve the great goals of liberty and justice we all seek.
>
> I believe, however, that it would be most helpful to clear the air once and for all in this regard, and I would appreciate it if you would send me any further comments you may wish to make with regard to the intended meaning of these two sentences.[70]

Goldwater and his writers paid the price of revenge; they already faced a hostile press, lagged in the polls, and had to wage an uphill battle in reuniting the party. Nevertheless, uttering those two sentences likely bolstered Goldwater, his colleagues, and his legions to prepare for what came next. They would need all the help they could get.

Backlash against Civil Rights

Goldwater's first task after the convention was to reunite the party. At the Republican Unity Conference in Hershey, Pennsylvania, Goldwater, running mate William Miller, Eisenhower, Rockefeller, Scranton, Romney, Nixon, and others met on August 12 to begin the healing process.[71] Designed for appearance's sake as much as for planning the campaign, the meeting got off to a positive start. After a call for unity from Eisenhower ("Let's get our souls bared so that when we go out we can put something together that is worthwhile, that can win, because, gentlemen, I am interested in winning") and an explanation of Goldwater's views toward extremism (the furor over the famous sentences had not died down), the conversation turned to civil rights.[72] Goldwater began by reiterating the position he stated in his acceptance speech:

I will use the great moral influence of the Presidency to promote prompt and peaceful observance of civil rights laws. It goes without saying that a Goldwater-Miller administration would take—and let me make this clear—within appropriate constitutional limits, whatever action is necessary to deal effectively with situations in this area that might develop disorders, riots, or any other form of mass lawlessness.[73]

Goldwater's language was telling, for he wanted to use the presidency as a bully pulpit rather than to pass additional laws. He wanted to persuade both sides, African American and white, to peacefully coexist. Ironically this was exactly the type of politicking Goldwater so often claimed to despise. Moreover laws were mentioned only in the context of what would be done when they were *broken* not how they might benefit desegregation proceedings.

Moderate and liberal Republicans, however, remained unsatisfied. Rockefeller, Romney, and others began pushing Goldwater about what would be done to attract and retain African-American voters. Charles Percy, who was running for governor of Illinois, told the group that in his state they were not about to give up on the African-American vote, and although "backlash" was an issue for many whites, he was confident that the Republicans would not take advantage of it. The backlash he spoke of referred to whites fleeing from the Democratic into the Republican party as a result of increasing attention paid to African Americans and, although still clearly a minority in raw numbers, African Americans' concurrent increase in political power within the Democratic party. Romney picked up on this point:

Now there isn't any question but that a good deal of the problem in Michigan is this question of whether the campaign is a racist campaign, and actually and particularly as they see the south wing in their support, you see, because this is a totally new alignment politically in the nation in recent years.[74]

Eisenhower responded to Romney's concern by stating that it was only an image problem "and not reality." Impossibly Goldwater, Miller, and Dean Burch, chairman of the Republican National Committee, all thought that as long as it was image and not reality, they did not have to worry. Eisenhower knew better, though, later remarking, "We are fighting an image now, whether [it] is party or what people think."[75] Miller's response to Romney demonstrated just how far removed the top echelons of the party were from the concerns of either liberal Republicans or African Americans. Rather than discussing how to stave off criticism in the coming campaign, Miller was more concerned with justifying the party's actions at the convention. Furthermore he had heard of no one *opposing* the civil rights plank who *he* knew; the culprits must have been rogue Re-

publicans. Finally the idea of possibly *supporting* a civil rights plank rather than
not opposing one never entered Miller's range of possibilities.

Goldwater planned to tackle the issue of civil rights by avoiding it: "I don't
even intend to talk about civil rights. I think it's such an explosive issue. And I
tried to get the President to hold off on this thing."[76] Goldwater turned the talk
back to farm issues, but Rockefeller returned to the problem of image, this time
linking the defeat of the extremism amendments with the Ku Klux Klan and how
African-American voters would perceive such a failure to speak out:

> ROCKEFELLER: Now Bill [Miller] makes a very able answer to George
> Romney's statement that we don't appeal to racism. We don't want this,
> and I am sure he is right. But Bill himself says we would accept Ku Klux
> Klan support.
> MILLER: No.
> ROCKEFELLER: I am talking about image; not the record, but the image.
> MILLER: You can't base the "ism" package on a quotation.
> ROCKEFELLER: But this is the impression, and we, the politicians, have to
> deal with the image.[77]

Fearing he did not get through to Miller and Goldwater, Rockefeller later told
Miller that "these issues need to be, not technically, but emotionally knocked
down as far as the American people are concerned if we in the industrial States
are going to do what is necessary for the national ticket and for our local tickets."[78] The RNC, however, decided not to follow Rockefeller's advice, preferring instead to concentrate on defusing Goldwater's image among white voters
and conceding African Americans to the Democrats. On the campaign trail the
issue caught up with him nonetheless.

On the same night that Barry Goldwater delivered his controversial acceptance speech in San Francisco, police in New York were moving into crowds of
African-American teenagers in an effort to avert a full-scale riot. Earlier that day
an off-duty police officer had shot and killed a fifteen-year-old African-American
boy who, when sprayed with a hose by a building superintendent, had attacked
the super and then the officer.[79] Two days later thousands of African Americans
took to the streets of Harlem to vent their rage over what they saw as a racially
inspired murder. When police yelled through bullhorns, "Why don't you go
home?" protesters responded, "We are home—this is our home."[80] The rioting
continued for another day, with conditions deteriorating so badly that police,
after firing thousands of rounds of ammunition, had to call for a resupply to be
trucked in from the Bronx, which was guarded by two officers armed with a
machine gun and a shotgun.[81]

Such incidents as the riots in New York helped give rise to a trend that would
benefit Barry Goldwater at the polls but would wreak havoc with his image as a

president for all of America, white and black. Backlash had the potential to shift votes from New Deal Coalition whites across party lines to the GOP. As the pundits Rowland Evans and Robert Novak noted in a column one month after the convention, "The phenomenon of the white backlashers is that members of white minority ethnic groups, normally steadfast Democrats, are so exercised about the Negro revolution that they will vote for Goldwater."[82] The columnists wrote about backlash as a theory that the GOP was not courting but was also not avoiding. If backlash did not take hold and white ethnics remained loyal Democrats, the Republican party might eventually become a party of white Protestants, their influence dwindling as the country's racial and ethnic diversity increased.

When the convention ended and the Goldwater campaign began gearing up for its final weeks, the issue of whether to use backlash was at the fore of more than a few strategists' minds. The party, of course, would never openly rely on nor play to such tendencies among white voters. Instead they told themselves that voters were independent agents, and if whites decided to abandon the Democrats because that party was courting a single interest in its coalition of special interests, that was their loss and the Republicans' gain. The issue, then, was trod around lightly but not too lightly. For example, the backlash potential in a region was almost always reported—in the same way that other bloc votes were reported—and those votes were factored into the district's evaluation. When Goldwater campaign staffers solicited reports from the field, a typical concern was how white ethnic voters who had voted Democratic in previous elections were responding to the civil rights movement and urban uprisings by African Americans. One such staffer, Ted Humes, served the GOP in this capacity in the industrial cities of the East and Midwest.

Humes, a lawyer, former CIA employee, and staunch conservative, had worked with the draft Goldwater forces to survey white ethnics' attitudes toward Kennedy in 1963. Raised in Pittsburgh, Humes spoke Polish and got along well in the Slavic communities.[83] After Goldwater won the nomination, Humes went back into the field and visited the ethnic communities of Cleveland, Buffalo, and Pittsburgh. Humes measured opinions in Cleveland and Buffalo during the week in which rioting broke out in New York City, and a short while later as he was surveying Pittsburgh, riots in Rochester hit the front pages. Humes's overall evaluation boded well for the Goldwater campaign: "As a result of this survey, conducted quite informally, I believe that the racial issue is enormously important within this group and that substantial blocs of normally Democratic voters are very likely to break for Goldwater on this issue."[84]

Humes found that a traditional economic and social conservative position was the norm for these immigrants or children of immigrants. Instead of waiting for or demanding assistance, they had suffered through years of deprivation until their hard work had paid off—usually exemplified by the better lives of their children. They did not understand why everyone in America could not do the same:

> They have brought themselves up by their own bootstraps neither giving nor asking favor and . . . they resent official government bequests of "rights" and "privileges" in the form of jobs, housing, legal immunities, etc., where the grantors had not earned them. This is definitely a sore spot with the preponderance of first and second generation Americans I believe.[85]

Politicians who made such concessions to African Americans, these conservatives believed, would "only whet their appetite for more in the future." Humes also found that even if the Poles, Czechs, and Serbo-Croatians did not know exactly why Goldwater had voted against the Civil Rights Act, they admired him for it since "somehow they equate this with resistance to continued clamor for 'civil rights' and its concomitants, rioting and disorder." Like other correspondents to the Goldwater headquarters, Humes never discussed the possibility that racism might affect voting behavior. Instead he attributed his survey responses to "emotions." Moreover, when couched in terminology that focused on what African Americans demanded instead of why the ethnics were responding so critically, the blame for the shift in voting was placed on the African Americans themselves, in effect making whites the victims.

Foremost on ethnics' minds, Humes found, was their concern about African Americans intruding into their neighborhood enclaves. Echoing the Slavs' own movements of sixty or eighty years before when they entered native-born Americans' neighborhoods, whites were adamant about keeping their streets free of African Americans. In a classic case of prejudice erupting over housing, Humes described the situation in the Herron Hill section of his native Pittsburgh, a formerly Polish district, where residents actively blocked blacks from buying property. Humes's subjects complained that they "had built their own homes and businesses and made their own way—nobody gave them anything—and these people think they can get anything they want by raising hell—without having to earn it." While these feelings would eventually help topple the Great Society, in August 1964 they boosted the confidence of the Goldwater forces, particularly when they found similar answers in cities with high white ethnic populations like Chicago, Milwaukee, and Gary.[86]

Wherever Goldwater forces went, they faced the issue of what to do about backlash. Should they use it while not encouraging it? Or should they make a concerted effort to lure African-American voters? In fact Goldwater could not really choose between these two options. After casting his vote against the Civil Rights Bill, any appeal he had to African Americans had been wiped out. Instead Goldwater's real choice was between exploiting or ignoring the backlash—or at least not giving aid and comfort to those who perpetrated such reactions. Reports from the Midwest told of the Republicans' dilemma:

There is no better example of the backlash at work than in Chicago. Bruce Biossat, Scripps-Howard columnist, reports that not only the well-publicized Polish sections are affected by it, but also the Italian, German, Ukrainian, and Lithuanian areas. An interesting sidelight is that the Poles' main objection to Negroes is in the housing problem rather than in job competition. The NAACP has been quick to recognize this, and they have mounted a massive registration drive.[87]

Humes's predictions seemed to be coming true; Indiana, Ohio, and Wisconsin reported backlash to be one of two or three main issues. Conservatives outside of the Goldwater camp also understood what was happening, and some decided that race was too crucial an issue to ignore.[88]

In late September 1964 *National Review* published a special report on "The Race Issue and the Campaign." Four conservatives gave their opinions on what should be done about the "Negro revolution," and each saw the potential for the New Deal Coalition's destruction. In "A Negro Minority vs. a White Majority?" Ralph de Toledano predicted that in its efforts to placate the African-American faction, the Democratic party, composed of a coalition of minority factions, was weakened and vulnerable. The New Deal Coalition, de Toledano said, worked because each minority group had a voice in the collective, and although powerless when separated, together they created a force that had dominated politics for more than thirty years. With the civil rights movement, however, the Democratic party submitted itself to African-Americans' demands and ignored white minorities crucial to the alliance's viability. De Toledano's conclusion was nothing less than chilling:

> The consequence, therefore, is that as the coalition of minorities approaches dissolution, the one minority which has claimed a priority will become the majority—a majority not in numbers but in influence. Already, Negro voters exercise an influence far beyond their numbers in such urban centers as New York and Chicago. Since the "white backlash" draws sustenance from political as well as racial frustrations, the move by some voters to the Republican Party can be expected to accelerate. And this, in turn, will make the Negro more important to the Democrats and leave them more dependent on the minority that was.[89]

De Toledano wrongly predicted that African Americans would become the dominant force in the Democratic party, but he was correct in noting how whites would react to increased attention to African Americans' needs.

Final Stretch

In the two months between the Labor Day campaign kickoff and November 3, a combination of forces helped assure that Goldwater could not be elected. Had one, two, or three been eliminated, perhaps the outcome might have been different; certainly if Goldwater had faced JFK rather than LBJ, a closer race would have been far more likely, perhaps to the point where Goldwater would have campaigned with an optimistic and aggressive attitude. Never a fan of stumping in the first place, Goldwater felt that competing against JFK would have been a challenge but that facing the dead president's memory as well as the consummate politician Johnson made the long hours and endless miles torturous. A report on the campaign tour through the Deep South, for example, told of complaints about the senator's speaking style ("often listless and sometimes stumbling") and his "obvious distaste for handshaking."[90] More damaging, however, was the campaign planners' inability to match Goldwater's speeches to the interests of the region he was visiting. When in St. Petersburg, Florida, the area with the highest percentage of its population on Social Security in the nation and considered a model city for its low crime rate and high degree of racial harmony, Goldwater spoke about "the breakdown in law and order" and civil rights problems. In Knoxville, Tennessee, Goldwater made the mistake of assailing the Tennessee Valley Authority, recalling the primaries when he said that the New Deal symbol should be privatized. Knowing that the candidate would only have a harder time in the rest of the country, the report concluded, "There will be few opportunities like this one again, as in Memphis where 100,000 greeted Barry Goldwater . . . and which the chief of police described as 'the largest ever.' An underdog cannot afford a 'largest ever' to be turned into an 'opportunity missed.'"[91]

The period of inactivity between the end of the Republican convention and the campaign's official beginning on Labor Day weekend crippled the state and local organizations. Ted Humes fumed about the five- or six-week hiatus, when the momentum simply stopped cold: "From the time the convention closed in S.F. until about Sept. 1 not a damn thing was done; I will always consider this fatal."[92] The only people working, claimed Humes, were the irregulars—the citizen groups. Moreover they were strapped for funds and were not told of the candidate's schedule, even when his appearance at a regional event would have garnered crucial votes.

Many of the problems emanated from Goldwater's advisers. Instead of acknowledging what the grassroots effort was doing for the candidate, Kitchel, Baroody, and the others sealed Goldwater off from his legions, which left the supporters feeling abandoned and unappreciated. Humes recalled how one Goldwater delegate from Pennsylvania, Ed Swartz, was treated by the inner circle when at the convention:

> [Swartz] knocked himself out for Bary [sic] in central Penna and came up to 15th floor to see his hero; palace guard wouldn't let him in and foisted Ed onto me. He was understandably mad about not being able

to meet his hero and . . . this attitude influenced his labors for the rest of the campaign.[93]

Humes realized that while Kitchel, Baroody, and the others did the planning, it was the workers who pounded the pavement, knocked on doors, and distributed literature. While Goldwater did not enjoy shaking hands, he and his circle might have realized that everyone had to make sacrifices, no matter how insignificant they seemed.

Unlike the draft and the primaries, the organization did not make better use of the wide variety of political culture—both nascent and created—that was available to them. When he was engineering the nomination bid, Clif White often worried about workers' intensity and efforts peaking too soon. Campaigns lasted a long time, and building momentum was critical. Kitchel and the others, however, did not seem to worry about these larger issues; in their decision to "stand down" the mechanisms for five weeks, they must have realized that they were bound to lose momentum. During those weeks they essentially abandoned the citizen groups, did not hold rallies, failed to respond quickly to mail sent to the RNC headquarters, and gave the impression that they were willing to let Johnson set the tone of the campaign. White and other planners had been cautious, believing that they would burn out the campaign volunteers if they pushed them too hard or too soon. That should have been the least of their worries. Some campaign workers had waited years for the chance to see their man grab the brass ring, and they were not about to give up now. As early as 1963, for example, Polly Yarnell, executive secretary for Citizens for Goldwater, wrote to the future candidate:

> To date, we have distributed over thirty thousand petitions. In addition, we have communicated directly with over 2,700 state and federal Republican legislators; all officers of the Republican National and State Central Committees; 1800 conservative citizens' groups, as well as hundreds of individuals who have heard about our activities and contacted us. We are currently contacting the 4,450 delegates and alternatives who attended the 1956 and 1960 Republican National Conventions—2,275 have already been contacted.[94]

For such dedicated volunteers the last five weeks of the campaign should have been the culmination of months or years of hard work. Instead the candidate and his immediate backers decided to settle for an outcome they believed was inevitable.

Much of the reticence had to do with Goldwater's (and maybe others') deep-down belief that he could not win and that the real victory lay in consolidating the conservative movement in preparation for future elections. Still it should have been obvious to the election team that people were clamoring for Goldwater, so responses like ignoring citizens' suggestions about the campaign or failing to distribute materials to citizen groups were tantamount to turning their backs on the grassroots.

Nearly all conservatives blamed unfair reporting by the press. Lee Edwards commented, "The news media were tilted decisively against Goldwater and etched into the minds of Americans a distorted image of the Republican challenger."[95] Some of this was certainly true; in this time when journalism was still a "gentlemen's" profession, when reporters made implicit agreements with their subjects to avoid damaging stories, Johnson was the president, and Goldwater became an easy target simply by opening his mouth. Journalist Theodore White, however, painted a markedly different picture. Summarizing the main dilemma, White wrote, "How could one be fair to Goldwater—by quoting what he said or by explaining what he thought? To quote him directly was manifestly unfair, but if he insisted on speaking thus in public, how could one resist quoting him?"[96] Goldwater was no political novice; he must have realized how speaking off-the-cuff would play in the papers the next day. His handlers at the time, as well as conservatives later on, attributed it to his *lack* of Machiavellian desire and his inherent inability to say anything other than the truth.

The Johnson campaign exploited Goldwater's missteps. In one memorandum for the president, an aide called for treating Goldwater "not as an equal who has credentials to be President, but as a *radical*, a preposterous candidate who would ruin this country and our future."[97] The Johnson campaign's famous "daisy commercial," shown only once as a paid spot, depicts a young girl pulling the petals off a daisy as she counts up to ten. When she reaches ten, the camera zooms in on her eye as a voice-over counts down from ten. At zero, the screen explodes with an image of a hydrogen bomb. Johnson's voice intones, "These are the stakes: to make a world in which all of God's children can live, or to go into the darkness. We must either love each other, or we must die." The message was clear: with Goldwater's finger on the nuclear trigger, anything could happen. The Johnson forces could attack using "humor, barbs, jokes, ridicule. If we lambaste him in rebuttal, if we answer his charges seriously, if we accept him as a legitimate candidate, we will be elevating him."[98] The press, of course, loved such copy. Ultimately, though, the working press warmed to Goldwater, and reporters would question him until his thoughts were sufficiently clarified so as not to cause complete embarrassment. Goldwater also took a liking to the reporters in tow, giving them gold souvenir lapel pins that read EASTERN LIBERAL PRESS.[99]

Finally the intraparty rivalries and the chasm between the conservatives and moderates left Goldwater without the traditional institutional support enjoyed by the frontrunner of a political party. Although parties are often split until a nominee is chosen, ideally the convention soothes wounds laid open months earlier. At the Cow Palace, however, each side decided to dress their comrades' wounds with salt—Hatfield's keynote address and Goldwater's acceptance speech being only the most obvious examples. Moreover neither side yielded ground on issues it believed were crucial to the identification of the GOP—most obviously extremism and civil rights. Instead of waging a single-front war the conservatives were forced to deal with the Democrats and the moderate Republicans, as well as being harassed by sniping from those in the business establishment who thought that Goldwater's instability might be bad for the economy.

Each day Goldwater stumped the Republicans moved further apart, while the Democrats united behind Kennedy's memory and Johnson's political genius. Though no election outcome is foreordained, by mid-September the contest between Johnson and Goldwater had essentially been decided. Even conservatives with impeccable credentials, who had raised money, written opinion pieces, and rallied the troops, realized they had no chance. At a September dinner for student leaders Buckley stunned his audience by speaking of Goldwater's "impending defeat."[100]

Johnson's 61%–39% victory was the landslide he wanted—a mandate that freed him from the shadow of a martyr, surpassed Franklin Delano Roosevelt's victories, and validated his visions. The continuation of legislative efforts to support the civil rights movement, the Great Society, and the war in Vietnam was ensured.

Losing the Election, Winning the Party, Discovering Limits

Within days of the defeat, letters began piling up in Goldwater's and Kitchel's mailboxes, which urged them not to give up the fight. The rallying cry that "27 million can't be wrong" echoed from one end of the country to the other. One writer, upset about rumors that the GOP might formally split into conservative and liberal parties, declared that at last Republicans and conservatism were intertwined and, for all intents and purposes, inseparable:

> These twenty-six [sic] million people voted and gave their financial support to the *Republican party* and the *Republican* candidate for President. They did not give their support to a mere conservative philosophy. They supported the great American of this generation who stood for honesty in Government, states' rights, and responsibility, unselfish devotion to the principles of freedom of all the people, and the substitution of a strong foreign policy for the fumbling and appeasement being practiced by the Democratic-Socialist administration.[101]

Another writer put it simply, "A battle was lost, not the war."[102] If it were just a battle, however, it was a Waterloo.

Goldwater received countless letters that urged him to stay in politics, which he did, rewinning his senate seat in 1968. Others tried to help him figure out where the team had gone wrong. One of Goldwater's friends pointed to "the 'defection' of Republicans who had never really been Republicans," the slanted reporting of the press, the circumstances surrounding LBJ's ascension, and the reluctance of much of America "to recognize an appeal to liberty and responsible individualism—atrophied by decades of brainwashing."[103] Retired General A. C. Wedemeyer found uncannily similar reasons: "the two most important factors were: a) the BRAINWASHING . . . and b) THE FOUR HORSEMEN (Scranton, Romney, Rockefeller, and Eisenhower)."[104] While Wedemeyer pointed to the Republican leadership and Goldwater's friend blamed the voters' ignorance, both believed that true conservative leadership had to assert its hegemony within the party.

In his own analysis Kitchel found four lessons in their loss. First, while facing overwhelming odds, they achieved a great deal, particularly in alerting the country to the dangers their constitutional republic now faced. Second, for now, Goldwater was the "only one truly effective leader," and his withdrawal from politics might well "cause those [conservative] forces to disintegrate and the chance for survival to be lost." Third, while Kitchel thought that the GOP was still the best choice for conservatives to develop and transmit their philosophy, were the party to be recaptured by liberals, "your duty and that of those whom you represent may require a third party effort." Finally, no matter how hard they worked for conservatism, they would have to "overcome, or at least to neutralize, the influence of the country's news media as currently constituted and motivated."[105] Kitchel was not alone in his thoughts; conservatives everywhere were evaluating the last eleven months and plotting their next steps.

The 1964 election was a milestone in the growth and development of post–World War II conservatism. Unlike 1952 conservatives did capture the party, which proved to the country that a modern version of their philosophy was politically viable. This blend of anticommunism, nineteenth-century classical liberalism, and traditionalism was a new political formula that, although failing its immediate test against New Deal ideology, did capture the organization that would propagate its views more effectively than any other medium. Conservatives succeeded in providing the Republican party with a set of ideological beliefs out of which it could fashion practical programs to run the country. When the Great Society's economic programs went belly-up or succeeded in antagonizing enough Americans who paid for but believed they did not benefit from its programs, Republicans had an antidote ready to administer. Should enough Americans begin to question liberal social engineering, Republicans had a solution at hand. Should Vietnam heat up to a point where American soldiers began joining the battle en masse, Republicans had a plan to deal with what they considered to be a containable brush-fire war. What conservatives did not provide, however, was the stimulus to spur a majority of Americans to make such a choice. That impetus would not come until events between 1965 and 1968 pushed much of the public to reconsider who and what they had voted for in 1964.

While conservatives did provide an ideological agenda for the GOP, they did not succeed in unifying the party behind their cause. Goldwater's run taught conservatives that they could not simply ignore moderates and liberals in their party. Conservatives quickly realized that in order to win under the Republican label, they would have to appeal to—or at least not deliberately alienate—more moderates than they did in 1964. Although conservatives did capture the party, they also learned that some concessions were necessary to secure the votes they needed to gain power. But how would conservatives take such steps without trading their ideological souls for votes?

In the 1964 election Republicans faced a strong economy, a relatively small war that seemed to be under control, a popular president, and a public that did not want a third leader in fourteen months. No matter what ideology conservatives might have thrown at this set of circumstances, they would have come up short. The election then showed them that while a philosophical base was important to guide the general direction of the movement's programs, they would have to be less ideologically driven when facing situations that demanded more practical alternatives. Such a realization led the conservative leadership to become more reactionary in the sense of responding to events and circumstances and to tailor their ideological presentations to fit into a more politically relevant context. Events between 1965 and 1968 provided the perfect stage for conservatives to hawk their wares, even if some thought that their chief salesman, Richard Nixon, was not adequately conservative.

Shifting the ideological agenda to the right while tailoring these same beliefs to respond more precisely to current events helped to establish limits on conservative ideology and action for the next sixteen years. To capture power conservatives realized they could not simply preach the free market and a strong national defense and expect the public to agree without question. Conservative candidates who followed in Goldwater's footsteps knew that they had to focus on breaking issues: the war, law and order, the civil rights and Black Power movements, the emerging counterculture, and an economy that had begun revealing fault lines. Conservative planners finally understood that the American people were not about to give Goldwater or anyone like him a mandate to implement such conservative change. There were real limits as to how far the public would let ideology swing to either the left or the right, and Goldwater's vision exceeded the rightward limit. Subsequent conservative candidates learned from Goldwater's mistakes and realized that while they might fully believe in such conservative tenets, they would need society's evidentiary assistance to convince the public that these were, in fact, the most practical solutions. Of course some skilled politicians like Ronald Reagan learned to test and sometimes exceed those limits. Goldwater, however, did not possess Reagan's skills, and even if he had, his agenda was simply too far to the right and came at the wrong time for most Americans to accept. But Goldwater's willingness—indeed, his insistence—not to play the politician and to deliver his message to the voters straight was vital to the conservative movement; he and his advisers staked out the boundaries within which conservatives would stay until the people asked for such leadership.

The year 1964 also proved to be the hammer that shattered the protective coating over the Democratic Deep South. While inroads had been made at local and state levels, it was not until Goldwater that the states of Mississippi, Alabama, South Carolina, Georgia, and Louisiana had gone for a Republican conservative. Furthermore African Americans in the Deep South went over- whelmingly for Johnson, while whites went with Goldwater, which previewed the polarization that would become so widespread over the next two decades.

Ted Humes's predictions that white urban ethnic voters would flock to Gold- water were not completely fulfilled, yet voting patterns did hint that such a shift might occur in the future. Although Humes's polls had been taken during times of urban unrest in other cities, a strong economy and relative quiet in the North and Midwest dampened the backlash about which Goldwater campaigners talked so much. Four years later, however, with explosive events recurring almost daily, Humes's theories came true (with more than a little encouragement from the Republicans themselves), and the urban Catholic and ethnic vote shifted solidly to Nixon.

Conservatives and Republicans learned in 1964 that they could no longer ignore the radical Right. Instead of hoping that the faction composed of a vari- ety of activist and interest groups would either remain quiet or simply melt away, conservatives realized that if they wanted to form an inclusive conservative movement that pulled in large numbers of Republicans, they would somehow have to neutralize the far Right. Dozens of post-election analyses blamed the Goldwater campaign for allowing extremists to infiltrate the organization and to propagate their own group's ideas rather than those of the candidate himself. The *St. Louis Post-Dispatch*, for example, offered reprints entitled "Ultraconser- vatism in the 1964 Presidential Election," a series of eight articles explaining how groups ranging from the John Birch Society to neofascists ended up with major roles in the campaign.[106] Writing in *National Review*, George H. W. Bush, a loser in the Senate race in Texas, blamed Goldwater's problems partially on the far Right:

He himself spoke constructively and forthrightly but the negative image remained. It remained partly because of the so-called "nut" fringe. An undecided voter would be pounced on by some hyper-tensioned type armed with an anti-LBJ book or an inflammatory pamphlet. The unde- cided voter wouldn't get a sensible message on where Goldwater stood, he'd get some fanatic on his back tearing down Lyndon. Goldwater didn't want to repeal Social Security but some of his more militant backers did. He didn't want to bomb the UN but these same backers did. They pushed their philosophy in Goldwater's name, and scared the hell out of the plain average non-issue-conscious man on the street.[107]

Clearly if responsible conservatives wanted electoral victories, they would have to begin freezing out those to their own right.

Such a proposition still gave some conservatives second thoughts. Any decision to exclude conservatives, no matter how broadly defined, would dash their hopes of uniting all believers behind the Republican party. Furthermore such actions bordered on Machiavellian politics; as conservative ideologues had feared, the political operators would start selling each other out for votes. Realistically, though, it was obvious that conservatives faced a choice between making concessions to win back responsible conservatives and moderate party regulars, who had been frightened off by the far Right, or remaining ideologically pure and staying above—and thus out of—the messy game of politics. Most conservatives chose the former, and beginning in 1965 the JBS and other radical rightists felt their power ebbing as conservatives distanced themselves from their dedicated, yet misguided, relatives.

Finally, and perhaps most important, 1964 demonstrated that those conservatives who were outside of the traditional power structures within the Republican party had a voice in their party and in their movement in general. Goldwater and the campaign proved to be too much for most Americans, which taught future office seekers that they would be more successful running on a philosophy that responded to explosive, contemporary issues than on an ideologically driven agenda seemingly too removed from daily life in America. At the same time, however, conservatives of all hues realized that previously unincorporated conservatives had provided much of the driving force behind Goldwater's candidacy. From Youth for Goldwater to Citizens for Goldwater to community organizations and civic groups, conservative Americans took part in the 1964 campaign like few others in their lifetime. One week before the election, for example, the Goldwaters received a letter from a resident of San Antonio, Texas, who remarked, "I have been on a campaign every day praying for Barry and you to be residents of the White House. I have worked diligently. Been spending my grocery money each week for you."[108] A young woman from Des Plaines, Illinois, wrote:

This is my second election but the first time I've ever donated money to or actively worked for a candidate. Ed and I have worked day and night covering 5 precincts for you. Three of them are definitely yours and we're very hopeful of the other two. It really isn't much territory in comparison to the whole country but we're hoping their [sic] are other people like us.[109]

Thousands got involved in politics at every level, and after their hero had lost, they did not lose their inspiration but continued to raise money, canvass, get out the vote, and support conservative social causes.

Most historical examinations of the 1960s depict the decade as a time of expanding political participation, most obviously for African Americans, women, and students. Conservative Americans are almost never included in such a roster, yet 1964 marks the point at which participation shifted from those who had run the party since before the war to a time when new energy, often in the form of vigorous young thinkers, joined the ranks and snatched power away from the old guard. In addition the Republican party became less tied to big business and more reliant on individual contributions. In 1960 the Nixon campaign solicited about 40,000 individual donations. By 1964 Goldwater forces, led by fundraiser Richard Viguerie, unleashed wave after wave of direct-mail campaigns—sending 15 million letters in all—and collected $5.8 million from 650,000 contributors. According to Goldwater biographer Robert Goldberg, "Only 28 percent of the Republicans' income, as compared to the Democrats' 69 percent, came in donations of five hundred dollars or more."[110]

On election day Goldwater reportedly had close to 500,000 campaign workers in the field. Considering that number equaled almost one out of every fifty-four people who voted for him, such a turnout was truly astonishing. Believing they were right about the issues, but that the press, the Democrats, and confusion within the Republican party prevented the truth from emerging, many Republican insiders caught Goldwater fever and after the loss pledged to re-dedicate themselves to achieving a conservative victory in 1968. For example, at a speech to the Arizona Federation of Republican Women, Republican National Committee member Margie Braden told her audience:

> I congratulated you before; now let me congratulate you again on being members of a Party which has found itself. . . . Now we can see clearly what we used to think vaguely and I can safely say that for the first time the majority in this room knew why we were working so hard in a campaign and why we must not even think of giving up now. We lost the campaign, but in analyzing the results of the recent election, I am convinced that our problem was not that the voters disagreed with the Republican stand, but that they did not comprehend the issues. The Republican Party does not need a new program, as much as it needs more salesmen—and these salesmen shall have to be ourselves.[111]

Braden realized that the process all of those women had gone through and contributed to had created a solidarity that would be tough to break. Moreover Braden's urgings that the women act as "salesmen" was not an isolated recommendation.

One year after the election noticeable changes were already taking place in the manner in which conservatives conducted themselves, as well as what they knew they had to do to win the next time. One such indicator came at the Young Republicans' annual meeting at Miami Beach in mid-June 1965. Tom Van Sickle, a strong Goldwater supporter, won the chairmanship in a fairly close race. This was not surprising, considering that YRs were usually more conservative than the party in general. What was unusual was the platform the group adopted. The body affirmed planks that supported the Civil Rights Act of 1964 and a pending Republican voting rights bill. Van Sickle announced that while he thought both planks were unconstitutional, he would "wholeheartedly endorse" both.[112] Leading the way for their elders, the Young Republicans understood that they could not ignore trends in American society to the detriment of their political power. Had they remained steadfastly opposed to civil rights legislation, for example, they would risk the loss of thousands of moderate young Republicans. Conservatives did not drop their ideological tenets; they merely subverted them to more pragmatic policies, which would draw people into their vision for America.

Finally, when Ted Humes analyzed the campaign for a friend, he mentioned a point remarkably similar to the one Margie Braden made in her speech to the Arizona Republican women:

> This is why I agree with the [*Wall Street Journal's*] analysis of the election; that conservative truths were not rejected, [but instead] our biggest need is salesmen for conservatism, and Barry was just our only focal point, he happened along when the movement ripened, and he was charismatic but not anywhere near profound enough to carry a campaign.[113]

Humes was exactly right. Goldwater was not the right salesman for conservatism. He disliked campaigning, was impatient with those who could not understand him, and equated sticking to conservative principles with not compromising, even if in the end he damaged the cause. But enough salespeople had received promotions in 1964 to ensure that future crusades would be well-stocked with conservative representatives. And within a couple of years of Goldwater's defeat, two names appeared as evidence of this new wave. Both had made careers for themselves on the fringes of politics, but neither had previously been a candidate for public office. Entering from stage right onto the political scene then are William F. Buckley, Jr., and Ronald Reagan.

BUCKLEY FOR MAYOR

On June 24, 1965, William F. Buckley, Jr., met with the media at the Overseas Press Club in New York City to declare his candidacy for mayor of New York. Toward the end of the question-and-answer session, reporters asked what would happen if Buckley actually won:

> BARRY FARBER (WOR): But you are asking people to vote for you. If you win, will you serve?
>
> BUCKLEY: Yes, I think I will.
>
> MR. SHERIDAN: What was your answer to that?
>
> BUCKLEY: If elected I will serve.[1]

Buckley, typically a confident raconteur, was unusually hesitant in his response. A busy man, Buckley was in no position to abandon his longstanding commitments. His journal, *National Review*, of which he was the principal stockholder, was still struggling financially.[2] His thrice-weekly syndicated column, duties as *National Review*'s chief editor, and his various speaking engagements each amounted to full-time jobs in and of themselves. Already a public figure, campaigning to lead the world's most well known and complex city was not something he needed to do to gain publicity.

Three days after his announcement Buckley received a letter from a Brooklynite, which echoed the thoughts of thousands of New Yorkers and tens of thousands of Americans:

> My happiness knew no bounds when you decided to run for Mayor of New York City on the Conservative ticket. Up until that moment, I had no one to vote for. You said your chances of winning may be slim, but I don't agree. I think your chances of winning are excellent, at this time.[3]

Less than a year after the debacle of the 1964 presidential election, Goldwater conservatives remained steadfast in their belief that the country would come to its senses and throw off the liberal yoke. Unwilling to concede defeat, Buckley's admirer, like millions of others, saw 1965 as the beginning of another crusade to put conservatism at the center of America's political spectrum. In the months following Goldwater's defeat, however, the direction of the conservative movement was once again uncertain.

In 1965 and 1966 conservatives worked diligently to engineer their own re-naissance; they refused to lie down and accept the stunning defeat. Rather, tak-ing the philosophy embodied in Goldwater conservatism, they searched for new opportunities through which they could pursue the American voter. The first real chance came in the form of Buckley, who offered to carry the movement's standard in 1965. Aided by a growing backlash against the surging Great Soci-ety, Buckley relentlessly pursued an agenda based on political idealism. The fracture in the Republican party, compounded during 1964, had not been prop-erly healed, and Buckley realized that he was stumping not only for a set of ideo-logical beliefs but that without some sort of unity among conservatives and Republicans, the presidency would remain as elusive in 1968 as it had in 1964.

Facing John Lindsay, a liberal Republican running as a fusion candidate by joining forces with New York's Liberal party, Buckley's campaign served as a test case for conservatives across the country. To call Buckley an underdog was an understatement; Republicans comprised only 22% of the New York City vote, and the New York Conservative party, founded in 1962, could claim only 15,000 registered voters, or about .005% of the city's electorate in 1965.[4] Moreover Buckley confronted issues similar to those that had felled Goldwater. Still the election mattered: one of the first campaigns after 1964 to attract national at-tention, strong Buckley support could prove valuable for the movement and demonstrate that conservatism was more quick than dead.

GOP and Conservatism after Goldwater

The Republican party and the conservative movement in 1965 were in very dif-ferent situations. After their poorest showing since the Roosevelt era, many Republicans openly questioned the survival of the two-party system. Conserva-tives, however, saw a kind of victory amidst the campaign wreckage. The cry of "27 million can't be wrong" rang from town to town, and many realized that if their power could be harnessed once, it could be harnessed twice. The party leadership, however, was forced to consider how it could recover from a loss caused in part by popular perceptions that it was controlled by extremists. Im-mediately following the election, Republican leaders retreated, with Goldwater and a number of top officials jetting down to Jamaica to escape the withering assault by the press. After the New Year, however, they reconvened, proceeded to take stock, and assessed which paths might lead to recovery.

Trying to ensure that circumstances similar to 1964 would never recur, the Executive Committee of the Republican National Committee met in an execu-tive session on January 21, 1965, bringing together a collection of insiders to hash out the role of the RNC in party strategy. The gathering came at a time of upheaval; RNC Chairman Dean Burch had been under pressure from party powerhouses to resign, and he quickly became another symbol of the split be-

tween the Goldwaterites and the pejoratively named "me-tooers," who favored
an inclusive party at the expense (conservatives believed) of true conservative
philosophy. Still the titular head of the party, Goldwater saw the pressure to oust
Burch as a repudiation of himself and his followers and vowed to fight the removal. But when power brokers like Dwight Eisenhower and Clif White joined
the anti-Burch contingent, it became obvious that the movement was serious,
and for the sake of the party Burch resigned.[5]

Meeting under a cloud of controversy in Chicago the twenty participants
discussed what could be done to challenge the Democrats, heal their battered
party, and chart a course that would establish electoral hegemony by 1968. Burch
opened the meeting with a speech that came straight to the point: "We don't
have any appeal to people and that's what we've got to change. I think one of
the reasons we don't have any appeal for people is all we do is fight each other.
Until such time as we learn how to run a Party, we aren't going to be able to run
the United States."[6] But try as they might, the issue of factionalism always returned, and its most immediate incarnation was the shuffling of RNC chairmen.
Burch described his own ouster as "more or less a forced resignation," to which
one participant replied, "A lot of people feel they have been betrayed."[7] Burch's
replacement with Ray Bliss, a GOP state chairman from Ohio, brought outcries
from some at the meeting, not because they did not like Bliss but because of the
method of his selection—no rank-and-file input, no democratic procedure, and
no choice to offer alternative candidates. The year 1964 had taught grassroots
conservatives to challenge the power structures of the GOP, and yet here they
were, ignored again.

Not everything was bleak for the Republicans. Financially the party was in
the black, having raised $17.9 million in 1964 alone. Fundraising techniques
mirrored those of conservative organizations, and nearly one-third of all the funds
were from direct-mail solicitations.[8] Direct-mail contributions averaged $15.21,
with most of the mailings resulting in very high return ratios. State quotas provided about 15% of all monies. While some states managed to raise only half of
their target funds, others far surpassed theirs. Mississippi brought in a whop-
ping 1700% of its quota. Republican dinners raised a surprising 13% of the
total; one dinner alone poured more than a million dollars into the coffers. Television appeals raked in hundreds of thousands of dollars; one appearance by
Burch raised more than $800,000 in a single evening, which surpassed even
Reagan's famous "A Time for Choosing" telecast in 1964, which had brought in
$700,000.

With so much financial support for the GOP, were leaders simply overreact-
ing to Goldwater's defeat? Many Republicans realized that in the wake of JFK's
assassination virtually no one would have been able to defeat LBJ, so perhaps it
was best to look to 1968. Yet something *was* missing from the party, although
no one knew quite how to articulate it. Dean Burch thought that the GOP sim-

ply no longer appealed to people. "The greatest requirement of this Party is acceptability on the part of voters out in the field," he said, not noting that such a statement was contrary to everything practiced by conservative Republicans in 1964. Before Burch and his colleagues could concern themselves with winning another election, they had to minister to their party since, as one participant put it, "I just think we have had enough bloodletting." Wearily, Burch replied, "Isn't much blood left. This Party is bled white."[9]

The GOP needed to prevent splinter groups and factions from further weakening an already tenuous coalition. Financial contributions during an election year indicated that until that point, conservatives and most Republicans saw the party as the standard-bearer. But what would happen in 1965, with few nationally watched elections and 1966 and 1968 still far away? Confidence could slip even further, which would help those already distracted look to third parties or organizations that challenged the GOP line. One Executive Committee member thought she saw such challenges appearing as early as January 1965:

> I anticipate from this something of an exodus of some people of strong convictions into splinter organizations . . . to the point that their time, effort and money will be taken out of the Republican Party as a Party and go into say just conservative organizations under whatever title and educational value they may follow. But they in a sense will be lost to us in the organization unless we make every effort to keep them within the Party and not . . . let this exodus occur.[10]

Here was a real threat to the GOP. Republicans who joined splinter groups would have their loyalties tested, and if the GOP were not performing up to their rigid standards, the party would lose out. Burch was pessimistic and argued that "party unity is something that will be achieved when we win an election." But could a divided party win an election?[11]

With the party so ruptured, conservative organizations immediately regrouped in an effort to establish hegemony over the GOP, each other, and perhaps even the Democrats. Soon after the January meeting of the RNC, a poll showed almost a perfect three-way split in the party. Thirty percent of Republicans believed that the GOP should move in a liberal direction; 37% wanted conservatism to be the party's trademark; and 33% were undecided.[12] The poll also substantiated what Burch had said in Chicago: image mattered. A substantial 29% of those Republicans surveyed believed Goldwater was "radical," a figure far too large for any presidential contender. Only 3% thought of Johnson as a radical. Though the 37% who wanted the party to move further to the right was giddily encouraging, conservatives realized that if they did not gain political power through focusing on concrete issues the average voter cared about most—including taxes, the relationship between the federal and state governments, the civil rights movement, crime, and changing cultural norms—their ideological agenda would never be fully implemented. A number of conservative groups decided to concentrate on local and state politics in an effort not only to force that 37% figure higher but also to recalibrate the 53%–25% split between Democrats and Republicans.

The biggest dilemma facing conservatives was whether to work within the GOP to increase the 37% who wanted to see the party move to the right or to strike out on their own and use independent coalitions to persuade activists and voters that the GOP was a great vehicle, as long as a conservative was in the driver's seat. As it turned out 1965 offered some New Yorkers the chance to examine and make such a choice, when New York City's mayor, Democrat Robert Wagner, decided to resign at the end of his third term. Although city politics were famous for their hyperbole, no one could have predicted that the race would be a continuation of 1964, as liberals and conservatives squared off in an ideological contest of wills.

Golden Boy of Conservatism

In 1965 New York was the financial capital of the world, and if not the cultural center, it was a close second to Paris, London, or Rome. Yet amid all of the pecuniary and creative wealth, there remained the unsettling knowledge that New York also symbolized all that could go wrong with cities.[13] Air and water pollution, terrible traffic congestion, a severe lack of low-income housing fit for human habitation, skyrocketing crime, an educational system that seemed to be collapsing at all levels, and a budget deficit that was predicted to reach $412 million were only the most severe obstacles.[14] Like other cities New York's middle class was fleeing to the suburbs, relying on the Long Island Expressway or the Holland Tunnel to keep them distanced enough to maintain their sanity.

The new mayor's performance would be a litmus test; if New York could solve its problems, other cities might too, which could return the American metropolis to its customary position as an incubator of democracy and American creativity. Moreover, following on the heels of the 1964 presidential election, these local races might indicate whether the public's mandate for Lyndon Johnson actually supported Johnson's liberal programs or simply Johnson the man. In a situation where issues might supersede personalities, would the groundswell of conservatism remain intact, thus indicating, as the conservatives repeated, "27 million can't be wrong"? Thanks to William F. Buckley, Jr., New York City in 1965 offered an opportunity to find out.

Born to wealth and conservatism in 1925, Buckley came from a family in which ideas mattered. From a young age he displayed a mix of pomposity, intellect, and wit. When he was only six he wrote a letter to the king of England and demanded payment for war debts. With an overbearing father and nine siblings, Buckley learned many of his debating skills at the dinner table, where the elder

Buckley "made them defend their intellectual and political positions. The dinner table was his place for checking them out, a place where . . . if someone had something bright to say, it could be offered up for the family—and perhaps the guests—to pick apart."[15] After attending private schools in New York and England, Buckley went on to the University of Mexico for a year and from 1944 to 1946 served as a Second lieutenant in the army. When he returned he continued his studies at Yale, where he made a name for himself as editor of the *Yale Daily News*. Giving a hint of what was to come, Buckley's caustic editorials railed against liberal and atheistic influences on campus. After brief stints as a Spanish instructor at Yale and an employee of the CIA, Buckley wrote *God and Man at Yale*. Only twenty-six when the book was released in 1951, it catapulted him into the inner circle of conservatives in the United States.[16] Assaulting the notion of academic freedom as a liberal ploy to teach atheism and collectivism, Buckley called on the university to permit alumni to influence departmental hiring, textbook choices, and course offerings. In essence Buckley believed that since the original purpose of the university—to train men of the cloth—had been abandoned, its fundamental moral values had also been lost, which made the institution a hothouse for socialist and other un-American teachings.

In late 1954, Buckley decided to found a journal of conservative opinion, which he tentatively titled *National Weekly*. In the prospectus sent out to wealthy conservatives, who might subscribe to a portion of the privately issued stock, Buckley described the role of his journal:

> NATIONAL WEEKLY will endeavor, in short, to counteract the reprehensible journalistic trend toward a genteel uniformity of opinion, and even of style. This nation, we contend, is not yet ready for that decadent, lukewarm mood of indifference which permeates our liberal press and, insofar as editorial convictions are concerned, makes most national journals indistinguishable from one another. NATIONAL WEEKLY is committed to what once was called personal journalism—the manly presentation of deeply felt convictions. It loves controversy.[17]

But Buckley wanted more than just an iconoclastic magazine. Just as the *New Republic* and the *Nation* had influenced a generation of college students to help create the New Deal or more general magazines like *Time* and the *New Yorker* had, in Buckley's words, contributed to the "passiveness with which the citizenry at large submitted to so total a revolution as Mr. Roosevelt's," *National Weekly* hoped to inaugurate a new era of conservatism.

Within a decade of the magazine's founding (the name had quickly changed to *National Review*) Buckley was a symbol for the insurgent conservative movement. Only thirty-nine years old in 1965 Buckley had developed close ties to conservatives from former Vice President Richard Nixon to Whittaker Chambers, famous for fingering Alger Hiss as a communist. Buckley's magazine's influence grew (even if it remained on financially unstable ground for years), and it soon cropped up in the offices of politicians, publishers, and influential intellectuals across the country. Before 1965 Buckley seemed content to write his syndicated column, edit *National Review*, appear in debates, and speak about politics. Then he decided to run for mayor of New York.

Long before 1964 *National Review* had strongly supported Goldwater and had called for him to lead the party into a new era of conservatism. When Goldwater lost, *National Review* did not spend weeks analyzing what went wrong but instead returned to its customary assault on Johnson and the Great Society. When Mayor Robert Wagner announced his intention to step down, the New York Republican party, dominated by liberals, hoped that perhaps this would be the year when they would finally break the Democratic lock on the city. But when John V. Lindsay, liberal Republican congressman from the "silk stocking district" of New York's Upper East Side, announced his intention to run and then sought—and won—the endorsement of the New York Liberal party as a fusion candidate, conservative Republicans faced a choice. They could support the party even though the party line had suddenly been usurped by someone who more closely resembled a Democrat than a Republican. Or they could attempt to remain true to their principles even as the GOP threatened to collapse again. For conservatives Lindsay's endorsement by the Liberal party reduced voters' choices to a liberal Democrat (Abraham Beame, who would have been the city's first Jewish mayor) or a liberal Republican, the differences all but undetectable.

Buckley claimed three theoretical reasons for running. The first was to become mayor, a goal everyone knew was essentially impossible.[18] Second he could help the Conservative party outpoll the Liberal party, an achievable goal. The Conservative party of New York state, founded in 1962, was designed to wrench the state GOP back to the right and away from liberals like Nelson Rockefeller and Jacob Javits, who dominated Albany and New York City and did so with conservative assistance. The third goal was simply to beat Lindsay. While it might have seemed antithetical to some conservatives to help elect a Democrat over a Republican, conservatives did not consider Lindsay a Republican but a liberal, and he was seen as a serious threat to capture the 1968 presidential nomination. To defeat Lindsay during liberalism's high tide would greatly diminish his chances for higher office. Lindsay's version of fusion, in which the Liberal party and moderate Republicans endorsed his candidacy, not only promised to continue the liberal stranglehold on city politics, but it openly threatened the two-party system. A Lindsay bargain with the Liberal party, never made public, supposedly entailed channeling one-third of all patronage to the Liberals. Lindsay allegedly pledged that "under no circumstances would I use the office of the Mayor to promote the interests of the Republican Party."[19] With a Republican in the mayor's office who worked for Democratic and Liberal goals, conservative Republicans would be exiles in their own land.

In May 1965 Buckley had written for his syndicated column a piece entitled "Mayor, Anyone?" Reprinted in *National Review* in the June 15 issue, it asked what could be done about the "crisis of the American city."[20] Because candidates were forced to pander to the myriad voting blocs in the city, reasoned Buckley, they could not offer a platform that might actually grapple with the problems that so thoroughly paralyzed those same communities. What if one simply offered a platform and did not worry about offending, say, Italians or Jews or African Americans and decided to forget "for the moment, the legal technicalities involved"? Buckley outlined ten points as a first attempt at offering a conservative ideology that could govern the metropolis. Crime could be controlled by stiffening penalties for juvenile delinquents (or making their parents responsible for their behavior) and encouraging community groups to patrol their own neighborhoods. Taking a libertarian stance Buckley called for repealing antinarcotic laws. To quell racial problems African-American and Puerto Rican entrepreneurs would be exempted from income and property taxes if they established businesses in depressed areas. No commercial traffic would be permitted to load or unload goods between 8 AM and 6 PM. Labor unions would have to let independent contractors compete on the open market. Gambling would be legalized. Anyone could operate a taxi. Anyone on welfare who was not a mother would report for "duty" every day to earn his or her dole. Students would attend the school closest to where they lived.

Around the time that Buckley wrote the column, the Conservative party, led by J. Daniel Mahoney, began to search for a worthy candidate to challenge the Liberal party and Lindsay. After Buckley's column was brought to his attention, Mahoney called Frank Meyer, an editor at *National Review*, to inquire if Buckley was available. Meyer reported that Buckley had tried, unsuccessfully, to convince William Rusher, the magazine's publisher, to run but was now seriously considering the race for himself. By June 7 Buckley had agreed to run, and he quickly won approval from the party's downstate county chairmen.

Buckley's official announcement, on June 24 at the Overseas Press Club, was as much an outline of a national conservative agenda as a declaration of his candidacy. While the speech expounded upon issues like crime, race relations, labor unions, welfare, and education, it stood out for its commentary on the relationship between the city and the federal government. The federal government had hamstrung the states and prevented cities from taking effective action. A mayor could talk about fighting crime, said Buckley, but he "would not have enough power, given the series of recent Supreme Court decisions in which the rights of the alleged transgressor are regularly preferred over the rights of the established victim."[21] With cases like *Gideon v. Wainwright* (and later *Miranda v. Arizona*), implied Buckley, a police force could not be expected to control criminals. In education, although the mayor might want to promote a moral or even holy atmosphere in the chaotic city schools, he was prevented from doing so because "the Supreme Court of the United States [had] ruled against even such prayers as are satisfactory to the spokesmen of the three major faiths practised [*sic*] in New York City." Buckley proposed that New York might do best by asserting its independence from the federal government and paying more attention to self-reliance than handouts:

> But increasingly the government of New York becomes the vassal of the government at Washington. . . . Mr. Lindsay and Mr. Wagner are almost always to be found egging the government at Washington on in its extravagances. And then—necessarily—approaching the government at Washington as supplicants, begging it to return to the City some of the income it has taken from it. . . . Against such economic circumlocutions as these, and the attendant mockery of self-government, someone, somewhere, ought to speak out. I propose to do so.

Buckley targeted his appeal at those New Yorkers who saw big government as a plague. The right person in the mayor's office might superimpose a scaled-down version of Goldwater's vision on the city. By drawing the line between the corrupted Republican party and the Conservative party, Buckley offered a chance to get even for 1964, as well as the possibility that 1968 would be a very different year.

New York Conservative Campaign

Buckley's campaign did not get going until the late summer.[22] While the delay might have resulted in setbacks similar to those the Goldwater forces experienced in the month between the July convention and Labor Day, Buckley did not have a lot of money to spend on the campaign. Marvin Liebman, a professional PR man and close associate of many conservative activists, originally estimated the campaign's total cost at $18,000, but the Buckley forces spent more than $200,000.[23] While assembling a campaign from scratch was not an easy task, Buckley surrounded himself with some of the most adept organizers in the conservative movement. Liebman, like the others, had ties spanning the country, and in his self-appointed role of fundraiser and organizer, he set to work applying his pioneering direct-mail techniques, using lists developed during the New York and national Goldwater campaigns. James Buckley, Bill's brother, who was later elected senator from New York on the Conservative party ticket (the party's biggest coup ever), oversaw the day-to-day operations, including placing advertisements, coordinating volunteers, and setting schedules. Neal Freeman, a young *Review* contributor, was Buckley's aide-de-camp, shuttling him from meeting to speech to fundraising dinner.

From the beginning Buckley refused to do what all politicians—particularly in New York—did: go to ethnic fairs, meet with representatives of voting blocs, or venture "into Italian or Jewish areas in order to eat pizzas or blintzes."[24] In effect Buckley would not kiss babies. He wanted the press and public to focus on his ideas as a conservative. The tactic did not make him many friends, and in some cases he gained a few enemies.[25] The strategy came from his own disgust with the hypocrisy of the exercise (and perhaps with his aversion to meeting the masses of New York face to face) and Liebman's low-budget campaign, which called for a limited number of appearances at rallies, combined with as many radio and television spots as fundraising would allow. Knowingly or not, Liebman took his campaign plan from William McKinley's 1896 crusade, which is famous for the candidate's rarely leaving the front porch of his house, while enthusiastic citizens rallied around McKinley manager Mark Hanna's ingenious strategy of bringing the voters to the nominee. Neither one a man of the people, both patricians had to devise ways to make their conservative strategy appeal to the average voter. McKinley and Hanna promised prosperity, while Buckley promised a return to rationalism and sensible government.

By mid-July the Buckley machine was starting to churn. Besides Buckley the Conservative slate included Rosemary Gunning for president of the City Council and Hugh Markey for comptroller. The first woman ever to run for citywide office, Gunning was well known in her native Queens for organizing a grassroots effort to oppose busing and supporting "neighborhood schools."[26] Markey, from Staten Island, had previously run under Conservative auspices for city councilman-at-large. All three were Irish Catholic, another nod to Buckley's refusal to do things for politics' sake. "Balancing the ticket" meant proposing the most qualified candidates according to their views, not race or religion.

One of the main goals of the organization, although rarely articulated, was to force city Republicans—and Republicans across the country by proxy—to decide where their loyalties lay. Would voting Republican mean supporting Republican principles? Because Lindsay's organization commanded far more resources than Buckley's, the Conservative ticket decided to make their intentions known in as many demographic and geographic sectors as possible, hoping that voters would seek them out. In July, for example, when the campaign was supposedly in limbo, Neal Freeman tried to secure an official endorsement from the Young Republicans. Moving in on official GOP turf was risky, especially since Lindsay was a past president of the Young Republicans of New York. But such a daring move could force the chapters to decide whether they were independent from the state GOP. Freeman knew the risks but believed that the potential benefits outweighed the costs. Without aggressively pursuing the traditional bases of power in the city, the Buckley campaign would be forced to the fringes, another third party ignored by the voters. But for such bold measures like Freeman's to succeed, a campaign needed the financial backing to spread the word from top to bottom.

Soon after Buckley declared his candidacy, Liebman revised upward his initial estimate of $18,000 and began doing what he did best: raising money through direct-mail solicitations. While some letters targeted the New York area specifically, many more went out across the country. The national appeal was simple: each election like the one about to take place in New York represented a threat to the gains made by conservatives in 1964. Liebman quickly drafted a letter he called his "hard-sell" fundraiser to send to conservatives around the nation:

> Right now, in New York City, the battle for the future is on.
>
> The Liberals intend to reconquer the Republican Party, and wipe out the hard-won gains made by conservatives in 1964. If he is elected Mayor in November, you can count on Lindsay being a leading presidential candidate in 1968.
>
> . . . We conservatives *cannot afford to lose this battle*. But we don't *have* to lose: 1964 settled *one* question for good and all: conservatives have the talent, organization, and money and *guts* to stop this threat to the Republican party. All we need is the *will*.
>
> . . . In 1964 we said "wait until next time." Next time is *now*, on the sidewalks of New York. Every dollar you send means another vote.[27]

Liebman's sense of urgency echoed the final days of the Goldwater campaign, although now desperation initiated the solicitation process. Richard Viguerie, an innovator in the use of computers in direct mail and Liebman's protege from his days in Young Americans for Freedom (a conservative youth group founded in 1960 by Liebman and Rusher), soon got in touch with his mentor. Viguerie offered to sell Liebman two lists:

> 13,000 contributors of $100 to the Republican party or to national conservative organizations in 1964 and 1965. The list is available for $30. per M [thousand].
>
> 10,000 contributors in 1965 to one or more conservative organizations. Everyone [*sic*] of these names contributed as a result of direct mail. This should easily be the best list available commercially. The list is available for $30. per M.[28]

One month later Liebman sent out a test mailing from two lists, one of 10,000 contributors of $500 or more to the Goldwater campaign and the other 15,000 contributors of $100 or more to Goldwater. The second list comprised 180,000 names, and if the tests proved successful, Liebman was prepared to go after the other 165,000 within a fortnight.[29]

With people like Viguerie on board, Liebman and his troops were in their element. They had prospered in other campaigns—for Goldwater, against communist China, and for John Tower in Texas, the state's first Republican senator since 1870. Nevertheless, in order to turn a mayoral race into a national campaign, the Buckley forces had to exploit the already established conservative network. Turning a local race into a national issue was not easy, and they were vulnerable to the institutional strife common in political undertakings.

Even though campaigners relished their underdog status, the internal workings were often strained, particularly since the organization was divided between Buckley (and his aides) and the Conservative party. Power struggles were not unusual among the men (except for Rosemary Gunning and Priscilla Buckley, the candidate's sister and an editor at *National Review*, few women played leadership roles) with fiefdoms frequently coming under contention. Part of the difficulty lay in designing Buckley's image. Freeman thought that a three-pronged approach would work best, and he suggested positioning Buckley as the "statesman, the thinker, the man who addresses his brilliant mind to the problems of the city and their root causes" against Lindsay as a "blintz-eating, shoulder-kneading intellectual lightweight."[30] Buckley would represent the "conservative *Republican* tradition"; Lindsay's group the "professional anti-Republicans." Finally Buckley could be seen as "young, attractive, athletic, yes— dashing—[and] is afraid of nothing." Lindsay, on the other hand, "shies from debate, evades the issues, kowtows to the power interests: the newspapers, the Rockefellers, the political bosses, the pressure groups."

Buckley ran into problems in two other areas within his campaign. Tied to the image problem and Buckley's personality was the question of whether he was running as a "serious" candidate or as a kind of joke. The problem began when Buckley held his first press conference. Asked how many votes he expected, "conservatively speaking," Buckley replied, "Conservatively speaking, one." Later, asked what he would do if he won the election, Buckley answered with a straight face, "Demand a recount."[31] Buckley's dry wit appealed to voters; they loved listening to his speeches, as they anticipated how he would surreptitiously insult his opponents or speak evil of liberals using his enormous vocabulary.[32] But his wit also got him into trouble with supporters, particularly those in the Conservative party. Though his confidence bordered on hubris, Buckley was not a politician and did not know the ins and outs of day-to-day campaigning or how a candidate's words would be picked apart by the press. Eventually he was forced to issue a confidential memorandum to members of the Conservative party:

> First, let me assure you that I take this campaign, its purposes, its prospects and my own involvement in it, with the utmost seriousness. In the following senses alone, it could be said that I am not a serious candidate: 1) I do not *expect* to win the election. And 2) I cannot, for the reasons I gave to the County Chairmen of the Party when I discussed with them the question of whether I should be your candidate, give my candidacy my full time. In that respect, I alone of the candidates running for Mayor am not "serious."[33]

Unlike Goldwater, who understood but despised political behavior, Buckley did not know and did not care to learn what it meant to be a candidate. He ran the campaign on his own terms, and he preferred to discuss the issues rather than plan how he could poll more votes.

But even Buckley learned a little about politics. Following his gaffe at his first press conference, he declared that he had come to understand something about running as an underdog:

> The truth, however, is often a subversive distraction in politics: because grass roots enthusiasm seems to rely heavily on at least the hope, if not the probability, of victory. I have, as you may have noticed from the tatterde-malion reports of the opening of our headquarters last week, evolved a new formula for coping with questions about my expectations for our ticket, namely, that while I do not believe we are going to win, I *do* believe in miracles.[34]

Buckley kept his eye on the prize: a national conservative agenda that could act as a delivery system for undeniable truths. While presumably about New York, Buckley's campaign often addressed the struggle over control of the national GOP. As he told members of the Conservative party in his confidential memo-randum, "On [the campaign's] success the future hopes of the national Republican Party may very well depend; from which it may follow on its success, the future of the country may well depend." And he was surrounded by advisers who thought along these lines.

Other conservatives also focused on how Buckley could be a symbol, albeit fleeting, of the conservative Republican renaissance. For example, Neil McCaffrey, president of the recently founded Conservative Book Club, provided Buckley with a steady stream of suggestions. McCaffrey saw the bending and possible dissolution of party lines as more than just a sacrilegious event. If Lindsay usurped the Democratic mantle, there would likely be disaffected Democrats as well as Republicans. Buckley should take advantage of this moment of permeability by reaching out across traditional boundaries:

> The kind of campaign Bill will be running will appeal as much to Demo-crats as Republicans. It will strike deeper chords and aim at a level at which Party labels dissolve. I think this might call for a subtle shift in Party ap-proach: you won't be talking so exclusively to disaffected Republicans. Here, in turn, lies the larger interest of the campaign. Bill will be doing what Barry should have done. If the campaign goes well it will presage the Party realignment (under Republican auspices, we hope) on which the hope of a constitutional republic is riding.[35]

McCaffrey realized that with Lindsay dissolving party lines and getting blamed for the chaos, a dramatic new range of opportunities opened up, particularly since registered Republicans were so outnumbered in the New York area. The "subtle shift" McCaffrey wrote about had not taken place a year earlier. Some thought that the white ethnic backlash would carry over into more mainstream voting blocs, but the Republicans did not capitalize on the nascent expressions of disaffection pervasive before the July convention. Buckley would be in a perfect position to exploit Lindsay's lack of party loyalty; the conservative could fish out voters from the political stream by using ideology rather than party line as bait.

Although Buckley might have preferred a campaign without advertising, where his philosophy was spread word of mouth through ever-widening concentric circles, his advisers knew differently. From the outset Liebman had recommended television and radio as the most cost-effective ways of delivering the candidate's message. A newspaper strike midway through September cut short a source of free advertising for Buckley, whose language skills made him a favorite of reporters. Radio was probably the best compromise for the campaign. One of the medium's benefits was an ability to target, with a relatively high degree of accuracy, the audience one wanted to reach. The Buckley campaign felt that its best prospects for winning votes through a radio campaign lay in reaching older families, families with school-age children, upscale households with incomes of $10–15,000 and higher than average education, and Catholics.[36] Needless to say, all of the targeted voters were white.

Campaign planners fairly accurately predicted which voters would comprise the Buckley constituency. Within the conservative Republican bloc, Buckley scored well with such ethnic groups as Italians, Irish, Germans, and Central Europeans. At his best Buckley received more than 25% of the vote in parts of the Bronx and Queens, places where registered Republicans were relatively well represented (anywhere from 30% to 38% of the voters). While it was expected that he would do well among Catholics, a full 22% of his votes came from white Anglo-Saxon Protestants, and another 26% came from German Lutherans.[37] Jews and African Americans barely supported Buckley, giving him 3.4% and 1.1% of his total vote, respectively. Due in part to his ability to speak Spanish, Buckley did make fleeting attempts at courting the Hispanic communities, although his programmatic agenda negated any language connection that might have gelled, and Lindsay's and Beame's generous budgets for Spanish language material helped keep this constituency away from Buckley.

Buckley did not garner as many or as well-known endorsements as Lindsay or Beame, but he did manage to draw some attention to himself vis-à-vis his relationships with other conservatives and the Republican party. While Beame eventually won the support of Lyndon Johnson, Buckley won the endorsement of Barry Goldwater, a fact he ended up not making public. The timing of the endorsement would have been perfect since the newspaper strike would end in a few days, and when it did the senator's testimonial would dominate local front-page news. Although Buckley and the others wanted to make the campaign a national referendum on conservatism, they knew that using Goldwater could backfire. If Buckley did not match the 800,000 votes Goldwater got in the New York area in 1964, the Conservative party and hence the movement would be seen as backsliding. The fact that Goldwater had run on the GOP ticket as a presidential candidate, thus creating a level of name recognition unmatchable by any other kind of campaign, would be ignored in the postmortem assessment. Moreover had the Conservative party performed admirably, analysts would have given credit to Goldwater instead of the local candidates. It was a lose-lose situation, they believed, so the Goldwater endorsement was shelved.[38] Buckley must have also realized that while Goldwater's name meant instant cachet in some circles, it was also a great risk in others. Like it or not, Goldwater had been repudiated one year earlier, and his image—an aloof campaigner who had little patience for the nuts and bolts of politics—was dangerously similar to Buckley's. While Buckley came off as a patrician swooping in to save the city and the GOP, Goldwater still embodied the westerner who dabbled in populism and extremism and could be wildly unpredictable. No conservative would ever risk offending the godfather of post-McCarthy conservatism, but one could not allow an association with Goldwater to sink one's ship just outside the harbor.[39]

Unwelcome Support

Buckley intended his campaign to focus solely on issues, and to a large degree he succeeded in keeping the emphasis off personalities and on the city's problems. But two general themes dominated the campaign's time and energy and required disproportionate amounts of effort to avoid pitfalls similar to those that had trapped Goldwater. Buckley first had to expunge any negative association between his campaign and potential supporters from the radical Right. Second many of Buckley's stances on issues, including welfare, busing, education, and crime, had overtones that could be interpreted as racist in nature.

While Buckley had long disavowed support from any openly racist or hate-inspired groups, as a leader of the conservative movement he attracted their underwriting nonetheless. Furthermore those suspicious of ties between Buckley and the radical Right had good reason to worry. Beginning in the mid-1950s, when Buckley was still establishing his name among conservatives across the country, he associated with a wide range of people, some of whom would later turn up as leaders on the far Right. Perhaps Buckley's closest relationship with any of these individuals was with Robert Welch.

Extremism created two problems for Buckley during his campaign. *National Review*'s outspoken stand against the JBS and extremism in general threatened fundraising both inside and outside of New York. Soon after Liebman mailed one of the first fundraising letters over the signature of Frederic Coudert, a New York attorney, former congressman from New York, and chairman of the Buckley for Mayor Committee, replies like the following started coming back to the campaign headquarters:

> Unfortunately, Mr. Coudert, your letter came on the heels of a particular column written by Mr. Buckley containing as vicious an attack on The John Birch Society as I have ever read anywhere at any time. Until then my wife and I were wholeheartedly supporting Mr. Buckley's candidacy.
>
> . . . if [Buckley] writes . . . a complete retraction equal in significance and length to the column of August 5th, I will send you the contribution you ask for. And at such time, my wife and I (and thousands of Birchers) might even reconsider voting for Mr. Buckley in November.[40]

Buckley, however, was not cowed by such threats. Two weeks before the election he devoted the October 19 issue to the relationship between the JBS and the conservative movement. In a six-part feature the editors included three of Buckley's columns (including the one that inspired the above reply), pieces by Frank Meyer and James Burnham, and questions and answers about the JBS. Buckley was not about to avoid controversy by delaying a story in the *Review* for the benefit of his campaign. If the Birchers were well organized enough to limit Buckley's fundraising apparatus, then so be it.

The other, more serious problem extremism raised was the possibility that voters believed that Buckley was somehow associated with one or more of these groups. What should Buckley do when, unsolicited, an extremist organization offered its help in the campaign? Two organizations openly backed Buckley's candidacy without his sanction. Willis Carto's Liberty Lobby, a grassroots organization originally founded as a congressional watchdog and to push through an amendment repealing the income tax, supported Buckley by distributing literature to members and nonmembers alike. In the past the Conservative party had sometimes used Liberty Lobby materials to gauge New York politicians' voting records, and in Lindsay the lobby had found public enemy number one.[41]

The other group to give Buckley its unauthorized support was Kent and Phoebe Courtney's Conservative Society of America. In mid-October the Courtneys mailed a letter and pamphlet to conservatives across the country and urged them to spread the word by circulating the pamphlet to voters and anyone interested in the future of the Republican party. The Courtneys saw the election as a referendum on the GOP, with Lindsay, Bliss, Scranton, Rockefeller, Romney, and Nixon facing off against Buckley, Goldwater, the Conservative party, and the CSA. Defeating Lindsay, believed the Courtneys, would make "apparent to even the Liberal Republicans that the people of New York, and of this entire Nation, will not support candidates who consistently support legislation which is detrimental to the welfare of our Constitutional Republic."[42] The CSA pamphlet "Beware of Lindsay!" spoke of the growing power within the GOP of liberals, their desire to banish conservatives from the highest ranks, and how the New York election was Lindsay's stepping-stone to the 1968 presidential candidacy.[43]

While Buckley might have derived some benefit from Carto's and the Courtneys' assistance, undoubtedly it was Lindsay and Beame who reaped the rewards from the association. During an appearance on "Meet the Press" two weeks before the election Lindsay launched a full frontal attack on Buckley, which focused on his association with the far Right and the split in the GOP:

> Now if [Buckley and other Conservative party candidates] claim that they are the right kind of Republicans—I don't think they are, I think they represent the forces of the radical right. . . . So I charge that this is a purely negative effort that has nothing to do at all with the two-party system. In fact, I don't think that the doctrine suggested by Mr. Buckley here, and his colleagues, has anything to do with conservatism. And true conservatives, I think, ought to think twice before they support this kind of action.[44]

The involuntary association between the far Right and Buckley provided ample ammunition for the candidates on the Left, justifying a series of attacks on Buckley based on the dangers of extremist elements rising up to hoot and holler for a Goldwater disciple. But even with Lindsay's and Beame's attacks, Buckley handled the situation better than the Goldwater forces ever had, and in the process he established a precedent that other conservatives would follow when faced with similar predicaments. Partially due to his long-time and well-publicized split with the JBS, Buckley stuck to the image of the nonpolitician, a man unwilling to bend his principles to pursue votes. Rather than giving tacit approval to any of the far Right organizations, Buckley made it clear that he would not speak in coded language about them nor invite, as Goldwater had, the honest, God-fearing members while repudiating the various leaders. Although such a tactic might work to convince a few extremists to defect, on the whole everyone knew it amounted to a pro forma approval of a powerful collection of voters and volunteers.

Issues and Answers

Buckley did not concentrate on repudiating the far Right; instead he hoped to ostracize its adherents by focusing on issues more relevant to New York City. By substituting mainstream topics on which conservatives could comment without fear, the campaign effectively stole much of Lindsay's and Beame's thunder. Buckley applied distilled conservative philosophy to the distinct problems of New York City and gave voters a chance to connect conservatism with their own lives. Nowhere was this more obvious than in issues relating to race.

The candidate and his advisers all agreed that the party should focus on welfare, education, and crime, perhaps adding a fourth concern about inefficient city government. Opinions of these issues often split along race and class lines, and the Conservative party knew that these topics generated the greatest emotional appeal among voters. While there is no evidence that the party tried to use race as a factor to divide whites and blacks, it must have been conscious of the potential for white backlash, as well as the increasing discontent in northern cities as the civil rights movement left the South. With Buckley the frontman for the ticket, it would be his ideas that came across as representing the party, and so special attention was paid to his position papers and statements. Campaign manager James Buckley believed three objectives should be kept in mind:

a) To formulate a comprehensive conservative position as to the management of cities in general, and the solution to New York's problems in particular.

b) To continue the job of educating the electorate in the temporal application of eternal truths.

c) To secure the largest possible number of votes without compromise of ideological positions—with the strategic objective of knocking out the Liberal Party.[45]

Two of the three objectives focused on dilemmas that conservatives believed would help shift the balance from failing liberal policies to a more reliable conservative agenda. Moreover since these opinions were supposedly not created solely for the election—they were "eternal truths"—conservatives had a built-in defense; they were not trying to antagonize race relations by focusing on potentially explosive issues. Rather these were the items around which liberals had built up empires of sloth, inefficiency, and inequality.

Buckley's welfare proposal was an indictment of New York's and America's increasing reliance on the government-as-provider. Rather than supplying emergency and temporary relief, welfare, Buckley said, had evolved into an institution in which recipients grew accustomed to their monthly stipends, even to the point where they would forfeit a job since that income was deducted from their dole.[46] Furthermore welfare "encourages degenerate and socially disintegrating attitudes and practices" and is administered so inefficiently that a public burden had become even more costly.[47] Citing statistics that showed an average increase in yearly costs of nearly 14%, Buckley championed the classical conservative solution of taking the burden off government and putting responsibility back into the hands of the community. Since New York had no residency requirement for a person to receive benefits, Buckley thought imposing a one-year minimum residency would help separate the truly needy from the free-loaders. Rather than having any outside income deducted from their monthly benefits, "welfare recipients should be allowed to retain a sufficient proportion of outside earnings so as to provide them with the incentive to seek gainful employment." Besides the residency requirement Buckley's most controversial suggestion involved setting up a pilot program to investigate moving "chronic welfare cases" to locations outside of the city. Citing exorbitant costs and an often dangerous environment, Buckley believed that families, particularly, would benefit from a program that could provide for their special needs.

Unapologetically patronizing in its intention to ship unwanted residents out of the city, Buckley's proposal created a stir through his direct, sometimes harsh, language, which drew fire from every liberal politician and organization in the city. The *New York Herald-Tribune* called his relocation program "reminiscent of the 'labor camps' which mark man's darkest hours."[48] Beame challenged Buckley's figures on how much money actually went to welfare recipients who had been residents of the city for less than a year. As the exchanges grew more vitriolic, however, it became apparent that welfare was being discussed without reference to race. Part of this tactic came from a memo from James Buckley, who suggested that "racial statistics and civil rights implications should be eliminated . . . as purely racial questions are irrelevant to how one should handle persons receiving Welfare payments (e.g., residency, obligation to work, etc.)."[49] Buckley took a different tack than Goldwater, aligning himself against liberals instead of African Americans.

Buckley presented a convincing case for his ability to look beyond race. In both public discussions and private correspondence Buckley discussed his views of race relations more bluntly than either Lindsay or Beame. Responding to a query about his views on the races in New York, Buckley replied simply:

> I would have hoped that it went without saying that I am as shocked and
> saddened by the injustice and incivility to Negroes as any other man, white
> or black. If in fact there is any doubt in your mind on this point, let me say
> it now: I believe the white community has been responsible for inexcus-
> able abuses of not only the civil liberties of Negro citizens, but of the basic
> natural rights to dignity and self-esteem. I join you in lobbying for an early
> trial on the assassination of Malcolm X. I believe a full public investigation
> of Malcolm's death would reveal not only the sordid details of that par-
> ticular incident, but a wealth of insights into the relationship between the
> races in New York City.[50]

Although Buckley certainly did not support affirmative action nor programs that targeted minorities, he did sympathize with the African-American predicament more than the media or many minorities gave him credit for. But because he did not let race trump ideology—in this case letting the injustices done by whites to African Americans justify continuing a lenient welfare system—he appeared to oppose equality among the races, particularly as the struggle in the South stalled and violence began spreading north. Such a strong, unyielding ideologi-

cal stand had become an albatross around Goldwater's neck, and it threatened
to do the same to Buckley.

In liberals' eyes Buckley's position on public education edged him closer to
wearing a racist cloak. Decrying the white flight from the city schools Buckley
described a system in which the percentage of white students had dropped from
62% to 34% between 1946 and 1964, while African-American and Puerto Rican
students were represented by percentages twice as high as in the population at
large. The high dropout rate combined with the dismal performance of those
who did stay in school convinced Buckley that the educational system was no
longer working. The candidate's proposals, however, were just as shocking to
some as the statistics that caused them. Busing would be discontinued, since
"the purpose of education is to educate, not to promote a synthetic integration
by numerically balancing ethnic groups in the classroom."[51] Buckley argued,
"Mature, self-confident and mutually respectful relations between the races are
more a byproduct of sound moral education than the automatic result of [an]
integrated school." The "neighborhood school" offered a universal solution, since
it heightened parent-teacher contact and got the local community involved with
the school. Buckley did not bother to elaborate on how a ghetto neighborhood
would suddenly have the money, resources, and time to help its school in an
equivalent way to a school on, say, the Upper West Side. And, as conservatives
believed about all bureaucracies, Buckley called for a reduction of support personnel and shrinking the infrastructure of the school system.

More than any other proposal, the Conservative party's plan for revamping
the school system closely resembled the desires of segregationists. By ignoring
environmental effects on students, families, and economic resources, Buckley
and his advisers attempted to skirt the race issue by saying it simply did not matter.
With such disparity among neighborhood schools in New York, the approach
would work only with those people who were happiest with the status quo, where
de facto segregation was the norm, and whites dominated the best public schools.
With his education policy Buckley went "hunting where the ducks were," knowing that his anti-busing position and neighborhood schools program would warm
the hearts of whites fearful of African-American encroachment in their neighborhoods. To ask a community with limited resources to increase its involvement with its schools, particularly in the midst of racial upheaval across the region and country, smacked of race and class condescension. Ghetto dwellers
wanted action not uplifting words telling them how they should feel. Buckley
must have known that he was alienating the African-American population; rele-
gating students to schools where learning was often an accidental process more
reliant on luck than policy meant that the statistics Buckley found so heinous
would only worsen. Furthermore improving race relations by asking African
Americans to focus on "sound, moral education" rather than improving hous-

ing, unemployment, or the physical plant where the education took place was not what would quell the demonstrations or calm the hallways. Until their schools began looking the same as those of whites, African Americans would not be satisfied.

While the problems of welfare and the public schools affected the city with varying degrees of immediacy, crime was the single issue that made New Yorkers wonder whether putting up with urban living was really worth it. During the decade prior to 1965 the crime rate shot up, and incidents in the first three months of 1965 had outpaced the previous year by 6.6%.[52] Random violence forced some denizens to hibernate in their homes for safety. Buckley proposed fighting crime using traditional methods: increasing police patrols, making laws tougher on the suspects than the victims, tightening up parole and probation so that criminals stayed in jail longer, and making the parents of juvenile delinquents accountable for the actions of their children. Buckley's most controversial position, however, was his opposition to civilian review boards for police officers. Initiated by citizens who wanted a check on police behavior, review boards offered a chance to evaluate the police in their neighborhoods. Buckley and other conservatives thought that civilian review boards would limit police effectiveness. One of the paradoxes was that the African-American communities called for review boards loudest, yet the police were not the problem, Buckley believed. Implementing civilian review would restrict police but leave the streets more dangerous for African Americans, who were the "most numerous victims of lawlessness."[53] A perpetrator's familial or racial background was unimportant, argued Buckley: "However understandable it may be that it is a result of my delinquency as a parent that my son has become a thief, thievery is wrong; and the supreme duty of civil society is to prevent that thief from marauding upon innocent civilians. That is the function of policemen. That and *only* that."

Buckley's willingness to dissect the city's problems, particularly those with racial overtones, was indicative of a plan that fell within a tightly bounded set of ideals. Hoping to convince blacks that increased policing would help them by protecting the lawful and eliminating the lawless, Buckley's message had to contend with the sometimes racist actions of white police in black neighborhoods, as well as the paternalism implied by the solution. He did not try to make excuses for his positions; those who did not agree were invited to vote for someone else. But for all of his political acumen, Buckley was anything but a politician, and his inexperience showed most obviously in his dealings with racially charged issues. The fault was not Buckley's alone; his advisers were as stubborn about their beliefs as the candidate. Ed Bell, freshly graduated from Columbia and a rapidly rising star in the *Review* crowd, told Buckley to distinguish between African Americans and Puerto Ricans. "The latter group contains many elements which have adjusted to American life in a commendable way, and they hate to be lumped with the 'Negro problem' en masse (in fact, Puerto Rican crime rates are much lower than Negro crime rates)."[54] Bell also thought that focusing on the Italian community would draw a lot of votes not in the least because "they are also very sensitive to the Civilian Review Board threat. You made excellent use of this last in the Sunday debate, but I think we must go further to dramatize it." Neil McCaffrey urged Buckley to "take a few such issues—on which your opponents are so notoriously weak—and keep hammering at them: crime, welfare, the police review board."[55] Buckley did not attempt to draw the city together to search for solutions to problems that supposedly affected everyone. And he offered the perfect excuse for proposing solutions that seemed to slight minorities: he was simply describing the problem honestly and proposing remedies that jibed with his conservative ideology.

Under a Microscope

The 1965 mayoralty election was a political analyst's dream; as a headline from the *Chicago Sun Times* put it, "N.Y. Race Full of Meaning—Pick Your Own." Even without Buckley the contest would have been interpreted as a referendum on the fitness of both parties. With each promoting liberalism as its overriding philosophy, the voters had to decide between the two. Was choosing Beame a ratification of the Great Society and Johnson's other programs? If Lindsay won, would that constitute approval of a liberal GOP, or was it simply a repudiation of Beame's specific programs? Was a vote for Beame a vote against liberal Republicanism? With Buckley added into the race, the permutations increased exponentially. The *Sun Times* article noted possibilities that ranged from a Lindsay victory as a signal to the national GOP to swing left or to liberal Republicans to begin gearing up for the 1968 election, to a Lindsay defeat giving hope to conservatives like Ronald Reagan who would "get a big boost—and if he won, might raise the prospect of a Grade B movie actor as a presidential candidate in 1968."[56] If Beame won and Buckley could take credit for stealing some of Lindsay's votes, the Liberal party and the Conservative party might trade places on the totem pole, no small feat in the heavily Democratic city. If Lindsay won, particularly by a significant margin, the moderates and liberals in the GOP would have sent a powerful message to the conservative wing, in effect labeling 1964 as an aberration and charting a new path for both the party and politics in general.

For many analysts the possibility that the Conservative party, a body so small it was easier thought of as a fifth or sixth rather than third party, might act as the spoiler was intoxicating. Buckley's plan to punish Lindsay "for his refusal to support Goldwater for President in 1964" had most of the GOP taking sides about whether it was really best to conduct business in such a public way.[57] In defeating Lindsay Buckley might discover a paradigm for gradually reversing the liberal tide within the GOP. But that program included language about race that, while reinvigorating the party, could further divide the nation. The Goldwater forces had chosen to avoid using the possibility of white backlash and had preferred instead to let their abandonment of African Americans serve as a sign to those who opposed integration and the civil rights movement. But if Buckley's pointed language worked, it might force Republican leadership to choose between remaining (or returning to) the party of Lincoln or narrowing their focus to conservatives and disenchanted Democrats.

As the race entered October pundits and politicians around the country began weighing in on the chaos in New York. Some Republicans believed that continuing the split from 1964 damaged all Republicans' chances, although they also felt that if Lindsay truly desired unity, he should have supported Goldwater a year earlier. The *Indianapolis News* took a hard line against Lindsay's call for party support:

> The episode is on the whole very instructive. It shows very neatly the double standard of political morality employed by the Liberal community. When their man Lindsay was gunning down Goldwater, that was a fine display of "conscience"; but when Bill Buckley starts siphoning off votes from Lindsay himself, that is an affront to "party unity."[58]

Lindsay's apparent hypocrisy was too much to resist for many journalists, particularly those who had supported Goldwater in 1964. The *Baton Rouge State Times* called Lindsay "the newest angry man," which referred to his frustration with Buckley and the party conservatives who refused to contribute time, money, or endorsements. The *Omaha Morning World-Herald* called Buckley "amazing" and lauded his "breaking all the rules of political campaigning and telling the truth—the whole truth—as he sees it."[59] George Crocker, a columnist for the *San Francisco Examiner*, believed that Buckley was the only viable solution for a city whose problems had not only been ignored by years of liberal administrations but were exacerbated through faulty programs, a situation that would continue unabated with Lindsay's election:

> During the long, liberal binge, the city has degenerated and is a scandal to the nation. Its bonds have lost prime rating. East Side, West Side, all around town, New York walks in fear. Riverside Drive after dark is a lethal obstacle course; Central Park a no-man's land. Social workers and psychiatrists swarm like locusts through its swollen welfare agencies, confused and confusing. The wedding of politics and nonsense was consummated here long ago.[60]

Liberal media sources assailed Buckley, fearing him to be Goldwater reincarnate. The *New York Times* fired the opening shots; the day after his announcement to run, an editorial asked, "What Makes Buckley Run?" Since there was a notable lack of public outcry for his candidacy, the editors believed that the

conservative was running because "he, and the Conservatives, wish once again
to do as much damage as they can to the liberals in the Republican party."[61] The
Times also provided valuable ammunition for the Buckley forces when it stated,
"If anything was needed to confirm the soundness of [Lindsay's] credentials as
a liberal, this opposing candidacy by the editor of The National Review, bible of
the conservative movement, is gilt-edged proof." In one sentence, the ultimate
liberal authority legitimized what all conservatives knew: Lindsay was an impos-
tor. The *New York Herald-Tribune* chastised Buckley for threatening to make
the contest an event for "staging esoteric debates."[62] The paper did not want to
deny him the right to compete, but the thought of turning the campaign into
more of a circus than it already was or doing anything that might block the election of Lindsay meant another "vote to continue the Tammany rule."

Perhaps the most insightful commentary came from the *Bath* (Maine) *Times*,
a daily with a circulation smaller than that of the *Yale Daily News*. The editors
saw Lindsay as representing "the new breed" of Republican, a candidate who
was "trying to make everyone in heavily Democratic New York forget party affiliation."[63] If Buckley successfully blocked Lindsay's rise to power, the nation could
expect a return to 1964, only this time the dangers would be even greater:

> If as good a candidate as John Lindsay can be defeated by the conserva-
> tive withdrawal, the conservatives will not only have more power but will
> have the incentive to launch a national campaign to defeat liberal Repub-
> licans in an effort to turn the GOP into a "conservative" stronghold. How-
> ever, this faction is not conservative in the sense of wanting to preserve
> the best of the past while moving into the future, but it is reactionary in
> the sense of wanting to return to the past in spite of what has happened
> since.[64]

The editorial made an important point: a Lindsay defeat would give conservatives in the GOP reason to return to their 1964 strategy, a dangerous move for
the party after what the voters had indicated that year. Maybe, though, that was
only true when placed in context of the specific circumstances of a Goldwater-
Johnson match-up, all played out against a backdrop of Kennedy's still recent
death. In either case, if Buckley successfully elected Beame not only would the
party reconsider rejecting conservatism, but the split between liberals and conservatives would likely not heal before 1968.

New Life for Conservatism

Toward the end of the campaign, Neal Freeman was assigned the task of responding to Buckley's mail. Replying to a woman in the Bronx, Freeman made
clear the purpose behind the $200,000 operation: "Our campaign has nothing
to do with Mr. Lindsay's repudiation of Sen. Goldwater last year. It has to do,

rather, with the *future* of the Republican Party."[65] Buckley's campaign was not about revenge; conservatives did not have time, money, or energy to waste on such a grand effort. The election sent a signal to Republicans and Democrats alike: conservatism was not dead and was not about to die. Buckley received 13.4% of the vote, or 341,000 out of a total 2.6 million cast, which represented a number equal to half of the registered Republicans in the New York City area.[66] And for each of those votes, the campaign spent only 72 cents, as opposed to Lindsay's $2.24 and Beame's $2.08.[67] The conservative strength was still there, and while the coalition had seemed strong in 1964, one year later it had solidified even more.

Liberals suspected that the show of force for Buckley came from the far Right; as the *New York Times* editorialized, "It will be important to try to determine the extent to which the lunatic fringe rallied to his banner, as distinct from those interested in principles that could truly be considered conservative."[68] The campaign had little trouble winning those conservatives who supported his stance on such issues as welfare reform, law enforcement, a return to local schools, and an end to busing. But Buckley also took votes from both Lindsay and Beame. Assessments poured in from all sides, but only a few seemed to comprehend the trends that had been activated in the previous five months. Neil McCaffrey submitted one of the more lucid analyses, pointing out similarities between 1965 and 1964:

> The pattern unfolds. George Wallace polls primary totals last year that rival, *up North and among Dems only*, Barry's *total* vote in the same areas. The Wallace votes weren't from Klansmen. They were from the same fed-up, disenfranchised, basically conservative Dems who had earlier switched to Ike and cheered for Joe [McCarthy].
>
> I don't mean to make you nervous, but Bill got Wallace Democrat votes.[69]

McCaffrey presciently described the coagulation of a new bloc that he believed would offer the most serious challenge yet to the New Deal/Great Society Coalition:

> The point is simply that the new conservative consensus, if it is ever to be fashioned, will be an authentic national majority whose major concerns are crime, forced integration, moral collapse, patriotism, labor exorbitance, taxes, and a cautious anti-Communism that shrinks equally from nuclear roulette and Communist expansion.

With a few exceptions and omissions, McCaffrey predicted the major issues for conservatives—and soon a majority of voting Americans—over the next decade. That New York might have held a referendum on the Great Society did not bode well for the Democrats. For such a hardcore nonpolitician to garner

13% of the vote in an overwhelmingly Democratic city indicated that serious cracks might be developing in the New Deal Coalition. Analysts besides McCaffrey picked up on these points, including a perceptive editorial in the *Mobile* (Ala.) *Press*. After gloating over Johnson's loss of "his boy, Abraham D. Beame," the paper considered how Buckley's showing had to be interpreted as a protest vote from the stronghold of Democratic politics: "If there was conservative sentiment expressed in the New York results—and there certainly was—then the Democrats might as well expect even stronger resistance in the rest of the nation."[70] New Yorkers, the Alabamans believed, were fed up with the usurpation of states' rights in order to finance their crumbling city, as well as the years of Democratic mismanagement that had brought them to such a juncture. Finally the paper expressed what many conservatives thought the election had proved:

> If the Republican leadership had the political judgment a national party is supposed to have it would now join ranks on policies considerably right of the Democrats. Up to now, many Republicans have seized upon policies closely resembling the leftwingism of the Democrats.

But they and other conservatives seemed to forget one thing: Lindsay had won, not lost, and the results could also be interpreted as a victory for liberal Republicanism.

Buckley's own analysis of the vote did not register shock at Lindsay's victory. He thought the election proved two things: that New York was a very " 'liberal' community" and that the Conservative party represented "the crystallization of a vote of responsible protest."[71] But behind Buckley's cool demeanor, he and other conservatives wondered how they would stop the moderate and liberal wings' momentum from advancing to where conservatives would have to consider seriously a third party.

As it turned out, however, Lindsay's victory boosted conservatism. Had Lindsay lost and Beame won, conservatives might have been deceived about their actual power and believed that they held more sway than they actually did. The liberal victory forced conservatives to continue rethinking their approach and contemplating how to cast a wider and tighter net. To increase their percentages over 1964 and 1965 tallies and to bolster the faction's vitality, they would have to resume searching for a combination of strategy and candidates that, while not sacrificing ideology, emphasized solutions and a way of life appealing to most Americans.

Liberal Republicans had reason to be hopeful; with candidates like Lindsay their future seemed limitless. The Ripon Society, an organization founded in 1962 by a group of liberal Republicans at Harvard, triumphantly reported what Lindsay meant to the party. Much like the results of 1964, said the society, 1965 showed how people "said 'no' to narrow and exclusionist politics and 'yes' to broad and inclusive appeals."[72] With candidates like Lindsay, the GOP could once again become the "party of Lincoln" and open itself to minorities in the tradition of Rockefeller, Scranton, Romney, and others. Lindsay had polled a remarkable 40% of the African-American vote, including such Democratic strongholds as the Bedford-Stuyvesant area of Brooklyn. Lindsay also did well among young voters, another bloc most recently loyal to Kennedy and Johnson. The Ripons saw the Buckley threat as a group of conservatives who had been, and probably would be, around forever: "In sum, the Buckley adventure proves little less than the existence of a disaffected conservative minority—about 13 to 14 per cent of the New York City electorate." Buckley's threat foreshadowed a Republican renaissance; Lindsay was "the first leader his Party has given to our generation. He must now definitely be considered a leading Republican Presidential contender."

Conservative Republicans saw things differently. Columnist George Crocker refuted the Ripons' assumptions, stating bluntly that "[Lindsay] has about as much chance of ever being nominated for President at [a] GOP national convention as Robert Welch has of winning the Nobel Peace Prize."[73] Crocker railed against Lindsay's background, citing the fact that he had cosponsored legislation with James Roosevelt to abolish the House Committee on Un-American Activities. But most important, said Crocker, was the understanding that conservatism was not a sudden brainstorm, which would crumble in the absence of electoral victories:

> There is a misconception in many minds that conservatives "learned their lesson" in 1964 and will henceforth only put up liberal candidates. To think of this is to have a shallow opinion of representative government. Conservatism is not just a political technique, to be tossed overboard when an election is lost. It is something deep and indestructible. It is a philosophy.

In essence Crocker's analysis of the 1965 election in New York brought conservatism full circle from its postwar roots. Echoing Russell Kirk, Raymond Moley, Albert Wedemeyer, and Buckley himself, Crocker realized that the gap between conservative theory and political and social practice was narrowing. When the two met conservatism would be triumphant. Crocker's faith was unshakable, and he and other conservatives prepared to hunker down and reenter the trenches in the fight for their own party.

At first glance there were few possibilities of finding a candidate who would abide by a conservative philosophy and appeal to the voters. Goldwater was out of elected office. The RNC had tossed out Dean Burch and replaced him with Ray Bliss, making the governing body more accessible but diluting the committee's solidarity for the time being. What other conservatives were there? Possibilities included John Tower of Texas, John Ashbrook of Ohio, and Walter Judd of Minnesota, but none really had the national appeal or name recognition that even Buckley now commanded. There was, however, one man who did hold a great deal of hope for conservatives. Never having held elected office, this man was nevertheless better known than most politicians. Some even compared him to Buckley as he pushed for conservatism when all electoral signs pointed the opposite way. As pundit Robert Donovan wrote in his analysis of the New York City race, "Like Ronald Reagan in California [Buckley] is trying to prove that right-wing conservatism still is on the march despite the Goldwater debacle of 1964."[74] With the collapse of the movement a real possibility, Reagan was one of the last hopes for conservatives.

A NEW KIND OF CONSERVATIVE

RONALD REAGAN

On March 27, 1965, Ronald Reagan, a Republican with only three years of official party membership but a long conservative resume, addressed a San Diego gathering of the California Republican Assembly (CRA), one of a few citizen groups that acted as an adjunct to the party. Reagan was not officially running for any office and was not championing a candidate or program. Instead he appeared because he was the most dynamic force in American political conservatism in 1965, and any group that wanted to make a big media splash, raise funds for its cause, or simply energize its members, got the former Democrat to stop by on, as he called it, his "mashed potato circuit." While most observers of California's political situation predicted that Reagan would throw his hat into the ring for the 1966 gubernatorial election, the primaries were still a year away, and everyone knew that anything could happen in the state's supercharged political atmosphere.

Like Buckley's followers Reagan's supporters saw him as a means to regrouping and partially reconfiguring the conservative movement. Equally important, however, was the fact that each man helped the GOP maintain its general program of rejecting the New Deal and the Great Society, while helping the Goldwater harshness to dissipate in the two years following his defeat. By the time Reagan spoke to the CRA gathering, his message had been honed during years of rightward drift, and the combination of his acting skills and his ability to understand what his audiences wanted to hear made his pronouncements irresistible. Never pessimistic about conservatives' chances, Reagan knew what the shell-shocked troops needed: a pat on the back for a job well done in 1964 and a warning not to become complacent:

> In these post-November days, many of us have a feeling of uncertainty, as if a gun had sounded ending the game and we don't know whether to turn in our suits or start getting ready for a return match. Actually, nothing has changed. What was true before the campaign started is still true. And what was false then is still false. Even if the vote was unanimous.[1]

Reagan reminded his listeners that the communist threat, the breakdown of American morality, and the growing welfare state meant that what Goldwater had said months ago was still true and in the balance hung everything that made America exceptional. As columnist George Crocker wrote about Buckley's defeat, conservatism was more than just a "political technique," it was a lasting philosophy.

As William F. Buckley, Jr., had demonstrated in New York, conservatism was far from dead in 1965. But on the national scene the GOP needed to revamp its approach from selling ideology to selling a personality; the remnants of Goldwater's frontal assault needed to be whitewashed. For the Republican party Ronald Reagan was the most crucial element for such a makeover. The ideology was still there; it needed an exponent who could make the ideas not just palatable but mouth watering. Ideology only went down easily when a party was establishing its foundation; afterward, even parties of principle needed charismatic leaders were they to succeed in growing beyond third- or fourth-tier status.[2]

Goldwater had placed principle before personality, but with the party principles solidly in place, all the movement needed was a person to unite it behind a conservative GOP and complete the missing half of the 1964 equation. The conservative movement always preferred to support a Republican party that adhered to its beliefs rather than a third party, but without a candidate who would ensure that principles were followed, activists had little choice. Even though the party had been hurt badly by its association with extremism, most Republicans willingly looked to new candidates to offer a respite from the internecine rivalries of the previous year.

California was the perfect place to test whether conservatism had indeed weathered the storm; just as its 1964 primary had catapulted Goldwater to the nomination, a conservative's election to its helm would indicate to the entire nation that not only was conservatism alive, but it was stronger than ever. The enthusiasm of the Goldwater campaign coursed powerfully through citizen groups like the CRA and the rival United Republicans of California (UROC). The state was not lacking in issues; between the Watts riots of 1965, protests at the University of California at Berkeley, air pollution (the newly dubbed smog seemed almost as ubiquitous as the redwoods), a rising crime rate, a yearly influx of nearly 300,000 newcomers, a widening "morality gap" between the generations, and a growing fiscal crisis in which the state's mounting debt threatened to rage out of control through ever-expanding governmental programs, conservatives could not have chosen a better litmus test for the theories of 1964. Governor Edmund "Pat" Brown was ripe to be plucked out of Sacramento. Though the state's massive budgetary woes were well publicized, few people really knew what the state's debt actually was. Equally important Brown's public image was shaky. Once described as "an affable owl," he was nearly unrecognizable to many Californians.[3]

If Buckley's mayoral bid was a testing ground for eastern conservatives in 1965, the 1966 California gubernatorial race would perform the same function on a national scale for the Republican party and the conservative movement. Coming at the same time as the midterm congressional elections, California would indicate whether progress had been made since 1964, or if polls projecting growing Democratic affiliation were indeed accurate. The uncertainties for the Republican party and the conservative movement were overwhelming. No one knew which faction would control the party in the next presidential election. Or if the party would split as it had in 1964. What would be done about those on the far Right, who hoped to swing more voters into their ranks and force their agenda onto the national scene? And, most crucially, *who* could possibly unite the two entities, party and movement, to defeat the Democrats?

Reagan's campaign was engineered to revive—or perhaps more accurately to spark—wide-scale conservatism by capturing the most valuable state in the union. California held forty electoral votes and had long since usurped Maine's traditional bellwether role. For many conservative Californians and non-Californians, Reagan embodied *the* hope for a conservative country. Not only did he have a record of years of devotion to conservative principles, but unlike Goldwater he also had a congenial public personality. Reagan represented the conviction that conservatism could leave the realm of the extraordinary to become the ordinary, the status quo rather than the enfant terrible.

Making of a Conservative

Born on February 6, 1911, to a shoe salesman and a housewife, Reagan's early years, first in Tampico and then Dixon, Illinois, were the stuff of small-town America, where the future actor and politician learned about community spirit and what it meant to work together to achieve a common goal. Although Reagan's boyhood and teenage years were not easy (his father was an alcoholic and never successful at his trade, and the depression hit the family hard), his mother taught him that good work could take him far, optimism that stayed with him throughout each of his careers.[4] At Eureka College in Illinois, Reagan became the Big Man on Campus, lettering in three sports and leading a student strike against the trustees when they tried to change the curriculum. After graduating with a degree in economics and sociology, Reagan took a job as a radio sports announcer, where he began honing his acting skills by providing play-by-play for football and baseball games he could not see, only hearing statistics telling him what had just happened. After he made a trip to Hollywood in 1937, Warner Brothers hired him for $200 a week, a great deal of money at the time, and provided a way out of the Midwest. Spending the war years as an army captain, Reagan narrated propaganda films and, as he used to remind people, "flew a desk" in Hollywood.

After the war Reagan was elected to the first of his six terms as president of the Screen Actors Guild, a union with communist members. A New Deal Democrat at the time, he resisted the possibility that liberal causes could be fronts for the CPUSA or similar groups. In 1948 Reagan's first wife, Jane Wyman, divorced him, and he entered a transitional period in his life. He was hired by General Electric to host "General Electric Theater," a television show that earned some of the highest ratings of the 1950s. Married to his second wife, Nancy Davis, daughter of a famous Chicago surgeon and for a brief time a Hollywood actress, Reagan gained a measure of stability, which provided him with an opportunity to reevaluate his position on a number of political issues. It was during this time, as he traveled the country speaking to GE employees and sharpening his ideology, that he converted from New Deal Democrat to a proponent of limited government, anticommunism, and individual responsibility in all areas of human relations.[5]

The zeitgeist in which Reagan's adult political ideology developed was, on the surface, the antithesis of his parents' political roots and what he had believed until the late 1940s and early 1950s. Through his work with GE and the Screen Actors Guild, Reagan began to see the inherent dangers in the state as provider. Although he did not change his party affiliation until 1962, he expounded on the benefits of capitalism as an organizer of social relations and on how the overbearing state and social engineering effectively defeated the natural order among people. Undergoing a gradual but continual transformation, Reagan voted for Eisenhower in 1952 and 1956 and campaigned for Nixon in 1960. The Supreme Court's power grabbing, warming relations with the Soviets, and an increasingly strong central government helped convince some Americans, including Reagan, that change, conservative change, was needed. Reagan's presentations to GE workers also persuaded him that conservatism instead of liberalism was the best solution to the country's problems. Going from factory to factory Reagan saw what free-market capitalism could achieve, and when he looked out into the faces of the workers he understood that any ideology that threatened what had produced such abundance, whether liberalism or communism, must not be allowed to spread any further.

By the late 1950s and the first two years of the 1960s Reagan was giving a stock speech not only to GE employees but also to civic and industrial groups nationwide. The demand for his services grew to the point where he was forced to choose between selling refrigerators for GE and selling an ideology years in the making. Reagan and GE parted company in 1962, but by that time the former actor was making a comfortable living on the banquet circuit. His early speeches demonstrated both his belief system and his oratorical skills. On October 18, 1961, in San Jose, California, for example, Reagan gave one of his stock performances at a Republican fundraising dinner. The fact that he was still a registered Democrat at the time made his words that much more powerful, and "Losing Our Freedom on the Installment Plan" never failed to bring an audience to its feet. In this permutation of his common themes, Reagan lashed out against liberals who meant well but almost certainly hurt the country:

The only common denominator needed to get these liberals to campaign for any particular piece of legislation is the extent to which it strengthens and adds power to the central government.

. . . Professor [Arthur] Schlesinger recently on television said that the welfare state is our greatest defense against revolution. Well that just isn't true. Our greatest defense against world revolution and communism is devotion to individual liberty, and the preservation of a free economy based on private ownership of property.[6]

Reagan's audiences were inevitably conservative, but he still labored to ensure that they would hear his words and reach the epiphanies that told them their country was heading down the wrong path. Quoting statistics that demonstrated the absurdity of government subsidies and overwrought planning, Reagan deliberately held back from reaching conclusions, knowing that the audience could fill in the blanks and thereby feel the effect more powerfully. In another speech, "What's at Stake," Reagan set up the federal government as an enemy of the people, although he reminded them that it did not have to be that way:

How many of us realize that we've lost the Fourth Amendment to the Constitution—our protection against search and seizure? Because today, federal agents, if they suspect a man of violating a regulation—not a law, a regulation—can invade his property without a warrant, can impose a fine without a formal hearing let alone a trial by jury, and if the fine isn't paid they can seize or hold his property or sell it at public auction to ensure payment of the penalty.[7]

In his attacks on the Supreme Court and the federal judiciary, Reagan's call to arms was not so different from that of Robert Welch. Big government not only threatened the economic stability of the country but also the individual freedom of every citizen, the keystone of the American experiment. Washington bureaucrats seemed determined to "improve" people's lives in the name of "progress," but the end result of such action would invariably lead to disaster:

These people who were so concerned in the [1960] campaign for the fate of the individual farmer had concealed in the fine print a provision that they recognized there were probably two million too many farmers in the country. And so they had proposed that the Department of Agriculture had the right to declare which two million farmers would be removed from the soil and returned to jobs in the city.[8]

Here Reagan blended a number of themes. The Jeffersonian and Jacksonian rural idyll was threatened by the central government, a sort of cabal imposing arbitrary state planning on the agriculture industry, literally uprooting farmers from their soil and dumping them in the evil city. The government's agency overruled any individual decision and gave citizens no choice about their life paths, a scenario close to the Soviet dictatorship. Whether or not Reagan had any evidence for such a plan was of little importance; sooner or later Americans would suffer. Although the number of farmers in America had been declining for decades—in 1966 there were only 4 million, down from twice that only twenty years before—the image of the farmer still held a powerful place in most Americans' minds, certainly in the minds of the conservatives who Reagan addressed.[9]

Equally important to what Reagan said was how he said it. Relying on nearly an entire life's work in the spotlight, Reagan's timing and delivery were impeccable, and he knew how to judge what an audience needed at various moments during a speech. When discussing the excesses of liberalism his voice took on a tone of disgust. Describing the standoff between the superpowers he adopted one of resiliency and imperviousness. Detailing the plight of an everyday American like the farmer, he became empathetic and displayed the side that reminded his listeners of his humble origins. His one fault in public speaking was exposed when he strayed from his planned remarks. While he was a good off-the-cuff speaker, he relied on phrases that had been committed to memory, and if pushed further he often found himself floundering and hoping that an answer would materialize that fit the question. For example, Reagan would hear a particularly persuasive story told by a constituent about governmental red tape, commit it to memory, and then simply recall it whenever he wanted to illustrate the evils of big government. As one biographer put it, "It was as if someone had hit the 'play' button on a tape cassette recorder."[10]

Reagan's style and substance came together most tellingly in "A Time for Choosing," also known among conservatives as "The Speech." Conceived and financed by a group of conservative California Republicans who had seen Reagan speak at the Coconut Grove nightclub in Los Angeles, Reagan's stock speech was more compelling than anything Goldwater could muster. After Reagan agreed to the request, the backers decided to film one of his speeches live. Technical problems, however, prevented the taping.[11] Reagan then suggested that rather than simply speaking directly to a camera, he should speak to a studio audience. Thus one day in late October 1964 a group of Los Angeles Republicans arrived at a large NBC studio in Hollywood. Taking their places in the theater seats, this audience both made the setting more realistic and made Reagan feel more comfortable since he was used to talking to such gatherings.[12] Addressing the audience rather than the camera, Reagan turned the half hour into a combination family meeting and political rally, in turn exhorting, shocking, sympathizing with, and inspiring his audience. At first, however, the audience members, neophytes at being on television, were transfixed by the cameras, forgetting to react to Reagan's finely tuned delivery. After a little while, though, they relaxed, and the taping went smoothly. When the tape was passed on to the

Goldwater campaign, Goldwater advisers Denison Kitchel and William Baroody initially rejected the speech.[13]

After a brief debate, however, the address was aired on October 27, 1964, and it instantly became a watershed in Reagan's political career. Marshaling all of his experience over the previous decade and a half, Reagan culled the best pieces of his stock speeches to create an appeal not only for Barry Goldwater but also for conservatism in general. Reagan followed his usual outline, established how unsound the current administration and previous liberal administrations had been, and wondered how so many in leadership had been blind for so long. Interspersing statistics like "since 1955 the cost of [the agriculture] program has nearly doubled. . . . In the last three years we have spent $43 in the feed grain program for every dollar bushel of corn we don't grow," Reagan led the audience through a primer of what conservatives believed and sold them a combination of fear and hope.[14] A master of the anecdote, Reagan told stories that not only illustrated a point but enabled viewers to imagine themselves in similar predicaments and facing similar choices:

> Not too long ago two friends of mine were talking to a Cuban refugee, a businessman who had escaped from Castro, and in the midst of his story one of my friends turned to the other and said, "We don't know how lucky we are." And the Cuban stopped and said, "How lucky *you* are! I had someplace to escape to."

After discussing the problems with agriculture policy, Reagan slipped effortlessly into a critique of urban problems: "Meanwhile, back in the city, under urban renewal the assault on freedom carries on. Private property rights are so diluted that public interest is almost anything that a few government planners decide it should be." Railing against centralized planning and the knee-jerk liberal desire to correct every apparent injustice in the country, Reagan made point after point with humor ("We have so many people who can't see a fat man standing beside a thin one without coming to the conclusion that the fat man got that way by taking advantage of the thin one!"), incredulity ("They have just declared Rice County, Kansas, a depressed area. Rice County, Kansas, has two hundred oil wells, and the 14,000 people there have over $30 million on deposit in personal savings in their banks. When the government tells you you are depressed, lie down and be depressed!"), and contempt:

> Not too long ago, a judge called me here in Los Angeles. He told me of a young woman who had come before him for a divorce. She had six children, was pregnant with her seventh. Under his questioning, she revealed her husband was a laborer earning $250 a month. She wanted a divorce so that she could get an $80 raise. She is eligible for $330 a month in the Aid to Dependent Children program. She got the idea from two women

in her neighborhood who had already done that very same thing. Yet anytime you and I question the schemes of the do-gooders, we are denounced
as being against their humanitarian goals.

Reagan brought his audience to the only logical solution: Barry Goldwater.
Casting the candidate as not only a true conservative but an honest, upstanding
citizen, Reagan related a story told to him by an ex-GI:

> It was the week before Christmas during the Korean War, and he was at
> the Los Angeles airport trying to get a ride home to Arizona, and he said
> that there were a lot of service men there and no seats available on the
> planes. Then a voice came over the loudspeaker and said, "Any men in
> uniform wanting a ride to Arizona, go to runway such-and-such," and they
> went down there, and there was a fellow named Barry Goldwater sitting
> on his plane. Everyday in the weeks before Christmas, all day long, he
> would load up the plane, fly to Arizona, fly them to their homes, then fly
> back over to get another load.

Reaction to the Speech should have given conservatives some idea of the
jewel they had suddenly unearthed, which sparkled before a national audience.
Messages to the Goldwater committee urged them to repeat the telecast immediately. Telegrams to Reagan glowed. "Great, Ronnie, Great," wrote John
Ford, the film director. "Phones ringing around the clock here since your telecast. Our deepest thanks and congratulations for a magnificent presentation"
came from none other than F. Clifton White. Goldwater's own senatorial staff,
in a tacit acknowledgment that their boss had a tendency to muddy the waters
when he spoke, responded, "We heard your great speech last night. A thousand thanks for a tremendous message made so clear."[15] Additionally some
telegrams asked the question that would become commonplace in the next
few years: "I heard your talk tonight. I know you're an actor but are you running for President[?]"[16]

Besides his familial background, his experiences in college and Hollywood,
and his work for GE, Reagan's political ideology demonstrated an ability to
draw on sources that, while perhaps contradictory in another set of circumstances or compiled by another individual, made perfect sense when distilled
through the former actor. What distinguished Reagan from other conservatives was his embodiment of the principle of fusion in his own person. The
combination of anticommunism, traditionalism, and libertarianism, labeled
"fusion" by *National Review* writer and editor Frank S. Meyer, contained the
most promise for uniting the movement. Goldwater's fusionism, however,
appeared to give credence to the fringes, which dampened his appeal to Americans who might believe what a fusionist believed but did not necessarily describe
themselves as "conservative."

For a New Deal Democrat to emerge unscathed after a transformation to Goldwater conservative would normally seem impossible, particularly in the charged atmosphere of the first half of the 1960s. Yet Reagan suffered only minor bruises and deftly controlled the accusations that he was a turncoat who could not be trusted. Reagan himself took on much of the responsibility of convincing his potential constituency of his genuine conservatism. Besides his numerous speeches and appearances, he replied to virtually every person who wrote to him, a practice he continued through his eight years in Sacramento. Although form letters eventually took their place, Reagan crafted individualized responses, more evidence of the style of his conservatism that won him praise from diehards within the GOP and the conservative movement and eventually from wavering Democrats.

By the 1966 campaign Reagan had defined a friendly, accessible conservatism, which still met the requirements of the Goldwater wing of the GOP. Only a few days before the general election Reagan responded to a writer for a Japanese-American community group's newsletter, who had remarked about the "danger of Reagan." Rather than dismissing her as a lost cause (or, as Goldwater might have done, not replying at all), Reagan located himself solidly within a set of values that were inarguably American:

> When you state that I am a "self-acknowledged conservative" you do not adequately define or explain what I actually mean by "conservative." My definition of a Republican conservative is an American of integrity, progressive in his creative thinking, who strives to make this a better place in which to live and raise children, and accomplishes that result by the application of hard work and sound common sense. A conservative Republican is a good American citizen with both feet on the ground.[17]

Who could argue with such a description? Not only had Reagan described an ideal, apolitical citizen of any country, but he had also outlined a set of values highly prized by immigrants or children of immigrants, as his reader was likely to be. Indeed conservatives did have a prize on their hands. The only remaining question was: could the movement and the Republican party set aside their internal differences long enough to get this man elected?

Party and Movement in California

If New York City in 1965 was a test case for conservative principles within and without the GOP, California in 1966 offered a similar scenario as the gubernatorial election promised to serve as a referendum on the future of conservatism and liberalism. If Reagan became the Republican nominee, he would have to contend with a variety of factions across the party's spectrum. While some extremists believed that Reagan was too good to be true and must therefore be some sort of rogue designed by America's enemies to woo conservatives into letting down their guard, most believed that Reagan promised the first fighting chance since Goldwater and perhaps even a better one.[18] But even if most conservatives supported Reagan, their enthusiasm and proclivity to latch onto controversial issues could end up splitting the Republican party, as had happened with Goldwater. The two major conservative citizen groups in the state, the UROC and the CRA, had undergone a role reversal in the time following Goldwater's defeat. While both came out in early support of Reagan as the candidate to take on Pat Brown, the CRA, formerly the more moderate of the two, suddenly called for an end to the income tax, a probe investigating the UN, and support of a constitutional amendment to overturn the Supreme Court's 1965 reapportionment decision.[19] Such radical action caused at least a handful of CRA members to bolt and seek instead "an organization dedicated to responsible middle-of-the-road Republicanism."[20] Their words were anathema to both the CRA and the UROC, but the newly formed California Republican League (CRL) welcomed them with open arms. Condemning the JBS and espousing a brand of Republicanism that Rockefeller or Romney would have agreed with, the CRL was an upstart group, with a mere 3,000 members in 1965 (by contrast, the CRA had 20,000 and the UROC anywhere from 7,000 to 15,000). The CRL acted as a watchdog group for moderate Republicanism and attempted to ensure that Birchers did not infiltrate the ranks and that Birch-oriented groups did not gain too much power. Similar to the CRL, the California Moderate Democrats appeared soon after, supported Reagan, and drew cross-over members from the GOP.

By 1965 the UROC, founded in 1963 by dissident CRA members, who thought their original group was too liberal, had switched places with its forebear and now held a moderate position it believed would be more practical.[21] But both organizations suffered from public images that led moderate Californians to believe that these interest groups wanted nothing less than to swing their party and state to the far Right. Perhaps due to the fever pitch at which many of the members operated, the groups seemed destined to endure an ongoing cycle of self-destruction and rebirth, with factions splitting off even as new recruits and affiliates joined their ranks. The Conservative party of California, for example, openly supported the John Birch Society and welcomed "all disillusioned Republicans and Democrats who are witnessing the take-over of their parties by Socialists who publicly advocate fundamental Communist doctrine and Communist programs that have destroyed all countries that tried them."[22] The diversity of such citizen groups posed a massive problem for the Republican party: since factionalism was still an unsolved issue in California, what should be done about groups like the CRA, UROC, and the Conservative party? Should it dare a repeat performance of 1964, where the big tent collapsed even as the elephants hoisted it into place, or would the winnowing begun in 1965 be completed and forgotten before the 1966 primaries? Either way conservatives risked a misstep that could cost them Sacramento and perhaps make their most promising candidate in years look like damaged goods.

Reagan himself believed that the grassroots would continue their internecine battles until the party leaders and candidates themselves put a halt to it. Writing to a Republican Central Committee officer in Stockton, Reagan outlined his strategy, which would later be known as the Eleventh Commandment:

> I have stated that I will not speak critically of any Republican and that I will wholeheartedly support whoever is the nominee of the Party.
>
> . . . I am the only one of the suggested candidates who has made such a statement. I have hoped, but my hope has been in vain that by continuing to say this I could in a sense force other candidates to say the same thing. Unless the candidates are willing to take the lead in this, we have no chance of unifying the Party at the grass roots.[23]

Not only would the candidates benefit from such a practice, implied Reagan, but the grassroots might model themselves after their leaders. Reagan hoped that by promoting unity from the top down, conservative leaders could neutralize the factions that seemed most likely to scare away moderate voters. While it was wishful thinking that extremists and unflinching hardcore conservatives would melt away in the hot California sun, and while Reagan did not want to lose the support of either group (particularly the latter, since he identified himself as such), he had unshakable faith. By focusing on his opponent, making extremism a nonissue, and framing conservatism in a positive light, the former actor thought it possible to unite the movement and the party in 1966.

But the prognosis for California that year was grim. Though facing a governor who had made his share of mistakes and whose state had been cursed by more than its share of the country's problems, the Republican nominee would still oppose an incumbent Democrat in a state where Democrats outnumbered Republicans 3–2.[24] Instead of riding Goldwater's coattails to an easy nomination and victory, Republicans had to ask themselves whether they would even publicly associate with their party's most recent presidential contender. One conservative who grappled with this problem was Thomas A. Lane, a retired major general in the army who had made a name for himself as an author and political commentator on the banquet circuit. In September 1965 he openly admitted, "Conservatives have been clobbered." The problem, remarked Lane, was that the conservative movement has "simply lacked a vehicle through which to express their concern and determination."[25] The Goldwater campaign had abandoned moderates and failed to convince unions that it supported their cause. Then Goldwater was "smeared" with the "trigger-happy" label, and the party had responded defensively rather than simply guaranteeing victory in Vietnam.[26] But the real problem had stemmed from the liberal-conservative split. In all previous elections, when a liberal had been nominated over a conservative, party discipline had held, and the conservatives, often against their better judgment, had supported the Eisenhowers and Nixons rather than the Tafts and Goldwaters. But 1964 had proved that, as among thieves, there was no honor among liberals. If the moderates could not be trusted to support a conservative, any effort that might shift control away from the status quo might be forever sabotaged.

Lane believed that to guarantee a policy that expressed their beliefs, conservatives would have to look to a third party. But, he asked, "Why should the party majority accept such dictation from a liberal minority? Why must party loyalty be a one-way rule, binding only on conservatives?" It should not, he answered, and forming a third party would be tantamount to surrendering, perhaps for good. Conservatives needed to reassert themselves, since "the conservative Republican has an obligation to save the Republican Party by fighting for control of it." Presciently Lane saw two prerequisites for this transformation to take place. First "conservatives must find another leader who will fight to recover party control." But that was a big order to fill; it could be years before such a man emerged. Second conservative Republicans needed a win, and Lane knew that "the campaign of 1966 will be won or lost at the state and district levels of political action." Yet for all of Lane's analysis, some crucial problems still loomed. Conservatives would have to make the compromises necessary to win, or they would simply eke out revenge against the liberal wing. The divisions within the movement might prove insurmountable, which would throw the effort back into the turmoil whence it came. Finally, although Lane thought a national leader would emerge in the next few years, who could run and win at the state level? Lane's predictions and the accompanying questions would be put to the test sooner than he thought, in the rough-and-tumble arena of California politics.

Producing Reagan

Rarely in twentieth-century politics is the advent of a viable candidate traceable to a small, tightly knit group of backers who simply want to see their man (or, less frequently, woman) elected to public office. Ronald Reagan, however, attracted such attention, and in 1965 a clique of California millionaires decided that, based on Reagan's experience campaigning for Nixon in 1960 and the Republican ticket in 1962 (including liberal Thomas Kuchel) and his performance in the Speech, he offered the best chance of unseating Governor Brown in 1966.[27] Behind the effort stood men like Holmes P. Tuttle, an entrepreneur in Los Angeles; A. C. "Cy" Rubel, chairman of the board of the Union Oil Company; and Henry Salvatori, founder of the Western Geophysical Company.[28] Tuttle and the others, however, had to act cautiously; they did not know whether Reagan would be open to such a scheme. In 1960 Reagan had been "approached by a group of people about running for either the Senate or for Governor." But the actor was not ready, and he recalled, "This was a proposal so out of line at the time with anything I had thought of in connection with myself that I refused without even a hint of maybe."[29] Moreover Reagan was the host of the popular television series "Death Valley Days," a position he would be forced to give up as a candidate. Thus Tuttle and the others advanced tentatively but made it clear that he was the man they wanted. Reagan worried about the costs—both financial and personal—of running such a massive campaign, although sponsors labored to convince him that these would be taken care of. Knowing that Reagan would be more inclined to agree to a complete package, the group next approached the public relations firm of Spencer-Roberts, which had run Rockefeller's primary campaign in 1964 and had a track record of thirty-four wins and seven losses, all for Republicans. Stuart Spencer and William Roberts did not jump at the chance to manage Reagan since, recalled Roberts, "We had heard that Reagan was a real right-winger and we thought that a right-wing kind of candidacy would not be a successful one. We'd also heard a lot of other things— that Reagan was a martinet, that he was difficult to work with."[30] But an arranged meeting between Reagan and the two planners eased their fears, since the potential candidate demonstrated an ability to listen and speak candidly and was easy to converse with.

Although the small group of backers could have easily financed the initial stages of Reagan's bid, Spencer and Roberts realized that they had to begin mending California's GOP fences. The simple fact that Reagan's supporters had hired Spencer-Roberts began the healing process for party insiders, since the firm had worked, albeit unsuccessfully, for Rockefeller in 1964. Spencer-Roberts decided to form the Friends of Ronald Reagan, a group that would aim at the primaries a year away. This tactic was meant to unify the state's Republicans behind Reagan and expand the circle of people who felt responsible for making the party whole again. To initiate fundraising as well as to introduce Reagan as a politician, not an actor, Roberts penned a letter, which Rubel signed, that asked recipients to join Friends of Reagan:

> Ronald Reagan, out of a deep sense of duty and dedication, is willing to serve his Republican Party as its candidate for Governor, providing a substantial cross-section of our Party will unite behind his candidacy.
>
> To this end, Mr. Reagan has agreed to exhaustively explore the depth of feeling and the possible commitment to such an endeavor. To assist him in the necessary exploratory activities, we have formed FRIENDS OF RONALD REAGAN. Our single goal, at this time, will be to help him in every possible manner in arriving at a considered and thoughtful decision.
>
> We feel Ronald Reagan deserves this opportunity.[31]

Although the letter was meant to test the fundraising waters (it did swimmingly, raising almost $135,000), it also called readers to dedicate themselves to rebuilding their party. If Republicans could not put aside their differences, the Democrats would retain their hegemony for another four years.

Spencer and Roberts had other reasons for solidifying the party. To win in the heavily Democratic state, it was estimated that a Republican would need 90% of his party's votes plus 25% of the Democratic votes.[32] In 1964 such unity within the GOP had been unthinkable, and Democratic crossover was minimal. In 1966, however, the picture had changed: with increased animosity toward the civil rights movement and the Great Society and the growing division over Vietnam, some Democrats had begun looking rightward, and more moderate Republicans had moved into the conservative category. Moreover such a coalition would be attainable with the right candidate and management. But the bottom line was that, unlike 1964, when Goldwater supporters dismissed moderate Republicans as traitors, Reagan would have to court moderates and convince them that not only was he a legitimate candidate but also that he would listen and respond to their concerns. Spencer and Roberts, however, had reasons to be hopeful. In polls as early as May 1965, the numbers indicated that Reagan might provide the glue for which the California GOP had been searching:

> Many political observers believe the Republicans haven't a ghost of a chance of staging a political comeback if they don't set some limits to their internecine warfare, persist in trying to destroy the availability of any new potential party luminary before he has had any real chance to shine. We normally would be of the same mind, but . . . *maybe* Ronald Reagan is above party.[33]

When asked whether it made a difference if Reagan were the Republican, Democratic, or Independent nominee in 1966, those queried demonstrated that Reagan did well in all categories, which led the researchers to conclude, "The people are voting strong for Reagan as a man rather than because he represents a party," exactly what Spencer and Roberts intended. Any personality attached to the GOP would be immutably identified with one wing or another of the party, which would only continue the sniping and infighting.

As the Republican picture became clearer and the primary match-up between Reagan and George Christopher, former mayor of San Francisco, became obvious, the Reagan forces commissioned polls to investigate how he would run against Christopher.[34] Questioning Republicans only, the survey showed that respondents disliked Christopher—a fellow Republican—for attacking Reagan, which led analysts to believe that the Spencer-Roberts strategy of enforcing unity was paying off. Most revealing, however, were Reagan's numbers regarding what voters liked and disliked about him. Reagan's sincerity and honesty came through clearly, as did his apparently distinct political philosophy. On the other hand, 77% of respondents commented negatively on his lack of political experience (26% did not like the fact that he was a former actor). Even though that number seemed daunting, Spencer-Roberts undoubtedly took it as a sign of progress; among all of the other issues listed, including extremism, supporting the John Birch Society, associating with Goldwater, and a lack of public stature, dissatisfaction reached only 6% in any one category (extremism), levels that could be easily controlled.[35]

Spencer-Roberts, the Tuttle group, and an ever-expanding Friends of Ronald Reagan had confidence that their man could continue his strong showing as the primary came and went.[36] But would Californians respond positively to Reagan's efforts at becoming a politician? Moreover *could* Reagan become a politician? Though he had excellent public speaking skills, his grasp of complex state issues was weak, and his reputation as a sincere and honest person depended in part on living up to the claim that he actually understood state government. To attack this problem Spencer-Roberts hired Stanley Plog and Kenneth Holden, behavioral psychologists who ran the Behavior Science Corporation in Van Nuys, California. Plog and Holden culled Reagan's speeches and writings and came up with seventeen distinct issues, each of which received a portion of eight black briefing books, which traveled with Reagan as he criss-crossed the state.[37] With Plog and Holden's references, Reagan developed a number of pat answers to common questions. He also learned to employ, as commentators called it, "a sort of wisdom-by-association technique also used by President Kennedy."[38] When unsure of an answer, Reagan knew how to shift the topic subtly to more familiar territory and never conceded that he did not know the answer to the original question.[39]

The Reagan team ran strongly against Governor Brown throughout 1966. Although Brown began the year leading Reagan, by April the tide had turned for good.[40] By the time of the June 7 primary, little doubt remained that Reagan was the strongest candidate the Republicans had seen since Earl Warren's days. Reagan beat Christopher by a 2–1 margin and outpolled Brown in raw votes, 1,385,550 to 1,334,286, no small feat for a state with 1.5 million more Democrats than Republicans.[41] The Reagan forces spent at least a half million dollars on the primary alone, which left little to chance, even against a notably weak opponent.[42] Congratulations from Goldwater, Nixon, and thousands of conservatives poured in to the headquarters, which told the candidate and his advisers, as Nixon said, that they "should continue to rely primarily on your obviously talented public relations team and on your own good judgment. This combination seems to have served you very well thus far!"[43]

Reagan's primary showing gave the first indication that the Democrats faced a real challenge. Prior to June the Democrats were relying on the composition of the California electorate to win the election. The June returns, however, woke them from a deep slumber. Even the White House got a dose of the bad news. The Democratic party in California, an aide to President Johnson noted, was in shambles. Allegiances split between Sam Yorty, mayor of Los Angeles, and

Edmund Brown. Now that Brown had won the primary, would Yorty throw his weight behind Brown? Yorty, said the aide, would not decide until October, which left open the threat that the conservative Democrat might back Reagan and draw his followers over to the Republican camp.[44] Another report from California recounted two other pieces of bad news. First, "The President's 'image' is not too favorable in Minnesota, the Dakotas, California, and Connecticut."[45] Second, after a meeting in San Jose, Reagan left a powerful impression on Walter Ridder, one of the owners of the Ridder publishing industry:

> [Ridder] went in prepared to dislike Reagan but found him interesting, well-informed, articulate, with a political philosophy a bit left of Goldwater, but basically a strong conservative. Ridder on the basis of talking, I believe, to Jess Unruh [a powerful assemblyman] and Mayor Yorty, thinks neither of them will exert themselves for Brown and that Brown is the under-dog. He also believes that if Reagan were elected, he would be a good potential and a strong candidate for the Republican nomination in 1968.

Simply put, Reagan was a Democrat's worst nightmare, a chisel that might finally dislodge one of the keystones of the Democratic bloc and possibly send the castle keep, once thought impregnable, crumbling to the ground.

As the campaign picked up speed, Spencer and Roberts learned to handle their candidate so that he could exploit his communication gifts, while avoiding being probed too deeply about issues that might reveal his shortcomings. Reagan was no Lyndon Johnson, who thrived on fast-paced, eighteen-hour days; he needed a nap in the afternoon before a dinner speech, and his handlers quickly incorporated the break into his routine. But his relatively limited campaigning appeared to match Brown for its energy and engagement—or, thanks to the Spencer-Roberts image, that is what it seemed like to the press. *Time*, for example, wrote that Reagan "has been running 18 hours a day as if the Dead End Kids were after him."[46] Furthermore Plog and Holden's black binders helped the former actor grapple with the issues, and he increasingly impressed journalists.

To expand Reagan's appeal beyond his movie and television image and to gain credibility among moderate Republicans and conservative Democrats, Spencer and Roberts generated a number of front groups to give the appearance of a broad-based coalition. Common in almost every twentieth-century campaign, Reagan's front groups were unusual, particularly when compared to those from 1964. Rather than making them appear to be grassroots creations, the Spencer-Roberts organization made it obvious that all of the groups under their control strived for the same end through similar means. Unlike the Goldwater campaign, where a wide range of citizen groups acted with impunity, mapped their own courses, and often ignored directives from campaign headquarters, as many of

Reagan's front groups as possible were chartered through the headquarters. Spencer and Roberts made the groups politically transparent. Youth for Reagan, for example, told its members, "We are selling fun with a purpose!" and "We are selling insight into the mysterious world of a political campaign!"[47] Californians for Reagan consisted of Democrats recruited to appeal to conservatives in their party, who were likely to swing over in the general election. Brown was finished, they argued, and now it was time to turn FDR's picture to the wall and bring new blood to Sacramento.[48] The Citizens Committee to Elect Ronald Reagan Governor sponsored cocktail parties, raffles, and barbecues; organized telephone committees; and hosted Nancy Reagan whenever possible, since she was a celebrity in her own right.[49] Operation Houseclean, chaired by Republican insider Goodwin J. Knight, targeted disaffected Democrats and asked them to question how Brown had managed to charge taxpayers for so much, including his sixteen relatives on the state payroll, purportedly making a combined $165,000 each year. And what about the state assemblyman who "charged the State $12,000 for mileage for less than one year for a committee that never held a meeting?" Other Operation Houseclean advertisements urged Democrats to "join the 1,215,134 Democrats who voted against the Brown Machine in the June primary. Help your party do a thorough housecleaning in Sacramento."[50] Reagan's handlers also targeted ethnic groups and created organizations for Mexican Americans and Asian Americans.[51] Essentially the Reagan campaign created a faux grassroots movement toward which Californians so inclined could gravitate, which minimized the chances of rogue fronts causing trouble through well-intentioned but misguided initiatives.

With limited spontaneous popular front activity, the Reagan campaign still had to create an atmosphere that conveyed a sense of Reagan as a man of the people, as the quintessential outsider, and as the rightful heir to California's tradition of innovative politics. Here again the campaign benefited from the actor's experience. Besides the requisite rallies, speeches, and appearances on news shows, the organization branched out to capture those who might not normally participate in a political campaign. A four-minute 45-rpm "floppy" record of a Reagan speech was pressed and mailed to 137,000 Democrats just before the general election.[52] Without Reagan's dynamic speaking style, such a gimmick would have been unthinkable. No opportunity was wasted to employ Reagan's photogenic looks, and a number of films were produced for community screenings or local broadcast. But those in charge of such public relations devices as films and radio addresses faced an unusual problem in selling Reagan: the voters' biggest complaint about him was the fact that he was a former actor with no experience outside of Hollywood. If films and advertisements reinforced this image, Reagan would be, in effect, battling himself when he claimed to be a politician untainted by previous experience and free of patronage debts. One proposal for a film centered on this problem, and its goal was to convince audiences that Reagan was not acting but analyzing problems and implementing solutions. The treatment, by Gerald Popper, a public relations consultant from Hollywood, suggested a series of "key issue" films, which would deliver hard-hitting facts while they involved their audiences in the give-and-take they saw on the screen, which was not a slick and overproduced Hollywood film.[53] Reagan would take a back seat to the style of the film; the method would draw out the man, rather than vice versa:

> Rather than projecting as an actor, we would rather have Ronald Reagan functioning as a commentator reporting from the pertinent scene. A man who knows the state's problems because he has learned them, not solely from books and lengthy reports, but from going out on the street and getting—first hand—the reactions of his fellow citizens. He is questioned and answers those questions. The answers may come quickly . . . sometimes there is an effort in phrasing the answer. Credibility![54]

Reagan would be intentionally *under*produced. He might deliberately stumble a bit in giving his answers, which would demonstrate that he was not perfect and had to think before he spoke. After years on the GE circuit, Reagan had to be cautious not to revert back to responses he had polished over the years. Popper reemphasized the importance of the film's style: "No Hollywood slickness here . . . but a newsreel style coverage that spells authenticity . . . plays up our candidate as someone vital . . . a man knowledgeable and experienced."

Brown's forces tried a number of approaches to beat back the conservative onslaught. One advertisement harped on Reagan's lack of experience as a politician and his wealth of experience as an actor:

> The Governor's office in Sacramento is not a movie set with painted doors and an artificial fire in the fireplace. It's the real room. And into this room, every day, come real people—Californians—to discuss real problems with a real Governor.
>
> No one doubts that Ronald Reagan would *look* believable behind that desk in Sacramento. But what are his qualifications to *be* a Governor?[55]

But Brown and his handlers knew that Reagan had the upper hand when it came to dynamism, popularity, and simple sex appeal. They needed not only to attack Reagan personally but also his connections to the scandal California Republicans had experienced since 1964. Being an actor was not a crime and usually not considered un-American. But supporting the John Birch Society or similar far-right groups often connoted illegal or at least unstable behavior. Brown's solution to the Reagan problem was clear from the outset: focus on extremism and help push the Republicans to disintegrate into chaos.

Weapon of Extremism

Concentrating on extremism, believed the Brown forces, would test Reagan's ability to keep the 90% Republican and 25% Democratic coalition from breaking apart. Not only would conservative Democrats be more reluctant to join a Republican who was supported by (and possibly supported) conservatives who attacked all Democrats as leftists or communist sympathizers, but liberal Republicans would also be likely to flee, fearing a return to 1964. Reagan would have to contend with the same people Goldwater lost—people like Margaret Meier, a liberal Republican organizer in southern California. A fire still raged in Meier, and she immediately sprang into action to help bring down Reagan. She did not need Brown to tell her that Reagan had connections to the far Right; her own research had convinced her long ago. In addition to investigating which Birchers were running for office (a study she conducted every election year), Meier used her vast network of sources to obtain a list of contributors to the Reagan campaign and spent hours combing through the names in an effort to match them to far-right issues and organizations.

Meier (and Brown) had a lot of material with which to work. Reagan's main campaign gimmick, for example, a plan he called the Creative Society, was coined by a famous far rightist, William S. McBirnie. In late 1965 McBirnie had been ruminating over a point Henry Salvatori made during a planning meeting. Reagan would need to overcome his lack of legislative experience while proposing "a program which fires the imagination of the voters."[56] Reagan needed a "positive program, packaged in some kind of a slogan or neat description: New Deal, Fair Deal, New Frontier, Great Society, New Order, etc." Why not propose a plan that was simultaneously positive and in opposition to the dominant strain of liberalism? McBirnie believed that the Creative Society was the solution to Reagan's problem, and in 1966 Spencer-Roberts and Reagan did indeed adopt the slogan and invented a program meant to capitalize not on government largesse but on private potential, a throwback to pre-depression/New Deal welfare capitalism.[57] Although the Creative Society was forgotten soon after Reagan took office, a controversy blew up in the faces of Reagan, Spencer, and Roberts when McBirnie was unmasked as its creator. If the issue of extremism were allowed to get out of control, Reagan might fall short in either of his crucial constituencies: liberal Republicans or conservative Democrats. To fight the extremism smear, Reagan would be forced to enter territory he had every intention of avoiding, which was exactly what Brown wanted him to do.

Campaign issues included the environment and conservation (a topic on which Reagan got himself into trouble when he said, speaking of California's redwood trees, "I mean, if you've looked at a hundred thousand acres or so of trees—you know, a tree is a tree, how many more do you need to look at?"), education, student protests, taxes and the state budget, and, most of all, race-related issues.

Reagan had voiced his opposition to the 1964 Civil Rights Act, and his emphasis on law and order echoed much of Goldwater's race-coded language, especially after the Watts riots of 1965. Nevertheless Reagan seemed genuinely concerned about attracting African-American voters, even though the prospects were dismal. A consultant to Spencer-Roberts, for example, wrote to a friend:

> Recent surveys indicate that our candidate's political image among Negro voters of both parties is practically zero. However, these same polls tend to show that Reagan can win the primary election without strong Negro support. Despite all this, Mr. Reagan insists that there be total Negro involvement in every phase of his campaign.[58]

Like Goldwater Reagan might have written off African-American voters as impossible to reach (it seems that most of his advisers did so). But like Goldwater again Reagan came from a background in which he had been taught that racism was wrong and that one should work for harmony among all peoples. The only time Reagan publicly lost his temper during the entire campaign was at the March National Negro Republican Assembly convention in Santa Monica, where George Christopher drew a parallel between Reagan and Goldwater regarding the 1964 Civil Rights Act. Reagan rose to his feet and yelled at the audience, "Don't anyone ever imply that I lack integrity. I will not stand silent and let anyone imply that—in this or any other group."[59] Reagan stormed out, and although he returned to the meeting, had the gaffe occurred closer to the primary or general election, the actor's skills might not have covered it over so seamlessly.

But extremism was the most crucial measurement for how much the GOP had changed since 1964 and how it might perform in future contests. Not only would the Democrats undoubtedly use the topic as one prong of their attack, but unlike some campaign issues, which materialized out of thin air, there actually was evidence to tie Reagan to various right wingers. In 1962 Reagan had worked on an unsuccessful congressional campaign for John Rousselot, who later became one of the country's best known Birchers, right behind Robert Welch and Edwin Walker in name recognition.[60] In 1962 Reagan was the campaign chairman for Lloyd Wright, who opposed liberal Republican Thomas Kuchel in that year's Senate race. Wright was an extremist by any measurement, who called for a punitive war with the Soviets and an all-out endorsement of the JBS. Moreover, because of Reagan's connections to conservative politics after so many years on the lecture circuit, he knew, whether only by name or as an acquaintance, virtually everyone who mattered in the conservative movement, broadly defined. For example, Reagan was friendly with Evetts Haley, Jr., publisher of the *Cow-Country Commentary*, a self-described "monthly report of conservative action." Haley, whose father wrote the infamous 1964 tract *A Texan Looks at Lyndon*, which attempted to connect LBJ with a number of illegal and pro-communist organizations, offered subscribers to his journal "a free copy of the pamphlet 'Our Nordic Race'" and believed that "history proves that no diluted race can achieve greatness."[61] Reagan's adherence to a big-tent approach dissuaded him from excluding people like Haley from his everyday correspondence.

In 1966 the national Republican party was only slightly less divided about what to do about extremism than it had been in 1964. Buckley's campaign had taught some lessons, namely that a conservative could get by without directly inviting the Birchers or the followers of Kent and Phoebe Courtney to join the cause. *National Review*'s stepped-up attacks on the JBS and similar groups had helped ally much of the conservative intellectual community, and those who disagreed with Buckley either kept quiet or aided the far Right. But extremism was still out there, waiting like a time bomb.

Leaders on the far Right kept up a continuous correspondence with conservative figures and let them know that groups like the JBS still had tens of thousands of members who could be mobilized on short notice.[62] Implicit in much of the correspondence was the threat that if conservative politicians tried to read the far Right out of the Republican party, there would be hell to pay at the polls. Ben McMillan, chairman of the board of Hussmann Refrigerator in St. Louis and a member of the JBS since attending Welch's first two-day seminar in 1958, wrote to Reagan at the end of 1965 and asked him to take a closer look at the JBS. Hoping to persuade Reagan not to condemn the society when he announced his intention to seek the Republican nomination, McMillan wrote that he had seen the "recent statement . . . condemning membership in the extremist organizations, and with that, of course, I entirely concur."[63] McMillan, like almost all Birchers, did not think of himself as an "extremist." He was simply a loyal American willing to do his part to save what he treasured so dearly. Reagan's reply hinted at how Spencer-Roberts's strategy would deal with the issue in the coming year. "I'm going to do my utmost to take this entire subject out of the campaign dialogue," he wrote.[64] The Republicans would never consider raising the issue, so it would be up to the Democrats to revive the apparition.

After the June primary the California Poll, a nonpartisan survey meant to assist both parties equally, released the results of a survey on issues about which citizens seemed most concerned. In a "Memo to Ronald Reagan and Pat Brown," publisher Mervin D. Field wrote, "The issues that the public wants you to discuss during the campaign, in order of their importance, are state taxes and government finance, schools and education, welfare programs, the race problem, transportation and freeways, and air and water pollution."[65] Neither extremism nor the John Birch Society appeared on the list. Ominously for Brown, 55% of those surveyed believed that Reagan would do a better job handling the issues. Never one to take defeat lying down, Brown and his advisers went on the offensive and deployed extremism as their main weapon. About two months after the primary the Brown forces produced a slick, twenty-four-page exposé called "Ronald Reagan: Extremist Collaborator." Detailing everything from how "fright-wing" money supported Reagan to how his advisers comprised a "rightist 'brain trust'" to Reagan's background and relationships with known extremists to Reagan's refusal to disavow Birch support, the document searched high and low for any connection—no matter how flimsy—between the candidate and those on the far Right. Desperate to link Reagan with 1964 and Goldwater, the Democrats did their best to stir up the internecine battles that infused conservative circles by presenting Reagan as a front man for the extremists. While the Democrats did uncover some connections of which the average voter was probably not aware, the over-the-top tone of the document reeked of desperation.

Brown knew that his best chance at trapping Reagan lay in his ability to force the conservative to choose between repudiating the JBS and other extremists and openly accepting their support and thus implicitly bolstering the Democrats' cause. Besides increasing the prominence of the issue in his stump speech, Brown tried various tactics to get Reagan to make a public statement or, borrowing from the anticommunists' use of the Fifth Amendment in the HUAC hearings, to turn Reagan's silence into an admission of guilt. Brown sent a telegram to Reagan and urged the candidate to "settle between ourselves the role the issue of political extremism will play during the campaign ahead."[66] Brown thought this was a win-win situation for him; either Reagan would accept the challenge and disavow extremism, or he would prove his guilt by his inaction. Brown wanted Reagan to repudiate the JBS, the CPUSA, and the KKK, withdraw his support for JBS members running for the state assembly, and remove any publicly identified extremists from his campaign staff. "Once you take these steps, I will no longer consider extremism a valid campaign issue." Reagan did indeed seem to be in a bind.

Reagan had a number of options with which to deflate extremism. Just after he declared his candidacy in early January 1966, a friend forwarded a suggestion from an advertising consultant about how to handle "the remnant tag ends of [a] John Birch sympathizer label."[67] The ad man thought that Reagan should not wait to be smeared by a Democrat. Instead he suggested:

> Reagan could set up a speech in San Francisco to the ADA, the Civil Liberties Union, the NAACP or maybe the Teacher's Union (whatever its name). They all suspect Birchism. He could emphatically state his rejection of John Birchism and his reasons for it. At the same time, he could establish a truer level of his conservatism (and liberalism), and his reasons for them. He could film the whole thing, excerpt it for TV spots, edit it for meetings in hostile territory, and silence most of the smeary whisperings in a hurry by meeting the suspicion head on.

Reagan did not take this advice, and here again Spencer and Roberts proved their worth. They realized that addressing the issue risked blowing it up to the proportions Democrats wanted to see. Acknowledging the problem, in effect, *created* the problem. If Reagan could ignore the topic, not encourage the issue to start showing up on the polls, and effectively counterbalance the Democrats' attacks, the point would be moot, and the advantage would swing to the Republicans. Reagan decided to pursue a combination of tactics. If he could ignore extremism, he would. As he told a friend, the GOP might hold together "if only we can keep some of the kooks quiet."[68] If others could speak to the issue without bringing the candidate into the picture, that would suffice for the first contingency plan. Forced to make a public statement at a news conference or during an interview, Reagan would follow Barry Goldwater's and William F. Buckley's leads by condemning Robert Welch, while praising the JBS members for their Americanism and patriotism.

Most interesting of the three tactics was the second. George Rochester, a member of the Democratic state Central Committee (the same group that produced the "Ronald Reagan: Extremist Collaborator" handbook), former state assemblyman and state senator, was tapped by the Reagan forces to act as a virtual one-man army to combat charges of extremism. Lucky to find someone with as much enthusiasm as Rochester, the Republicans instantly understood the advantages of having a Democrat answer Democratic charges. Rochester was fed up with the inefficiency and bureaucratic largesse that pervaded the Brown administration. During September and October Rochester set aside his law practice and threw himself into the task of repelling the Democratic attacks. Producing pamphlets like "A Democrat Answers the Cranston-Brown Hullabaloo about the John Birch Society," Rochester rebutted Cranston and Brown's accusations, first by referring to the *Report of the California Un-American Activities Committee*, an investigatory panel continued under the Brown administration, which found that the JBS was not secret, anti-Semitic, racist, anti-Catholic, or pro-Nazi, and then by conducting his own investigation in which, to defuse Cranston's charges of clandestine operations, Rochester looked up and listed the JBS's address and phone number from the telephone book.[69] By using language like "hullabaloo," Rochester also poked fun at his fellow Democrats and implied that they were trying to make something out of nothing. Rochester wrote letters to the editor, had his pamphlet serialized in a number of southern California papers, appeared on radio and television shows, and generally tried to take as much of the heat off Reagan as possible. With people like Rochester helping him on the front lines, Reagan worried far less about the issue than the Democrats wished.

By the first week in October the Democrats conceded that the extremism issue had failed, and for the last month they turned to attacks on Reagan's character and personality. In their assault on Reagan's lack of experience and his acting career, they unwittingly led Spencer-Roberts to one of the biggest campaign coups ever. The problem of selling Reagan's *inexperience* did not remain a problem for long; he became the consummate outsider, a man uncorrupted by past

political allegiances and ready to clear out entire chunks of the state government
if need be. In the end Brown could do little more than watch as he fell further
and further behind. The final tally showed Reagan crushing Brown by a million-
vote margin, the 58%–42% landslide percentage eerily close to the Johnson-
Goldwater results.

Three separate sets of forces conspired to help extremism die a quick and
relatively painless political death, initially in the California conservative movement and later as a national political force. First Reagan's and Spencer-Roberts's
strategy smothered the attacks that the Democrats brought against them. And
personalities like Goldwater, Nixon, and Buckley signified the support by the
upper echelons of the movement for the candidate's decisions.[70] Second Brown's
bumbling attempts to label Reagan an extremist backfired when, instead of sticking, the labels slid off Reagan's slick coating and fell away, impotent. Brown might
have been the first to experience what was later known as Reagan's "Teflon"
personality. The upshot was that Brown's attacks seemed unfair to the voters;
Reagan, ever the diplomat, deflected the charges by asking the candidates to
focus on such issues as taxes and education, which made Brown seem like he
was simply attacking Reagan's character, a mistake when the antagonist was a
career politician and the protagonist a skilled actor. Finally, compared to 1964,
the voters themselves were thoroughly uninterested in extremism. Although
Welch was still a mouthpiece to be reckoned with, public extremist pronouncements had fallen off sharply since Goldwater's defeat. Even though the JBS and
other groups still had tens of thousands of dedicated members on their rolls,
the sense of urgency was missing from the public debate. Real issues replaced
extremism: taxes, crime, education, the environment, and the war in Vietnam
all seemed far more important than whether or not a candidate associated with
people from a group that long ago had been exposed by the klieg lights of the
press.

Cutting off the millstone of extremism from around their necks amounted to
nothing less than a turning point for conservative Republicans; now they could
unite around an individual rather than an ideology and allow for the possibility
of support from their liberal brethren. The man became the ideology, and the
ideology became the man, an osmotic process that demonstrated that what Goldwater had hoped to do, but at which he had failed so miserably, was actually
possible. Casting off extremism also permitted moderate and liberal Republicans to view conservatives as more reliable and less unpredictable, which opened
the door for a broader coalition in support of a candidate who represented a
belief system in which all factions could find value. This *lack* of extremism made
conservatism—and Reagan—much more palatable, since if Goldwater and 1964
was the benchmark for the press and public, Reagan and 1966 represented a
sharp decline in outright attention paid to the issue. The net gain in respectabil-
ity among Republicans and conservative Democrats was immense; the sense that

conservatives had freed themselves of extremist influence meant they now treated issues with a greater degree of "objectivity." Any improvement over 1964 registered exponentially on the Richter scales of moderate Republicans and conservative Democrats. If the GOP had not already started returning to the center, it could give that appearance while maintaining its right-leaning stance on most issues.

Party and Movement Merge

In analyzing the results of Reagan's primary victory over George Christopher in June 1966, pollster Louis Harris uncovered a trend in California he believed might augur a shift in national politics. Harris found that "for all its accent on the new and the young, California is going conservative."[71] Southern California had actually increased from 40% to 50% conservative in the wake of Johnson's landslide, while the rest of the state had seen a jump from 18% to 30%. Harris found that one-third of the Democratic votes in the primary could be considered conservative, a protest "against purported mollycoddling of Mexicans and Negroes on the welfare rolls, against demonstrations and 'sex orgies' at Berkeley, and against 'softness' in handling the riots in Watts." But Harris's most stunning finding came in what would be the long-term effects of the conservative shift. Predicting the change long before Reagan had won the office, Harris looked at the big picture and saw that Reagan would benefit from those who had broken the trail he now traveled down:

> In 1928, Al Smith lost for President but brought out the big-city Catholic vote that provided a central pivot for Franklin Roosevelt's new majority in 1932. In 1948 Tom Dewey lost but brought into being new suburban Republican power which largely formed the basis of victory for Dwight Eisenhower in 1952. Now conservatives are hoping that when Barry Goldwater lost in 1964, he crystallized a new right-of-center vote in America. It may be too soon to say that the biggest state, often volatile, is the U.S. trendsetter; yet it is now possible this new conservative bloc could provide Ronald Reagan with victory in California in 1966—and in the nation in 1968 or 1972.

While Harris was off the mark on the year that Reagan would be elected president, he was accurate about the new conservative coalition. Since the 1950s conservatives had been foiled either by personality or program, each in turn preventing crucial elements from coagulating. The Reagan campaign marked the moment when conservatives realized that not only did they number in the millions, but that they could also put together a winning organization. With the Eleventh Commandment, or "Thou shalt not speak ill of other Republicans," well on its way to becoming a pillar of the GOP, Reagan was the right candidate at the right time, and he helped to unify the movement and the party in California under the same banner. But what would it take to see the same drama played out on a national level?

A vitriolic editorial in the *Philadelphia Inquirer* aptly summed up the Republicans' dilemma: they needed to overcome the infighting, which had come to characterize the party even more than its ideology. "There will be no Republican unity, for instance, if Ronald Reagan, on the heels of his spectacular victory in California, is made the target of continuing abuse by Republican 'liberals' hoping, thereby, to gain advantage in the coming Presidential race for George Romney," wrote the editors.[72] Suggesting that the party should focus on beating the Democrats rather than itself, the editors urged all factions to lower their voices and worry about victory first and ideology second. Conservatives would do best, for example, if Barry Goldwater would "crawl back into the political solitudes to which the voters sent him, and call a halt to the sniping at Romney and other Presidential possibilities." Liberal Republicans, on the other hand, "should stop lecturing Governor-elect Reagan and heaping their malice on him as though he came through the election—on a million-vote margin—with unclean hands." The image of unity was more important than the fact of unity, a point made clearly but ignored at the Hershey conference soon after Goldwater's nomination in 1964. While the problem had not been solved, the distance traveled since 1964 led many observers to believe that if the GOP stayed the course, it would only be a matter of time before their man was in the White House.

Buckley's and Reagan's campaigns were the most coherent expressions of conservatism after Goldwater, and in many ways they trumped the senator's efforts at bringing the party around to their ways. Soon after Reagan was elected, the congratulatory letters and telegrams began rolling in, and RNC Chairman Ray Bliss told the newly elected governor, "We look forward under your leadership to seeing California once again return to its rightful position as the great Republican citadel of the West."[73] A few months after his inauguration, Congressman John Ashbrook of Ohio told the governor, "You're the best shot in the arm the Republican Party has received in many years, in my humble opinion."[74] Reagan appreciated the compliments; he had toiled to achieve a victory few believed possible before that autumn, and the help had come from every corner of the conservative movement. One of those most responsible for keeping national attention focused on California was William F. Buckley, who Reagan thanked with a sincere letter:

> What I really want to set out to write [is] a heartfelt thank you for kind words spoken and written for morale-building when morale was low, particularly morale-building for Nancy. Seriously, I want you to know I'm deeply grateful.[75]

Reagan took the oath of office at fourteen minutes after midnight on January 3, 1967. Focusing his inaugural address on the Creative Society, the governor said little about what kind of programmatic administration his would be; he did, however, demonstrate to Californians what kind of man he was and what was truly important to him. At the end of the speech Reagan motioned to the top of the Capitol Building and told the crowd:

> If, in glancing aloft, some of you were puzzled by the small size of our state flag . . . there is an explanation. That flag was carried into battle in Viet Nam by young men of California. Many will not be coming home. One did, Sergeant Robert Howell, grievously wounded. He brought that flag back. I thought we would be proud to have it fly over the Capitol today. It might even serve to put our problems in better perspective. It might remind us of the need to give our sons and daughters a cause to believe in and banners to follow.
>
> If this is a dream, it is a good dream, worthy of our generation and worth passing on to the next.
>
> Let this day mark the beginning.[76]

As much as Goldwater and his campaign had come to be recognized as a defining moment among conservatives, Reagan too became an object of reverence. If Goldwater had articulated the need for a broad-based conservative coalition, Reagan succeeded in demonstrating that it was possible to assemble one that would not only refrain from offending liberal Republicans and conservative Democrats but would actually attract them too. His decreased reliance on outright ideology meant that voters would be attracted or repelled by the candidate alone, a variable he and his handlers controlled far more easily than ideas. That extremists were nudged out of the formal coalition meant that although their presence was unofficially acknowledged, these activists began migrating into other, more respectable conservative organizations and focusing on the issues that would make headlines in the next decade: busing, abortion, taxes, foreign policy, education, and social engineering. Reagan did not allow himself to commit the Goldwater gaffes, which had cost the Arizonan the support of liberal Republicans and conservative Democrats. Reagan would not be forgotten by America anytime soon, particularly by the Democrats.

Reagan's 1966 election helped instigate a sea change in national politics. With such a stunning victory over a long-time loyal Democrat in an overwhelmingly Democratic state, Reagan proved that the conservative Republicans were far from dead and that liberals and Democrats had reason to worry. Five months into Reagan's first term, the Johnson White House produced an analysis of California politics in which the Democrats were reported to be "in a general state of shock and pessimism," facing "a fluid situation with respect to the various power groups in the state, with no one moving to take control."[77] The party itself was "increasingly in the hands of moderate liberals, with the CDC [California Democratic Committee] clubs increasingly dominated by the New Left and alienated from the moderate liberals of the party leadership," a scenario that played right into the hands of the Republicans. Leadership was divided, and those who made the plans were "younger, inexperienced people—the old guard is passing away or dropping out of sight." Traditional Democratic strongholds dissolved in the face of the Republican onslaught, and even "the labor rank-and-file defected in large numbers to Reagan and the Republicans, and even a lot of the local leadership of the labor movement went in this direction." The report concluded depressingly, *"The consensus is that if the President had been running on the ticket in 1966, he would have been defeated in California"* (italics in original).

For the Democrats to contain the Republican wave before it breached the California border and moved eastward, they would have to figure out how to deplete the growing political capital of the Right, an inventory that grew each day that riots broke out and liberals called for more programs like the Great Society.[78] The weaknesses seemed few, however, with the White House report recommending pressuring Reagan about possibly increasing taxes and the Republicans placing the open housing question back on the ballot in 1968.[79] In essence the Democrats had little with which to attack Reagan. Even worse, from the moment Reagan had declared his candidacy in 1966, rumors of a presidential bid had abounded. The White House was particularly concerned that Reagan would leave office to throw his hat in the ring in 1968. In a late August memo Vice President Hubert Humphrey described a talk he had had with Goldwater:

> He tells me that Reagan does not want to run for President and will not take a second spot on a Rocky ticket. He said he told Reagan that this was not his time and that Reagan shouldn't kid himself into believing he could beat Johnson. Goldwater said he told Reagan that the same little old ladies in tennis shoes that used to cheer and clap for him did the same thing for Bob Taft and Tom Dewey. . . . He also told me that he didn't think Reagan was ready for the Presidency.[80]

But Goldwater (and hence Humphrey and perhaps Johnson) underestimated the depth of Reagan's support even as early as nine months into his first term. Thousands of Californians wrote to their governor and urged him not only to be a "favorite son" candidate but also to use the delegates as leverage for his own campaign.[81] Only sixteen days later presidential aide Fred Panzer telexed a soon-to-be released Harris Poll to Johnson at the LBJ Ranch:

> Reagan is known to 86 per cent of the electorate, and has made a "remarkable" impact in a short period, says Harris. He is looked on as a "conservative" by 51 per cent of the American people. Only 12 per cent believe he is a "radical." By contrast in 1964 nearly half the voters thought Barry Goldwater was a "radical." Thus Reagan's philosophical image is close to

that of rank-and-file GOP identifiers, 55 per cent of whom consider themselves "conservatives." He is the only GOP candidate to run ahead of LBJ in the South.[82]

Playing on such racially oriented issues as riots and welfare, Reagan had helped shift many labor, agricultural, and urban ethnic votes into the Republican camp. The absence of radicalism was due not only to this transformation in public attitudes toward what was tolerable in society but also to the lack of extremism surrounding Reagan, a factor that had conspired to help sink Goldwater in 1964. The separation of the images of conservative and radical represented a major step forward for conservatives, one that would not have been possible without Reagan and his 1966 campaign. Moreover the New Left greatly aided the conservative Republicans. As radicals like the Weathermen and the Black Panther party stole the spotlight from moderate groups like the original incarnation of Students for a Democratic Society, the term *radical* became more strictly associated with the Left than the Right. The John Birch Society and other extremist groups, while still in existence, slunk into the shadows, the exact opposite of the Weathermen's 1969 Days of Rage in Chicago or the Black Panther shootouts with the police.

By early 1968, although presidential polls showed LBJ defeating Reagan, the margin was smaller than the LBJ landslide over Goldwater, and Reagan had not yet campaigned nationally. By December 1967 77% of those surveyed thought that Reagan was correct in putting "a firm hand to race riots," 65% thought he was "charming and sincere," and fully 55% believed he "represents a new approach to politics, different from most politicians."[83] Reagan's biggest burden was his acting background, which 53% of those surveyed thought was "not [the] kind of experience needed to become President."

Reagan helped accelerate a trend already in motion, which was energized by actions on the Right as much as those on the Left. Unlike Goldwater Reagan stayed within the limits of tolerable conservative ideology, and the boundaries he established set a precedent for conservatives in the years to come. Two years into Reagan's first term as governor, the outlook for conservative Republicans on a national level could not have been more different than it was in 1964. The psychological distance traveled over the short temporal span made it seem like an entire political cycle had come and gone. An American Conservative Union report, issued one month before the 1968 presidential election, asked, "How Conservative Are Americans?"[84] Finding that most voters took conservative stances on major issues affecting the country, the organization predicted that, with the exception of medical care, Americans wanted to move away from Great Society programs and that "clearly conservatism is the philosophy of the American people." Although many conservatives did not consider Richard Nixon to be a conservative in the Taft-Goldwater-Reagan tradition, neither was he a liberal in the Rockefeller-Romney-Lodge tradition. More Machiavellian than either liberal or conservative, Nixon implemented a combination of conservative and liberal programs that angered almost all liberals and split conservatives over what grade to award him.

By 1966 the factions that had largely defined conservative political culture for the half decade prior to Reagan's triumph had been tamed. While extremist groups still demanded Chief Justice Earl Warren's resignation, for example, the general public no longer saw such calls as representative of the GOP. For many Reagan's victory was the algorithm that would bring together moderates and conservatives under the party banner in future races. Moreover Democratic attempts to link extremists with Reagan or his predecessors fell flat, which signified the shift from a conservative agenda based on ideology—embodied by Taft, Goldwater, and to a degree Buckley—to one grounded in personality and contemporary events and issues. Of course factions, particularly the extremists, still played a political and cultural role, although it was not one that they had originally envisioned. The confidence Republicans gained in 1966 allowed them to deflect attempts by factions, particularly extremists, at bullying the party into accepting compromising positions and permitted them to demonstrate their newfound ideological purity. The absence of extremism helped eliminate the public's doubts, which so frequently had derailed previous conservative bids, and cleared the way for platforms that reflected the three strands of ideology (traditionalism, anticommunism, and libertarianism) more clearly than ever before. The party's shunning of factions, however, did not end their organizational lives. Freed from their tenuous links to the party, splinters began pursuing agendas the GOP had never contemplated.

The shift from pure ideology to electoral pragmatism could not have happened overnight. Nor could it have happened without such individuals as Buckley, Reagan, and dozens of less well known conservatives. The contrast they provided against the backdrop created by Goldwater and the earlier waves of conservatives, those who sidled up to extremists more readily than moderates, was extreme in its own right, and few failed to notice the change. Ideology, of course, was not dead, and in fact its importance grew after 1966. As the conservative movement became more united, ideology acted as the mortar that held together the sometimes uneven building blocks that comprised the party platform. The difference between 1964 and 1966, however, was that ideology moved from the foreground to the background, replaced by men who could expound on such ideas without seeming fanatical.

Three weeks after Reagan's gubernatorial victory, *National Review* cartoonist C. D. Batchelor penned a drawing of the steamship *California* sailing east into a "liberty" sunrise, flying the banner "conservatism" as the clouds of "welfare giveaways" and "bloated bureaucracy" dissipated overhead. Captioned "Under a New Flag and toward the Sunrise," Batchelor's cartoon aptly summed up the conservative pride over California.[85] But now the steamship needed to reach those states ideologically landlocked or embargoed after thirty years of liberal rule. By 1968 the answer lay in a new feature of the conservative movement, which had taken its place among the readily identifiable personalities and philosophies. The growth of conservative interest groups rose from a combination of the migration of extremists out of their own circles into areas devoted to more mainstream issues and years of work behind the scenes, which prepared such alliances for the era of the post–New Deal Coalition. Forgetting the orderliness and battle lines of the previous thirty years, conservatives, increasingly united yet still at odds on a number of points, faced a hardscrabble liberal opposition with seemingly uncontrollable tentacles. Taking advantage of the backlash against the race and rights "revolutions," conservatives forged a new bloc dependent as much on liberals' actions as their own. These factions, once detrimental, acted as the final catalyst in creating the conservative hybrid. While the GOP had a larger purpose than simply letting one branch destroy the other to gain hegemony, these private organizations helped focus the movement in its final stage, melding the Republican party with the movement to gain an electoral advantage that, were it not for Watergate, would have been fully played out in the 1970s instead of the 1980s. These organizations, previously extras in the movement, now stepped forward to take center stage in the grand production that would lead to an even grander finale.

PASSING THE TORCH

ORGANIZATIONS AND ISSUES

1968–1972

One month after Ronald Reagan's resounding victory in the California Republican primaries, Russell Kirk, perhaps conservatism's leading ideologue, posed the question "New Direction in the U.S.: Right?" in the *New York Times Magazine*. Kirk sought to pick apart the political events of the previous two years and to dispel the false impression that conservatism was a moribund ideology. At the same time the radical Right had become a non-issue, Kirk noted, the far Left had increased its activity tenfold, pressuring those in office "who fail to do anything effective about this form of political insanity, or who retain some connection with the radical groups."[1] Radicals on the Left who tried to shut down army terminals, marched with Viet Cong banners, and supported black nationalism all played into the hands of conservatives old and new.

Since the Goldwater campaign, said Kirk, "a good many conservative-minded folk, neophytes in practical politics in 1964, have since learned what to do and what not to do in primary and general elections." Leading the charge would be people like Reagan, said Kirk, a conservative who "is more supple than Mr. Goldwater and more willing to work." Given the right conditions, Kirk intoned, "one can imagine a conservative crusade that would make the work of the Goldwater volunteers in 1964 seem a feeble gesture."

By 1968 it was no longer a question of whether the GOP would be wrested from the liberals, but *who* would embody the conservative philosophy, carrying the movement and the party into the next decade. The transition from a party of principle to a party of personality marked a new sophistication; still unknown, though, was how to make a conservative GOP the majority party in America.

The period between 1968 and 1972 saw the maturation of a number of independent conservative organizations whose roots stretched back to the early 1960s. These splinter groups, although disdained by GOP operatives, carried the momentum forward even as the focus on Republican grassroots activism and movement culture declined precipitously. The collapse of extremism aided their legitimacy and gave the impression of ideological objectivity. But as party adjuncts gained strength Kirk and others knew that conservatives needed to focus on controversial events and the liberal agenda, with ideology coming second or sometimes not at all. Careful to remain within the philosophical limits established by the American public, such groups as Americans for Constitutional Action, the Free Society Association, the American Conservative Union, and Young Americans for Freedom all struggled to keep conservatism vital.

Replicating the urgency of 1964 these organizations provided the GOP with an unquantifiable advantage over the Democrats by 1968 and helped the party reach a wider audience of voters and financial donors. The transition from the grassroots politics of 1964 to a politics of fundraising, information dissemination, and individual training went as smoothly as it did for conservatives because of these independent organizations. Adjuncts could keep conservative ideology dynamic, and, perhaps most relevant to the post-1968 period, these bands would train a new generation of conservatives and groom them for various slots in the GOP. Liberals, ironically, moved in the opposite direction. Johnson's 1964 campaign had been a hierarchical wonder in which planners left little to chance. By 1968 the Democratic party had been buffeted by the forces of liberal citizen movements, responded to many of their demands, and thus squeezed out traditional constituencies in favor of those who had rarely had a voice in the proceedings.[2] While the effort was noble, it also backfired and gave conservative Democrats one more reason to move into the GOP.

Forebear: Americans for Constitutional Action

Americans for Constitutional Action (ACA) was one of the earliest national groups devoted to the election of conservative politicians. Founded in 1958, ACA quickly took a position alongside the Republican party and acted as a watchdog over representatives and those hoping to win elected office.[3] A consciously designed antidote to Americans for Democratic Action (ADA), ACA planned to charter local chapters, educate its members about the workings of Congress, and generally promote conservative values. Its principles urged members to live according to rules set by a combination of religion, limited government, and the Founding Fathers, in other words, traditionalism:

> Man derives directly from the Creator, his rights to life, to liberty and to the means of acquiring and possessing property. These rights are inherent and inalienable. They are not mere privileges granted by government, subject to withdrawal at the whim of government.[4]

ACA intended to infuse politics with a sense of righteousness and harness the power of upright individuals as a defense against the Leviathan. But ACA went further than simply reiterating what the founders had said. "To secure the blessings of liberty," its charter read, "we must preserve a free market economy, with government acting only when necessary to protect individual rights and to prevent predatory action in the market place."

Although ACA originally planned to charter chapters across the country, the grassroots component of the organization never made significant headway. Instead, to measure how incumbents and potential representatives fared against the group's somewhat nebulous criteria, ACA invented the ACA Consistency Index, or simply the ACA Index. Representatives were evaluated in two dimensions:

> *For* safeguarding the God-given rights of the individual and strengthening constitutional government.
>
> *Against* group morality, a socialized economy and centralization of government power.[5]

Infinitely elastic, such criteria helped analysts at ACA decree, for example, that a vote supporting the Nuclear Test Ban Treaty violated their standards since it increased susceptibility to Soviet advances—both technological and strategic—and thus heightened the risk of a socialized economy. Each representative and senator received yearly rankings as a percentage total; a score of one hundred indicated a perfect record.

Soon, when the press, much of the conservative public, and politicians themselves needed a measurement of a congressperson's conservatism, they turned to the ACA Index. But such a system actually worked against ACA's initial plan, which was to encourage local chapters to pursue grassroots activism. The efficiency of the ACA Index made it difficult for members to understand why gathering in person was necessary when everything they needed to know was sent to them via the U.S. Postal Service. Nevertheless ACA officials implored their members to do more than just read the scores at election time to determine who would receive their vote. In 1961 and 1962 ACA produced three manuals: "Your Decision," with an introduction by John Tower; "Your Challenge," with an introduction by Barry Goldwater; and "Your Victory," with an introduction by Strom Thurmond. Each manual sought to teach members "not to be repelled by the words 'political action.'"[6] ACA couched its lessons in terms that sought to make political organizing a fun and productive activity, although one requiring "dedication" and "hours of hard work." After a few private meetings to choose officers and set an agenda, an open gathering would be staged to recruit citizens less likely to get interested without some promise of socializing, entertainment, or other activity, which might have been political in nature but was also cultural. This movement culture—in the form of a speaker, film, cocktail party, dinner, or rally—could attract less dedicated citizens, who would still work to see conservative values upheld in an election.

But the ACA faced a number of difficult choices about its image, internal structure, and whether to rely on grassroots activity. Almost from the beginning

ACA had to define itself repeatedly as a *conservative* organization, which, as retired Admiral Ben Moreell, the group's chairman noted, was "*not* a Republican organization."[7] In this time before Goldwater and when the conservative movement was still gathering steam, the ACA had to separate itself from the GOP without standing in opposition. ACA's solution was to focus less on the grassroots activities it had hoped to inspire in 1961 or 1962 and to shift its gaze to higher-level political organizing, where the ACA Index and other information comprised the benefits of membership. This change of direction, which prevented the group from ever becoming a citizen-based network of chapters (like the JBS), was meant to guide and exert influence on the GOP. By 1966 only nineteen chapters existed in the country, although ACA still had a complete program in place if new chapters formed spontaneously.

Electing politicians who conformed to ACA standards cost a lot of money, which made fundraising a top priority. The price of operating ACA, while not low, was reasonable as far as national lobbying organizations went: the 1966 estimated budget was $162,900. But adding in candidate assistance increased expenses to $437,900.[8] Without a grassroots network supplying chapter dues or crucial legwork in a campaign, ACA had to rely almost solely on direct-mail fundraising. Although direct mail was not a new technique by any means, few nationally focused groups with an agenda as broad as ACA's relied on it before the mid-1960s. But ACA leaders were ambitious and proposed, for example, to raise $100,000 over a period of seven months. Using lists borrowed and purchased from organizations, including 18,000 American Conservative Union supporters, a list of 12,000 Dean Burch advocates (collected during and after his ousting as chairman of the RNC), 3,000 "conservative prospects," and 25,000 new names, ACA projected netting $20,000 each month in an all-out effort to fill the coffers. Surprisingly former ACA contributors comprised only 1,000 of the 58,000 total names, an interesting comment on the business of buying and selling lists of potential contributors.[9]

Money was a constant worry for ACA. As Chairman Moreell wrote to the ACA president, retired General Thomas A. Lane:

> The last money report I saw indicates that we did well in February, but not nearly as well as we have to do to finance a decent job in the 1966 elections. I believe it showed we collected about $25,000 for January and February 1966. We need more Chapters! Some of the "fat cats" might come through if we had that tax exemption.[10]

To gain a tax exemption, however, meant marketing the group as a nonpartisan educational organization, a highly unlikely scenario. Moreover Moreell's desire for more chapters was also likely to amount to naught, which would still leave ACA relying on "fat cats" and direct mail. Nevertheless ACA made out well: in

1965, an off-election year, it raised $123,000. In 1964 it had set a record and pulled in $187,000, a number it hoped to surpass in 1966.[11] While these figures were respectable for almost any private, citizen-based political lobbying group, they were especially staggering when compared to the revenues of comparable liberal groups.[12]

After 1966 the national ACA and its handful of local chapters tried valiantly to influence voters and public opinion using more than just the index. Chairman Moreell and President Lane sought to distinguish themselves from other conservatives and pushed for candidates who would carry forth the vision enumerated in the founding principles. To make matters more complex Lane and Moreell were suspicious of some fellow conservatives, especially those who had changed their opinions on important matters. In late 1966, for example, Moreell told Lane that he did not trust *National Review* contributor and former socialist James Burnham. Moreell thought Burnham had never fully refuted his background, and now he was acting as Buckley's "'guru,' the 'great teacher.'"[13] Moreell's defense of the JBS was not surprising; he acknowledged "that there has always been 'indirect association' between the ACA and the Birch Society. . . . Governor [Charles] Edison, General [Bonner] Fellers, Howard Buffett and others on our Board have had and still have a direct relationship with the J.B.S."[14] Unwilling to disavow extremist forces of the past—the same forces that had helped drag down Goldwater—ACA ended up as part of the old guard of splinter groups.

In the end ACA continued relatively unchanged from its founding in 1958: it produced the index biannually and relied on direct mail to support its few programs and to fund candidates and incumbents. Try as it might, it would not be the organization to lead the movement into the post-1968 era, in which issues more than conservative philosophy dominated the political forum. ACA did fill a niche, however, by acting as a counterweight to ADA and as a reliable and trustworthy extension of the GOP. But even after the revolution in conservative activism inspired by the JBS and the Goldwater movement, ACA had learned little about putting Americans to work for a cause.

On the other hand, ACA did learn from the events of 1963–1964. It was one of the few groups to remain fiscally viable, and it did so without recruiting tens of thousands of workers to stock chapters or canvass neighborhoods. Perhaps it was not necessarily the citizen activities that made a group effective but instead the money it raised, a degree of maturity (both internally, in controlling its staff, and externally, controlling its image in the media), and the relatively low-risk venture involved in a top-down effort that made ACA outlast most liberal and conservative groups. Finally, though ACA sought to mold the GOP in its image, it rarely, if ever, opposed the party outright. ACA's presence offered a model for other groups to emulate, a picture of stability in a movement that still lacked guidance to carry it into the new decade.

Upstart: Free Society Association

In early 1965 Denison Kitchel, an Arizona lawyer and Barry Goldwater's former campaign manager, wrote the former senator regarding the problem of maintaining the nucleus of the 27 million voters who had indicated their preference for a conservative president. Kitchel recounted the facts that, by this time, every conservative leader knew: "Those 27 million voters represented approximately 40% of those voting at the election and 80% of the number needed to win the election."[15] While Kitchel simplified the Goldwater constituency dramatically, in essence suggesting that voters had an ideological imperative to support the Arizonan and that few simply voted Republican habitually, he accurately described the newfound power of conservative numbers. In the vacuum caused by the party's failure, individuals and organizations rushed pell-mell toward the head of the pack, everyone hoping to lead the unsteady movement. Kitchel worried that extremist groups "such as the John Birch Society and the Billy Hargis and Kent Courtney claques" would reroute many of "these rudderless 27 million into a third party movement labeled 'conservative.'"[16]

To create a bulwark against extremism and to avoid a fragmentation of the conservative movement, Kitchel proposed the Free Society Association (FSA) to take the helm of the rudderless masses and help them avoid foundering on the shores of liberalism. Kitchel estimated that it would take $250,000 to get the FSA off the ground. J. Howard Pew, a multimillionaire whose foundation often donated generously to conservative causes, had already committed $50,000 of his own money. Kitchel thought that "another $50,000 has been virtually assured." But after a solid year of backing Goldwater, could those individuals who had parted with $5 or $10 be counted on to finance a supposedly nonpartisan group? With rivals breathing down their necks, Kitchel and the others might not have time to wait for those monies to trickle in. From where would the remaining $150,000 come?

Kitchel knew exactly where the money was stashed: in the treasury of the Citizens for Goldwater-Miller. More than $300,000 remained tucked away, inaccessible to the RNC, and only Goldwater and Miller could determine where the money went. Goldwater complied with Kitchel's wishes and told the trust's executors about "the need of some central committee or group to control and formulate the efforts of the many conservative organizations now springing up in the country."[17] Goldwater asked that a check for $150,000 be sent to FSA as soon as possible. "I realize these funds were raised for Goldwater-Miller," said the former candidate, "but they are not going to do anybody any good just sitting in a bank, and we have work to be done." If the money belonged to the citizen committee, however, what prevented Goldwater from simply giving it to various Republican groups or committees? Somehow Goldwater seemed to have the impression that the FSA was not like competing conservative groups. More likely, however, Goldwater was taking aim at his party, which now shunned him in the aftermath of the November devastation.

The Free Society Association was one of the more curious conservative groups to spring up after 1964. Lasting just over four years FSA helped transform citizen-based organizations, which relied on a combination of activism and lobbying, into a two-tiered structure, with organizations resembling ACA rather than the JBS on top and groups devoted to specific causes, which relied upon grassroots activism, directly below. In many ways FSA was an attempt to breed the broad-based citizen movement, pioneered in the Goldwater campaign, with its immediate predecessor, the eastern Republican establishment, a culture composed of insiders and big donors.

Chartered quickly, FSA purported to have three distinct purposes. The first was to teach the nation about the principles upon which "our constitutional republic and free society were founded," to solve problems using these principles, and to distinguish between a free society and "the creeds of 'extremist' groups whose basic and laudable purpose may be the preaching of anti-communism but whose hallmark . . . is irresponsible leadership and untenable positions."[18] Kitchel needed to be clear about distinguishing FSA from extremist groups; not only had his brief membership in the JBS recently come to light, but using such phrases as "constitutional republic" to describe the United States put FSA uncomfortably close to extremists like the JBS, which was fond of telling Americans, "It's a Republic Not a Democracy—Let's Keep It that Way!" FSA's second purpose was to provide a "nonpartisan haven" for those who agreed with its principles but did not want to "misguidedly channel their interests and energies into the many 'extremist' organizations now aggressively seeking new members." Finally FSA hoped to "provide leadership and direction for action at the community level . . . in the form of educational, discussion, and study groups."

That FSA paid so much attention to heading off possible attempts at diverting Republicans into third-party efforts or extremist groups made it as much defensive as offensive. Although Kitchel and his colleagues chose the name "because it offers both a timely antithesis to the highly publicized and socialized 'Great Society' and a timeless identification with the overriding objective of true conservatism," on the surface FSA seemed most concerned with holding the movement together long enough to get to 1966 or 1968, when another election might reunite the masses.[19]

Once FSA had received its seed money, Kitchel and Goldwater went on the stump to promote their creation around the country. In a speech before the Southern California Republican Women in Los Angeles, Kitchel showed off tactics that many conservative groups would employ in the coming years. Asking rhetorically why they had gathered on that day, Kitchel described "a strange virus [that] is eroding the moral and political strength of the United States of America and threatening to destroy the institutions which have made it the greatest and the freest nation in the history of the world."[20] The source of the virus, said Kitchel, was the radical Left and its host of associated movements, which sought "to remold American society. They aim toward mass control of a mass society—not individual freedom in a free society."

The destruction had begun, and it was now up to those Americans who believed in a free society and traditional conservative principles to halt the downward spiral before it was too late. But how could an individual do anything in the face of rioting students or burning ghettos? That is where FSA stepped in. As Kitchel boasted, "The Free Society is a non-partisan crusade for political education. It is not a political action group. It is not an arm of the Republican Party, or of any other party. It will not endorse political candidates. It will not participate in political campaigns." In effect FSA was billed as a no-risk proposition, which particularly appealed to groups like the Republican Women. FSA was not about writing letters, marching, electing its members to school boards, or canvassing neighborhoods to support a conservative candidate. Instead, by reading the group's literature, sending in one's dues, and simply *thinking* along the same lines as others in FSA, a "grassroots organization designed solely to inform millions of Americans of the basic facts concerning the great political issues of the day" would congeal. In this respect Kitchel was far ahead of his time, deemphasizing political action as defined by the Goldwater campaign. Moreover, unlike the GOP, Kitchel was not afraid to trot out Goldwater as the group's honorary chairman, a man who personified "the principles of the free society for millions of Americans." Kitchel predicted that within the coming year FSA's roster would be several hundred thousand names long and in a few years would comprise millions.

From the outset Republican reaction to FSA was hostile. Newly appointed RNC Chairman Ray Bliss already had enough trouble trying to rebuild the party, and adding an unknown ingredient into the mix could spoil all of the remedial work done until that point. Fearing that FSA was focused on the 1968 presidential race, Bliss thought it would siphon off contributions, put money out of reach for the 1966 congressional elections, and thus possibly sink the GOP even further.[21] In late August 1965 the Republican Coordinating Committee held a closed-door session to discuss what to do about the splinter groups. Attended by Eisenhower, Goldwater, Bliss, and other top Republicans, the meeting raised no one's confidence about the party. Symbolically Goldwater left the meeting before the discussion turned to the role of groups like FSA.[22]

Many conservatives had trouble placing FSA within the conservative framework constructed during the previous two years. While not an extension of the GOP, the FSA was also not in league with the JBS or similar groups. But Kitchel and Goldwater did not inspire confidence among some conservative leaders. Russell Kirk helped lead the attack against FSA. Kitchel and his cronies, wrote Kirk in his nationally syndicated column, "appear to have justified a paraphrase of Madame Nhu's bon mot: 'If you have Goldwater's staff for your friends, you don't need any enemies.'"[23] Alluding to Kitchel's inability to manage grassroots conservatism, Kirk implied that the Arizonan would be no more likely to work effectively with the members of his group than with the millions of Americans who had wanted Goldwater to win. Of course some of Kirk's antipathy was on behalf of the *National Review* circle, which had helped draft the senator, only to be frozen out once the formal declaration was made.[24] Kirk's paraphrase of Madame Nhu, however, could also be reversed and applied to the relationship between FSA and the rest of the conservative movement; with fellow conservatives like Kirk and Bliss, FSA would never lack for enemies.[25]

Taking the offensive, the FSA tried to counter the criticism that greeted its founding. Kitchel worked the press and fed stories to reporters that emphasized how as a nonpartisan educational group the FSA differed from the GOP. The implication was that if the Republicans behaved well, the support of the FSA constituency would wash over them like a cleansing rain. Besides giving speeches Kitchel and the other officers appeared on talk shows to promote the association as an up-and-coming group that served the conservative cause. Not long after the group's founding, Lynn Mote, FSA's executive director, appeared on "Washington Viewpoint," an opportunity worth its weight in gold. When asked if the entire coalition from 1964 was targeted for FSA membership, Mote replied, "I don't want to call them extremists—but people of very extreme conviction of the '64 election might prefer something more of an activist nature than we see ourselves in the Free Society Association."[26] Mote detailed some of the group's projects, such as what framers of the Constitution meant at the time the Federalist Papers were written, and also tried to tackle the question on everyone's mind: if 1964 showed the strength of a conservative coalition, and those bonds had now started to tear apart, how would FSA recruit new workers for the struggle? Mote was optimistic but nebulous:

> We hope that if we can inform 100,000 or 500,000 people, or possibly a million at some time, in a little more depth in some of the important legislative problems and public policy problems of the day—they can then be pretty good missionaries for an intelligent and sound conservative point of view, and we know, of course that widespread membership that is well informed can do much more to identify and convince people along conservative lines.[27]

Mote sought to create a critical mass: when enough people talked and thought about conservative principles, a fresh wave of conservatism would sweep over the country, independent of party or association. But Mote's reach exceeded FSA's grasp. For hundreds of thousands of missionaries to spread the word across the United States required more than simply paying dues and receiving newsletters.

Until its demise FSA attempted to carry out its programmatic plan, hoping that this, along with continuous membership drives, would help the group reach a self-perpetuating critical mass. Producing as many newsletters and bulletins as possible, the FSA quickly turned out announcements dealing with the 1965 elections, the New Left, and other issues members might find useful in rounding out their conservative educations.[28] It did not take long, however, before liberal Republicans began charging that the FSA analysis was shortsighted and factually incorrect. Caught up in the same battle that had raged since early 1964, Kitchel and the others did little to mend fences.

As the years passed and FSA became more comfortable as a disseminator of information, it also began making policy recommendations. In late 1966, for example, the group produced a set of guidelines for television coverage of elections and urged that networks refrain from announcing winners until the results were actually tallied.[29] FSA also undertook political surveys to help determine how it framed its material and its relationship to the GOP. One survey of five southeastern states, for example, detailed "a trend away from Johnson . . . due mainly to excess Federal spending, centralization of authority in Washington, and the handling of the Viet Nam situation."[30] Birchers, the survey reported, "no longer consider themselves members of the Republican Party," and third-party movements were in the works in a number of areas.

Still FSA edged toward trouble. One of the earliest series of accusations against the group labeled it "excessively rigid," as the post-1964 political arena demanded a more flexible approach and inclusion of moderates. Kitchel tried to refute the charges by saying that FSA was not a Goldwaterite party but rather an attempt at "a new 'climate of thought' whose effect would be to move the whole national spectrum toward the right."[31] But even as Kitchel assured reporters that FSA welcomed all conservative viewpoints, he seemed unwilling to compromise his vision of how the country would look once a few million FSAers began voicing their opinions in kaffeeklatsches or voting booths. By recentering Americans' notions about politics, what to expect from their government, and what to expect from each other, Kitchel's revolution was more of the mind than of the streets. If his ideas were labeled "rigid," then he would have to suffer under the misnomer; what would take FSA from fledgling group to trendsetter would not be a middle-of-the-road ideology. But such thinking only served to worsen the problems and made the association's primary function—recruiting—difficult and, at times, impossible.

Like many organizations in the post-Goldwater era FSA initially went through a membership boom-and-bust cycle. Kitchel and Goldwater had hoped that it could snatch up a few hundred thousand of the 27 million in its first year, but it fell dramatically short of that goal. After FSA's first six months the organization had made virtually no inroads into the conservative constituency and had drawn its members only from areas like southern California, Chicago, and the

New York metropolitan area—places primed by Goldwater and Buckley. All of California, for example, had barely 7,000 members, with more than half residing in Los Angeles County.[32] Kitchel and his colleagues had not figured out how to penetrate those areas of the country that did not already have an active conservative community. A year after its founding FSA's roster had topped out at 40,000—a significant improvement over its first six months but still below the projections used to sell the group to prospective members and donors. And FSA discovered lagging membership meant lagging income, although it claimed that within the first year it had amassed $500,000, usually failing to tell reporters (and members) that almost half of that had come from two sources. In public FSA kept a stiff upper lip and reported that newsletters were going out to 60–75,000 individuals per month, with another 5,000 going to libraries and other public reading rooms.[33] But without better fundraising and a more lucid purpose, FSA seemed destined for the organizational dustbin.

While FSA had a fundraising operation that rivaled any conservative group, it also found itself caught in a Darwinian struggle in which only the top few organizations would do more than simply survive. Within a few months of its founding, FSA faced tough competition in the direct-mail arena. Since most conservative groups relied upon lists rented from either direct-mail innovator Richard Viguerie or competing groups, too many mailings in too short a time made all of the solicitations ineffective. By late August 1965, for example, FSA got word that the American Conservative Union had used a Goldwater for President list and had hit the jackpot, raking in almost $36 per contribution, a staggering amount for any direct-mail solicitation. After such a success, FSA heard, the ACU was eager to start a new list based on a Republican National Committee solicitation. To compete, mused one FSA official, a mailing of a half million names might do the trick.[34] Sending out waves of 500,000 letters was neither cheap nor accurate in targeting the conservatives who Kitchel anticipated would comprise the backbone of FSA. But he could not afford such luxuries; in the scramble for money, the slowest usually lost.

Over the next three years FSA never let up in its quest to recruit new members or bring in funds. Two days after Christmas 1965 Ron Crawford, head of membership services, proposed another mass mailing to a wide range of lists:

> 15,000 Fulton Lewis, Jr., Mailing List; 10,000 Conservative Book Club Expires [lapsed purchasers]; 75,000 Conservative Book Club Buyers; 33,000 Illinois for Goldwater; 65,000 New York Conservative Party; and approximately 15,000 initial mailings on the RNC list ($50 and less) to Connecticut, Colorado, and Delaware, which were missed on the original mailing. Sometime this month we also plan to mail the 200,000 testing from Krupp's in Los Angeles.[35]

But if Kitchel had promised to separate his group from extremist organizations, the decision to mail to supporters of Fulton Lewis, Jr., would do little to further that goal. Moreover mailing to Conservative Book Club readers, Goldwater supporters, New York Conservative party members, and the like also ensured that some of those who became members would not receive clean bills of health were their principles to be inspected. But the prospects of an instant windfall were hard to resist.

Even the presence of hundreds of thousands of potential contributors did not solve FSA's two problems: how to recruit new conservative blood and how to find a niche among the half dozen or so conservative groups that had sprung up since 1964. Faced with competition from the ACA, the American Conservative Union (ACU), and Young Americans for Freedom (YAF), FSA soon found itself trailing in the race to head up the movement. Kitchel and the others seemed reluctant to pursue their own message; not wanting to cave into the one solution that might possibly save the group—direct action at the community level—they focused on raising money and refused to admit that they were a group without a clear identity or purpose.

The end came quickly for FSA. Kitchel's projected 1968 budget included a fund for publications but little else. By June 1969 association members received a letter informing them that "we are closing up shop."[36] Why did FSA fail to carry the conservative movement forward into the next era? The most obvious answer—its lack of any kind of grassroots program—tells only part of the story. Some conservative groups promoted their causes successfully without relying on JBS-style rallies, meetings, and direct actions, which suggests that FSA's failure was more complicated. Even without the movement culture relied upon by conservative groups during the first half of the decade, the leaders of FSA never considered that members would *want* to do more than read what spewed out of the Washington office. FSA's terrible relationship with the GOP further damaged its chances at becoming the sole group responsible for educating conservatives about contemporary issues.

Without some sort of campaign, theory (even as extreme as Welch's conspiracy), or larger purpose, FSA floundered, never clear how it fit into the post-Goldwater movement.[37] Ironically FSA most closely fit the mold of a pre-1964 eastern Republican group, where letterhead titles, the amount of money raised, and the cocktail party guest list were the benchmarks of success. Finally the leaders of FSA never seemed to have in their hearts the devotion necessary to make such a project come to fruition. They recruited 40,000 members with little effort, but those people joined for reasons at odds with Kitchel's original purpose; their impetus came more from the past, from Goldwater, than from the future. If ACA and FSA were not the organizations to lead the movement into the next decade, some other group would need to bridge the two eras.

Adjunct: American Conservative Union

In late 1960 Marvin Liebman, the well-connected conservative public relations operator, sent a memo to a number of conservative leaders around the country and proposed the founding of Americans for Conservative Action (different from the ACA discussed earlier), a counterpart to the ADA. Nothing came of the effort as conservatives like Goldwater argued that the election of conservatives to Republican seats was the more important goal for the movement.[38] Liebman filed the proposal, in case it might come in handy in the future. Four years later, less than a week after Goldwater had gone down to a crashing defeat, Liebman dug out his original plan and sent it to Robert Bauman, chairman of Young Americans for Freedom, a group Liebman had helped found in 1960. While much of the document was outdated, said Liebman, "The balance of the material might be worth exploring in terms of our proposed new operation."[39]

It was natural, then, that Liebman would propose a group that might take the reins and lead conservatives out of the desolation of 1964. Deciding not to revive Americans for Conservative Action in its original form, Liebman settled on the name American Conservative Union (ACU), since:

> I believe this name has the ring of permanence, whereas the use of the word "committee" leaves the impression of an organization of temporary nature.
>
> I believe it is the closest we can come to the A.D.A. without being repetitive of existing conservative organizations.
>
> The name of the organization should include the word "conservative" for philosophical reasons and for very practical financial reasons.[40]

Unlike Kitchel, who named the Free Society Association without pondering how it would fit into the range of already-existing conservative organizations, Liebman's plan helped establish his group as part of the larger movement and plugged a gaping hole in the tenuous dike.

Liebman proposed three general goals for the ACU. "Unification of the Conservative Movement" would be accomplished through coordinating conservative leadership, developing a new structure "willing to speak and act in terms easily understood and generally acceptable to the public," and cultivating a "'leadership cadre' rather than a mass group."[41] Liebman's second goal focused on "responsible political action," or infiltrating and recruiting from both parties to develop a congressional constituency, induct a "reliable membership of limited numbers in all fifty states," and eventually influence elections on all levels. Finally Liebman hoped to shape public opinion by using many of the same methods outlined in the first two objectives: starting publications, issuing press releases, creating a speakers' bureau, holding conferences, and even making formal attempts to change the media's opinion of conservatism, a daunting task in November 1964.

Exactly one month after Goldwater had lost Liebman and Bauman had the legal papers drawn up for the founding of the ACU. The following day Liebman wired a number of conservative leaders across the country and invited them "to meet in Washington to discuss the organization of the American Conservative Union." Just as Kitchel had hoped that FSA could head off extremist groups before they filled the leadership vacuum, Liebman said the same without being explicit: "We believe that there is a vital need for such an organization at this particular juncture of American history. There are literally millions of American citizens who seek conservative leadership in the months and years ahead."[42] But the fact that defeating extremism was not one of the group's long-term goals, but only a subtext, meant that its purpose was larger than simply fighting the Robert Welches and Kent Courtneys of America.

Two weeks later eight men and one woman gathered at the Statler-Hilton Hotel in Washington to launch the operation. Congressman Donald C. Bruce of Indiana was elected chairman, Congressman John Ashbrook of Ohio vice chairman, Robert Bauman became secretary, and Frank S. Meyer, *National Review* editor and writer, became treasurer. Advisory panels, like the Committee on Political Action, led by William Rusher, and the Committee on Arts and Sciences, led by author John Dos Passos, helped flesh out the ACU's programmatic agenda.[43] Directly linking the GOP to the ACU at the highest level by having two young but respected conservative congressmen take the helm paid further dividends. Recruiting Bauman from YAF meant that not only would former YAFers feel comfortable with a familiar name in a leadership position, but that many of YAF's tactics, techniques, and contacts would travel to the new group. The inclusion of *National Review* staffer Meyer (and the invitation to William F. Buckley, who attended the founding meetings and was elected as a director) ensured that those previously frozen out of conservative activist politics due to the control of the Goldwater campaign by the Arizona Mafia would be reintegrated under the auspices of the ACU.

The most significant action taken at the founding meeting concerned the ACU's relationship with the John Birch Society. Buckley proposed that no one in a leadership position at the JBS be permitted to join the ACU's board of directors, the advisory assembly, or as an associate. Both Buckley and Bauman thought such a policy was best kept confidential, that the discussion be excised from the minutes (except from the original copy), and that a public statement detail the relationship between the two groups. While no single author took credit for the statement, it sounded suspiciously like Buckley's doing:

> The question inevitably arises, What is the relation between the American Conservative Union and the John Birch Society? The answer is: There is no relation between the two organizations. The directors of the ACU take a view of world affairs substantially at variance with that taken by

Mr. Robert Welch in his most publicized writings. Under the circumstances, the leadership of the ACU will be wholly distinct from that of the John Birch Society.[44]

Refusing to condemn the JBS rank and file, ACU leaders at least hoped to distinguish themselves from Welch and his brain trust. Under Liebman's tutelage the ACU refined its goals and clarified its major purposes in preparation for going public. In the race among conservative groups, the ACU showed a great deal of promise as it entered the starting blocks.

Less than one month later, however, *National Review* publisher William Rusher wrote to Buckley, "The ACU is not in good shape at all." First, said Rusher, Congressman Donald Bruce, the chairman, was adamant that he would not work with Robert Bauman, who had left his post at YAF to come to the ACU. Rusher thought, "This may be dismissed as simply a personality clash, and perhaps surmounted, but I am afraid it reveals, instead, a very deep fissure in Bruce's personality."[45] Bruce was reluctant to delegate power to anyone smarter than himself, thought Rusher, and others on the board agreed. "If I am correct," mused Rusher, "then the ACU is doomed from the outset to administrative and executive mediocrity." Next the financing "is just barely trickling in." Big donors were cautiously waiting to see if the group would get on its feet, not realizing that their money would help make that possible. Henry Salvatori, one of Reagan's strongest backers in the California gubernatorial race, "does not consider that he ever made a firm pledge of $50,000." Finally, and perhaps most significant, Rusher reported that when Goldwater was informed about the ACU, he apparently replied, "Oh, yes. You know I tried to stop that. But it won't get far. That's the *National Review* crowd—you know: Frank Meyer, Bill Rusher. When I listen to those guys I start looking under the bed."

Six weeks later William J. Gill, a close friend of Clif White, wrote to Don Bruce to recommend a structural change:

My own feeling is that you have to build from the grassroots up. Coordination from Washington is fine (God knows we need it!) but I think you are going to have to give people at the precinct level a little more to hang onto than a membership card and a note of thanks for their financial contribution. They must have something to *do*, besides write checks.[46]

Gill had put his finger on the fundamental problem for conservative groups in the post-Goldwater era: where would the balance lie between grassroots activism and top-down organizing? Like FSA, the ACU would have to confront the fact that the norm for conservative groups in 1965 was based on the political culture of 1964, a model rooted in the JBS and other extremist organizations.

Gill was not the only one to point out the origins of the quandary in which the ACU found itself mired. Neil McCaffrey, a young staffer at *National Review*, wrote to his colleagues associated with the ACU to warn them of the group's looming problems. Agreeing with Gill, McCaffrey thought that now that the JBS was on the decline, the ACU was a natural to move in and replace extremist activism with responsible activism. McCaffrey suggested that the ACU begin bonding with PTAs, women's clubs, and Republican clubs. "Give them a conservative organization that moves (like the Draft-Goldwater Movement)," said McCaffrey, "and you will find that this wins more converts than a thousand attacks on the Birchers."[47] But McCaffrey's urgings did not answer the fundamental question haunting the ACU: did it want to be an activist group?

The ACU's troubles quickly worsened. In October 1965 Chairman Bruce resigned when he disagreed with the board of directors over whether he could speak at a We, the People! rally in Chicago. The gathering, sponsored by such extremists as Kent Courtney, was exactly the kind of event the ACU hoped to avoid, and now its leader wanted, in effect, to join the enemy.[48] Although the press did not immediately pick up on the strife raging within the ACU, by early 1966 the group's problems were public knowledge, and everything from Bruce's ouster to the resignation of several founders and staff members to the serious fundraising problems threatening the group's very existence all damaged the ACU's public image.[49]

Unlike FSA, which seemed to wallow in its problems and to offer few alternatives to check its rapid downward spiral, the ACU quickly began examining solutions to the wide range of challenges it now encountered. Buckley urged his fellow board members to take an inventory of the organization and its achievements to date. "How many in-depth projects have been completed?" inquired Buckley. How was the ACU dealing with affiliate organizations? What kind of an impact had it made in Congress? And how had the ACU performed in regards to the money it had spent so far?[50] William Rusher implored *National Review* to play up the ACU in the coming months, particularly in light of the ongoing controversy raging between the JBS and the magazine. As the JBS declined, further expanding the leadership vacuum, Rusher did not think that the ACU could entirely fill the void left by the JBS:

> I most emphatically do not encourage you to assume that we can (or that we should) best Robert Welch at his own game. The ACU will probably not amass a membership as large as that of the John Birch Society; certainly it won't command anything like the same financial resources. . . . But, provided you do not set your sights impossibly high, I think the ACU may reasonably hope to serve as a substitute medium of effective action of the salvageable members of the John Birch Society.[51]

The ACU's first action to stave off what seemed like imminent collapse was to boost its fundraising efforts. Liebman proposed that Richard Viguerie take over fundraising entirely for the ACU. But even with Viguerie on its side, the

ACU needed to develop a more cohesive program to balance its books. Although it was one of the top half dozen organizations (based on the prestige of its leadership alone), for it to survive it needed to search for alternatives to direct mail. Following the strategy of a political campaign—particularly one designed by Clif White—Liebman wanted to name state finance chairmen in all fifty states and establish annual quotas to decentralize some of the heavy burden. With the goal of raising $10,000 each month, the plan also included a series of dinners that, at $100 a plate, might bring in $20,000 each month, as well as a new effort to affiliate conservative groups with the ACU to boost membership, which might possibly rake in another $1,000 each month. Direct mail would eke out another $60,000 annually, while "special projects" like producing rental films might match the direct-mail revenues. The prospective total of $41,000 each month must have seemed outrageous to some board members; for the troubled organization suddenly to begin pulling in tens of thousands of dollars after barely remaining viable smacked of the hubris that had led to the downfall of more than one conservative group.[52]

But even with the proposals urging the ACU to turn to alternative fundraising methods, its leaders fell back on what they knew best: direct-mail solicitation. By May 1965 Liebman had recommended a test mailing of 50,000 letters to a range of constituencies, from the *National Review* prospect list, to the Conservative Book Club list, to the Republican donors list.[53] By September the first returns showed promising results. Some lists averaged as high as $13 per contribution, which signified a constituency willing to give if approached properly. Unfortunately the sheer number of responses was depressingly low; less than 1% of the solicitations garnered responses, and often the rate was even lower.[54] After sending nearly 50,000 pieces of mail, the ACU had raised little more than $5,000, a poor showing for one of the supposed leaders of the movement. But Liebman knew that the group needed to gain momentum before it could expect big payoffs, and so he urged David Jones to rent Viguerie's 300,000-name list for a massive blanketing of the national conservative community.[55] Whether Liebman's confidence was well placed or whether the ACU simply caught the lucky end of a developing trend, repeated direct mailings helped the group turn the corner and begin to stabilize its finances. In 1967 four "outside" (non-ACU-generated) lists grossed $80,000 at a cost of some $35,000, and the 1966 membership lists produced $61,000 at the low cost of $8,000.[56] By mid-1967 William Rusher reported to the editors at *National Review* that "the ACU is in by far the best shape of the four so-called 'splinters.'"[57] For leading the organization out of the wilderness, Rusher credited Jones and Ashbrook, as well as a heavy reliance on Young Americans for Freedom alumni. As Rusher explained, "Sophisticated conservatives now turning the corner into their thirties, who don't want to, and in any case can't, play college politics forever" were joining the ACU and forming "a valuable, NR-oriented reservoir of talent."[58] Tying the ACU to

YAF might make a kind of postcollege conservative fraternity, one more step in creating the "conservative establishment."

Whether the ACU would emerge as the movement's lead organization depended as much on its relationship with fellow conservative groups as on its own inner workings. The FSA, ACA, and the ACU all acted cordially toward each other, never openly challenging each other's leadership or programmatic agenda. After FSA's formation in mid-June 1965, the ACU issued a press release welcoming Goldwater and Kitchel to the arena. ACU Chairman Donald Bruce wanted Kitchel to discuss what it would mean for FSA to work in the same field as the ACU: "It has been apparent to me that there will be attempts to drive a wedge between ACU and the Free Society Association. You can be assured I will do everything within my power to prevent this from happening."[59] Kitchel, however, tried to keep close tabs on the ACU and monitored that group's early problems even as his own organization slipped toward the precipice.[60] In August 1966 Goldwater issued a press release touting, "Four Major Conservative Organizations to Cooperate and Coordinate." ACA, ACU, FSA, and YAF, said the release, would "for the first time closely coordinate their work to avoid duplication and to make all of their individual efforts more effective." Apparently Goldwater called the meeting, held at his Washington apartment, in order "to bring the leading conservative organizations together to talk about cooperation and coordination that is long overdue but has been largely overlooked."[61] Even if such a meeting took place, however, little came of the senator's efforts.

It did not take long, though, before the word was out that the ACU could be trusted to bring the movement closer together rather than wrenching it further apart. For example, Walter Judd, a Republican congressman from Minnesota, told a constituent, "I certainly agree with your desire that [the ACU] be a means of unifying rather than of multiplying conservative organizations."[62] Internally the ACU constantly assessed its leadership capabilities and tried to figure out, as David Jones described, how best to "place the ACU in its proper role at the vanguard of the American Conservative Movement."[63] Not known for their self-criticism or ability to accept recommendations to change their ways, the ACU's fresh attitude represented a major shift in how conservative groups would be run in the future.

If the ACU wanted to lead the movement into the next decade, it needed to distinguish its programs—both to inspire political action and to generate movement culture—from the myriad of other groups operating on the same band width. Like other groups the ACU's first order of business was self-promotion, and it produced dozens of pamphlets, bulletins, and newsletters describing its principles and goals. One, entitled "Get on Target with the ACU!" described the battle between the Right and Left for "the uncommitted." Whichever side could attract the undecided voter would control the entire political arena, while the losing side ended up with nothing: "Success or failure lies in influencing the majority—the uncommitted. For too long conservatives have aimed their arrows and ideas only at each other."[64] The monthly newsletter, *Battle Line*, contained sections on presidential politics, Congress, "party machinery," leading names in the GOP, and state politics. Much more professional in appearance than, say, FSA's newsletter or even Welch's JBS *Bulletin*, the multiple references to the GOP made the ACU more like an adjunct of the party than an independent group.

Where the ACU did run into problems was, not surprisingly, in deciding what it would *do*. As chairman of the Political Action Committee, William Rusher had to decide how to allot the group's human resources. Less than three weeks after his appointment a woman from Saugerties, New York, inquired whether the ACU was prepared to take over the task of coordinating the hundreds of local conservative groups, each with often just a handful of people, in order to prevent "the vast numbers of conservatives who worked for Goldwater-Miller" from becoming "discouraged and scattered through neglect."[65] Moreover, for all of the hoopla generated in the wake of the founding, the group had only 6,526 members.[66] Clearly something was lacking in the ACU's presentation.

Rusher and the others sought to distinguish the ACU from competing groups by carving out a niche where its unique programs would reflect the body's founding principles. One suggestion involved hiring Fulton Lewis III, a well-known extremist, to produce a film called *Operation Insurrection*, a graphic look at the communist-inspired rioting that was taking place with alarming frequency in black ghettos. Borrowing its title from *Operation Abolition* (which Lewis had narrated and edited), *Insurrection* claimed that the riots were not the fault of the indigenous blacks, but because they were pushed to the breaking point by outside agitators they essentially had no choice but to lash out in anger.[67] Curiously this theory was no different than that of Robert Welch about communists inspiring the civil rights movement in the South. But after Donald Bruce, Frank Meyer, and Rusher viewed some of the initial footage, Meyer urged that the film not be released until the script was revised.[68] Such attempts at creating a movement culture rang hollow since they supported no greater cause. Unlike a political campaign where a film supported a candidate, trying to sell ideology on its own was nearly impossible, and the ACU did not make it clear how an individual member would effect change through participation in a larger group. The more the ACU struggled with fundraising and recruitment, the more it seemed to have made the wrong decision regarding its corporate structure.

Over the next four years the ACU increasingly borrowed tactics that echoed pre-1965 activist groups, although it never fully made the transition into a political action group. By 1966 the ACU had developed a "political action" program, complete with kits to help set up local chapters. With topics in the main handbook like "Putting Your Team Together," "Opening the Door," "A Systematic Approach to Victory," and "Fund Raising," the ACU's decision to entertain direct action allowed it to blend Birch and ACA tactics.[69] The new approach to field work boosted the entire organization's morale; now, with chapters appearing across the country, a sense of belonging—so crucial to creating a political movement greater than a collection of individuals with a common interest—slowly emerged and with it pride in an expanding membership.

By mid-1967 the ACU had incorporated an activist component into its overall program, although compared to the JBS or YAF it erred on the cautious side. Perhaps due to its goal of developing a "leadership cadre" rather than a mass movement, the ACU was particular about who joined its Political Action Program. Instead of holding open information sessions in community centers or in a member's home, like the JBS, or recruiting at political rallies (or college campuses) like YAF, the ACU relied on word of mouth and hoped that trusted members would recommend responsible, upstanding members of their communities (both professional and civic) as potential activists. After a speaking engagement at the University of Oregon in April 1967, for example, Rusher struck up a correspondence with William Moomau, a conservative with connections to YAF, the Young Republicans, and the ACU. Moomau recommended J. David Hosfield as a potential leader to launch the ACU in Oregon. Hosfield, said Moomau, was an architect in Eugene who "reads *National Review* and *Human Events*. He has never been a member of the John Birch Society so far as I have been able to determine. . . . Mr. Hosfield is in his early 30's and a member of the Lane County Young Republicans."[70] Though Rusher did not bring Hosfield on board, he continued to scour the state for leaders and by early 1969 was asking his friends, "Now that the election is over, I wonder if this is an appropriate moment to raise with you afresh the question of chartering a state chapter of the American Conservative Union in Oregon."[71]

As the ACU stabilized its membership, income, and programs, it took on the air of a more established organization. The group produced a series of reports and studies, including *The ADA Report* (1967), *The Democratic Margin of Victory (DMV) Report* (1967), which described how the Democrats won elections by swinging the undecided over only for elections, *The COPE (Committee on Political Education) Report* (1967), and *The GRI (Group Research Incorporated) Report* (1968), which sought to expose GRI, a left-wing research association, as a fraud. By 1970 the group was openly criticizing Richard Nixon, particularly for his handling of Vietnam and welfare. Just before Nixon's new welfare plan came up for congressional debate, the ACU issued "The Nixon Welfare Plan . . . Solution or Socialism?" a twenty-five-page analysis that urged members of Congress to fight its implementation:

> The Nixon program, despite its doubtless sincere intentions, will in the long run greatly exacerbate the "welfare mess" for three basic reasons:

1) It makes welfare more comfortable when it should be made less comfortable.

2) By moving toward a guaranteed income, it makes welfare more respectable, more of a "right" when it should be made less respectable, less of a "right."

3) It drastically increases the number of recipients, thus risking corrupting 12 million more American citizens, when desperate efforts ought to be made to decrease the number of persons receiving unearned checks from government.[72]

Nixon, said the ACU, was moving toward social engineering, trying to guarantee opportunities like attaining a certain income level as rights in and of themselves, when they were in fact not guaranteed at all. After having unanimously endorsed Nixon in 1968, the ACU's turn against him demonstrated its continued independence, even as its connections to the GOP remained tight.

By the late 1960s riots, lawlessness, welfare, Vietnam, national defense, the counterculture, and a general breakdown of morality all received continuous attention through publications and infrequent organized political actions. The ACU was convinced that most Americans were in fact conservative and that, given the right information, they would make the logical choice in politics and in their private lives. By 1969 the group had developed programs to support the Anti-Ballistic Missile System, championed by Nixon to ward off Soviet attacks; instituted a refined system of donating money to various conservative candidates and incumbents, which mimicked the ACA agenda; and had even begun investigating such issues as the voucher system to finance schools, after it appeared that the Supreme Court decision to strike down prayer in schools would not be overturned by a constitutional amendment. To further its efforts toward financing conservative candidates, in 1969 the ACU set up the Conservative Victory Fund (CVF), an offshoot that focused solely on researching candidates' positions and allotting monies to a variety of local and state politicians. By October 8, 1970, the CVF had accumulated $99,000.[73] One year later, through direct mail, the CVF had raised some $400,000 at a cost of $240,000, with the profit handed over to candidates.[74]

By the mid-1970s the ACU had incorporated a tax-exempt foundation called the ACU Education and Research Foundation, which financed the National Journalism Center, an institute run by M. Stanton Evans to train conservative journalists to take their places in the liberal establishment. The group also established the American Legislative Exchange Council, a body focused on state legislatures.[75] Now that the ACU was dug in, it tried to bring other conservatives around to its moderate political activism. In 1975, for example, Liebman suggested that perhaps the ACU might get a number of conservative leaders

to sign a single fundraising letter, thus making "the ACU seem like *the* reposi-
tory of Conservative wisdom and wit, over and above internal political battles."
Liebman's recommended leaders included Goldwater, Ashbrook, James Buckley
(New York senator and William's brother), Jesse Helms, Reagan, Strom Thurmond,
and even George Wallace.[76] The ACU also learned how to choose its battles;
even if it won only a few, those it picked were often closest to conservative
Americans' hearts. Virtually every conservative group after 1975 fought to save
the Panama Canal from being turned over to the Panamanians in 2000. To do
its part the ACU produced a half-hour documentary on the canal, which it tele-
vised accompanied by a toll-free number that viewers could call to pledge contributions to the ACU. The documentary brought remarkable results. In five
months the ACU received 58,000 pledges at an average of $14.41, a yield of
between $550,000 and $626,000 in total expected income. The campaign was
not cheap, costing nearly $400,000, most of that in air time, and the treaty was
still ratified in 1978. But the net profit was still almost $250,000, not bad for a
five-month effort, and the names generated by the campaign could be used over
and over in the future.[77] William Rusher later recalled that fundraiser Richard
Viguerie said that nearly a half million voters had had their names added to his
lists as a result of the Panama Canal controversy, a crucial resource that could
be tapped in 1980.[78]

The ACU succeeded where others failed for a number of reasons. First it
managed to find a workable middle ground between grassroots politicking and
centrally organized fundraising and lobbying. Although the ACU's Political Action Program was never effective, its existence helped members feel connected
to a movement and not just an ACA-like group that collected and redistributed
funds. Second the ACU realized, unlike ACA or FSA, that it needed the support of key Republican figures were it to navigate the fine line between acting
independently and pushing the GOP toward the right. By including John Ashbrook, Donald Bruce, and Peter O'Donnell, among others, the ACU remained
cognizant that without the party their work would probably amount to naught.
Third, linking GOP and *National Review* personnel, the ACU planners realized,
could help unify the movement after the fractious events of 1964. With the influential support of Buckley, Rusher, Meyer, Liebman, and others, the ACU
knew that it could win the conservative intellectuals over to methods that would
bring victory. Fourth, unlike FSA, which was slow to respond to difficulties and
failed to recalibrate its objectives, the ACU, although hesitantly at first, rethought
its strategies in light of the disappointing results of 1965–1966. With the help of
a rejuvenated direct-mail campaign, the ousting of Donald Bruce, and the beginning of a pseudograssroots political wing, the organization performed at a level
that satisfied both the directors and members. Fifth, the ACU branched out and
added the CVF and other spinoffs in order to remain viable and flexible into the
next decade. These operations showed members and potential members that

the ACU would be around even after its goals had been met. Sixth the ACU filled a niche by taking conservatives who had "graduated" from groups like YAF or smaller, defunct organizations and giving them a political home separate from the GOP. By continuing to train conservatives to capture power, the ACU carried on the work of the Goldwater movement, although now it concentrated on neither a specific candidate nor an ideology but on a set of universally applicable principles. The ACU succeeded where others failed because its design deliberately pulled the remnants of the Goldwater-era movement into the post-1965 period; it realized that new strategies and tactics were necessary to initiate the renaissance. Even after periodic mistakes the ACU emerged as the responsible independent conservative group of the late 1960s and 1970s.

Leading Edge: Young Americans for Freedom

In the September 3, 1960, *National Review Bulletin*, a small announcement asked college students from around the country to meet

> to establish a continuing youth organization dedicated to the achievement of political objectives. The conference will be held in Sharon, Connecticut. . . . Weekend expenses (including bus fare and hotel rooms) will be about $16.00. Meals will be gratis.[79]

In addition to the advertisement, known conservative college activists received invitations. From September 9 to 11 approximately one hundred students from forty-four colleges across the country met at Great Elm, the palatial estate of the Buckley family, to draw up a list of goals and strategies for the as-yet-unnamed group. On hearing the new group's name—Young Americans for Freedom (YAF)—William Rusher remarked, "I remember not liking the acronym much—and liking it even less when Liebman . . . became the first to point out that this made the rest of us Old Americans for Freedom, or OAFs."[80]

Before the conference Douglas Caddy, a one-time organizer of the Student Committee for the Loyalty Oath in 1958 and of National Youth for Goldwater for Vice President in 1960, asked M. Stanton Evans, a journalist from Indiana (who later led the ACU's National Journalism Center), to outline a set of ideological maxims for the fledgling youth group.[81] Evans wrote what came to be known, with only minor changes, as the Sharon Statement. The objective of the document, wrote Evans retrospectively, "was to set down as concisely as possible the major themes of American conservatism. . . . In broad terms, the manifesto was meant to embrace both the 'traditionalist' and 'libertarian' schools within the conservative community."[82] When determining the balance between the federal and state powers, the states would retain hegemony wherever possible. The market economy would regulate all human economic needs and wants. Communism posed the most severe threat to America. Finally, foreign policy decisions would be determined by posing the question "Does it serve the just interests of the United States?"[83]

Throughout the 1960s YAF clung fast to its original beliefs and attitudes as embodied in the Sharon Statement. The statement, however, was as important for what was left out as for what Evans and the others included. By deliberately remaining vague about specific goals (other than defeating communism), YAF accommodated the extreme diversity within conservatism, particularly in the volatile world of youth politics. The statement was also forward-looking; similar to Students for a Democratic Society's (SDS) Port Huron Statement of 1962, it described not just how things were but how they could be. Finally the statement avoided any associations with either specific individuals or political parties. At Sharon in 1960 YAF voted against endorsing Nixon for president, since "YAF was less interested in partisan politics than in standing forth for conservative values, and . . . Nixon seemed at best a feeble champion of the conservative cause."[84]

More than the other three splinter groups that worked to influence the GOP and the conservative movement, YAF's focus on youth and its response to a single issue—in its case the New Left—enabled it to carve out a niche in the otherwise crowded world of conservative organizations. Moreover YAF was the exception to the post-1965 rule that grassroots activism was no longer a viable organizing strategy for national conservative groups. Because it tended to concentrate on a specific issue and constituency, YAF recruited using tactics from 1964 and also relied on a movement culture that it lifted almost intact from its enemies on the Left. Like the ACU, which eventually marketed itself as the next stage in a comprehensive conservative training program, YAF took neophytes and schooled them in a blend of extremist tactics and responsible ideologies; it provided an exciting introduction for young people committed to seeing the conservative capture of the White House and Congress.

By 1963 YAF reported a membership of 10,000 on college campuses alone.[85] Although the organization at the national level created relatively few paid positions, the chain of command was as well defined as any burgeoning corporation. As YAF expanded rapidly in the late 1960s, paid positions often doubled or even trebled, growth that eventually forced budget cuts in the early 1970s. In addition a National Advisory Board, made up of such congressmen as Strom Thurmond, conservative luminaries in academia like Ludwig von Mises, and successful businessmen, helped to spread the word and vision of YAF.[86]

An elaborate system of regional conferences, leadership seminars, and state workshops sprang up to heighten and satisfy interest in youth conservatism. Most important, however, were the annual national conventions, which met just before the start of the autumn academic term. A time to connect with others in the movement, the national conventions—which always received widespread press attention—served as perhaps the first formal training ground for YAFers. Delegates lobbied for platform planks, caucused for national board members, and, if the convention was during a presidential election year, argued over the possible endorsement of a YAF standard-bearer.[87] Candidates for the national board campaigned months in advance, produced pamphlets and posters, and garnered endorsements from better-known YAFers. Like so many YAF activities, what ultimately mattered most was the *impression* such pageantry made on the participants, not the actual outcome itself. With a thousand or more YAFers in attendance, listening in rapt attention to conservative heroes (like Strom Thurmond, Barry Goldwater, William F. Buckley, and even John Wayne), caucusing sessions that often lasted late into the night, and plenty of social occasions to mingle with the conservative elite, a national convention was a young conservative's utopia.

What motivated students during the 1960s to join a group that might alienate them from the apparently prevailing political and ideological fashions of their peers? In 1963 sociologist Lawrence Schiff studied what types of college students embraced conservatism, and he observed a "desire to appear as the dutiful son," a chance to achieve upward mobility, and the ability "to justify, in an otherwise youthfully attractive package, a parental obedience streak that is somewhat out of place in our contemporary peer-oriented culture."[88] Schiff offered three perceptive conclusions about YAF. Observing the 1963 national convention, Schiff noted, "The style of the movement . . . was a passive, though frequently enthusiastic, obedience to duly constituted leaders, strict hierarchical social organization and a general dependence on adult figures to provide both programs and direction."[89] Schiff saw not only a docility on the part of the students but a concerted effort by adults to control their charges. Second Schiff believed the movement had no real future; conservative movements "all speak to a largely unrecognized proclivity toward posturing rather than program that constitutes one important quality of the complex current conservative impulse in America."[90] Since YAF preached style over substance, Schiff did not foresee any real conservative momentum. Finally, though unaware of his accuracy, Schiff proposed the theory that much of YAF's appeal was based on "the program's ideological emphasis on *risk-taking* and *romanticization of achievement-oriented behavior*" (Schiff's italics).[91]

Sociologist Richard Braungart found the majority of YAFers were males who "indicated positive attitudes toward high school authorities and [had] pleasant school experiences."[92] YAFers were also more likely than SDS members to have positive relationships with their parents and to practice religion more actively. The families from which YAFers came often had Republican parents, Catholic or Protestant traditions, a less-educated lower- to middle-class working father, and an ethnic background that was more likely to be Northern European than Eastern European.[93] Braungart concluded, "Family political status proved the strongest indicator of student politics, with students adhering to the political status of their parents."[94]

YAFers themselves were quite conscious of their social status particularly when compared to SDS members. They almost seemed to revel in their working-class backgrounds; the more they could define themselves as outside the eastern Establishment, the stronger the underdog spirit and sense of purpose that flowed through the movement. Paradoxically, however, YAF always flaunted its members from such elite schools as Harvard, Yale, and Stanford. Nevertheless YAFers made it a point to differentiate between their own social backgrounds and those of their rivals in SDS:

> At Harvard, Douglas Cooper said simply: "There's a world of difference between the middle-class and the upper middle-class. SDS kids are often the sons and daughters of doctors and lawyers and they harbor real guilt that they are where they are without somehow earning it. We're more blue-collar and middle-class," he said. "We're Staten Island. They're Scarsdale."[95]

The YAF organ, the *New Guard*, read more like a college alumni magazine than a guide to political theory and practice. In sections like "YAF & the Right Scene," members not only read about policy updates and their opponents but also about what their fellow activists were doing both personally and politically ("Lee Buchschalcher has been appointed state chairman in Missouri . . . Tulsa YAF members sponsored an all night vigil on behalf of the POWs. More than 100 attended . . . Wayne Thorburn is honeymooning in New Orleans").[96] Conservative students were not socially vacuous, and the writers and editors at the *New Guard* realized this with ever-increasing clarity. In 1966, for example, a YAFer gave a positive review to Bob Dylan's most recent album, while advertisements for YAF used popular lingo like "YAF a Go Go"—only somewhat facetiously—to gain attention and acceptance.[97]

YAF actions and events, which ranged from rallies in support of anti-Castro Cubans to threatening boycotts against American companies that traded with eastern bloc countries, supported what slowly became a contrived social community. In what was perhaps YAF's biggest media coup ever, Marvin Liebman organized a conservative rally at Madison Square Garden two years before the 1964 presidential election. The *New York Times* accorded it front-page coverage, and periodicals on the Left and Right took notice.[98] The 1962 rally was more than just a gathering to celebrate such personalities as John Tower and Barry Goldwater; in the same way that Populist gatherings of the 1880s contained moments when "a farm family's wagon crested a hill en route to a Fourth of July 'Alliance Day' encampment and the occupants looked back to see thousands of other families trailed out behind them in wagon trains," feelings of unity and hope surely flooded over excited young conservatives as they walked up the ramps into the thundering auditorium.[99]

Between 1965 and 1969 YAF reoriented its programmatic goals to take advantage of developments in both foreign and domestic affairs. More than anything else, the New Left was a public-relations godsend to YAF. Perfect foils for the eager YAFers, SDS and other left-wing groups taught them how to counter liberal arguments and forced them to develop their own positions on the same subjects, necessary skills for any future politico. YAF would always have had an enemy in international communism, but for countless conservative young people, the struggle for America's moral high ground took place not between the forces of Washington and Moscow but between Orange County and Berkeley. In the end what mattered most was whether YAF actions taught members valuable lessons, kept them interested, and perhaps convinced other students to join. And unlike the ACA, FSA, or ACU, YAF addressed race and gender as emerging issues in youth consciousness.

Although blacks never consisted of more than 2%–3% of YAF's total population, YAF was never openly hostile toward any race, ethnicity, or religion. The Sharon Statement's libertarianism theoretically provided for equal treatment of all individuals. It also, however, presented an easy justification for opposing such programs as welfare, Social Security, and affirmative action. Each individual, YAFers claimed, was responsible for his or her own well-being; a statist government could only strip away God-given liberties and rights. Additionally the market economy was the apotheosis of efficiency. Thus programs like welfare and affirmative action promised undeserved advantages based on such arbitrary factors as skin color or gender, and those perquisites, while not only eliminating any reason to work hard would decrease the rights of another citizen in an equal but opposite direction.

Implicit in many YAF publications was the fact that while the New Left might have been "revolting," the radicals were still predominantly white. Groups like the Black Panthers took on added danger for YAFers. In the guise of libertarianism YAF instituted actions like organizing a petition drive to place an initiative on the California ballot to repeal a state law that required "racial quotas" in schools: "The method to achieve these quotas will be through mandatory busing of schoolchildren."[100] Most observers, however, found little or no evidence of racism: "YAF publications scrupulously avoid even hinting at racial malice in their attacks on black militants, blasting instead their tactics rather than their demands."[101] Perhaps critics, expecting a Klan-style attack on blacks, were instead surprised by YAF's seemingly color-blind philosophical defense.

Although YAF was overwhelmingly male-dominated, its attitude toward women, like blacks, was complex. Libertarian philosophy encouraged women to take leadership positions on both state and national levels, and it was not unusual for women to serve as chapter chairs or on the national board. On the other hand YAF always maintained that women should fulfill traditional duties as wives, mothers, and homemakers. The YAF women disavowed connections to "loonies who march, raise clenched fists, and dress like slobs," which referred to the nascent feminist movement.[102] Instead, they maintained, "any well-adjusted woman, who works hard to raise her family and make their home a happy and comfortable place to live, looks upon her day-to-day tasks of cooking and cleaning as a way of expressing her love."[103] Despite such traditionalism women, though vastly outnumbered by men, appeared in demonstrations, news conferences, and leadership seminars and comprised a subtle but constant voice in YAF.

Just as the Left had activist-celebrities like Mark Rudd, leader of the Columbia University protests of 1968, or Tom Hayden, popular SDS leader and future politician, YAF had corresponding prophets. Besides older conservatives, such as the Buckleys, Goldwater, Reagan, and Liebman, YAF's national officers often spoke or debated on campuses across the country. Perhaps the most interesting of all YAF stars was Phillip Abbott Luce. Luce was the perfect conservative role model; in the early 1960s he was a member of the Maoist Progressive Labor party and often led student trips to Cuba. He came to realize his ideological mistakes, and by the mid-1960s was one of the more popular YAF lecturers and writers. Luce, who dressed like a hippie, inspired college students who agreed with intellectual conservatism yet did not want to become social outcasts. He realized that YAF needed "people with style and wit, people who are hip to the media. Like Jerry Rubin."[104]

Luce and other YAF speakers not only dramatized the ideological war taking place between YAF and the New Left, but they helped to increase membership and attention, broadening and deepening YAF's resources. YAF correctly realized that money would ultimately determine whether a new chapter could continue recruiting, demonstrating, and networking after the initial excitement wore off. Direct-mail requests took on an increasingly urgent tone, and by late 1969 Randal Teague was able to write to the national board of directors, "October was the biggest single month in YAF's history—$125,479.08."[105]

After 1966 YAF narrowed its programmatic aims to supporting U.S. policy in Vietnam and opposing the New Left on campuses; in the process it became expert at co-opting the Left's own social protest methods. One of YAF's most educational experiences grew out of Stanford YAF's successful (albeit temporary) thwarting of SDS takeovers of administration buildings and the Stanford Research Institute. Chapter Chairman Harvey Hukari, along with a "hard core" of twenty-five YAFers, would learn of the target of an SDS demonstration and then rush to arrive there first. Stanford YAF would then link arms and form a two-person-thick wall, or they would quickly sit down in the area that SDS had originally intended to occupy. YAFers also photographed SDS members and later turned the photos over to the police. YAF chapters across the country copied these tactics with varying degrees of success.[106] In addition YAF stole SDS organizing manuals, annotated them with countertactics, and shipped them off to YAF chapters around the country.

Other YAF actions in 1968 and 1969 included filing lawsuits against colleges that canceled classes for antiwar protests; demanding that colleges hire equal numbers of conservative professors; planning in San Francisco for a "Right-Wing People's Park," where they would lay sod and plant trees in the parking lot of the liberal *San Francisco Chronicle*; promoting the wearing of blue buttons as a symbol of peace on campuses; and opposing the draft on the grounds that it produced low morale in the armed forces and could be replaced by a voluntary system.[107] While these actions gained media coverage, in the end YAF demonstrations were more important to YAF members than to either left-wing students or the population as a whole. YAFers knew, as one organizer recalled, that "the left dominated the debate."[108] The demonstrations and threats against the Left attracted other conservative students, created fundraising opportunities, and most important, held the interest of YAFers, who often felt alone in their struggles.

Although YAF nearly collapsed in 1969 after a fight between the traditionalists and libertarians at the national convention in St. Louis, the organization picked itself up and, while it suffered regular internecine warfare, continued to train young conservatives to do their share in creating a conservative Establishment.[109] A number of YAF alumni did enter political careers, including student organizer Dana Rohrabacher who, after working first as a libertarian minstrel spreading the gospel through song from campus to campus and then as a journalist in the 1970s, became one of President Reagan's top speechwriters.[110] In 1988 he was elected to the House of Representatives from Orange County, California, and in 1991 received a 96% rating by the ACU. Jim Lacy, YAF's national board chair, served as a cabinet undersecretary at the Department of Commerce during the Reagan years. Former YAFer Michelle Easton won appointment as a cabinet undersecretary at the Department of Education. One of YAF's most infamous alumni, Tom Charles Huston, penned the famous Huston Plan, which called for the Nixon administration to combat the Black Panthers and the Weathermen by using such covert operations as wiretapping, mail opening, breaking into offices, and planting informants.[111] One YAF alumnus, Patrick Buchanan, joined Nixon's staff as a speechwriter and later campaigned for president, incorporating some of the tactics YAFers had used a generation before.[112]

Only YAF successfully bucked the trend of declining grassroots activism among conservative groups, and in the wake of the JBS's demise, YAF filled in as the one group through which young people could meet, work together to achieve results, and then move on to another project, staying busy in their fight against the Left. That it was a student group limited its effectiveness, but after the Twenty-sixth Amendment passed in 1971, more politicians took notice of their younger constituents.[113] The GOP was anything but impervious to the efforts of groups like YAF, and in the latter half of the 1960s and into the 1970s the party followed the lead of independent conservative groups and pursued a variety of issues it knew would divide the country along partisan and ideological lines.

Conservatives entered the 1970s well prepared to take charge of American politics, and even with Watergate they managed to make gains throughout a decade that could have represented a complete disaster. With the burden of extremism permanently shaken (or so it appeared), conservatives characterized an alternative force to the 1960s, an offering many Americans found too tempting to pass up. Reagan's victory in 1980 would mark the end of one journey and the beginning of another, but the overlap was clear to everyone. Conservatives had achieved their goal, even if the timetable had been mistaken and the route circuitous. In the end it only mattered that they had arrived.

By the end of the 1960s many Americans were convinced that the drug culture, civil rights movement, and student protests had overwhelmed the courts; that pornography and violence were now mainstays of the entertainment industry; that intellectuals, in their blind support of free speech, had lost sight of the social contract; and that the country had given in to African Americans' radical demands—all indicators that the country had lost its moral underpinnings. These believers spurred the conservative movement and the GOP to reenter the maelstrom with a vengeance. Moreover the combination of flourishing independent conservative groups and the collapse of extremism produced a new set of opportunities for conservatives within the party. The synergy created by these forces came together in the 1968 presidential election with stunning results.

With the impressive outcome of the 1966 election, the GOP had looked forward to 1968, knowing that not only was momentum on its side but also that liberals actively aided the party with each dollar spent on the Great Society, each student protest, and each publicized Black Power struggle.[1] At the 1968 Democratic National Convention in Chicago, where young people rioted in the streets and thoroughly embarrassed the party, the fate of the liberals—although not yet fully sealed—plunged toward its nadir. Demonstrators chanted, "The whole world is watching!" and hoped that television cameras would beam the revolution to the hinterlands. Most Americans, however, loathed the protestors. Polls showed overwhelming support for Chicago Mayor Richard Daley's brutal police tactics, and 94% of the 74,000 letters the mayor received in the two weeks after the demonstrations supported his actions.[2]

Even if Chicago had gone perfectly, the Democratic faithful who had managed to nominate Vice President Hubert Humphrey faced divisions wrought by antiwar supporters of Eugene McCarthy and conservative Democrats who stood up for Alabama Governor George Wallace. Nixon knew this and sought to capture the Wallace constituency wherever he could, particularly as the three camps of the Democratic party—the McCarthy antiwar movement, the Humphrey followers, and the Wallace faction—moved further apart. After years of upheaval McCarthy and Wallace supporters alike believed the middle road could not be taken were the country to move forward. Students canvassing for McCarthy urged each other to "Go Clean for Gene," cut their long hair, and dressed respectably so as not to scare off potential voters. Wallace supporters nodded in agreement when their candidate blamed the federal government for emasculating the states and letting rioters run rampant. "We ought to turn this country over to the police for two or three years," said the candidate, "and everything would be all right." The "briefcase-totin' bureaucrats, ivory-tower guideline writers, bearded anarchists, smart-aleck editorial writers and pointy-headed professors" had lost their common sense years ago.[3]

Democrats had reason to be worried. Although before the convention polls indicated that Wallace support would take two votes from Nixon or Rockefeller for every one taken from Humphrey or McCarthy, the upsurge, as a report to President Johnson warned, was

> a protest against change generated by the establishment centers of mass media, money and mortar boards. It is the protest of rural and small-town voters who fear the cities as a focal point of wealth, sin, dirt and crime. This is descriptive of the Goldwater voters. The union members who are attracted to Wallace also fear the direct threat of advancing Negroes into their neighborhoods, their schools and their jobs.[4]

The Democrats did little to check the impression that their party no longer centered on white ethnics, labor, and other party regulars who had for so long made up the backbone of the New Deal Coalition. Moreover, after revising the delegate selection process prior to the 1972 election, traditional Democrats wondered how they fit into what now appeared to be a party composed of women, African Americans, and other "rights revolution" constituencies.[5] Simultaneously the GOP continued to build on the revised legacies of Goldwater by, for example, fundraising from tens of thousands of small donors rather than relying on large contributors.[6]

When the Republicans had gathered earlier that summer in Miami, they had faced none of the dissension that plagued the Democrats. Nelson Rockefeller and other moderate Republicans had little chance against Nixon, who demonstrated an unsurpassed ability to refashion himself whenever politically expedient. Borrowing heavily from Wallace, Nixon called for law and order in the streets. Borrowing from Humphrey and McCarthy, Nixon promised to "bring us together" at home and to bring "peace with honor" in Vietnam. While many conservatives had initially backed Reagan as the 1968 nominee, they closed ranks behind Nixon, with more than a few regarding Wallace as an advocate of dangerous "collectivist welfare state" policies.[7] Nixon captured the presidency by the slimmest of margins, 43.4% to Hubert Humphrey's 42.7%, with Wallace's 13.5% share playing a key role. Nixon's election opened new paths; seven months later the liberal Republican trend personified by John Lindsay had nearly disappeared. In a *Newsweek* column, Stewart Alsop described how New York City had caught the "Orange County bug," and he compared conservatism to an epidemic, which infected those previously thought immune to politics. Though the cause could be white backlash, wrote Alsop, it was necessary to take a closer look. Rebelling against liberalism did not necessarily signify racism; it could just as easily mean that these whites were offended by government assistance targeted at blacks. Many thought enough had been done to aid particular minorities, and the more aid continued to pour into programs catering to non–working-class white families, the more resentment grew.[8] One year later a *U.S. News and World Report* survey found that the Orange County bug had indeed visited much of America, although its genus had been renamed the "silent majority." "People are fed up," responded one man to the interviewers. "They have their own worries. They are tired of being pulled and hauled and shouted at."[9] Increasingly, political confrontations between Americans were turning violent, which punctuated the rhythms of everyday life with fear.

In a survey of various trends in the United States, *U.S. News* found that protests over Vietnam had crossed into areas of life previously thought resistant to such disturbances. In New York, for example, on May 8, 1970, hundreds of construction workers, or "hard hats," stormed into a crowd of young protesters on Wall Street, injuring at least seventy. The hard hats then marched to City Hall and demanded Mayor Lindsay's impeachment.[10] Though Americans had grown used to the fact that students often comprised the nucleus of demonstrations, by the academic year 1969–1970, studying seemed to have taken on extracurricular status. Nixon's first year in office saw more than 1,000 demonstrations on more than 200 campuses; property damage ran into the millions of dollars; and the shootings at Kent State in Ohio and Jackson State in Mississippi resulted in at least seven deaths. Administrations appeared to acquiesce to their students, with schools like Princeton and Duke even allowing them to rearrange their autumn class schedules so they could take time off to campaign for peace candidates. Not all students, however, condoned the demonstrations. *U.S. News* also interviewed David Keene, national chairman of Young Americans for Freedom, who argued that students went along with the protests simply because they wanted to fit in: "These are the people who will be hurt. These are the ones who will be clubbed and busted. The leaders know what they are up to and will escape to fight another day." Keene could not have done a better job at reinforcing anxious parents' suspicions.

The violence associated with antiwar and student protests seemed to amplify traditional crime, or those transgressions not usually thought to be political in nature. Felonious behavior continued to skyrocket. In 1969 a murder was committed every thirty-six minutes, a rape every fifteen, an aggravated assault every two, and a burglary every sixteen seconds. In 1963 fifty-five police officers had been killed and 16,793 assaulted nationwide. Six years later those figures had jumped to seventy-three and 33,604. As far as most working- and middle-class Americans could tell, their fears that society was out of control were justified. Many put the blame squarely on the New Left, a coupling conservatives eagerly exploited.

In April 1969 William Rusher addressed his colleagues at *National Review* about his experiences debating the New Left on college campuses. Their enemy was America, and their "hatred . . . is not only deep, but extends to just about every aspect of the American government and society: its foreign policy ('imperialist'), its economic system ('capitalist' and 'exploitative'), its values ('hypocritical'), its culture ('materialistic'), its democracy ('phony'), etc., etc."[11] Rusher was not entirely dismissive, since most young adults were not malevolent and simply wanted to cause a ripple in the media and the Establishment, and sometimes they even managed to latch onto an issue that almost justified their behavior. But these students nevertheless represented a new breed: humorless ("Have you ever tried to tell a joke to a New Leftist?"), without parental guidance, and pushed by younger faculty members, who enjoy "their total dominance over these young people, and feed them just enough simplistic pseudo-Marxist catnip to keep them fine-tuned on the subject of America's inherent loathsomeness." Rusher saw no reason to take the New Left seriously as a political movement, but in his pity he ignored the fact that the threat was very real to those Americans who did not share his long-range vision.

Besides Wallace the one individual who capitalized best on the New Left and the general upheaval was Vice President Spiro Agnew. A little-known governor of Maryland before being tapped by Nixon, by the middle of 1970 he was receiving 250 speaking invitations a week. Acting as Nixon's Wallace, Agnew railed against riotous youth, crime, the antiwar movement, and intellectuals. His prognostications did not bode well for student protesters still willing to challenge the government:

> The criminal left belongs not in a dormitory but in a penitentiary. The criminal left is not a problem to be solved by the department of philosophy or the department of English; it is a problem for the Department of Justice.
>
> Black or white, the criminal left is interested in power. It is not interested in promoting the renewal and reforms that make democracy work; it is interested in promoting those collisions and conflicts that tear democracy apart.[12]

Agnew said what the silent majority wanted to hear. In fifteen appearances he raised $2.5 million for the GOP, a sign that conservatives were generally comfortable with the drift of the Republican party over the first years of the Nixon White House. Americans who wanted the pre-1964 status quo backed Agnew for his ability to paint an honest picture of the country, which happened to resemble perfectly the one they already had in mind. As Agnew said about the silent majority, "One reason the silent majority is so silent is this: They're too busy working to make a lot of noise."

Nixon and Agnew also used issues like busing to make connections between federal and local policies; they trusted that such parallels would help conservatives identify with the GOP. As early as 1968, for example, citizens in San Francisco began organizing against busing programs; they created Parents and Tax-payers, Save Our Schools, Citizens for Democracy, and Mothers Support Neighborhood Schools in efforts to reverse the growing trend toward what they perceived as social engineering. Similar movements occurred in virtually every major city. Moreover Nixon learned from Wallace how much ground could be gained from the busing issue. After Wallace's 1972 victory in the Florida primary, Nixon copied the Alabama governor's hard line and urged his chief of staff, H. R. Haldeman, to ensure that "our major effort should be to put our Democratic friends strongly on record in favor of busing and us on record against it."[13]

Midway through Nixon's first term, however, some conservatives began doubting their choice of 1968 and soon were wondering out loud if a new conservative candidate would be needed in 1972. Phyllis Schlafly's monthly report headlined, "Poll Says Nixon Can't Be Reelected" and detailed Republican dissatisfaction with Nixon's inability to keep his campaign promises. Predicting that Nixon would carry only 217 electoral votes, well shy of the 270 needed to win, Schlafly found conservative Republican disappointment with Nixon's performance in foreign and domestic affairs and in the policies he had implemented over the first two and a half years of his administration.[14] On such issues as welfare, where the American Conservative Union had led the assault, an overwhelming 66% of surveyed Republicans disapproved of Nixon's policies. The president received similar ratings on his ability to uphold national security, where his eagerness to promote the Strategic Arms Limitation Treaty was seen as giving in to the Soviets. In the August 10, 1971, issue of *National Review*, a conservative coalition came together to "suspend support of the Administration" and chose instead to seek new options as a way to pressure Nixon into complying with their wishes. The declaration, signed by Buckley, Rusher, and other editors from *National Review* and *Human Events*; the ACU Capitol Hill and executive directors; Dan Mahoney, director of the New York Conservative party; Neil McCaffrey, president of the Conservative Book Club; and Randal Teague, executive director of YAF, was a powerful warning shot across the administration's bow. Nixon, however, plunged forward, trying to ignore critics to his right and left.[15]

In early 1972 *National Review* endorsed John Ashbrook for president and spoiled the White House's hopes that since Nixon had endorsed Buckley's brother James in his 1970 bid for the Senate, Buckley could at least return the favor.[16] After returning with Nixon from his trip to China, Buckley promptly lit into the president, criticizing his efforts at détente with the communists. While Ashbrook had garnered only 10% of the votes in the New Hampshire primary, he reminded voters that there were other, true conservatives available, and that, although Nixon might win, they did not have to pay automatic homage to him.

Although Nixon trounced George McGovern in 1972 by the lopsided margin of 61%–38%, his troubles were really just beginning. Nixon's fall from grace, however, coincided with the advent of two new branches of conservatism: the neoconservatives and the religious Right. Arising out of the dissatisfaction with the radicalization of academia, culture, and activist politics, some liberals rebelled against what they saw as their bastard progeny and took up the cudgel of intellectual conservatism with a vengeance. Led by such public scholars as Norman Podhoretz, Nathan Glazer, Daniel Patrick Moynihan, Irving Kristol, and Midge Decter, and a slew of journalists like Morton Kondracke and Charles Krauthammer, the neoconservative movement gathered steam throughout the 1970s and positioned itself perfectly for the ascendancy of Ronald Reagan in 1980.[17] Following Buckley's style, neoconservatives criticized government programs and also made recommendations for change, many of which were implemented after 1981.

On the other end of the activist-intellectual spectrum, the Christian Right took its lead from groups like the John Birch Society and YAF and the Goldwater and Wallace campaigns. Putting one's body on a picket line or marching in opposition to the Equal Rights Amendment or the Supreme Court's *Roe v. Wade* decision became the updated versions of canvassing for Goldwater or rallying to support the men in Vietnam. More populist than neoconservatives ever wanted to be, the Christian Right also subsumed the New Right, a collection of general purpose conservative activist groups like the Conservative Caucus, headed by Howard Phillips, the National Conservative Political Action Committee (NCPAC), led by Terry Dolan, and even some of the conservative think tanks, which had sprung up after the 1960s.[18] Personified best by Richard Viguerie, who sought to create an agenda for the upstart conservatives, the New Right was a viable force for only a few years, although its tactics like direct-mail fundraising aided all factions of the movement well into the next decade.[19]

Like children, neoconservatives and the religious Right closely resembled their forebears, and yet they became independent entities, separate from but connected to the larger movement. Neoconservatives essentially imitated the pre-1965 GOP, in which ideology dominated. Refusing to worry about selling their belief system to the general public, these former liberals deliberately took the high road, confident that their ideas would trickle down to the masses after government implementation. Neoconservatives, however, tended to rely on intellectual activism and used articles, books, and conferences to spread ideas they hoped would one day become policy. The religious Right, on the other hand, copied the successful fundraising efforts of the JBS, ACU, and YAF and prayed that their primarily working- and middle-class constituency would open their wallets as they marched on the picket lines. Furthermore the religious Right closely mimicked JBS and YAF tactics, where media attention, movement culture, and constant activity helped keep a wide-ranging coalition united in spirit and purpose. That these two new conservative factions arrived at the opening of the new decade was not surprising. Extremists who had been shunned by the GOP and independent groups required outlets for their opinions. More important was the fact that conservatism was now essentially a conventional belief system in the American political spectrum. The GOP had shifted to the right, and a new populist conservatism was ascendant. For conservatives who did not trust the two-party system to represent their beliefs accurately, the co-optation of conservatism by the GOP signaled the need for a fresh era of activism to begin.

The conservative coalition grew throughout the 1970s as abortion, busing, the Equal Rights Amendment, the Panama Canal, and negotiations with the Soviet Union became mainstream concerns for Americans. Although three or four general factions comprised the broad movement, and competition among them was sometimes fierce, the sense of uncertainty so common among conservatives in the 1960s was no longer a factor. Among the traditionalists, the New Right, the Christian Right, and the neoconservatives, conservatism as a whole gained an element of stability, which made even self-criticism acceptable. Reagan's Eleventh Commandment, while still in place in some parts of the GOP, was pushed aside as factions argued openly about tactics and issues as they prepared for the elections of 1976 and 1980. Even more remarkable, considering that Watergate had stopped the GOP virtually dead in its tracks in 1974, conservatives remained confident that their work over the previous decade would pay off.

Spared the burden of extremism, all of the conservative movement's ships rose as the Left sank deeper into chaos. Thanks to the mistakes of the liberals and radicals during the second half of the 1960s and the work done by conservatives to take advantage of those gaffes, by the early 1970s conservatives were located comfortably in the center of the American political conversation. Responding to the 1960s and to conservatism's acceptance by mainstream Americans as a solution to the country's myriad problems, the GOP took advantage of the metamorphosis. Moreover the GOP helped solidify the electoral shift: any liberal policies Republicans implemented received enough support from moderate and liberal party members to hold the new coalition together. Part of this relocation from the fringes to the relative center came as a result of the movement's perceptiveness and willingness to scale back its ideology and rhetoric to remain within the limits that Goldwater had exceeded. Always somewhat flexible, these guidelines called for fiscal, social, and cultural conservatism without requiring drastic action or upsetting supporters' impressions about how the American government *should* act toward its citizens and other countries. Goldwater had challenged those notions, as had the John Birch Society and other extremists. Nixon, whether a "true" conservative or not, remained within the limits tested four years earlier and he pushed the envelope only in the directions that he knew Americans would follow.

Conservatives' use of specific issues, chief among them widespread youth protests, racial divides, rising inflation, and new demands by politically underrepresented groups like women, the elderly, African Americans, American In-

dians, Chicanos, and homosexuals, all helped independent organizations and the
GOP make the transition from being a movement based on ideology to one based
on issues. As organizations focused on matters like the Equal Rights Amendment or busing, new campaigns sprang up that relied on updated grassroots
campaigning, and local activism, instead of being the crux of the strategy to
achieve victory, was one integrated enterprise among many, holding members'
interest while lobbying and more sophisticated pressure could be brought to bear
on lawmakers and policy writers. While there was a marked decrease in movement culture compared to the events of 1964, conservatives of the late 1960s
and early 1970s learned not to rely so fully on a single tactic; though delivering
excitement and energy, that approach often contained little staying power.

Had the ways of the early 1960s been superseded by "modern" politics, with
direct participation considered less important than raising money and securing
endorsements? Had both pre-1964 and post-1964 conservatism been co-opted
with citizen activism limited to only what the GOP found acceptable? To a degree the answer was yes, since as the movement became more entrenched, self-
confident, and self-critical, it could ignore those participants who carried with
them the risks of extremism or simply crossed the boundaries of acceptable ideology. Such a reconfigured movement was exactly what the Republican party
had been looking for. But in other ways movement culture as embodied in
grassroots participation never fully died out; rather organizations that needed
to rely on activism to spread their word and attract media attention did just that.
They knew that if their efforts paid off they would gain a foothold in the burgeoning and revitalized movement.

Conservatism Triumphant

In 1963 William Rusher had urged fellow conservatives to take a risk. To break
the New Deal Coalition's lock on the presidency, he said, "It will take courage;
it will take imagination; it will compel the GOP to break the familiar mould [sic]
that has furnished it with every presidential nominee for a quarter of a century—
but it can be done."[20] With help from millions of Americans, Rusher and his
fellow activists were wrenching the Republican party rightward, inaugurating a
new era of American politics, and forever changing the tenor of the GOP and
the two-party system. Between 1957, when foreign and domestic events began
catalyzing nascent conservative ideology, and 1972, when the movement had
gained enough stability to help propel Richard Nixon to a second term, the conservative movement transformed the lives of virtually every American. Conservatives, of course, *meant* to change America—the irony inherent in such a metamorphosis was lost on no one, yet the scale surprised everyone.

If conservatism had seemingly triumphed by the end of the 1960s, the 1970s
constituted its first real test. Soon after Richard Nixon's reelection in 1972, the

American economy, which had enjoyed nearly unabated growth with low inflation since the end of World War II, suddenly faltered. In 1973 Nixon decided to take the dollar off the gold standard, which immediately dropped the currency's value. The Middle Eastern oil embargo caused prices to skyrocket and panic at the gas pumps. Americans drove from one station to another, topping off their tanks simply to ensure that they would always have enough fuel. A worldwide grain shortage sent food prices higher and, combined with rising inflation, stagnant wages, and increasingly obsolete manufacturing systems, made 1973 a turning point in American postwar history.[21] As the last American ground troops pulled out of Vietnam, one era, characterized by social and cultural unrest and economic stability, bled into another, during which the "me generation" and economic uncertainty reigned supreme.

The drama that was conservatism, however, continued to evolve, with many of its original actors still holding center stage. By 1974 even the John Birch Society had traveled full circle. Following fast on the heels of the 1973 Supreme Court decision in *Roe v. Wade* and jealously eyeing the rapid growth of the anti-abortion fervor, the JBS threw itself into the anti-abortion movement. MOTOREDE, or the Movement to Restore Decency, was a JBS front that concentrated almost solely on opposing abortion through citizen activism. Through letter writing, press releases, information packets, and films, it sought to convince Americans that abortion was morally repugnant.[22] "We can think of no matter more compelling . . . than the murder of tens of thousands of unborn infants every month," proclaimed the JBS.[23] Moreover the society linked liberalized abortion with its larger concerns of an overbearing government and external threats: "Unfortunately, this attack on life itself is just one part of a much more comprehensive and even more sinister campaign to regulate and regiment all existence." But if the anti-abortion movement was now the vanguard of extremist discontent, had the JBS actually moved toward the center, forced to play catch-up to those who led the protest? No; the JBS, under Welch's incessant if unpredictable guidance, retained its ability to tap into the pool of conservative dissatisfaction and if that meant entering the debate over abortion, busing, and the Panama Canal, or continuing with its campaign to defeat world communism, the organization knew how to further itself and its causes.[24]

As Welch continued to lead his organization down a path that guaranteed confrontation with both hardcore and moderate conservatives, his web of conspiracy stretched ever wider. In 1979, working with coauthor Medford Evans, Welch produced "False Leadership: William F. Buckley, Jr., and the New World Order." Welch and Evans told the story of Buckley's ability to exploit his position as a conservative leader in the hopes of seeking "a place in the Establishment which he professes to oppose, in the expectation of sharing influence with such as [*sic*] Henry Kissinger and the House of Rockefeller in a New World Order to be achieved through—in Kissinger's terms—'the experience of chaos.'"[25]

Tracing the development of their relationship, Welch recounted the evolution of the conservative movement from his perspective; he portrayed Buckley as a spoiler intent on grabbing power for himself, while the hard-working conservative community languished in anonymity.[26] Evans argued that Buckley had attacked Welch in the early 1960s "not because he thought Welch was wrong, but because he knew Welch was right." Applying Welchian logic Evans decided that if Welch's charges against Eisenhower were that wrongheaded, Buckley would have had no reason to "go to war" with Welch. Yet he did, thus proving Welch's hypothesis correct and making a case for the conspiracy emanating from conservatives themselves. Welch recounted Buckley's attacks from the early 1960s through the late 1970s and wondered why any so-called conservative would turn his sights on someone who had devoted his life to exposing the dangers of liberalism and communism.[27] While Welch and Evans offered a few hypotheses about Buckley's behavior, in the end they had to dismiss him and his cronies at *National Review* as jealous, mischievous, and dangerous, all qualities the conservative movement could surely do without.

Although Welch's star sank throughout the 1970s, the JBS remained the most recognizable and one of the largest organizations on the far Right. Later outstripped by groups focused solely on abortion, busing, and other politically charged issues, the JBS continued to attract adherents and even sponsored summer camps for teenagers to learn about "the Conspiracy."[28] Although the society made few forays into hands-on politics, it did celebrate Reagan's election in 1980. With the downfall of the Soviet Union and the collapse of European communism in the late 1980s, the JBS refocused its energies on the conspiracy originating from the United Nations, illegal immigrants, and a too-liberal government.[29] The mainstream GOP, however, no longer tolerated extremism, even if some candidates like Patrick Buchanan borrowed heavily from the tactics pioneered by the fringe in the 1960s.[30] Extremism, however, did aid mainstream conservatism in two ways. First its very presence outside of the core of the GOP made the party seem more judicious, since the boundary between the kooks and responsible conservatives was officially delineated. Second the strategies and tactics pioneered by extremists were co-opted by the mainstream and updated to increase their efficiency.[31] The professionalization of grassroots activity accompanied the continued expansion of such practices to a wide range of causes, with liberals often becoming equally proficient in their application. While direct-mail solicitors or conservative purists might have decried the extension of grassroots activism, they also knew that it was just such progress that had allowed conservatism to take center stage in 1964. But what had the revolution wrought? By the middle of the 1970s the president had resigned, former Vice President Spiro Agnew had pleaded nolo contendere to a number of charges, and nearly all conservatives considered Gerald Ford a poor substitute for a

Rockefeller or Lindsay Republican.[32] Some conservatives, therefore, began considering a third party.

William Rusher's *The Making of the New Majority Party* represented one attempt to capitalize on conservative frustration in 1975. A May 1974 Gallup Poll found that if Americans had to choose either the "liberal" or "conservative" party, 38% would choose conservative, while only 26% liberal (36% had no opinion). Two months later, however, another Gallup Poll found that only 23% of respondents would openly identify themselves as Republicans.[33] While the philosophy of conservatism remained strong, the Nixon-Agnew imbroglio had damaged the GOP so severely, said Rusher, that the ideology needed a new outlet. Rusher proposed a third party called the Independence party, which would run serious candidates at the local, state, and national levels. Extremism would not be tolerated in the slightest, and the organization could draw on previously successful populist models, like elements of the Goldwater campaign. Rusher hoped to recruit Reagan, pondered whether Wallace would draw the social conservative vote without alienating others because of his stance on segregation, and generally bemoaned the small pool of nationally known conservative figures who could help carry the party—and hence conservatism—to victory.[34]

Rusher's realization of the need for a sales force to continue the country's conversion to conservatism signaled that the lessons learned so harshly in 1964 had not been forgotten. A third party as a new outlet for activism also harked back to tactics pioneered between 1964 and 1966, when campaign organizations realized that they needed to work creatively with citizen volunteers, who demanded that their efforts achieve tangible results. While some activists had gravitated to the religious Right, the vast majority stayed within the folds of the GOP. When the party sagged, Rusher reasoned, the time was right to pluck them from the moribund institution and use their energy to reinvigorate conservatism. While the Independence party seemed as much an intellectual exercise as a blueprint for political change, the fact that a conservative with Rusher's historical dedication to the GOP had proposed such a radical solution meant that conservatism continued to expand both its constituency and its vision.

Organizer Marvin Liebman remained committed to promoting conservatism by creating ad hoc organizations dedicated to a variety of causes. Reasoning that such a strategy had worked well throughout the 1960s, Liebman took on clients as well as promoting his own causes. Following Nixon's lead, one of Liebman's most successful forays became the promotion of law and order, which spawned a number of temporary fronts. For example, Liebman tapped Senator James L. Buckley, Clare Booth Luce, and others to sponsor the ad hoc Citizens' Legal Defense Fund for the FBI in order to help defend current and former agents accused of breaching Americans' civil rights by wiretapping or other means of surveillance. The fund raised approximately $300,000 in little over a year, with some 15,000 individual contributions helping pay the legal bills of indicted agents.[35] More important than the money, however, were the names the mailings generated. Recycled in future direct-mail campaigns, donor names made Liebman's fronts into a self-perpetuating conservative fundraising machine. Combined with lists created during the previous fifteen years, Liebman, Viguerie, and other fundraisers helped finance Ronald Reagan's presidential campaigns in 1980 and 1984, along with such issue-oriented crusades as defeating the Equal Rights Amendment, opposing laws to guarantee rights for minority groups, and supporting the nomination of Robert Bork for the Supreme Court in 1987.

The lessons Liebman and his colleagues had learned about movement culture and its importance to conservative constituents continued to influence the direction of the movement and the GOP, although now that conservatism was no longer an underdog, meetings, rallies, and other events that generated a sense of belonging seemed to matter less.[36] If the movement culture of the Goldwater campaign had expired, what replaced it was serviceable enough. Later conservative hubris and subsequent disarray haunted candidates like George H. W. Bush in 1992, but in the early 1980s voters and observers alike took conservatism seriously, a remarkable transformation considering that the first iteration of the ideology was only three decades old. Conservative political culture's ability to remain viable at its core while expanding to include more centrist Republicans helped the GOP become inextricably linked to the movement, a coupling inconceivable in 1964.

Though race appeared as an issue exploited by conservatives and Republicans after the 1960s, more remarkable was how relatively infrequently the topic appeared in party platforms or on conservative organization's agendas. Following the lessons of such conservative organizations as the ACU and YAF, the GOP realized that it was easier to let the Democrats take the heat by failing to live up to their promises than to respond to the issue any more than absolutely necessary. Of course Republicans and conservatives did weigh in on the topic, at times risking accusations of racism in order to uphold their principles. Whether or not racism was at the heart of such tactics was almost impossible to determine conclusively.[37]

The New Deal Coalition had deteriorated substantially by the mid-1960s, yet it still had enough cachet to help elect liberal Democrats at the state and local levels throughout the 1970s and 1980s. And, as the elections of 1992 and 1996 demonstrated, conservatism did not fully replace liberalism as the dominant ideology. Conservatism, however, had not reached its limits. Beginning with the "Reagan Revolution" and continuing almost unabated since, young conservatives have taken up the torch of their forebears, pushed the ideology in new directions, and increasingly attempted to enlarge the coalition. Aided first by the growth on Wall Street in the 1980s, the reaction against liberalism on college campuses grew rapidly. The election of Bill Clinton in 1992 provided the perfect target for these intellectuals, many of whom were children of neo-conservatives. Tightly connected to such think tanks as the American Enterprise Institute, the Manhattan Institute, and the Heritage Foundation, such young conservatives as Dinesh D'Souza, David Brooks, Laura Ingraham, David Frum, Adam Bellow, and others contributed to periodicals like the *American Spectator* (which quickly grew to a circulation of 340,000, three times that of the usually liberal *New Republic*), opened publishing houses for conservative titles that could not find a publisher, and inundated Washington political life, securing internships in Congress and forming small circles within which they plotted their next assault on what remained of the liberal Establishment.[38]

While the ideas of young conservatives remained closely connected to those espoused by their counterparts in YAF in the 1960s, one crucial difference remained. For the most part YAFers were not of the elite, were almost always Christian, and often came from working-class backgrounds and attended public or sectarian universities. The new young conservatives, however, went to Ivy League schools, were frequently Jewish (for example, William Kristol, son of Irving Kristol, and John Podhoretz, son of Norman Podhoretz, two of the original neoconservatives), and enjoyed living life extravagantly, reveling in economic and cultural libertarianism. Moreover whereas the new young conservatives relished the bonds they formed between older and younger intellectuals, they failed to reach out to their peers who, in the 1960s, would have joined YAF, which left the next generation of activists open for recruitment by the religious Right. Still a powerful difference between the factionalism of the 1960s and that of the 1980s and 1990s remained: unlike organizations of the 1960s, which appeared to work at cross-purposes, the mosaic of conservative groups operating during and after the Reagan era reflected the movement's vitality. Rivalry among independent organizations and the Republican party resulted in innovative policies and campaign methods and demonstrated that the free market of conservative action and ideas worked. While not all factions participated in such an ideological round table (the religious Right, for example, remained unyielding on such issues as abortion and gay rights), the mainstream of the movement, even when not represented in the White House, prospered more than ever before.

Thirty years after the conservative movement captured the Republican party in 1964, the godfather of modern electoral conservatism reaffirmed his libertarian roots and shocked colleagues and followers by becoming an advocate for gay rights. "Why the hell *shouldn't* they serve [in the armed forces]? They're American citizens," argued Barry Goldwater.[39] Moreover Goldwater observed that the radical Right now consisted of "Pat Robertson and others who are trying to take the Republican Party away from the Republican Party, and make a religious organization out of it." The irony clearly escaped the standard-bearer; in the eyes of moderate Republicans in 1963 and 1964, conservatives had wrested

the party away from its customary leaders without regard to tradition or deco-
rum, had overthrown the eastern wing, and completely rearranged the power
structure. But in opening up the party to Americans in 1964 who had never
thought the GOP would welcome anyone except a Rockefeller or a Boston Brah-
min, Goldwater and his colleagues accomplished what the Democrats tried to
legislate within their own party four years later. In both cases, of course, the upheaval was too much for the voters to support and resulted in losses for the
Republicans in 1964 and the Democrats in 1968. But the enlargement of the
GOP to include constituents from the South and West signified that a new era
of politics had come to America.

By the late 1990s some observers noted that the conservative revolution had
begun to subside. In making such a claim, however, liberals implicitly had to
concede that conservatives formerly *had* dominated the public sphere, and only
now was their "hold on the national electorate" loosening.[40] Such an argument
was remarkable for a number of reasons, perhaps none more important than
simply acknowledging the progress of the conservative movement since the late
1950s. Moreover when liberal pundits failed to mention that forty years earlier
conservatives had been dismissed as "pseudoconservatives" and their ideas as
illegitimate "impulses," they further undervalued the hostile political atmosphere
that conservatives had actually overcome. On the other hand partisan chroniclers frequently offered teleological narratives, which gave the impression of
certain victory. What emerged from approximately fifteen years of conservative
struggle and growth was the extraordinarily universal acceptance that conservatives could indeed have a hold on the national electorate, whether they were
now losing it or not.

And what of the movement's other key players? William F. Buckley continued to write, speak, and prognosticate about politics and morality in America,
though he focused more on ideas of spirituality as he got older. Similarly William Rusher retired from *National Review* and became a syndicated columnist
and a fellow at the Claremont Institute. Ronald Reagan, crippled by Alzheimer's
disease, became a reclusive figurehead, his wife, Nancy, making his public statements for him. Many others passed on. Still Russell Kirk, Marvin Liebman,
L. Brent Bozell, Barry Goldwater, and other crucial figures had lived to see
Reagan installed as president. And their words and actions survived them. Kirk's
canon of conservative thought remained essentially unchanged and guided
politicians and activists alike. The bond formed between the movement and the
party held fast, and though it did not always provide a consistently winning formula, some conservatives felt that, if it required compromise, victory was not so
important. While the eastern Establishment of the GOP had included many
conservatives, conservatives also chose to open up the party to the rest of the
country and created one of the first broad-based political movements of the
1960s. Though a small group of highly educated intellectuals had initiated a trans-

formation of the political system, it was millions of Americans, inexperienced in politics, who made the ideas into a movement. While those same intellectuals sometimes found themselves frozen out of the politicking they had started and at other times found that the grassroots participation they had encouraged could not be controlled, they realized that democracy was a messy process and that eventually their side would triumph. The big tent was finally filling up, sans extremists and their ilk. And even if the vast majority had never read Kirk's *The Conservative Mind*, they intrinsically understood what ideology could and could not accomplish. In the end conservatives realized they had to act, a lesson taught time and time again in those crucial fifteen years.

When asked once how he would define conservatism, William F. Buckley noted that formulating a neat, one-sentence definition was almost impossible. Some questioners are never satisfied, observed Buckley, and those people, he quipped, "I punish by giving, with a straight face, Professor Richard Weaver's definition of conservatism as 'a paradigm of essences towards which the phenomenology of the world is in continuing approximation,' as noble an effort as any I have ever read."[41] In many ways the founders of the movement and their immediate disciples sought to join the phenomenology of the world and strived to push the canon of political, moral, and religious thought and action closer to that paradigm of essences. Though their creation did not meet their every expectation, they inspired others to continue what they had started. In the end conservatives learned the practical limits of their ideology, the importance of organization and action, and what made the difference between electoral success and failure. They had been lessons hard learned.

NOTES

ABBREVIATIONS

Buckley Papers   William F. Buckley, Jr., Papers, Manuscripts and Archives, Yale
                    University Library
FBI Documents   FBI file no. 62-104401 Sec. 40, Federal Bureau of Investiga-
                    tion, Washington, D.C.
FSA Papers   Free Society Association Records, Hoover Institution Archives
Goldwater Papers   Barry Goldwater Papers, 1964 Presidential Campaign /w, Ari-
                    zona Historical Foundation, University Libraries, Arizona State
                    University
HIA   Hoover Institution Archives, Stanford, California
JBS Records   John Birch Society Records, Brown University Library
JFKL   John F. Kennedy Presidential Library, Boston, Massachusetts
LBJL   Lyndon B. Johnson Presidential Library, Austin, Texas
Liebman Papers   Marvin Liebman Papers, Hoover Institution Archives
Meier Papers   Margaret Meier Papers, courtesy of Department of Special
                    Collections, Stanford University Libraries
Oregon Special   Division of Special Collections and University Archives, Uni-
Collections   versity of Oregon
Reagan Papers   Ronald Reagan Collection, GP: Campaign 66, Hoover Insti-
                    tution Archives
Rusher Papers   William A. Rusher Papers, Manuscripts and Archives Division,
                    Library of Congress

INTRODUCTION

1. Edwin A. Walker, "Who Muzzled the Military? Stop Communism!" December 12, 1961, New Left Collection, box 14, folder "Anti-Communist (Various)," HIA.

2. Fletcher Knebel and Charles W. Bailey II, "Military Control: Can It Happen
Here?" *Look*, September 11, 1962, 17–21; "Crackpots: How They Help Communism," *Life*, December 1, 1961, 6.

3. *Newsweek*, December 4, 1961.

4. Two perceptive essays on liberalism in twentieth-century America are Gary
Gerstle, "The Protean Character of American Liberalism," *American Historical
Review* 99, no. 4 (October 1994): 1043–73; and Michael Kazin, "The Agony and
Romance of the American Left," *American Historical Review* 100, no. 5 (Decem-
ber 1995): 1488–1512.

NOTES TO PAGES 4-15

5. See Alan Brinkley, "The Problem of American Conservatism," *American Historical Review* 99, no. 2 (April 1994): 414–15.

6. As one study has shown, "Subordinate group members who were discontented with the relative power of their groups and who saw an unjust system as the explanation for their power disadvantage were motivated to bring about change by participating in traditional types of political activities." See Arthur H. Miller et al., "Group Consciousness and Political Participation," *American Journal of Political Science* 25, no. 3 (August 1981): 508.

7. FDR and the Democrats relied primarily on white Catholic ethnics from the urban North combined with southern white Protestants; African Americans and Jews comprised the rest of the coalition. Facing such a powerful bloc forced Republicans to seek "wedge" issues in order to divide the coalition at its weakest points. These are discussed more fully in later chapters.

8. For example, spending for "income security" rose from approximately $6 billion in 1953 to $18 billion in 1960. Defense spending, on the other hand, actually fell from a peak of $50 billion to $45 billion over the same period. Bureau of the Census, *Historical Statistics of the United States: From the Colonial Times to 1970,* pt. 2 (Washington, D.C.: Government Printing Office, 1970), 1116–17.

9. Miller et al., "Group Consciousness and Political Participation," 495.

10. Ibid., 496–97.

11. Lawrence Goodwyn, *The Populist Moment* (New York: Oxford University Press, 1978), xviii.

12. For my purposes, the conservative "movement" will refer to the conscious collection of individuals and institutions working toward the political and social ascendancy of conservative ideology. "Movement culture" indicates the activities *within* the movement that aid in attaining the four stages through which a movement must pass.

13. William A. Rusher, *The Rise of the Right* (New York: National Review Books, 1993), 62.

CHAPTER 1

1. Lionel Trilling, *The Liberal Imagination* (New York: Viking, 1950), ix.

2. Taft had used anticommunism as one of his main campaign planks in 1948 and later claimed that he could not have stopped McCarthy even if he had so desired. See James T. Patterson, *Mr. Republican* (Boston: Houghton Mifflin, 1972), 448–49.

3. The idea of pseudoconservatism remained viable among many academics well into the 1960s and 1970s. By the late 1950s, however, some conservatives had retaliated with their own conception of the "pseudoliberal." Based not on a psychological deficiency but rather on a desire to centralize power, pseudoliberals deluded citizens by convincing them that the federal government could take care of all of their needs without their having to worry about taxes or loss of freedom. See "The Old Backward Look," Americans for Constitutional Action, n.d., National Republic Magazine Records, box 732, folder 4, HIA.

4. Reviewing the book, Kirk charged that the liberals had wrongly focused on the far Right, and he hoped to prove that most conservatives were responsible in their beliefs. Kirk fought an uphill battle, however, and it was not until the mid- to

late 1960s that the majority of conservatives separated themselves from the far Right and thus allowed conservatism to gain the political strength necessary to win the White House. Kirk quoted in George H. Nash, *The Conservative Intellectual Movement in America since 1945* (New York: Basic, 1976), 139. For an extended analysis of *The New American Right*, see William B. Hixson, Jr., *Search for the American Right Wing* (Princeton, N.J.: Princeton University Press, 1992), 9–16.

5. But some on the Left fervently attacked anticommunists as red baiters and worse, thus reducing political discourse to how much influence one believed the American Communist party actually possessed. See Harvey Klehr, John Earl Haynes, and Fridrikh Igorevich Firsov, *The Secret World of American Communism* (New Haven, Conn.: Yale University Press, 1995), 322–28.

6. Richard Hofstadter, "The Pseudo-Conservative Revolt," in *The New American Right*, ed. Daniel Bell (New York: Criterion, 1955), 41–42.

7. Ibid., 44.

8. Raymond Moley, "Address before Republican Precinct Workers," June 16, 1952, Raymond Moley Papers, box 135, folder "Cleveland Republican Precinct Workers Address," HIA.

9. Nash, *Conservative Intellectual Movement*, 254.

10. On the other hand, conservatives always knew how to spot a liberal. According to Buckley, "I confess that I know who is a conservative less surely than I know who is a Liberal. Blindfold me, spin me about like a top, and I will walk up to the single Liberal in the room without zig or zag, and find him even if he is hiding behind the flower pot." William F. Buckley, Jr., "Notes towards an Empirical Definition of Conservatism," in *What Is Conservatism?* ed. Frank S. Meyer (New York: Holt, Rinehart and Winston, 1964), 212.

11. Barbara Jeanne Fields, "Slavery, Race and Ideology in the United States of America," *New Left Review*, no. 181 (May–June 1990): 110. Lionel Trilling offers a similar definition; see *Liberal Imagination*, 277.

12. Melvin J. Thorne, *American Conservative Thought since World War II: The Core Ideas* (New York: Greenwood, 1990), 9. This paragraph draws on Thorne extensively.

13. M. Stanton Evans, "Techniques and Circumstances," *National Review*, January 30, 1962, 58.

14. Other influential conservative thinkers included Friedrich A. Hayek, Ludwig von Mises, Eric Voegelin, Richard M. Weaver, Peter Viereck, and Gerhart Niemeyer.

15. Kirk's father, however, was a strong opponent of "assembly-line civilization," a characteristic that powerfully affected his son. See Nash, *Conservative Intellectual Movement*, 69–72.

16. Russell Kirk, *The Conservative Mind: From Burke to Santayana* (Chicago: Regnery, 1953), 7–8.

17. Kirk's beliefs, however, provided enough flexibility for political and social actors to determine how much or how little action they took. When an issue seemed to require guidance in the political arena, conservatives could invoke the first tenet, in which political problems are moral problems and there is simply no choice but to act.

18. In perhaps the most literal demonstration of Kirk's ability to cross between the intellectual and the practical, in 1989 President Reagan awarded him the Presidential Citizens Medal.

19. George H. Nash, "The Conservative Mind in America," *Intercollegiate Review* 30, no. 1 (Fall 1994): 27.

20. For an insightful analysis of *Witness*, see Sam Tanenhaus, *Whittaker Chambers* (New York: Random House, 1997), 459–71.

21. Patterson, *Mr. Republican*, 449.

22. Samuel A. Stouffer, *Communism, Conformity, and Civil Liberties* (Gloucester, Mass.: Peter Smith, 1963), 39.

23. Ibid., 68. People were primarily worried about personal business or family finances, the health of themselves and their family, and other personal problems.

24. Ibid., 176. Those who did think they had known a communist used such reasoning as "I saw a map of Russia on a wall in his home," "He wrote his thesis in college on Communism," "He didn't believe in Christ, heaven, or hell," or "I just knew. But I wouldn't know how to say how I knew." Ibid., 176–77.

25. For a summary of Burnham's background, see Nash, *Conservative Intellectual Movement*, 91–93.

26. Burnham, however, continued to contribute to the left-leaning *Partisan Review* until 1953. Ibid., 118.

27. Richard Gid Powers, *Not without Honor* (New York: Free Press, 1995), 206. Here Burnham differed from other conservatives, such as Robert Taft, who wanted to force American communists into the open but not outlaw the party. See Patterson, *Mr. Republican*, 447.

28. James Burnham, *The Coming Defeat of Communism* (New York: John Day, 1950), 14.

29. Ibid., 25, 91.

30. Burnham also considered what he called "preventative war," or what some others called a "first strike." While he could not justify launching an all-out attack at that time, Burnham did believe that "whether or not to begin a full military war is a problem of expediency," and he said that the conditions required continuous evaluation to determine whether at some point a first strike was warranted. In any case, as long as the United States took the offensive in a political war, the chances of military conflict would be greatly reduced. See ibid., 145–48.

31. Ibid., 232.

32. Ibid., 276, 278. Burnham's optimism disappeared in his next works, *Containment or Liberation?* and *The Web of Subversion*.

33. "Matthews vs. Acheson," *Washington Post*, August 28, 1950, 6.

34. Ellis Haller and Philip Geyelin, "Officials Secretly Study a Bold Plan to Push the Iron Curtain Back," *Wall Street Journal*, October 16, 1950, 1, 8.

35. (Garden City, N.Y.: Doubleday, 1951).

36. William A. Rusher, *The Rise of the Right* (New York: National Review Books, 1993), 20. Not surprisingly *The Web of Subversion* was adopted by conspiracy theorists in the 1960s to prove that a number of administrations had turned a blind eye to the growing problem. In 1962 the patriarch of conspiracy theory organizations, the John Birch Society, reprinted the book using its own publishing house, Western Islands, and offered copies of the paperback for $1.

37. Nash, *Conservative Intellectual Movement*, 96–97.

38. Ibid., 142.

39. Quoted in ibid., 292.

40. For more on Wedemeyer, see Keith E. Eiler, ed., *Wedemeyer on War and Peace* (Stanford, Calif.: Hoover Institution Press, 1987).

41. Albert C. Wedemeyer, "Address before the Students of the University of Utah, 28 February 1952, and the Students of Brigham Young University, February 29, 1952," 7, Albert C. Wedemeyer Papers, box 10, folder 1, HIA.

42. Albert C. Wedemeyer, "Address before the Founders' Day Banquet, University of Utah," February 28, 1952, 2, ibid.

43. Raymond Moley, *How to Keep Our Liberty* (New York: Knopf, 1952).

44. Raymond Moley, *The Republican Opportunity* (New York: Duell, Sloan and Pearce, 1962), 46.

45. Raymond Moley, "Address before the National Coffee Association Convention," December 8, 1952, Raymond Moley Papers, box 136, folder 10, HIA.

46. *Brown v. Board of Education* was the landmark case that struck down the "separate but equal" doctrine codified in the 1896 decision *Plessy v. Ferguson*. Although legal action was slow to follow (partially due to the Eisenhower administration's fear of antagonizing the white South), *Brown* set the precedent for legal challenges to racial segregation.

47. *Historical Statistics of the United States, Colonial Times to 1970*, pt. 2 (Washington, D.C.: Government Printing Office, 1975), 1117–18.

48. It is important that libertarianism of the 1950s should not be perceived in post-1972 terms. There was no budding libertarian movement, no separate political entity, and people did not identify themselves as libertarians. "Classical liberalism" was the operative definition of the ideology that emphasized the primacy of the individual and warned against the danger of the state. It was not until 1972, with the formation of the Libertarian party, that the term began entering the mainstream political vocabulary.

49. James Burnham, "U.S. Political Spectrum," c. 1960, James Burnham Papers, box 3, folder 37, HIA.

50. James Burnham, "Litmus Propositions for Liberal-Conservative Test," c. 1960, ibid.

CHAPTER 2

1. William A. Rusher, *The Rise of the Right* (New York: National Review Books, 1993), 52.

2. John D. Weaver, *Warren: The Man, the Court, the Era* (Boston: Little, Brown, 1967), 287.

3. American Civil Liberties Union, *The Smith Act and the Supreme Court* (New York: American Civil Liberties Union, 1952), 4.

4. For accounts of Warren as governor, on the Supreme Court, and in politics in general, see Weaver, *Warren: The Man, the Court, the Era*; Jack Harrison Pollack, *Earl Warren: The Judge Who Changed America* (Englewood Cliffs, N.J.: Prentice-Hall, 1979); G. Edward White, *Earl Warren: A Public Life* (New York: Oxford University Press, 1982); Leo Katcher, *Earl Warren: A Political Biography* (New York: McGraw-Hill, 1967); Henry M. Christman, ed., *The Public Papers of Chief Justice Earl Warren* (New York: Simon and Schuster, 1959); and Earl Warren Oral History

Project, *Earl Warren: The Chief Justiceship* (Berkeley, Calif.: Bancroft Library Oral History Office, 1977).

5. See "Turmoil in Washington," *U.S. News and World Report*, June 20, 1957, 25; and Harold Lord Varney, "Earl Warren: Ike's Worst Appointment," *American Mercury* (August 1958), 5.

6. "The Week," *National Review*, June 29, 1957, 3.

7. See White, *Earl Warren: A Public Life*, 243–44; Weaver, *Warren: The Man, the Court, the Era*, 288–89; Katcher, *Earl Warren: A Political Biography*, 365–68; and Christman, ed., *Public Papers of Chief Justice Earl Warren*, 150–75.

8. Christman, ed., *Public Papers of Chief Justice Earl Warren*, 174.

9. See Weaver, *Warren: The Man, the Court, the Era*, 289; and Pollack, *Earl Warren: The Judge Who Changed America*, 189.

10. Harlan had supported the Smith Act in previous decisions, so many observers saw this ruling as evidence of Warren's growing influence over his fellow justices.

11. Christman, ed., *Public Papers of Chief Justice Earl Warren*, 187. See also Weaver, *Warren: The Man, the Court, the Era*, 289–90; and Pollack, *Earl Warren: The Judge Who Changed America*, 188. For an extended discussion of academic freedom, see J. Peter Byrne, "Academic Freedom: A 'Special Concern of the First Amendment,'" *Yale Law Journal* 99, no. 2 (November 1989): 251–340, esp. 289–93.

12. Burris Jenkins, Jr., "What's Wrong with this Picture?" *Journal American*, June 30, 1957, National Republic Magazine Collection, box 675, folder 5, HIA.

13. "Here's How the Supreme Court Is Stirring Things Up," *U.S. News and World Report*, June 28, 1957, 30. In the same issue, see "In the Court's Own Words," 35–38.

14. Forrest Davis, "The Court Reaches for Total Power," *National Review*, July 6, 1957, 33.

15. Ibid., 36.

16. Varney, "Earl Warren: Ike's Worst Appointment," 6. For what is surely a more accurate version of the events at the 1952 convention, see David W. Reinhard, *The Republican Right since 1945* (Lexington: University Press of Kentucky, 1983), 75–96.

17. "Has Congress Abdicated?" *National Review*, June 29, 1957, 5.

18. "What Congress Is Doing to Curb the Supreme Court," *U.S. News and World Report*, July 12, 1957, 50.

19. Ibid.

20. "The Supreme Court's New Line-Up," *Business Week*, July 6, 1957, 34. See also James Burnham, "Why Not Investigate the Court?" *National Review*, July 20, 1957, 83–85; Paulsen Spence, "The Constitution versus the Court," *American Mercury* (January 1959), 69–74, 97; James O. Eastland, "Box Score on the Supreme Court," *American Mercury* (September 1958), 27–28; "The Court Makes It Harder to Control Red Spies' Movements," *Saturday Evening Post*, August 2, 1958, 10; Telford Taylor, "Is the Supreme Court Supreme?" *New York Times*, October 5, 1958, 10, 80–82; L. Brent Bozell, "A Bill to Curb the Court," *National Review*, March 1, 1958, 200–201; and "Court and Civil Liberties," *America*, June 29, 1957, 355.

21. Michael R. Belknap, *Cold War Political Justice* (Westport, Conn.: Greenwood, 1977), 261. Belknap also points out how the Smith Act opened a door for

the growth of government surveillance agencies, in particular the FBI's Counter-Intelligence Program. See 281.

22. "Mr. Eisenhower Falls to the Summit," *National Review*, August 15, 1959, 263.

23. Only one of *National Review*'s editors favored Khrushchev's visit: Whittaker Chambers. See Sam Tanenhaus, *Whittaker Chambers* (New York: Random House, 1997), 512.

24. "What Khrushchev Intends," *National Review*, August 29, 1959, 293.

25. "How to Protest?" *National Review*, August 29, 1959, 293. One *National Review* editor shortened the sticker to "Khrushchev Welcome Here" and placed it on the front bumper of his car. "Not Welcome Here," *National Review Bulletin*, September 5, 1959, 4.

26. Letters to the Editor, *National Review*, August 29, 1959, 310.

27. See "Not Welcome Here," 3. The article mentions a full-page newspaper advertisement taken out by the Committee against Summit Entanglements (CASE), a front group led by John Birch Society founder Robert Welch. CASE was a trial run for Welch in the world of organizational anticommunism, not only providing experience in how to attract citizens but also getting his name out to thousands of engaged conservatives.

28. "A Call for National Mourning," advertisement in *National Review*, September 12, 1959, 323. This committee was formed by Marvin Liebman, a former liberal who became one of the key figures in the postwar conservative movement.

29. Advertisement in the *New York Times*, September 14, 1959, 15.

30. Advertisement for Khrushchev Protest Rally, *National Review*, September 12, 1959, back cover. For the text of Buckley's speech, see "The Damage We Have Done to Ourselves," *National Review*, September 26, 1959, 349–51.

31. John B. Judis, *William F. Buckley, Jr., Patron Saint of the Conservatives* (New York: Simon and Schuster, 1988), 175.

32. See *National Review Bulletin*, September 19, 1959, 3; and "For the Record," *National Review*, September 26, 1959, 347.

33. Dan Smoot, "Thirteen Days," *Dan Smoot Report*, October 5, 1959, p. 316.

34. Anon., n.d., Elizabeth Churchill Brown Papers, box 32, folder 7, HIA.

35. Maloney, "Turn Your Back and Say a Prayer," *Tablet*, August 22, 1959, ibid.

36. See "Anti-Khrushchev Protests Planned," n.d., Walter Judd Papers, box 222, folder 3, HIA. Hoping to spotlight the situation's irony, the committee issued a press release that cited violations of protesters' First Amendment rights. While wearing black armbands or carrying black flags, some Americans were forcibly removed from Khrushchev's parade route in their cities. For these conservatives their inability to protest freely represented yet another encroachment by the Leviathan. See press release "Committee for Freedom Scores Suppression and Arrests of Peaceful Demonstrators in Khrushchev Parade," n.d., in Judd Papers, box 222, folder 3, HIA.

37. See "K Goes Home" and "The Camp David Conference," *Time*, October 5, 1959, 19–21.

38. "First Look at No. 1 Red," *U.S. News and World Report*, September 28, 1959, 39–40.

39. "An Unwitting 'Paul Revere'?" *Newsweek*, September 28, 1959, 33.

40. "What Americans Think," *Newsweek*, September 28, 1959, 39.

41. Analysts in Hollywood knew immediately that something had gone wrong with the choice of films for Khrushchev to see. The trade journal *Variety* reported, "Nobody at 20th [Century–Fox] or the State Dept. seems to have had the foresight to know that Russians are quite puritanical, and that K's reaction might have been anticipated." Such mistakes would do economic damage to Hollywood in two ways: first by sending a message to film distributors abroad about the lack of sensitivity of American studios, and second by reinforcing the image many Americans had of Hollywood as an immoral place that rebuffed the church. See "Culture and the Can-Can," *Variety*, September 30, 1959, 1.

42. L. Brent Bozell, "They Gave the Orders," *National Review*, October 10, 1959, 387.

43. Gallup Poll Data, *Gallup Poll Reports, 1935–1968* (Princeton, N.J.: American Institute of Public Opinion, 1969), September 28, 1959, 325.

44. See "How Sincere Was Khrushchev?" *National Review*, October 24, 1959, 413–14. Robert A. Taft advocated such a strategy in 1951. See *A Foreign Policy for Americans* (Garden City, N.Y.: Doubleday, 1951).

45. Broad overviews of the culture of the Cold War include Richard M. Fried, *Nightmare in Red* (New York: Oxford University Press, 1990) and *The Russians Are Coming! The Russians Are Coming!* (New York: Oxford University Press, 1998); and Stephen J. Whitfield, *The Culture of the Cold War* (Baltimore: Johns Hopkins University Press, 1991).

46. *Masters* held one of the top three spots on the bestseller list for a total of twenty-two weeks. See the *New York Times Book Review*, April 6, March 4, June 1, August 3, and September 7, 1958.

47. For the sake of brevity, only Hoover's book will be examined here. For a review of Gordon, see C. P. Ives, "The Supreme Court: Two Views," *Modern Age* (Winter 1959–60), 87–90. For reviews of Skousen, see the *Freeman* 9, no. 8 (1959), 8; and *Intelligence Digest* 20, no. 240 (1958), 19. On Skousen, see also C. O. Garshwiler to Eugene C. Pulliam, September 30, 1959, Jameson Campaigne Papers, box 4, folder "Sept. 1–October 30, 1959," HIA.

48. Samuel A. Stouffer, *Communism, Conformity, and Civil Liberties* (Gloucester, Mass.: Peter Smith, 1963), 230.

49. Among the more notable books on Hoover are Richard Gid Powers, *G-Men: Hoover's FBI in American Popular Culture* (Carbondale: Southern Illinois University Press, 1983); Kenneth O'Reilly, *Hoover and the Un-Americans* (Philadelphia: Temple University Press, 1983); and Athan G. Theoharis and John Stuart Cox, *The Boss: J. Edgar Hoover and the Great American Inquisition* (Philadelphia: Temple University Press, 1988).

50. Hoover had worked for years to give millions of Americans the impression that he had a close, friendly relationship with them. Though he did not personally respond to their letters, his assistants implied that his counsel was there exclusively for them. Hoover also published articles in popular periodicals, which further deepened his connection to much of America. With essays like "Could Your Child Become a Red?" Hoover addressed what concerned parents in a forthright and simplistic way and provided what seemed like easy solutions that anyone could implement. See J. Edgar Hoover, "Could Your Child Become a Red?" reprinted by

Protect America League, May 19, 1952, Alfred Kohlberg Papers, box 86, folder "J. Edgar Hoover," HIA.

51. COINTELPRO became much more famous in the next decade, when the FBI used it against individuals and groups it considered radical or subversive. See, for example, Cathy Perkus, ed., *COINTELPRO: The FBI's Secret War on Political Freedom* (New York: Monad, 1975).

52. Richard Gid Powers, *Secrecy and Power: The Life of J. Edgar Hoover* (New York: Free Press, 1987), 340.

53. Ibid. In 1954, however, Eisenhower remarked that there were now only 25,000 members of the CPUSA and that Americans should let the FBI take care of them. It is not clear whether Eisenhower used inflated figures (possibly supplied by Hoover) to ensure continued support for the agency and its director. See Richard Gid Powers, *Not without Honor* (New York: Free Press, 1995), 272.

54. Hoover decided against dismantling the newly formed (and apparently effective) COINTELPRO-CPUSA and instead expanded its reach, which cleared the way for heightened surveillance on Americans of diverse backgrounds during the 1960s.

55. Powers, *Secrecy and Power*, 344. Powers goes on to say that the ghostwriters never received a dime of the book's profits, a fact that spurred the joke within the bureau, "*Masters of Deceit*, written by the Master of Deceit who never even read it."

56. Ibid., 344. ABC television later bought the rights to the book, but it was never filmed. See Powers, *G-Men*, 244.

57. J. Edgar Hoover, *Masters of Deceit* (New York: Henry Holt, 1958), 85–94.

58. Ibid., 84–85.

59. Ibid., 320–21.

60. Charles Poore, "Books of the Times," *New York Times*, March 15, 1958, 15.

61. One curator of the show responded to Eisenhower, "Some people think the President's paintings aren't so good either." Robert J. Donovan, "President Is Critical of Art for Moscow—Calls Levine Painting 'Lampoon,' 'His Not So Good Either,' Is Reply," *New York Herald Tribune*, July 2, 1959, in "American Art at the Moscow Fair," *Congressional Record—Senate*, July 2, 1959 (Washington, D.C.: Government Printing Office, 1959), 12548.

62. The most informative source on the uses of art in the Cold War is Jane De Hart Matthews, "Art and Politics in Cold War America," *American Historical Review* 81, no. 4 (October 1976): 762–87. Also see Christopher Lasch, "The Cultural Cold War: A Short History of the Congress of Cultural Freedom," in *Towards a New Past*, ed. Barton J. Bernstein, (New York: Pantheon, 1968). On the controversy over the State Department show Advancing American Art of 1946–48, see Neil Harris, "Museums and Controversy: Some Introductory Reflections," *Journal of American History* 82, no. 3 (December 1995): 1105–7.

63. Francis E. Walter, "The Moscow Art Exhibit," *Human Events*, June 24, 1959, 2.

64. Ibid.

65. The history of HUAC is a fascinating subject, which extends beyond the scope of this discussion. The Hamilton Fish Committee of the House of Representatives, founded in 1930, focused on the social unrest caused by the depression. Dies founded

HUAC in 1938 and coined the famous term *fellow traveler* in the process. For more on both, see Joel Kovel, *Red Hunting in the Promised Land* (New York: Basic, 1994); and William Gellermann, *Martin Dies* (New York: John Day, 1944).

66. Francis E. Walter, "Our Art Exhibition in Moscow," *American Mercury* (September 1959), 98–104.

67. Wheeler Williams, "The Truth about Modern Art," *American Mercury* (January 1959), 98.

68. Testimony of Wheeler Williams, "The American National Exhibition, Moscow, July 1959," in Hearings before the Committee on Un-American Activities, House of Representatives, July 1, 1959 (Washington, D.C.: Government Printing Office, 1959), 915.

69. Ibid.

70. Ibid., 916.

71. Testimony of Ben Shahn, ibid., 945.

72. Testimony of Wheeler Williams, ibid., 910.

73. "Leftists Open Drive to End House Group," *New York Times*, September 21, 1957, 8. For the best summary of the Emergency Civil Liberties Committee, see Jerold Simmons, *Operation Abolition* (New York: Garland, 1986), 128–77.

74. See "Lehman Opposes House Unit Shift," *New York Times*, January 3, 1959, 7; "Chairman Walter's Latest," *New York Times*, January 6, 1959, 32; and "Rayburn Scuttles Plan to Kill Panel," *New York Times*, January 16, 1959, 31.

75. HUAC held seven hearings between July 1, 1959, and the hearings in San Francisco in May 1960. See Richard N. Katz, comp., *The Legal Struggle to Abolish the House Committee on Un-American Activities: The Papers of Jeremiah Gutman* (Berkeley, Calif.: Meiklejohn Civil Liberties Institute, 1980), 31.

76. Walter Goodman, *The Committee* (New York: Farrar, Straus and Giroux, 1968), 426.

77. For some of the national controversy leading up to Chessman's execution, see E. W. Kensworthy, "Chessman Case Stirs New Furor," *New York Times*, February 21, 1960, 1, 45.

78. Simmons, *Operation Abolition*, 192.

79. Goodman, *The Committee*, 430.

80. Why the hoses were turned on has always been a point of contention between the two sides. HUAC supporters say that at first the hoses were turned on with only slight pressure to show the students what they faced. Those who got wet from this initial hosing became more agitated, conservatives claimed, and attacked a police officer. After the officer was rescued from the students, the hoses were turned on full force. Students claimed that they never attacked an officer and that the hoses were immediately turned on full force.

81. Walter quoted in W. E. Schmitt and A. O. Hanks, "San Francisco's Black Friday," in *Congressional Record—House*, May 18, 1961 (Washington, D.C.: Government Printing Office, 1961), 8391.

82. Walter was referring to the 1958 attack on Vice President Nixon's motorcade in Caracas, Venezuela. "'Operation Abolition' Authentic," *Enterprise* (Livingston, Mont.) June 22, 1961, in Francis E. Walter, "'Operation Abolition' Authentic," *Congressional Record—Appendix*, July 17, 1961 (Washington, D.C.: Government Printing Office, 1961), A5399.

83. "Don't Miss 'Operation Abolition,'" *Daily Plainsman* (Huron, S.D.), quoted in Karl E. Mundt, "Don't Miss 'Operation Abolition,'" *Congressional Record—Appendix*, June 1, 1961 (Washington, D.C.: Government Printing Office, 1961), A3892. The Minnesota Civil Liberties Union estimated that in February 1961 alone, 75,000 people saw the film. In addition to selling copies of the forty-five-minute film at $100 each, Washington Video Productions also produced a thirty-minute version for television. See Simmons, *Operation Abolition*, 197–98.

84. See, for example, James C. Davis's address to the House on March 13, 1961, in which he described reaching the chief of the Army Information Department, who informed him that he had purchased thirty-four copies of the film for showings on army posts. Davis, "Committee on Un-American Activities," *Congressional Record—House*, March 13, 1961 (Washington, D.C.: Government Printing Office, 1961), 3805.

85. "James Roosevelt Hanged in Effigy," *New York Times*, August 18, 1960, 18.

86. See, for example, Santa Clara Democratic Central Committee, "A Report on 'Operation Abolition,'" *Congressional Record—Appendix*, March 21, 1961 (Washington, D.C.: Government Printing Office, 1961), A1981; "Film Documentary on Riot Withdrawn," *Los Angeles Mirror*, April 13, 1961, ibid., A2484–85; for remarks by Fitts Ryan, see "The New York Times Views House Un-American Activities Committee," May 10, 1961, ibid., A3294.

87. Roosevelt to Colleagues, December 31, 1960, in Minnesota Civil Liberties Union Papers, box 4, folder, "HUAC 1961" quoted in Simmons, *Operation Abolition*, 230.

88. In 1969 HUAC renamed itself the House Internal Security Committee; it was finally abolished in 1975.

89. Gallup Poll data from surveys conducted on January 29 and May 5, 1961, in *Gallup Poll Reports, 1935–1968* (Princeton, N.J.: American Institute of Public Opinion, 1969), 337, 339.

90. Simmons, *Operation Abolition*, 201.

91. One historian has called the May 13 protests the "turning point in the national campaign to abolish HUAC." Simmons, *Operation Abolition*, 194.

92. Committee on Un-American Activities, *The Truth about the Film "Operation Abolition,"* pt. 1 (Washington, D.C.: Government Printing Office, 1961), 4.

93. Ibid.

94. Ibid., pt. 2, 22.

95. Ibid., 7, 23–28.

CHAPTER 3

1. From 1931 to 1933 Andrews was the Virginia auditor of public accounts; from 1945 to 1947 he served as the organizer and first director of the Corporation Audits Division, U.S. General Accounting Office; and from 1953 to 1955 he was U.S. commissioner of internal revenue. See the title page of the inventory of the T. Coleman Andrews Papers, Oregon Special Collections.

2. Robert Welch to T. Coleman Andrews, October 27, 1958, T. Coleman Andrews Papers, box 1, folder "John Birch Society 1," Oregon Special Collections. For an-

other example of Welch recruiting a businessman who would eventually join the council, see correspondence between Robert Welch and James W. Clise, August 13, 1959, October 1, 1959, and October 12, 1959, all in James W. Clise Papers, box 1, Oregon Special Collections.

3. T. Coleman Andrews, "Notes," T. Coleman Andrews Papers, box 1, folder "John Birch Society 1," Oregon Special Collections.

4. Ibid. When Andrews wrote about "wastefulness," he was referring to Welch's example of the Soviet's 1957 triumph with Sputnik. Welch and others thought that this was a ploy to force America to overspend on the race to space, which would eventually cause the country's downfall. President Ronald Reagan later employed this same strategy and used the Strategic Defense Initiative ("Star Wars") to help force the Soviet Union into bankruptcy.

5. Ibid. See also Robert Welch, *The Blue Book* (Belmont, Mass.: Western Islands, 1959), 37, 45, for Welch's statements on collectivism as a cancer that infects civilizations and that only "drastic surgery" can cure such diseases.

6. Welch, *Blue Book*, 146.

7. Ibid.

8. Glenn A. Green to Robert Welch, November 11, 1959, T. Coleman Andrews Papers, box 1, folder "JBS 1," Oregon Special Collections.

9. Liberal investigators Benjamin Epstein and Arnold Forster estimated enrollment at between 20,000 and 50,000 in 1964, although they also commented that "estimates of the membership by the press and other observers have varied from 50,000 to 100,000." Furthermore the authors extrapolated from 1961 Massachusetts tax returns an estimate of more than 24,000 members. See Forster and Epstein, *Danger on the Right* (New York: Random House, 1964), 11.

10. Myer Feldman, "Memorandum for the President. Subject: Right-Wing Groups," August 15, 1963, Papers of John F. Kennedy, Presidential Papers, President's Office Files, box 106, folder "Right Wing Movements, Part 1," JFKL.

11. As historian Richard Hofstadter put it, "Third parties are like bees: once they have stung, they die." Hofstadter, *The Age of Reform* (New York: Knopf, 1956), 97.

12. Welch, *Blue Book*, 53. See also G. Edward Griffin, *The Life and Words of Robert Welch* (Thousand Oaks, Calif.: American Media, 1975), 267–71.

13. See Griffin, *Life and Words of Robert Welch*, 80; and Carolyn Wyman, *I'm a Spam Fan* (Stamford, Conn.: Longmeadow, 1993).

14. "To a Fellow-Citizen of Massachusetts," September 27, 1949, Lucille Cardin Crain Papers, box 58, Oregon Special Collections.

15. Welch, *Blue Book*, 112.

16. Robert Welch to Henry Regnery, November 2, 1951, Henry Regnery Papers, box 78, folder 78–1, HIA. In an example of what is either bias or sloppy research, Griffin, in *The Life and Words of Robert Welch*, 169, claims that Regnery "wrote Welch and offered to have his company publish this letter as a small book."

17. Such efforts on Welch's part, however, eventually caused him to seek an increase of his own royalties, since the bulk of the distribution came from Welch's own organization. See Robert Welch to Henry Regnery, April 29, 1952, Henry Regnery Papers, box 78, folder 78–1, HIA.

18. Welch was also encouraged by like-minded friends to continue investigating America's political situation. After reading *May God Forgive Us*, Alfred Kohlberg, a

friend and confidant of Welch's, wrote: "May I direct your attention to something that is badly needed now. That is a book or pamphlet such as yours, written well as yours, telling where we should go from here. Do not think it is impossible, it is extremely easy. Practically all long-time students of Communism are in agreement on what should be done. None of them have yet been able to put it in popular and understandable form. It seems to me that maybe that is your job." Kohlberg to Welch, December 10, 1952, Alfred Kohlberg Papers, box 200, folder "Robert H. W. Welch, Jr., to 1956," HIA.

19. Robert Welch, *The Life of John Birch* (Chicago: Henry Regnery, 1954).

20. Harry Goldgar, unpublished memoirs in author's possession, 1994, 109. Goldgar adds that after the trial, signs reading "Lynch Saint Birch" appeared on Mercer's campus. Needless to say, such details of Birch's life were conveniently avoided and forgotten by Welch. Goldgar, 113. See also "Young John Birch Stirred a Furor," *New York Times*, April 23, 1961, 64.

21. See Griffin, *Life and Words of Robert Welch*, 112.

22. *Vital Speeches of the Day* 22, August 1, 1957, 623–27.

23. Ibid., 623.

24. In 1957 Welch was convinced that, if it stayed on its present course, Vietnam would fall to the communists within a few years.

25. William F. Buckley to Robert Welch, July 4, 1955, box 3, folder "Welch, Robert H. W., Jr.," Buckley Papers. Regnery introduced the two men in the 1950s. See William F. Buckley to Henry Regnery, February 1, 1962, Henry Regnery Papers, box 10, folder "WFB, 1956–1966," HIA.

26. Robert Welch to William F. Buckley, Jr., June 6, 1957, box 4, folder "Robert Welch," Buckley Papers.

27. In the 1952 election Republicans had gained twenty-two seats not to mention the White House.

28. Thus a Bircher could collect *The Black Book*, *The Blue Book*, *The White Book*(s) (bound collections of the society's monthly *Bulletins*), and *The Pink Book*, a periodical collection of articles about the society. Opponents of the JBS countered with the *John Birch Society Coloring Book*. See Meier Papers.

29. For a laudatory evaluation of the book, see Griffin, *Life and Words of Robert Welch*, 225–49. Far more common are analyses that accuse Welch of slandering Eisenhower and others, including Gerald Schomp, *Birchism Was My Business* (New York: Macmillan, 1970), 36–39; Milton A. Waldor, *Peddlers of Fear* (Newark, N.J.: Lynnross, 1966), 30–31; Forster and Epstein, *Danger on the Right*, 40–43; as well as a vast number of articles in periodicals, the most effective being those from *National Review* in 1962 and 1965.

30. Alfred Kohlberg to Robert Welch, September 2, 1958, Alfred Kohlberg Papers, box 200, folder "Robert H. W. Welch, Jr., 1957–," HIA.

31. Ibid.

32. Robert Welch to Alfred Kohlberg, September 4, 1958, ibid.

33. "Meet the Press," May 21, 1961, p. 2 of transcript in Lawrence Spivak Papers, box 158, folder "TV Transcripts: Welch, Robert, 5/21/61," Manuscripts and Archives Division, Library of Congress. Welch began inserting a disclaimer at the beginning of *The Politician* only after Kohlberg's September 2, 1958, letter. For example, in a copy of *The Politician* sent to Bryton Barron, a signed note from Welch stated, "Each

copy of the manuscript is numbered and this is No. [handwritten 4b]. I am asking you to consider it as on loan to you, for your eyes only, until it is returned. But I shall not ask for it back in a hurry, because if anything happens to me I should like to have a goodly number of copies safely out in other hands." Robert Welch to Bryton Barron, n.d., Bryton Barron Papers, box 10, Oregon Special Collections.

34. Lucille Cardin Crain to Robert Welch, February 18, 1959, Lucille Cardin Crain Papers, box 58, Oregon Special Collections.

35. J. W. Clise to B. E. Hutchinson, February 19, 1959, James Clise Papers, box 1, Oregon Special Collections.

36. Perhaps the most famous example of such an awakening is Whittaker Chambers's turn from communist to Alger Hiss's accuser. Chambers's autobiography, *Witness* (New York: Random House, 1952), is a powerful tale, which inspired many conservatives to take up the hunt in the 1950s. For Chambers's epiphany, see his "Foreword in the Form of a Letter to My Children," 3–21.

37. Howard Kershner to Robert Welch, February 6, 1959, Howard Kershner Papers, box 19, Oregon Special Collections.

38. Ibid.

39. A. C. Wedemeyer to Robert Welch, October 14, 1961, Albert Wedemeyer Papers, box 115, folder 9, HIA.

40. A. C. Wedemeyer to Robert Welch, September 5, 1961, ibid.

41. Robert Welch to A. C. Wedemeyer, October 10, 1961, ibid.

42. Arthur G. McDowell, form letter, May 5, 1961, ibid. See also A. C. Wedemeyer to George S. Birch, December 24, 1962, folder 10, ibid.

43. William F. Buckley to Robert Welch, December 16, 1958, box 6, folder "Welch, Robert," Buckley Papers.

44. Ibid.

45. Robert Welch to William F. Buckley, Jr., December 18, 1958, box 6, folder "Robert Welch," Buckley Papers.

46. Ibid.

47. Griffin, *Life and Words of Robert Welch*, 254.

48. T. Coleman Andrews to Robert Welch, January 14, 1959, T. Coleman Andrews Papers, box 1, folder "John Birch Society 1," Oregon Special Collections.

49. Robert Welch, "Confidential Report No. 1," December 19, 1958, T. Coleman Andrews Papers, box 1, folder "John Birch Society 1," Oregon Special Collections. Medford Evans was a professor at Northwestern State College in Louisiana who was fired, Welch claimed, because of his "uncompromising stand against Communism." See Welch, *Blue Book*, 75.

50. Robert Welch to T. Coleman Andrews, January 7, 1959, T. Coleman Andrews Papers, box 1, folder "John Birch Society 1," Oregon Special Collections.

51. Welch, *Blue Book*, 146.

52. Robert Welch to T. Coleman Andrews, November 27, 1959, T. Coleman Andrews Papers, box 1, folder "John Birch Society 1," Oregon Special Collections.

53. Although most of the men who agreed to be on the council remained on it for a number of years, some resigned after disagreements with Welch, and others were forced to resign. Andrews resigned once in 1962, withdrew his resignation, and then resigned permanently in 1963. Originally resigning because of disagreements with Welch over *The Politician* (or similar conspiracy theory arguments), Andrews's

second and final resignation came after he missed too many council meetings while tending to his ill wife. T. Coleman Andrews to Robert Welch, March 14, 1963. See also Welch to Andrews, March 20, 1961; Welch, Council Bulletin, November 16, 1960; Ben McMillan to Andrews, March 16, 1962; and Andrews to Welch, March 29, 1962, all in T. Coleman Andrews Papers, box 1, folder "John Birch Society 1," Oregon Special Collections.

54. Forster and Epstein, *Danger on the Right*, 39. Even as late as 1989, when fundraising seemed to do little more than keep the society alive, individual contributions of $1,000 or $2,000 were not unusual. See Field Staff Weekly Sales Report, box 10, JBS Records.

55. This argument is drawn from Lawrence Levine's interpretation of popular culture in nineteenth-century America, as well as his analysis of depression-era mass culture. See Levine, *Highbrow/Lowbrow* (Cambridge, Mass.: Harvard University Press, 1988), and "The Folklore of Industrial Society: Popular Culture and Its Audiences," in his *The Unpredictable Past* (New York: Oxford University Press, 1993), 291–319.

56. Member's Monthly Message Department, n.d., box 3, folder "MMM Dept.," JBS Records.

57. "Review and Setting Tone for the New Year," n.d., box 3, folder "MMM Dept.," JBS Records.

58. Laurence Swanson, "MMM Summary, Week of November 2, 1964," box 7, folder "64," JBS Records.

59. Ibid.

60. In areas with a higher density of Birchers, section leaders were situated between the coordinator and the chapter leader.

61. Although there are many examples of communists switching sides to become leaders in the anticommunist battle, two well-known figures were Whittaker Chambers and Nathaniel Weyl. Each spoke from an "expert's" perspective, and often their experience insulated them from criticism from the Left. See Chambers, *Witness*; and interview with Weyl, "I Was in a Communist Unit with Hiss," *U.S. News and World Report*, January 9, 1953, 22–40.

62. Bryton Barron, "Daily Notes 1960," Bryton Barron Papers, box 10, Oregon Special Collections.

63. Bryton Barron, "Daily Notes 1960 and 1961," entries for November 9, 1960, and January 16, 1961, ibid.

64. Leslie Zodun to Bryton Barron, April 10, 1961, ibid.

65. Membership for men cost $24 a year, while women paid only half that. While not elucidated upon anywhere, Welch (who set the rates) probably thought that more men than women worked and that they should pay more since they had more. It is not clear if Welch believed that men would be more active in the society or if he was surprised by the amount of women participants.

66. See Regional Office Memo to Chapter Leaders, n.d., Bryton Barron Papers, box 10, Oregon Special Collections.

67. On chapters, see ibid.; for presentations, see "A Presentation Meeting," n.d., box 4, folder "Presentations," JBS Records; for meeting questions, see "Suggested Questions for Discussion," Bryton Barron Papers, box 10, Oregon Special Collections.

68. Meier Papers.

69. See Fred W. Grupp, Jr., "The Political Perspectives of Birch Society Members," in *The American Right Wing: Readings in Political Behavior*, ed. Robert A. Schoenberger (New York: Holt, Rinehart and Winston, 1969), 83–113.

70. There is reason to believe that Grupp's data were flawed. For example, in 1961 Welch wrote to a friend that "approximately one-half of our members all over the country are Catholic." Additionally, declared Welch, "approximately one-half of our field staff throughout the country is Catholic, and around two-thirds of our employees here in the Home Office" (see Robert Welch to Neil McCarthy, April 22, 1961, Granville Knight Papers, box 3, Oregon Special Collections). Grupp's presentation also depicts the society in a deceptively static way, which gives an impression that membership was not subject to fluctuations in population, the political climate, or repercussions from events.

71. Grupp's findings are in stark contrast to those of Stanley Mosk, attorney general of California and author of the famous report on the John Birch Society. Mosk notes, "The cadre of the John Birch Society seems to be formed primarily of wealthy businessmen, retired military officers and little old ladies in tennis shoes." Mosk's comments, needless to say, enraged many on the Right. See Mosk, "Report on the John Birch Society," July 7, 1961 (Sacramento: State of California Office of the Attorney General), 1.

72. John Birch Society, "Leaders' Manual," n.d., box 41, JBS Records.

73. Ibid., 15.

74. Ibid.

75. Meier Papers.

76. "Leaders' Manual," 16, JBS Records.

77. Forster and Epstein, *Danger on the Right*, 22–24, 43.

78. "Leaders' Manual," 16, JBS Records. Fluoridation was a popular issue for some JBS chapters. Anti-fluoridationists believed that either the principle of adding a chemical to their drinking water or the actual fluoride itself was wholly objectionable. Anti-fluoridationists, however, never seemed to complain when water was treated with chlorine or other purifying agents.

79. See "Impeach Earl Warren?" n.d., Elizabeth Churchill Brown Papers, box 40, folder 14, HIA.

80. Robert Welch to T. Coleman Andrews, January 7, 1959, T. Coleman Andrews Papers, box 1, folder 2, Oregon Special Collections.

81. T. Coleman Andrews to Robert Welch, May 1, 1961, ibid.

82. Letter to "Honorable _____" [*sic*], March 20, 1961, ibid.

83. Robert Welch, "To All Coordinators, Section Leaders, and Chapter Leaders," June 18, 1963, box 4, folder "Prayer in Schools," JBS Records. Later, Welch's biographer G. Edward Griffin also added his voice to the denunciation in *The Great Prison Break: The Supreme Court Leads the Way* (Belmont, Mass.: Western Islands, 1970).

84. Robert Welch to T. Coleman Andrews, January 7, 1959, T. Coleman Andrews Papers, box 1, folder 2, Oregon Special Collections.

85. Robert Welch, "A Letter to the South on Segregation," first published in *One Man's Opinion* (September 1956), 28–37.

86. Welch believed that little had changed between the 1896 decision of *Plessy v. Ferguson* and 1954. In order to maintain this tunnel vision, Welch ignored such watershed events as the Great Migration, when blacks left the South in large num-

bers during the 1910s; World War I; the revitalization of the Ku Klux Klan; the Great Depression and New Deal; World War II; and the desegregation of the armed forces.

87. John Fall to [name expurgated], May 24, 1967, box 5, JBS Records.

88. Welch never substantially changed his position on the civil rights movement and always focused on the deceit he believed was used to instigate protests. Never one to shy away from controversy, in 1965 Welch gave an address at Howard University in which he called the United States "insane" and cited, among other examples, "Negro rioting sparked by Communist agitation." *Facts on File* 25, no. 1310, December 2–8, 1965, 450.

89. On civilian review boards, see information on the Support Your Local Police campaign in box 40; on tax reform, see information on TRIM (Tax Reform Immediately) in box 40; on Vietnam, see information on TRAIN (To Restore American Independence Now) in box 4; and on the Panama Canal, see box 1, all in JBS Records. More information on all of these campaigns also is available in various John Birch Society *Bulletins*.

90. In an August 17, 1964, memo from W. E. Dunham to Robert Welch, Dunham relates that a member on Long Island had informed him that on August 8, approximately 150 to 180 JBS members distributed some 80,000 flyers. The member told Dunham that "the police gave them overwhelming cooperation and that in almost every area the local police are 'in love' with the JBS." Memo in box 40, JBS Records.

91. One example of an early political campaign of sorts was the 1959 CASE (Committee against Summit Entanglements) program. Welch set up CASE as a front to prevent Eisenhower from meeting Khrushchev in 1959. See CASE memo "To Present Members and Prospective Members," August 7, 1959, T. Coleman Andrews papers, box 1, Oregon Special Collections.

92. Robert Welch, "A Statement for the Press," March 17, 1962, T. Coleman Andrews Papers, box 1, folder 3, Oregon Special Collections.

93. In this sense Welch was following a strand of conservatism that later emerged as a political force in its own right: libertarianism.

94. Robert Welch, "To Members of the Council," and form letter to Ezra Taft Benson, both August 1, 1963, T. Coleman Andrews Papers, box 1, Oregon Special Collections. Benson's son, Reed, had become a coordinator for the society in October 1962.

95. Robert Welch, "To Our Coordinators," November 7, 1962, box 3, folder "Education," JBS Records.

96. Ibid.

97. Robert Welch, "About Barry Goldwater," July 10, 1963, box 3, folder "Barry Goldwater," JBS Records.

98. Goldwater felt similarly about Welch: "I must agree with you that Bob Welch is politically naive to a marked degree. His dedication and his intelligence could be put to much better use if he didn't inject them into the political stream directly but by the circuitous route of candidates." See Barry Goldwater to Constantine Brown, September 1, 1960, Elizabeth Churchill Brown Papers, box 2, folder "Goldwater, Barry," HIA.

99. Although the society formally maintained its nonpartisan position throughout the 1960s, one journalist, Chip Berlet, reported finding a letter from Welch to

George Wallace in a collection of Birch Society documents that asked him to "adopt the Birch platform." Only days after the 1968 election, Berlet says, Welch wrote, "It is the ambition and the intention of Richard Nixon, during the next eight years, to make himself the dictator of the world." Welch urged Wallace to consider running in 1972 under Birchite principles, since "the people of this country are ready for an anti-Communist crusade behind some political leader who really means it." Apparently Wallace's political background impressed rather than disgusted Welch. This writer could not verify the existence of the document. See Chip Berlet, "Trashing the Birchers," *Boston Phoenix*, July 14–20, 1989, 10.

100. [Name expurgated] to J. Edgar Hoover, June 7, 1965, FBI Documents.

101. [Name expurgated] to Hoover, June 5, 1965, FBI Documents.

102. J. Edgar Hoover to [names expurgated], June 10, 1965, July 23, 1965, and July 20, 1965, FBI Documents.

103. "Memorandum from SAC, Buffalo, to Director, FBI," June 17, 1965, FBI Documents.

104. These cards, however, most likely belonged either to a Minutemen chapter or a similar paramilitary group. Unlike the JBS, the Minutemen actually practiced paramilitary maneuvers to prepare for the impending communist invasion. See J. Harry Jones, *The Minutemen* (Garden City, N.Y.: Doubleday, 1968); and California Bureau of Criminal Identification and Investigation, *Para-Military Organizations in California* (Sacramento: California Bureau of Criminal Identification and Investigation, 1965).

105. "Memorandum, SAC, Kansas City to Director, FBI, Subject: Research," July 15, 1965, FBI Documents.

106. [Name expurgated] to Walter Winchell, July 5, 1965, FBI Documents.

107. "Memo from Deputy Director, CIA, to Director, FBI," December 14, 1962, in CIA documents received under Freedom of Information Act, in author's possession.

108. In a news conference on February 7, 1962, for example, Kennedy attacked the JBS and called it "alien" to both parties; it had "no place in the Republican Party." Former President Eisenhower, said Kennedy, "has been as vigorous in his denunciations of the John Birch Society as I." *Facts on File* 22, no. 1112, February 15–21, 1962, 56.

109. Myer Feldman, "Memorandum for the President. Subject: Right-Wing Groups," John F. Kennedy Presidential Papers, President's Office Files, box 106, folder "Right Wing Movements, Part I," JFKL.

110. For more on Kennedy's attempts to control the Right using legal methods, see Elizabeth MacDonald, "The Kennedys and the IRS," *Wall Street Journal*, January 28, 1997, A16.

111. "Memorandum from Senator Gale McGee to Mike Feldman," August 14, 1963, John F. Kennedy Presidential Papers, President's Office Files, box 106, folder "Right Wing Movements, Part I," JFKL. The portrait McGee draws is similar to that of many academic observers, most notably historian Richard Hofstadter's connection between the Populists of the 1890s and supporters of McCarthy and the radical Right in the 1950s. See Hofstadter, *Age of Reform* and "The Pseudo-Conservative Revolt," in *The New American Right*, ed. Daniel Bell (New York: Criterion, 1955).

112. "Memorandum from Senator Gale McGee to Mike Feldman," August 14, 1963, John F. Kennedy Presidential Papers, President's Office Files, box 106, folder "Right Wing Movements, Part I," JFKL.

CHAPTER 4

1. In military parlance, an "admonishment" is a rebuke; at that time it was the lightest corrective measure the army could impose. See *Facts on File* 21, no. 1076, June 8–14, 1961, 218.

2. See John Lewis Gaddis, *Strategies of Containment* (New York: Oxford University Press, 1982), 88–126, 359.

3. While this NSC directive may be declassified, this author has not seen the original. After Fulbright wrote a memorandum on the NSC directive, Strom Thurmond demanded a copy from him and eventually received one, which he published in the *Congressional Record*. Fulbright's memorandum became famous among those on the Right; it was proof positive that liberals like Fulbright were out to sabotage the military. See *Congressional Record—Senate*, August 2, 1961, 14395–99. Most of the information included here on the actual NSC directive comes from Cabell Phillips, "Right Wing Officers Worrying Pentagon," *New York Times*, June 18, 1961, 1, 56.

4. For a digestible summary of the massive hearings, see U.S. Senate, *Report by Special Preparedness Subcommittee of the Committee on Armed Forces*, "The Use of Military Personnel and Facilities to Arouse the Public to the Menace of the Cold War and to Inform and Educate Armed Services Personnel on the Nature and Menace of the Cold War" (Washington, D.C.: U.S. Government Printing Office, 1962), 1–13.

5. U.S. Senate, *Hearings before the Special Preparedness Subcommittee of the Committee on Armed Services, United States Senate*, "Military Cold War Education and Speech Review Policies," pt. 3 (Washington, D.C.: U.S. Government Printing Office, 1962), 1162.

6. For representative works, see William H. Whyte, Jr., *The Organization Man* (New York: Simon and Schuster, 1956); and David Riesman, *The Lonely Crowd* (New Haven, Conn.: Yale University Press, 1958).

7. U.S. Senate, *Hearings before the Special Preparedness Subcommittee*, pt. 3, 1163.

8. Two studies that address POWs in the Korean War are Albert D. Biderman, *March to Calumny* (New York: Macmillan, 1963); and Stephen D. Wesbrook, *Political Training in the United States Army: A Reconsideration* (Columbus, Ohio: Mershon Center of Ohio State University, 1979), 22–27. Most observers credit Biderman with rectifying the misconceptions about the rate at which POWs cooperated with their communist captors.

9. See Edwin A. Walker, "Who Muzzled the Military?" address delivered December 12, 1961, Dallas, Texas, New Left Collection, box 14, folder "Anti-Communist, Various," HIA.

10. Roberts himself was dismissed in 1962 from the army for making an unauthorized speech to the Daughters of the American Revolution. Unlike Walker, who

resigned from the army, Roberts did not want to give up his military career. He successfully sued the army and received back pay, damages, and reinstatement to active service. For a wealth of information on the Pro-Blue program, see Archibald Roberts's Papers, cartons 1–5, Oregon Special Collections.

11. Walker's belief that the ACA Index was completely nonpartisan clearly illustrates how he saw the role of the United States vis-à-vis the communist enemy. Even though the ACA Index rated politicians on how conservatively they voted, Walker defended himself by saying, "The ACA Index had no partisan bias, as far as I knew. Even if it had some bias, as most documents do have, the index was factual and educational, as far as I could tell." U.S. Senate; *Hearings before the Special Preparedness Subcommittee*, pt. 4, 1419.

12. Russell Baker, "Walker Is Rebuked for Linking Public Figures to Communism," *New York Times*, June 13, 1961, 15.

13. See Sydney Gruson, "Walker Attacks Service Weekly," *New York Times*, April 17, 1961, 15.

14. The Defense Department found no connection between Walker's program and the JBS. See Department of Defense Directorate for News Services, press release, June 12, 1961, White House Name File, box 2910, JFKL.

15. "Walker Resigns," *Facts on File* 21, no. 1098, November 9–15, 1961, 417. In 1982 the army quietly reinstated Walker's pension. See Eric Pace, "General Edwin Walker, 83, Is Dead; Promoted Rightist Causes in 60's," *New York Times*, November 2, 1993, B10.

16. Walker spoke at both conservative and liberal schools about the dangers of communism and the communist-run civil rights movement. For Walker's visit to Stanford University, for example, see "Gen. Walker Charges Whites Control Negro Rights Groups," *Palo Alto Times*, October 29, 1964, 2.

17. After Walker's arrest, his stock among conservatives fell rapidly when the U.S. attorney general's office reported that he was psychologically unfit. Conservative periodicals that had supported Walker denounced his actions, and politicians who had offered their support managed to avoid the press, which left only the staunchest segregationists in his corner. For information on Walker's role in Mississippi, see correspondence in the Burke Marshall Papers, box 19, Mississippi File, and the RFK Papers, Attorney General's General Correspondence, box 11, folder "Civil Rights: Mississippi, 11/62–12/62," both in JFKL.

18. Perhaps Walker's most famous episode after his admonishment and the military-muzzling investigations came on April 10, 1963, when a sniper, later determined by the Warren Commission to be Lee Harvey Oswald, tried to assassinate the retired general. This time, however, Oswald missed.

19. [Names expurgated], MMM, n.d., box 6, folder "Tim Welch," JBS Records. Other MMMs called for a letter-writing campaign to convince the general to accept his pension so that he could put it to good use fighting communism.

20. May Orrell to Florence Dennis, May 5, 1961, enclosed in Florence B. Dennis to Bryton Barron, May 17, 1961 (emphasis in original), Bryton Barron Papers, box 10, Oregon Special Collections.

21. Clarence Manion to T. Coleman Andrews, November 7, 1962, T. Coleman Andrews Papers, box 1, folder 2, Oregon Special Collections.

22. [Name expurgated] to Home Office, c. August 5–9, 1963, and reply by D. A. Waite, August 15, 1963, both box 6, folder "Members' Letters Sent to Welch," JBS Records.

23. (Belmont, Mass.: American Opinion, 1963).

24. Walker's sidekick, Arch Roberts, became a nuisance to the society in the early 1970s when, barnstorming around the country on behalf of his program to end American involvement in the UN, he latched onto the JBS chapter system to book speaking engagements and solicit contributions. Coordinators were instructed to refuse Roberts's attempts to persuade chapters to take up his cause. See Thomas Hill to Ed [name expurgated], February 4, 1972, box 4, JBS Records.

25. *Independent American* 7, no. 4 (May 1961), 4, quoted in Eric Maxwell Odendahl, "The Maj. Gen. Edwin A. Walker Case: A Content Analysis of Four Prestige Newspapers, Four Iowa Newspapers, Three National News Magazines, and Eight Right-Wing Publications," Master's thesis, State University of Iowa, 1963, 103.

26. *Independent American* (April-May 1962), 1, University of Iowa Right Wing Collection, microfilm reel no. 164. The Courtneys were not the only conservatives— responsible or otherwise—calling for Walker to take political leadership. Book publisher Devin A. Garrity wrote to Strom Thurmond, "It is my personal hope that General Walker will run for the Senate seat now held by [Democratic] Senator [Ralph] Yarborough [of Texas]." Garrity to Thurmond, November 9, 1961, Devin Adair Garrity Papers, box 24, folder "T," HIA.

27. *Independent American* (April–May, 1962), 1. In the same issue the editors predicted that Walker was "gaining fast" in the gubernatorial primary in Texas and that he would finish as high as second or third. After Walker was arrested in Mississippi, the Courtneys shifted their focus, and Walker returned to martyr status.

28. (New Orleans, La: Conservative Society of America, 1961). See also Kent Courtney and Phoebe Courtney, *The Silencers* (New Orleans, La.: Conservative Society of America, 1965).

29. "Ten-Shun!" *National Review*, May 6, 1961, 273.

30. Ibid., 274.

31. Ibid.

32. Edwin A. Walker to William F. Buckley, Jr., June 15, 1961, in box 17, folder "Walker, E. A.," Buckley Papers.

33. William F. Buckley, Jr., to Edwin A. Walker, July 5, 1961, in box 17, folder "Walker, E. A," Buckley Papers.

34. "Let the Generals Beware," *National Review*, July 1, 1961, 407.

35. "Out: Not with a Whimper but a Bang," *National Review*, November 18, 1961, 326.

36. Medford Evans, "Citizen Edwin A. Walker: An Interview," *National Review*, December 16, 1961, 411–12. When Walker was arrested the following year in Mississippi, the magazine ran a short piece that focused on the potential violations of his civil liberties when a psychiatrist declared him unstable without ever examining him personally. See "General Walker, Stage II," *National Review*, October 23, 1962, 302.

37. Interestingly Kennedy thought that Americans should "address themselves to the kinds of problems which are created by Laos, Vietnam, by internal subversion, by the desperate life lived by so many people in this hemisphere and in other

places which the Communists exploit." Without too much trouble, one might easily draw parallels between what the president recommended and what Robert Welch recommended. "Transcript of the President's News Conference on World and Domestic Affairs," *New York Times*, April 22, 1961, 8.

38. "Are We Muzzling Those Who Know Red Tactics Best?" *Saturday Evening Post*, November 4, 1961, 82.

39. "Fair Play for General Walker," *Life*, October 6, 1961, 4.

40. "Crackpots: How They Help Communism," *Life*, December 1, 1961, 6.

41. Ibid.

42. See C. V. Clifton to Colonel Norris, April 18, 1961, White House Name File, box 2910, JFKL. As the number of letters and telegrams increased, the White House recorded the writer's name, address, and whether he supported or opposed Walker's removal. See daily tally sheets by Ralph A. Dungan, special assistant to the president, White House Name File, box 2910, JFKL.

43. Telegram from J. D. Wilson and C. E. King, June 5, 1961, ibid.

44. Mr. and Mrs. Curtis Spears to the president, August 25, 1961, ibid.

45. Frederick G. Dutton to Lucy K. Johnson, August 15, 1961, ibid.

46. Frederick G. Dutton to David K. Gillies, May 13, 1961, ibid.

47. Memo to Attorney General Robert F. Kennedy, prepared by Victor G. Reuther, Walter P. Reuther, and Joseph L. Rauh, Jr., "The Radical Right in America Today," December 19, 1961, reprinted in Victor G. Reuther, *The Brothers Reuther and the Story of the UAW* (Boston: Houghton Mifflin, 1976), 491.

48. Ibid., 495.

49. We, the People! pamphlet, 1961, in author's possession.

50. Walker and his patron, Strom Thurmond, did address (on separate occasions) the Freedom Club of Los Angeles, which sponsored patriotic rallies that featured famous anticommunists. For example, on January 11, 1962, Walker addressed an audience of 15,000 at the Los Angeles Sports Arena. See the *American Standard* 1, no. 1 (February 1962), 1, in Radical Right collection, box 12; Freedom Club *Bulletin*, November 30, 1961, Radical Right collection, box 9; and Freedom Club announcement, n.d., Radical Right collection, box 8, all in HIA.

51. Telegram from Archibald E. Roberts to multiple recipients, September 7, 1961, Archibald E. Roberts Papers, box 7, folder "Materials Concerning General Edwin A. Walker," Oregon Special Collections.

52. Charles R. Beauregard to J. William Fulbright, September 21, 1961, New Left collection, box 15, folder "Fulbright Letters," HIA.

53. Maryesther Williamson to J. William Fulbright, September 20, 1961, ibid.

54. After Roberts was dismissed from the army in 1962, he undertook a similar campaign on his own behalf, hoping to generate enough noise that the army would have to reinstate him. A short time later he successfully sued the secretary of the army and other Pentagon officials and won his reinstatement. In 1965, however, he voluntarily retired so he could work full time for his organization, the Committee to Restore the Constitution. See inventory for the Archibald E. Roberts Collection in Oregon Special Collections and the broadside "Critic of Yorty Sues U.S. Army over Dismissal," July 6, 1962, Radical Right collection, box 53, HIA.

55. James P. Duffy, *Who Is Destroying Our Military?* (East Elmhurst, N.Y.: Torchlight, 1966), 62.

56. *Congressional Record—Senate*, April 14, 1961, 5934.

57. Fletcher Knebel and Charles W. Bailey II, "Military Control: Can It Happen Here?" *Look*, September 11, 1962, 21. Air Force General Curtis LeMay, head of the Strategic Air Command and an outspoken advocate of the use of nuclear weapons against communist foes, might have served as a model for such fears. (He also served as the model for mad Air Force officer General Buck Turgidson in Stanley Kubrick's 1964 film, *Dr. Strangelove, or How I Learned to Stop Worrying and Love the Bomb.*) Besides sending reconnaissance missions into Soviet airspace to provoke the enemy, LeMay schemed to accumulate power he could use independently of presidential orders, particularly in time of nuclear war. See Richard Rhodes, "The General and World War III," *New Yorker*, June 19, 1995, 47–59.

58. In an interview in late 1961, for example, former President Eisenhower told Walter Cronkite, "I do believe that our officers, when they receive recruits, have the need for making certain that these men are loyal people, understanding that they are defending the United States and the things for which she stands—her ideals, her aspirations, her principles, her rights. I do not believe they should try to do this in terms of partisan politics whatsoever." See Leo Egan, "Eisenhower Says Officers Should Stay out of Politics," *New York Times*, November 24, 1961, 1, 23.

CHAPTER 5

1. Richard Wilson, "These Are Strange Bedfellows," *Los Angeles Times*, July 16, 1964, pt. 2, 5.

2. See Goldwater's autobiographies, *With No Apologies* (New York: William Morrow, 1979), and, with Jack Casserly, *Goldwater* (New York: Doubleday, 1988), and the biographies by Lee Edwards, *Goldwater* (Washington, D.C.: Regnery, 1995); and Robert Alan Goldberg, *Barry Goldwater* (New Haven, Conn.: Yale University Press, 1995).

3. Cabell Phillips, "Goldwater Busy Bolstering G.O.P.," *New York Times*, July 3, 1961, 16.

4. (Shepardsville, Ky.: Victor, 1960).

5. For a detailed account of how the book came about as well as a useful analysis of some of its main points, see Edwards, *Goldwater*, 105–30.

6. Phillips, "Goldwater Busy," 16; and Edwards, *Goldwater*, 139.

7. The best works are F. Clifton White with William J. Gill, *Suite 3505* (New Rochelle, N.Y.: Arlington, 1967); William A. Rusher, *The Rise of the Right* (New York: National Review Books, 1993); Stephen Shadegg, *What Happened to Goldwater?* (New York: Holt, Rinehart and Winston, 1965); Edwards, *Goldwater*; and Goldberg, *Barry Goldwater*.

8. Rusher, *Rise of the Right*, 69.

9. White, *Suite 3505*, 45.

10. The plotters were worried, however, that Goldwater might "pull a Sherman on us," a reference to General William Tecumseh Sherman who, when supporters pushed him to run as the Republican candidate in the 1868 election, declared, "I will not accept if nominated, and will not serve if elected." White, *Suite 3505*, 121–22.

11. Since Goldwater was up for reelection to the Senate in 1964, he used the cover of the Senate race to disguise his inquiries about finances, personnel, and time-tables for a presidential bid.

12. Anon. [probably Denison Kitchel], "Program," February 23, 1962, Denison Kitchel Papers, box 4, folder "Goldwater Presidential Campaign, Draft Goldwater Endeavor," HIA.

13. White, *Suite 3505*, 199–203.

14. Anon. [probably Kitchel], "Questions and Premises," December 23, 1962, Denison Kitchel Papers, box 4, folder "Goldwater Presidential Campaign, Draft Goldwater Endeavor," HIA.

15. White, *Suite 3505*, 137.

16. F. Clifton White to Barry Goldwater, June 7, 1963, Denison Kitchel Papers, box 4, folder "Goldwater Presidential Campaign, Correspondence General, 1963," HIA.

17. White, *Suite 3505*, 211.

18. F. Clifton White to Barry Goldwater, June 7, 1963, Denison Kitchel Papers, box 4, folder "Goldwater Presidential Campaign, Correspondence General, 1963," HIA.

19. Edwards, *Goldwater*, 180.

20. Ibid.

21. See Edwards, *Goldwater*, 327–30. Among other scenes in *Choice* was a shot of a limousine racing down a highway with beer cans flying out the window, homage to stories of Johnson careening around the LBJ Ranch.

22. Courtney Hafela, treatment for "The Conscience of a Conservative," n.d. (c. April 1962), box 85, folder "Conscience of a Conservative," Liebman Papers.

23. William F. Buckley, Jr., to Marvin Liebman, May 2, 1962, ibid.

24. Goldberg, *Barry Goldwater*, 143. Among the members of the organizing committee were Robert Welch, conservative industrialist Herbert Kohler (famous from the brutal strike at his Wisconsin plumbing supply plant), Kent and Phoebe Courtney, and other well-known conservatives.

25. *Facts on File* 22, no. 1132, July 5–11, 1962, 225.

26. As Goldwater wrote to one friend, "Frankly, I feel now that I should have stayed with my original intention of not actively campaigning, because I find a hazard in this, the scope of which had never occurred to me." See Goldwater to Jameson Campaigne, April 2, 1964, Jameson Campaigne Papers, box 1, folder "Letters after 1950," HIA.

27. White, *Suite 3505*, 158. Richard Kleindienst, one of the Arizona Mafia, sent a follow-up letter to the group's head, James O'Malley, which explained that "until the National Convention is concluded, the activities of your organization must be coordinated with the activities in the various states in connection with the primary goal of securing delegates for Goldwater at the convention." See Kleindienst to O'Malley, January 15, 1964, box 13, folder 50, Goldwater Papers.

28. White, *Suite 3505*, 159.

29. Maurice Van Nostrand to F. Clifton White, April 24, 1964, 1964 Presidential Campaign series, box 3, folder 6, Goldwater Papers.

30. Rowland Evans and Robert Novak, "Goldwater Volunteers Can Help—and Hinder," *Los Angeles Times*, August 21, 1964, pt. 2, 5.

31. Goldberg, *Barry Goldwater*, 190. For many young conservatives, the time spent working for Goldwater proved to be their formative political experiences and got them interested in the craft for the rest of their lives. See, for example, Margaret M. Braungart and Richard G. Braungart, "The Effects of the 1960s Political Generation on Former Left- and Right-Wing Youth Activist Leaders," *Social Problems* 38, no. 3 (August 1991): 297–315.

32. Goldwater, *Goldwater*, 154. In his 1979 autobiography Goldwater makes no mention of his hesitancy nor his conviction that he would lose.

33. Barry Goldwater to William F. Buckley, Jr., March 27, 1961, box 14, folder "JBS," Buckley Papers.

34. Transcript from "Meet the Press," November 19, 1961, Lawrence Spivak Papers, box 159, Manuscripts and Archives Division, Library of Congress. As Buckley later explained, "For a season or two, in Phoenix in the early sixties, joining the John Birch Society was on the order of joining the local country club." William F. Buckley, Jr., "My Secret Right-Wing Conspiracy," *New Yorker*, October 21 and 28, 1996, 124–26.

35. Goldberg, *Barry Goldwater*, 159.

36. "The Question of Robert Welch," *National Review*, February 13, 1962, 87.

37. Ibid., 88.

38. William F. Buckley, Jr., "Goldwater and the John Birch Society," *National Review*, November 19, 1963, 430.

39. From "Campaigning for the Presidency," PBS documentary, August 19, 1992, quoted in Goldberg, *Barry Goldwater*, 189.

40. Shadegg, *What Happened to Goldwater?* 124. In other states the book seemed to have a similar effect. Later the Johnson campaign was aware of Schlafly's and others' books, which portrayed the president in an unfavorable light. One aide wrote to Johnson, "The moment we moved West of Chicago . . . we began getting hit with warnings about the effect of three hate books, 'A Texan Looks at Lyndon,' 'A Choice Not an Echo,' and 'None Dare Call It Treason.'" The aide cautioned that the books were available at newsstands, that people were reading them, and that Johnson should not answer their charges personally. See Lawrence F. O'Brien to Lyndon B. Johnson, October 4, 1964, White House Central File, box 84, folder "PL 2, 10/2/64–10/4/64," LBJL.

41. Goldwater did not actually suggest using atomic weapons for such a purpose, but when asked what he would do about the situation in Vietnam, he replied that the supply route from China into North Vietnam would have to be interdicted and that "there have been several suggestions made; I don't think we would use any of them. But defoliation of the forests by low-yield atomic weapons could well be done." Goldwater was not proposing his own plan but merely summarizing possibilities that had made the rounds in the Department of Defense. See Goldberg, *Barry Goldwater*, 191; and Shadegg, *What Happened to Goldwater?* 124–25.

42. Goldberg, *Barry Goldwater*, 192.

43. Telegram from William Knowland to Richard Nixon, May 27, 1964, Denison Kitchel papers, box 4, folder "Goldwater Presidential Campaign, Correspondence General Jan. 1–Nov. 1, 1964," HIA.

44. Edwards, *Goldwater*, 222.

45. Shirley Katzander, press release, April 30, 1964, box "Goldwater Clippings," folder "Extremist Republicans," Meier Papers.

46. Margaret Meier, untitled list of extremist connections, n.d., ibid.

47. Furthermore conservative Republicans were more likely to vote in primaries than were centrist Republicans.

48. Arline Fry and Jack Blair, "Let's Set the Record Straight," n.d., box "Goldwater Clippings," folder "Local Republicans," Meier Papers.

49. As late as June 1, some polls had Rockefeller ahead by as much as nine points. Reporter James Reston from the *New York Times* thought that Goldwater and Rockefeller might neutralize each other ("a double knockout") and make way for a compromise candidate like Scranton or Nixon. See Reston, "California Vote Unlikely to Sway GOP on Nominee," *New York Times*, June 1, 1964, 1.

50. Rockefeller polled 61,307 to Goldwater's 38,699. "Vote Results at a Glance," *Palo Alto Times*, June 3, 1964, 5.

51. Russell Kirk, "The End of Liberal Republicanism Is Here," *Los Angeles Times*, July 26, 1964, F7.

52. Wallace Turner, "40,000 in Parade against Arizonan," *New York Times*, July 13, 1964, 18.

53. Alan Cline, "Civil Rights Marchers Hear Denunciations of Goldwater," *Palo Alto Times*, July 13, 1964, 19.

54. Goldberg, *Barry Goldwater*, 202. Another report, however, placed the numbers at fifteen delegates and twenty-six alternates. See John D. Morris, "Negro Delegates Drop Plans to Walk out as a Demonstration against Goldwater," *New York Times*, July 16, 1964, 19.

55. See, for example, Shadegg, *What Happened to Goldwater?* 131–68; Rusher, *Rise of the Right*, 119–24; Goldberg, *Barry Goldwater*, 201–9; Edwards, *Goldwater*, 253–80; Goldwater, *Goldwater*, 174–87; White, *Suite 3505*, 11–18, 377–408; and Theodore H. White, *The Making of the President—1964* (New York: Athenaeum, 1965), 200–231.

56. "Republican National Convention," *Facts on File* 29, no. 1237, July 9–15, 1964, 227.

57. Richard Bergholz, "Would Back Rights Law—Goldwater," *Los Angeles Times*, July 11, 1964, 1, 3.

58. Goldberg, *Barry Goldwater*, 202–3.

59. *Facts on File* 29, no. 1237, July 9–15, 1964, 230.

60. See "A Rights Protest Staged on Floor," *New York Times*, July 16, 1964, 19.

61. "Negro Spokesmen Bitter on Goldwater Nomination, Saying It Will Aid Racists," *New York Times*, July 17, 1964, 19.

62. Alan Cline, "Demonstrators Plan to Return," *Palo Alto Times*, July 16, 1964, 1.

63. "Transcript of the Keynote Address by Gov. Hatfield at GOP Convention," *New York Times*, July 14, 1964, 20. Hatfield had criticized extremists for at least a year before his keynote address, so what he said at the keynote should have been a surprise to no one. See Mark O. Hatfield, "Oregon Gov. Hatfield Answers Critics of Extremist Stand," *Los Angeles Times*, May 26, 1963, G3.

64. White, *The Making of the President—1964*, 211.

65. White, *Suite 3505*, 398–99. For concurring opinions, see also Rusher, *Rise of the Right*, 120; Shadegg, *What Happened to Goldwater?* 161–62; Goldwater, *Goldwater*, 183–84; and Edwards, *Goldwater*, 261–62.

66. Edwards, *Goldwater*, 268. See also Harry Jaffa, "Extremism and Moderation: Reflections on a Phrase," July 27, 1964, Denison Kitchel Papers, box 3, folder "Nixon, Richard, 1960–1968," HIA.

67. Goldwater, *Goldwater*, 185.

68. See, for example, Goldwater, *Goldwater*, 187; Edwards, *Goldwater*, 276; and William F. Buckley, Jr., "Uproar over Candidate's Famous Words Hints Caution Is in Order," *Los Angeles Times*, July 23, 1964, pt. 2, 5.

69. There are, however, problems with this story, since Goldwater annotated an early draft of the article Kitchel was writing and made changes in language that included what he himself said to Eisenhower, as well as how Eisenhower responded. See Denison Kitchel, "Explaining Things to Ike," January 2, 1975, draft version, Denison Kitchel Papers, box 5, HIA.

70. Richard M. Nixon to Barry Goldwater, n.d., Denison Kitchel Papers, box 3, folder "Richard Nixon, 1960–1968," HIA. For Goldwater's reply, see drafts in the same folder.

71. While Miller became Goldwater's running mate because he was relatively unknown, a Catholic, and could antagonize Johnson at will, he was not the only candidate for the job. Backers of George Wallace sent an emissary to San Francisco just before the convention began to offer the Alabaman's services. Goldwater, however, gently turned him down. See Dan T. Carter, *The Politics of Rage* (New York: Simon and Schuster, 1995), 220–21.

72. "Confidential Proceedings of Closed Session Meeting of Republican Unity Conference," August 12, 1964, 14, box 5, Ralph de Toledano Papers, HIA.

73. Ibid., 30.

74. Ibid., 59.

75. Ibid., 83–84.

76. Ibid., 70. Nixon later recommended against avoiding civil rights and suggested that the focus be placed on local, state, and private solutions, but Goldwater dodged the subject fairly adroitly during the campaign.

77. Ibid., 79.

78. Ibid., 80.

79. Theodore Jones, "Negro Boy Killed; 300 Harass Police," *New York Times*, July 17, 1964, 31. See also White, *Making of the President—1964*, 232–34.

80. Paul L. Montgomery and Francis X. Clines, "Thousands Riot in Harlem Area; Scores Are Hurt," *New York Times*, July 19, 1964, 54.

81. Francis X. Clines, "Police Exhaust Their Ammunition in All-Night Battle," *New York Times*, July 20, 1964, 1, 16.

82. Rowland Evans and Robert Novak, "Current Tactics May Transform GOP," *Los Angeles Times*, August 17, 1964, pt. 2, 5.

83. For Humes's biography, see Theodore Humes to Eduard M. Oetting, November 25, 1983, Theodore Humes Papers, box 1, folder 1, Arizona Historical Foundation.

84. Ted Humes, memorandum, August 8, 1964, Theodore Humes Papers, box 1, folder 2, Arizona Historical Foundation.

85. Ibid.

86. The Johnson forces also worked to make inroads into the ethnic communities. Although they did not use backlash, administration officials exploited their positions to deliver favors to ethnic communities. For example, the postmaster general told the president that he would give special priority to foreign language newspapers in major cities, which he would "accomplish . . . with appropriate fanfare." See John A. Gronouski to Lyndon Johnson, August 10, 1964, White House Central File, box 83, folder "PL 2, 8/15/64–8/25/64," LBJL.

87. "Regional Analysis—Illinois," n.d., box 3, folder 3, Goldwater Papers.

88. Democrats, of course, kept tabs on what the Goldwater forces were doing with the issue of race. One aide to Johnson mentioned, "When [racism] gets going organized labor can move right out from under its leadership en masse. I've seen it happen too often. Witness Polish Milwaukee and Baltimore County." See Henry H. Wilson, Jr., to Lawrence F. O'Brien, July 8, 1964, White House Central File, box 83, folder "PL 2, 6/15/64–7/23/64," LBJL.

89. Ralph de Toledano, "A Negro Minority vs. a White Majority?" *National Review*, September 22, 1964, 815.

90. Dick Thompson, "Memorandum on the Goldwater Tour of the South," n.d., box 3, folder 5, Goldwater Papers.

91. Ibid., 4–5.

92. Theodore Humes to William Gill, August 1, 1965, Theodore Humes Papers, box 1, folder 2, Arizona Historical Foundation.

93. Ibid.

94. Polly Yarnell to Barry Goldwater, May 13, 1963, Barry Goldwater Papers—political, box 15, folder 8, Arizona Historical Foundation.

95. Edwards, *Goldwater*, 341–42.

96. White, *Making of the President—1964*, 112.

97. Jack Valenti to Lyndon Johnson, September 7, 1964, White House Central File, box 84, folder "PL 2, 9/6/64–9/14/64," LBJL.

98. Ibid.

99. White, *Making of the President—1964*, 340.

100. Lee Edwards, *The Conservative Revolution* (New York: Free Press, 1999), 133.

101. Hale Houts to Denison Kitchel, November 19, 1964, Denison Kitchel Papers, box 4, folder "Goldwater Presidential Campaign, General Correspondence Nov. 21–Dec. 28, 1964," HIA.

102. Jaromir Vanecek to Denison Kitchel, December 10, 1964, Denison Kitchel Papers, box 1, folder "Correspondence General, undated 1950–1975," HIA.

103. Phillip Alexander Ray to Barry Goldwater, November 6, 1964, Denison Kitchel Papers, box 2, folder "Goldwater, 1964–1970," HIA.

104. A. C. Wedemeyer to Barry Goldwater, February 1, 1965, A. C. Wedemeyer Papers, box 133, folder 6, HIA.

105. Denison Kitchel to Barry Goldwater, January 6, 1965, Denison Kitchel Papers, box 2, folder "Goldwater, 1964–1970," HIA.

106. Copy in Denison Kitchel Papers, box 4, folder "General Correspondence, Nov. 21–Dec. 28, 1964," HIA.

107. George Bush, "The Republican Party and the Conservative Movement," *National Review*, December 1, 1964, 1053.

108. Mrs. Alex Paveglio to Barry Goldwater, October 27, 1964, Barry Goldwater Papers—political, box 7, folder "P," Arizona Historical Foundation.

109. Nicky Quance to the Goldwaters, October 27, 1964, folder "Q," ibid.

110. Nixon statistic in "Grassroots," *National Review*, November 17, 1964, 1001; Goldwater statistics in Goldberg, *Barry Goldwater*, 219.

111. Speech by Margie Braden, January 16, 1965, Denison Kitchel Papers, box 3, folder "RNC, 1959–1972," HIA.

112. *Facts on File* 25, no. 1287, June 24–30, 1965, 240.

113. Ted Humes to William Gill, August 1, 1965, Theodore Humes Papers, box 1, folder 2, Arizona Historical Foundation.

CHAPTER 6

1. "Text of First Press Conference," June 24, 1965, box 321, folder 235, Buckley Papers. Not surprisingly, Buckley's hesitancy is not mentioned in his account of the campaign, *The Unmaking of a Mayor* (New York: Viking, 1966). On his first press conference, see p. 110.

2. The publication did not turn a profit until the 1990s. See John B. Judis, "A Magazine and a Movement," *Wall Street Journal*, November 10, 1995, A14.

3. Lillian R. Mansfield to William F. Buckley, Jr., June 26, 1965, box 293, folder 3, Buckley Papers.

4. Statistics from Buckley, *Unmaking of a Mayor*, 328.

5. A good description of Burch's removal is in David W. Reinhard, *The Republican Right since 1945* (Lexington: University Press of Kentucky, 1983), 210–11.

6. "Executive Session of the Executive Committee of the Republican National Committee," January 21, 1965, 6, Ralph de Toledano Papers, box 6, folder 1, HIA.

7. Ibid., 11.

8. All statistics from ibid., 34–42.

9. Ibid., 87.

10. Ibid., 98.

11. Burch had reason to be pessimistic. In his February 1965 chairman's report, he noted that in 1940 40% of the country was registered Democratic, 38% Republican. In 1964 the numbers had moved to 53% and 25%. See "Chairman's Report: The State of Our Party, as of February 1965," box 1, folder "Dean Burch," FSA Papers.

12. Raymond M. Lahr, "30–37–33: That's the Shape—and Dilemma—of the GOP," *Louisville Courier-Journal*, February 28, 1965.

13. The contemporary literature on the problems and future of cities c. 1965 is immense. See, for example, John Peter, "Everybody's Going to Town," *Look*, September 21, 1965, 31; "The Way the U.S. Is Growing—What It Means," *U.S. News and World Report*, January 13, 1964, 82–85; and Bernard Weissbourd, "Are Cities Obsolete?" *Saturday Review*, December 19, 1964, 12–15, 66.

14. Terrance Smith, "Lindsay Experts See '65–'66 Deficit of $412 Million," *New York Times*, December 22, 1965, 1, 34.

15. Charles Lam Markmann, *The Buckleys* (New York: William Morrow, 1973), 23.

16. For more on *God and Man at Yale*, see the debates that sprang up directly after its release, for example, McGeorge Bundy, "The Attack on Yale," *Atlantic* (November 1951), 50–52; William F. Buckley, Jr., "The Changes at Yale," and McGeorge Bundy, "McGeorge Bundy Replies," both in *Atlantic* (December 1951), 78–84; Selden Rodman and Frank D. Ashburn, "Isms and the University," *Saturday Review of Literature*, December 15, 1951, 18–19, 44–45; Max Eastman, "Buckley versus Yale," *American Mercury* (December 1951), 22–29; Robert Hatch, "Enforcing Truth," *New Republic*, December 3, 1951, 19; and "Secular, Collectivist Yale?" *Newsweek*, October 22, 1951, 70.

17. W. F. Buckley, Jr., "Memorandum, Re: *A New Magazine*," c. September 1954, 4, Henry Regnery Papers, box 10, folder "W. F. Buckley, 1944–54," HIA.

18. Buckley, *Unmaking of a Mayor*, 299. A fourth, never-articulated reason was simply to get a book out of the experience. Even thirty years later one of Buckley's closest friends ventured that he ran so that he could write a book about being a politician-in-training. Less than a year after the election, *National Review* sported advertisements for his book, which promised to "lay bare the serious problems facing Americans at home today: the social revolutions ripping apart our big cities." See *National Review*, September 20, 1966, 917.

19. J. Daniel Mahoney, *Actions Speak Louder* (New Rochelle, N.Y.: Arlington, 1968), 285. While there is no compelling reason to believe that this quotation is not true, Mahoney, one of the founders of the Conservative party, had many axes to grind and used his book to get in his licks wherever possible.

20. William F. Buckley, Jr., "Mayor, Anyone?" *National Review*, June 15, 1965, 498.

21. "Statement by Wm. F. Buckley, Jr., Announcing His Candidacy for Mayor of New York," June 24, 1965, box 299, folder 61, Buckley Papers.

22. Marvin Liebman, a close friend and adviser of Buckley's, had written a memo prior to the June 24 announcement that suggested that he should "hold off any campaigning until Wednesday, September 15, the day after primary election day." See Liebman to Buckley, "Confidential Memorandum RE: Mayoralty Campaign," c. June 1965, box 63, folder "Memoranda," Liebman Papers.

23. Buckley, *Unmaking of a Mayor*, 101.

24. Ibid., 251.

25. Most famously, Freeman snubbed the Polish Pulaski Day Parade, which embroiled Buckley in controversy. See Buckley, *Unmaking of a Mayor*, 250–52, and correspondence between Freeman and Francis J. Wazeter, September 11 and 13, 1965, box 295, folder 29, Buckley Papers.

26. See Douglas Martin, "Rosemary R. Gunning, 92, Foe of School Busing," *New York Times*, October 7, 1997, C27.

27. Marvin Liebman, "Draft, 'Hard-Sell' Fund-raising Letter," c. July 26, 1965, box 63, folder "Memorandums," Liebman Papers.

28. Richard M. Viguerie to Marvin Liebman, July 29, 1965, box 9, folder "Buckley for Mayor—Correspondence," Liebman Papers.

29. Liebman to Arthur Andersen et al., August 28, 1965, box 63, folder "Memorandums," Liebman Papers.

30. Neal Freeman to Marvin Liebman, July 19, 1965, box 296, folder 45, Buckley Papers. The number of references to "blintz eating" in the documents pertaining to the election sometimes boggles the mind. It seems that the Buckley forces latched onto this image as one that represented a politician at his worst. In this case, John Lindsay the WASP trying to act Jewish for the sake of a vote.

31. Buckley, *Unmaking of a Mayor*, 111, 119–20.

32. As one adviser told him, "One of your main advantages has been that people are listening to you, not because of your profundity, but because they are afraid they might miss a witticism. The threat of humor wins a considerable captive audience that Lindsay and Beame are incapable of winning." Ed Bell to William F. Buckley, n.d., box 295, folder 30, Buckley Papers.

33. William F. Buckley to Conservative Party Officials, September 8, 1965, box 310, folder 154, Buckley Papers.

34. Ibid.

35. Neil McCaffrey to Bill Buckley and Dan Mahoney, July 7, 1965, box 293, folder 5, Buckley Papers.

36. Radio advertising proposal, "Who Are the Best Prospects?" c. September 1965, box 62, folder "Advertising—busses, subways, stations," Liebman Papers.

37. See table 8, "Religious and Ethnic Distribution (According to Vote Profile Analysis)," and table 9, "Twelve Assembly Districts in Which Buckley Attracted His Highest Percentage of the Vote," in Buckley, *Unmaking of a Mayor*, 333–34.

38. Ibid., 276–78.

39. Goldwater did support Buckley behind the scenes in any way he could, including sending him $1,000 in the final days of the race. See Goldwater to Buckley, November 1, 1965, box 305, folder 117, Buckley Papers.

40. Gerald F. Greene, Jr., to Frederic Coudert, August 16, 1965, box 9, folder "Buckley for Mayor—Correspondence," Liebman Papers.

41. See Lyn Shepard, "Response to Buckley's Platform Bothers Opponents," *Christian Science Monitor*, October 29, 1965, 3.

42. Kent Courtney to Fellow Americans, October 18, 1965, box 309, folder 142, Buckley Papers.

43. Conservative Society of America, "Beware of Lindsay!" 1965, ibid. Courtney was probably also responsible for a letter-writing campaign to voters that accused Lindsay of being procommunist. The letters were sent from New Orleans, the CSA's home, and borrowed a number of themes from the pamphlet. See "Constructive Step," editorial in the *Quincy* (Mass.) *Patriot Ledger*, November 2, 1965, 1–2.

44. "Meet the Press," October 17, 1965, transcript in box 320, folder 234, Buckley Papers.

45. James Buckley to William F. Buckley et al., September 9, 1965, box 324, folder 288, Buckley Papers.

46. William F. Buckley, "The Welfare Mess—A Vicious Cycle," October 1, 1965, box 298, folder 55, Buckley Papers.

47. To defend his conjecture that welfare encouraged "degenerate" behavior, Buckley invoked Daniel Patrick Moynihan's 1963 study of the African-American family, *Beyond the Melting Pot* (Cambridge, Mass.: MIT Press).

48. *New York Herald-Tribune*, October 13, 1965, quoted in Buckley, *Unmaking of a Mayor*, 179–80.

49. Jim Buckley to L. Brent Bozell, September 10, 1965, box 324, folder 288, Buckley Papers.

50. William F. Buckley to Miss S. Robinson, October 14, 1965, box 317, folder 199, Buckley Papers.

51. William F. Buckley, "The Crisis in the Schools—Whatever Became of Education?" October 5, 1965, box 298, folder 55, Buckley Papers.

52. William F. Buckley, "Crime—in New York It Pays," October 13, 1965, box 298, folder 56, Buckley Papers.

53. "Statement by William F. Buckley to the New York City Council on the Proposal to Establish a Civilian Review Board for the New York City Police Department," July 13, 1965, box 299, folder 61, Buckley Papers.

54. Ed Bell to William F. Buckley, n.d., box 295, folder 30, Buckley Papers.

55. Neil McCaffrey to William F. Buckley, September 29, 1965, box 293, folder 5, Buckley Papers.

56. Carelton Kent, "N.Y. Race Full of Meaning—Pick Your Own," *Chicago Sun Times*, October 31, 1965. See also Robert Gruenberg, "High Stakes in N.Y. Mayor Race," *Chicago's American*, October 31, 1965, both clippings in box 306, folder 124, Buckley Papers.

57. Robert J. Donovan, "Buckley 'Threat'—An Analysis," *New York Journal-American*, clipping in box 301, folder 82, Buckley Papers.

58. "Time for 'Unity'?" *Indianapolis News*, October 21, 1965, clipping in box 304, folder 105, Buckley Papers.

59. "The Newest Angry Man," *Baton Rouge State Times*, October 18, 1965, and "Amazing Mr. Buckley," *Omaha Morning World-Herald*, October 28, 1965, both ibid.

60. George N. Crocker, "Hot Race in New York," *San Francisco Examiner*, October 24, 1965, pt. 2, 2.

61. "What Makes Buckley Run?" *New York Times*, June 25, 1965, 32.

62. "Enter Mr. Buckley," *New York Herald-Tribune*, June 25, 1965, 28.

63. P. W. C., "Why the New York City Election Is Important," *Bath* (Maine) *Times*, November 1, 1965, clipping in box 305, folder 122, Buckley Papers.

64. Ibid.

65. Neal B. Freeman to Nellie Marquardt, October 16, 1965, box 294, folder 15, Buckley Papers.

66. In comparison Henry Cabot Lodge, a liberal Republican presidential write-in candidate in 1964, received a total of 341,841 in all primaries combined.

67. Buckley, *Unmaking of a Mayor*, 335.

68. "The Buckley Vote," *New York Times*, November 3, 1965, 38.

69. Neil McCaffrey to Bill Buckley et al., November 3, 1965, in box 293, folder 5, Buckley Papers.

70. "New York Election Results Has Hints for Great Society," *Mobile* (Ala.) *Press*, November 4, 1965, clipping in box 304, folder 105, Buckley Papers.

71. "Statement by Wm. F. Buckley on the Outcome of the Election," November 3, 1965, box 298, folder 59, Buckley Papers. In the same folder see also "Mr. Buckley Analyzes the Results of a Lindsay Victory."

72. "A Second Mandate to Republicans: A Ripon Society Report and Analysis of the 1965 Elections," n.d., box 318, folder 207, Buckley Papers.

73. George N. Crocker, "A Dem under the Skin," *San Francisco Examiner*, November 14, 1965, pt. 2, 2.

74. Robert J. Donovan, "Buckley 'Threat'—An Analysis," *New York Journal-American*, box 301, folder 82, Buckley Papers.

CHAPTER 7

1. Ronald Reagan, "Address to California Republican Assembly in San Diego," March 27, 1965, transcribed from cassette tape in Kurt W. Ritter Collection, box 1, HIA.

2. This idea is drawn from George H. Mayer, *The Republican Party, 1854–1966*, 2d ed., quoted in Lewis Chester, Godfrey Hodgson, and Bruce Page, *An American Melodrama* (New York: Viking, 1969), 184–85.

3. Lou Cannon, *Ronnie and Jesse: A Political Odyssey* (Garden City, N.Y.: Doubleday, 1969), 77.

4. Reagan would often tell the story of Christmas Eve 1931 when, instead of receiving his expected Christmas bonus, his father got a blue slip telling him he had been fired. For an analysis of how Reagan used this story in 1965 and in 1979 when running for president, see Lou Cannon, *Reagan* (New York: Putnam, 1982), 31–32.

5. Reagan's life has been described in a number of works, all of which tell virtually the same story. See, for example, Cannon, *Reagan*, 17–97; Cannon, *Ronnie and Jesse*, 3–8, 29–43; Anne Edwards, *Early Reagan* (London: Hodder and Stoughton, 1987), 9–159; Lee Edwards, *Reagan: A Political Biography* (San Diego, Calif.: Viewpoint, 1967), 11–64; Bill Boyarsky, *Ronald Reagan* (New York: Random House, 1981), 12–72; and Bill Boyarsky, *The Rise of Ronald Reagan* (New York: Random House, 1968), 11–92. For Reagan's own account, see his autobiography, written with Richard G. Hubler, *Where's the Rest of Me?* (New York: Duell, Sloan and Pearce, 1965). Edmund Morris's controversial authorized biography, *Dutch* (New York: Random House, 1999), contains fictional elements.

6. Ronald Reagan, "Losing Our Freedom on the Installment Plan," October 18, 1961, transcribed from cassette tape in Kurt Ritter Collection, box 1, HIA.

7. Ronald Reagan, "What's at Stake," October 10, 1962, Stockton, Calif., transcribed from cassette tape, ibid.

8. Ibid.

9. U.S. Bureau of the Census, *Historical Statistics of the United States: Colonial Times to 1970* (Washington, D.C.: Government Printing Office, 1975), 127.

10. Cannon, *Reagan*, 115.

11. Cannon, *Ronnie and Jesse*, 71.

12. See Ronald Reagan, *An American Life* (New York: Simon and Schuster, 1990), 139–40.

13. After Kitchel and Baroody rejected the national broadcast, the Californians who sponsored the speech (not coincidentally, the same people who engineered Reagan's gubernatorial bid) aired it in California using their own money. The broad-

cast raised so much money in one night that they told the Goldwater forces that they could pay for a national broadcast themselves. Kitchel and Baroody continued to hesitate, so Goldwater phoned Reagan, who told the senator, "It's not really that bad, Senator, and I don't think it will do you any harm." Goldwater never called back to cancel the speech, which convinced the Californians that they knew more about how to sell conservatism than the Goldwater forces. See Cannon, *Reagan*, 103.

14. Ronald Reagan, "The Speech—Goldwater Campaign 1964," October 27, 1964, box 38, folder "The Speech," Reagan Papers.

15. All telegrams October 28, 1964, box 38, folder "The Speech," Reagan Papers.

16. Wilma Batz to Ronald Reagan, November 1, 1964, ibid.

17. Ronald Reagan to Kats Kunitsugu, November 1, 1966, box 7, folder "K," Reagan Papers.

18. Some extremist groups had believed Goldwater was a communist dupe, intent on leading the country into the arms of the Soviets. These suspicions sometimes continued with Reagan. For example, Myron Fagan, head of the Cinema Educational Guild and author of such works as *Eisenhower, A Truman Trap*, and *Red Treason in Hollywood*, believed Reagan was disingenuous in his anticommunism and that Nancy, his second wife, came from a liberal family that had "welcomed Eleanor [Roosevelt]," which led him to believe that Nancy Reagan was a communist. Reagan met with Fagan in 1965 to attempt to convince him otherwise, although it is unclear if he was successful.

19. Rob Wood, "CRA Calls for End to Income Tax," *Redwood City* (Calif.) *Tribune*, March 29, 1965, 7.

20. Some CRA members began working against Reagan when it became clear that he would likely be the frontrunner among Republican candidates, but instead of attacking him about his policies, they took the extremism issue and turned it on its head. In September 1965 John Rousselot, former congressman from southern California and former JBS area coordinator, reportedly told the press that he would either attack or support Reagan—whichever would help the candidate most.

21. See Jerry Rankin, "United Republicans Back Reagan; CRL Charges Birch Infiltration," *Redwood City* (Calif.) *Tribune*, May 21, 1965, 16; and Bill Boyarsky, "UROC Adopts New 'Practical' Look, Elects Reagan-Backer," *Redwood City* (Calif.) *Tribune*, May 3, 1965, 17.

22. E. Leach, "Press Release of the California Conservative Party," n.d., box 18, folder "Correspondence—JBS," Reagan Papers.

23. Ronald Reagan to J. Marshall Cless, January 3, 1966, box 38, folder "Republican Party," Reagan Papers.

24. Brown, however, was only the second Democratic governor the state had seen in the twentieth century. The first was Culbert L. Olson, who was born in Utah Territory in 1876 and served from 1938 to 1942.

25. Thomas A. Lane, "Essential Elements of a Conservative Program" (originally published as "Find New Leader, Win Back Control of Party, Conservatives Told," *Cincinnati Enquirer*, September 12, 1965), T. A. Lane Papers, box 11, HIA.

26. Ibid.

27. During his liberal days, Reagan had also campaigned for Hubert Humphrey in Humphrey's first bid for the Senate in 1948 and for Helen Gahagan Douglas in her Senate fight against Richard Nixon in California in 1950.

28. See Cannon, *Reagan*, 102–7.

29. Ronald Reagan to John A. McCone, October 3, 1966, box 9, folder "M," Reagan Papers. To this writer's knowledge, Reagan never mentioned this incident in any other context, and no chronicler of his life has ever recounted the proposition.

30. Quoted in Cannon, *Reagan*, 104.

31. Form letter from A. C. Rubel, n.d., box 10, folder "Reagan Workers," Meier Papers. For Roberts's authorship, see Cannon, *Reagan*, 106.

32. "Why Republican Hopes Are Rising," *U.S. News and World Report*, June 20, 1966, 32.

33. J. Clements Marketing Counselors, "The Voice of 300 Californians in the Yellow Zones," May 7, 1965, box 35, folder "Polls," Reagan Papers.

34. A note of intrigue accompanies Christopher's run for the nomination. In polls conducted in early 1966, Brown was the loser when faced against Christopher but a winner when matched against Reagan. With this knowledge, Brown approved a plan to discredit Christopher and hired researchers and consultants to dredge up information on his 1939 conviction for violating a "fair-trade" milk-pricing statute. Although the violations were technical and the conviction was old news in northern California, Christopher's home turf, when spread around the southern half of the state, the accusations forced Christopher to go on the defensive. While Reagan probably would have won the primary anyway, Brown's machinations came back to haunt him as he was relegated to the category of common, dishonest politician. See Cannon, *Reagan*, 109–10.

35. Opinion Research of California, "A Public Opinion Issue and Attitude Survey concerning the Republican Gubernatorial Primary Election in the State of California," March 12–13, 1966, box 35, folder "Polls," Reagan Papers.

36. Reagan defeated Christopher by a margin of 1,417,623 to 675, 683, while Brown defeated Samuel Yorty, mayor of Los Angeles, by only 400,000 votes and polled only 140,000 votes more than all his challengers combined, a foreboding sign for the Democrats.

37. Reagan, however, often insisted that he did his own research and speech writing. In a letter to the *Sacramento Bee*, Reagan complained bitterly, "No one has ever written a speech for me. Indeed, I have always done my own research." Reagan to the *Sacramento Bee*, September 10, 1965, box 12, folder "S," Reagan Papers.

38. David S. Broder and Stephen Hess, *The Republican Establishment* (New York: Harper and Row, 1967), 274.

39. To supplement the candidate himself, the Reagan campaign created an army of speakers who could represent his views at gatherings, debates, and workplace visits. The "Ronald Reagan for Governor Speaker's Manual" included a breakdown of the types of audiences a speaker might encounter, six different speeches one might use, and what to do when facing a hostile crowd. In some ways the campaign's plan resembled World War I's Committee on Public Information's "Four-Minute Men," who fanned out around the country to give brief inspirational and patriotic speeches. See "Ronald Reagan for Governor Speaker's Manual," 1966, Kenneth Hall Papers, box 1, HIA.

40. See "Reagan Era Chronology," n.d., 2, Ronald Reagan Subject Collection, box 41, folder "RR Collection: Reagan Era Chronology, 1964–1974," HIA.

41. "Why Republican Hopes Are Rising," *U.S. News and World Report*, June 20, 1966, 32.

42. For the budget see "Reagan for Governor Committee," n.d., box 10, folder "Reagan Contributors (B)," Meier Papers.

43. Richard Nixon to Ronald Reagan, June 9, 1966, box 10, folder "N," Reagan Papers.

44. Memo from Robert E. Kitner to the President, June 25, 1966, Confidential File, box 150, folder "RE," LBJL. Yorty did nothing to dispel the rumors that he would back Reagan, saying, "I always felt that Reagan was the only candidate Brown could possibly beat. But in view of his tremendous showing, which I think was quite a surprise, I think he has a very good chance." Farley Clinton, "Ronald Reagan: A Light in the West," *National Review*, June 28, 1966, 613.

45. Memo from Robert E. Kitner to the President, June 21, 1966, Confidential File, box 150, folder "RE," LBJL.

46. "Ronald for Real," *Time*, October 7, 1966, 31.

47. Richard Thies, "Membership Recruitment Kit—Youth for Reagan," n.d., box 36, folder "RR—committees," Reagan Papers.

48. See George Rochester and Y. Frank Freeman, "Attention Democrats Only!" n.d., George Rochester Papers, box 1, folder "Politics—pre-1966 and 1966," HIA.

49. See Bob Spare and Jim Taylor to Region I Republican Headquarters, Central Committee Chairmen, and Club Presidents, October 3, 1966, box 3, folder "Reagan," Meier Papers.

50. See "Is It True," October 29, 1966, and "Democrats," November 1, 1966, both in box 3, folder "GOP—I," Meier Papers.

51. See "Mexican-American Democrats Support Reagan," *Ya Basta*; and Mexican-American Democrats for Reagan Committee, "The Hour of Decision," August 1, 1966, both in box 35, folder "66 Campaign—RR Material," Reagan Papers.

52. Bob Spare and Jim Taylor to Region I Republican Headquarters, Central Committee Chairmen, and Club Presidents, October 3, 1966, box 3, folder "Reagan," Meier Papers.

53. Gerald Popper to Bill Roberts, n.d., in box 35, folder "RR Material (2)," Reagan Papers.

54. Gerald Popper, "Format for Ronald Reagan Key Issue Films," n.d., box 35, folder "RR Material (2)," Reagan Papers.

55. "Governor's Office," n.d., box 34, folder "EGB: Material against RR," Reagan Papers. Later Brown expanded upon the acting reference by broadcasting a documentary called "Man versus Actor," which showed him speaking to an integrated classroom and reminding the children, "I'm running against an actor and you know who shot Lincoln, don'tcha?" See Cannon, *Ronnie and Jesse*, 86.

56. Wm. S. McBirnie to Ronald Reagan, November 30, 1965, box 34, folder "The Creative Society," Reagan Papers,

57. In 1968 conservative publisher Devin Adair Garrity published a book of Reagan's speeches under the title *The Creative Society*, perhaps the best attempt at making the slogan into a viable program. Reagan returned to these ideas when he became president in 1981.

58. Martin L. Dinkins to Ulysses W. Boykin, December 21, 1965, box 19, folder "B-C," Reagan Papers.

59. See Cannon, *Reagan*, 111.

60. When Rousselot was elected to the House in 1960, Spencer-Roberts managed his campaign. He lost his bid for reelection in 1962 but was elected in 1970 after the death of Congressman Glenard P. Lipscomb. Rousselot served until 1982, when he stepped down and became a special assistant to President Reagan for the year 1983. See Edwards, *Reagan*, 86; and *The Biographical Directory of the U.S. Congress, 1774–1989* (Washington, D.C.: Government Printing Office, 1989), 1746–47.

61. *Cow-Country Commentary* 1, no. 3 (December 1964), 1, 5, Radical Right Collection, box 3, HIA.

62. Perhaps most obvious to the GOP was the upward spike in the membership rolls of the JBS and other organizations following Goldwater's defeat. After yet another affirmation of the downward direction of the country, Americans flocked to join activist groups, which made an already difficult dilemma more troublesome for the Republicans. See Robert E. Dallos, "Goldwater's Flop Stirs Rush of the Embittered into Far-Right Group," *Wall Street Journal*, March 26, 1965, 1, 21.

63. Ben McMillan to Ronald Reagan, December 15, 1965, box 8, folder "M2," Reagan Papers. See also Goldwater to McMillan, October 8, 1965, ibid.

64. Reagan to McMillan, December 24, 1965, ibid.

65. Mervin D. Field, "California Voters Concerned with Many Issues; Most Presently Rate Reagan Better Able to Handle Them," *California Poll*, June 24, 1966, box 35, folder "Polls," Reagan Papers.

66. Edmund G. Brown to Ronald Reagan, September 10, 1966, box 34, folder "Birch Society," Reagan Papers.

67. Charley Lahey to Ernie Marshall, January 7, 1966, box 18, folder "Correspondence—JBS," Reagan Papers. See also Marshall to Reagan, January 7, 1966, ibid.

68. Quoted in Kurt Schuparra, *Triumph of the Right* (Armonk, N.Y.: Sharpe, 1999), 129.

69. George Rochester, "A Democrat Answers the Cranston-Brown Hullabaloo about the John Birch Society," c. October 1966, George Rochester Papers, box 1, folder "Birch Society," HIA.

70. Spencer-Roberts, however, was careful not to bring Goldwater in to campaign for Reagan, understanding the associations that would instantly form in many Californians' minds. When asked why Goldwater was not coming to the state, Reagan responded, "I believe [the issues in this election] are between the candidates and the people." This tactic also challenged Brown not to rely on President Johnson's support. See "For the Record," *National Review*, July 12, 1966, 700.

71. Louis Harris, "Analyzing the Swing to the Right Wing," *Newsweek*, June 20, 1966, 32.

72. "GOP Problem: Unity," *Philadelphia Inquirer*, c. November 10, 1965, clipping in box 38, folder "66—Press/Media," Reagan Papers.

73. Ray Bliss to Ronald Reagan, November 11, 1966, box 23, folder "Letters of Congratulations," Reagan Papers.

74. John Ashbrook to Ronald Reagan, March 14, 1967, box C-760, folder "Governor Personal—A," Reagan Papers.

75. Ronald Reagan to William F. Buckley, December 7, 1966, box 18, folder "Correspondence—Misc," Reagan Papers.

76. Ronald Reagan, Inaugural Address, January 1, 1967, box 40 GP: Research Unit, folder "Creative Society," Reagan Papers.

77. Report, "Estimate of the Political Situation in California," May 1, 1967, WHCF PL, box 33, folder "PL/ST 5 4/9/67–10/7/67," LBJL.

78. On what Reagan and southern California meant to the rest of the nation, see James Q. Wilson, "A Guide to Reagan Country," *Commentary* 43, no. 5 (May 1967): 37–45.

79. Republicans had yearned to repeal the Rumford Act, which in word guaranteed fair housing opportunities for minority groups but in deed operated in a clumsy and inefficient manner.

80. Hubert H. Humphrey, "Memo for the Files," August 23, 1967, Confidential File, box 76, folder "PL/Name Political Affairs/Name," LBJL.

81. As a favorite son candidate, the state's delegates would be pledged to Reagan until he released them to a specific nominee, thereby ensuring—or at least giving the impression of—party unity. For more on Reagan's near-candidacy, see Chester, Hodgson, and Page, *An American Melodrama*, 437–99.

82. Memo, Fred Panzer to the President, September 8, 1967, WHCF PL/2, box 88, folder "PL 2, 8/23/67–9/18/67," LBJL.

83. Memo, Fred Panzer to the President, January 16, 1968, WHCF PL/2, box 88, folder "PL 2, 1/1/68–1/22/68," LBJL.

84. American Conservative Union, "How Conservative Are Americans?" October 9, 1968, box 15 GP: Research Unit, folder "American Conservative Union 74," Reagan Papers.

85. C. D. Batchelor, "Under a New Flag and toward the Sunrise," *National Review*, November 29, 1966, 1206.

CHAPTER 8

1. Russell Kirk, "New Direction in the U.S.: Right?" *New York Times Magazine*, August 7, 1966, 20.

2. The most lucid explanation of this phenomenon can be found in Thomas Byrne Edsall with Mary D. Edsall, *Chain Reaction* (New York: Norton, 1992).

3. One of the founders of ACA, John Synon, had a record of working for the election of conservatives although not always in the most respectable ways. Hired by the oil industry in the 1940s to discredit liberal Republican Earl Warren, Synon had moved on to become a red baiter in the 1950s. After helping found the ACA, he drifted into the White Citizens' Council movement in the South and opened a press that published such works as *Breeding Down*, an account of the "mongrelization" America could expect with the civil rights movement. He was also a close associate of Alabama Governor George Wallace. See Dan T. Carter, *The Politics of Rage* (New York: Simon and Schuster, 1995), 201–2.

4. ACA, "Application for Charter as a Local Chapter," n.d., T. A. Lane Papers, box 3, folder "ACA—Special," HIA.

5. ACA, "The ACA Consistency Index," 1964, T. A. Lane Papers, box 3, folder "ACA Op. Plan 1966," HIA.

6. "Your Decision," 1961, box 136, folder 3, Rusher Papers.

7. Ben Moreell to Roger E. Reynolds, August 31, 1962, Henry Regnery Papers, box 52, folder 14, HIA.

8. See "Minimum Budget, January 1, 1966 to December 31, 1966," n.d., T. A. Lane Papers, box 3, folder "ACA—1966," HIA.

9. Charles A. McManus to Admiral Ben Moreell, "Interim Report," June 30, 1966, T. A. Lane Papers, box 3, folder "1966—ACA," HIA.

10. Ben Moreell to T. A. Lane, n.d., T. A. Lane Papers, box 3, folder "Moreell—1966," HIA.

11. Thomas A. Lane, "Annual Report, 1965," January 29, 1966, T. A. Lane Papers, box 3, folder "ACA—Special," HIA.

12. ADA's income in 1960 was $126,292, yet it still ran a significant deficit. It was not until 1968, when the group resorted to direct mail and was rewarded with membership contributions of approximately a half million dollars, that the group entered the black. See Steven M. Gillon, *Politics and Vision: The ADA and American Liberalism, 1947–1985* (New York: Oxford University Press, 1987), 153, 213.

13. Ben Moreell to Tom Lane, November 18, 1966, T. A. Lane Papers, box 3, folder "Moreell—1966," HIA.

14. Ben Moreell to Charles A. McManus, May 20, 1966, ibid. McManus was executive director of ACA.

15. Denison Kitchel, Memorandum to Senator Goldwater, April 11, 1965, box 5, folder "Goldwater (DK Personal)," FSA Records.

16. A photo of Kent Courtney affixing a bumper sticker to his car reading "27,000,000 Can't Be Wrong" appeared in newspapers across the nation soon after Goldwater's defeat. See Sterling F. Green, "Right Wing Ignores Defeat, Gears for 1966 Elections," *Chicago Sun Times*, April 4, 1965, 24.

17. Barry Goldwater to Stetson Coleman, April 15, 1966, box 5, folder "Goldwater (DK Personal)," FSA Records.

18. "Memorandum on the Free Society Association" (probably authored by Denison Kitchel), n.d., box 12, folder "Organizational Materials/Memorandum," FSA Records.

19. Ibid.

20. Denison Kitchel, "Speech before the Southern California Republican Women," November 19, 1965, box 8, folder "Kitchel, D.—Speeches," FSA Records.

21. See Arthur Krock, "In the Nation: The Impoverished Republican Party," *New York Times*, July 1, 1965, 30.

22. David S. Broder, "Splinter Groups Vex GOP Parley," *New York Times*, August 31, 1965, 14. See also Jerome S. Cahill, "GOP Dissuading Donors on Aiding Goldwater Group," *Philadelphia Inquirer*, September 2, 1965, in DNC Series I Papers, box 48, folder "Republican Party—1965, Free Society," LBJL.

23. Russell Kirk, "Goldwater Blunderers Are Back," *Louisville Times*, July 28, 1965, ibid.

24. Writing retrospectively, William Rusher, one of the draft engineers, described the FSA as "a rather scholarly little group" with its main drawing point being that it controlled "some (though not all) of the mailing lists generated by the campaign." But Rusher agreed with Kirk that "the Arizona Mafia had lost a good deal of its in-

fluence on November 3, and even Goldwater personally, though as beloved by conservatives as ever, could no longer give orders to the troops and expect them to be obeyed unhesitatingly." See Rusher, *The Rise of the Right* (New York: National Review Books, 1993), 133.

25. The FSA also made enemies of Birchers, who thought Kitchel was trying to upstage Robert Welch, as well as moderates, who thought that Kitchel was aligning the group with Welch and other extremists.

26. Transcript for "Washington Viewpoint," August 15, 1965, DNC Series I Papers, box 48, folder "Republican Party—1965, Free Society," LBJL.

27. Ibid.

28. See *News from the Free Society* 1, no. 3 (November 1965), ibid. Later newsletters covered such topics as "Black Power—It's Gonna Be a Long Hot Decade," "There Really Is a Republican Party," and "1984 Is Closer than We Think."

29. See "Right-Wing Group Hits TV Election Reporting," *Washington Post*, November 25, 1966; and "Election Guessing," *Baltimore Sun*, December 1, 1966, both in DNC Series I Papers, box 48, folder "Republican Party—1965, Free Society," LBJL.

30. Fred Mynatt, "Political Survey in 5 Southeastern States," December 10, 1965, box 10, folder "Mynatt, Fred," FSA Records.

31. Bruce Biossat, "FSA Tries to Accent Positive," *North Idaho Press*, December 30, 1965, box 1, folder "Misc. C & D," FSA Records.

32. Ronald Crawford to Denison Kitchel, December 6, 1965, box 3, folder "Crawford, Ronald—Correspondence," FSA Records.

33. Walter R. Mears, "First Year of 'Free Society' Reviewed," n.d., DNC Series I Papers, box 48, folder "Republican Party—1965, Free Society," LBJL.

34. Memo from Ron Crawford to Jean, August 23, 1965, box 1, folder "ACU," FSA Records.

35. Ron Crawford to Denison Kitchel, December 27, 1965, box 3, folder "Crawford, Ronald—Correspondence," FSA Records.

36. Denison Kitchel to Members and Friends of the Free Society, June 1, 1969, box 10, unlabeled folder, FSA Records.

37. As one headline described it, "'Free Society' Loses Top Man and Self," David Broder, *Washington Post*, February 13, 1969, box 10, unlabeled folder, FSA Records.

38. See Barry Goldwater to Marvin Liebman, January 30, 1961, box 59, folder "Americans for Conservative Action," Liebman Papers.

39. Marvin Liebman to Robert Bauman, November 9, 1964, box 57, folder "Background of ACU," Liebman Papers.

40. Marvin Liebman, "Recommended Name for New National Organization," n.d., ibid.

41. Marvin Liebman, "Goals of the *American Conservative Union*," n.d., ibid.

42. Telegram from Marvin Liebman to unknown person, December 5, 1964, box 57, folder "Background of ACU," Liebman Papers.

43. See "Minutes of the Meeting of the Board of Directors of the American Conservative Union," December 18–19, 1964, Stefan Possony Papers, box 215, HIA.

44. Ibid.

45. William Rusher to William F. Buckley, February 2, 1965, box 35, folder "Inter-Office Memos (1)," Buckley Papers.

46. William J. Gill to Donald Bruce, March 17, 1965, box 132, folder 6, Rusher Papers.

47. Neil McCaffrey to John Ashbrook et al., January 19, 1966, box 135, folder 8, Rusher Papers.

48. See "Minutes of the Meeting of the Board of Directors," September 17, 1965, Stefan Possony Papers, box 215, HIA. See also Robert Bauman, "Statement by the American Conservative Union," September 17, 1965, box 58, folder "Board Mtgs. of ACU," Liebman Papers.

49. See, for example, Paul Hope, "Bickering Splits Conservative Union," *Washington Star*, April 15, 1966, DNC Series I Papers, box 48, folder "Republican Party Splinter Groups—1965," LBJL. In 1965 Buckley also decided to resign, although he based his decision on potential conflicts of interest he might have between the ACU and *National Review*.

50. William F. Buckley, "Confidential Memorandum," March 30, 1965, box 58, folder "Confidential Memoranda," Liebman Papers.

51. William Rusher to Bill Buckley et al., August 26, 1965, box 35, folder "Inter-Office Memos (2)," Buckley Papers.

52. In the ACU's first five months, it raised an impressive $105,519. See "Financial Statement, American Conservative Union, through March 31, 1965," box 131, folder 8, Rusher Papers.

53. Marvin Liebman to Donald Bruce, May 20, 1965. One year later the ACU could draw on Buckley for Mayor lists, the Committee of One Million list, and even Liebman's special VIP list. See Ed to Joanne Mantikos, May 26, 1966, both in box 57, folder "ACU," Liebman Papers.

54. See "Summary—First Large Mailing," September 23, 1965, box 58, folder "ACU—Mailings," Liebman Papers.

55. Marvin Liebman to David Jones, June 2, 1966, box 57, folder "ACU," Liebman Papers.

56. John Jones to Board of Directors, November 5, 1967, Stefan Possony Papers, box 215, HIA.

57. The four splinters to which Rusher referred were ACA, FSA, ACU, and YAF.

58. William Rusher to the Editors, May 22, 1967, box 132, folder 8, Rusher Papers.

59. Donald Bruce to Denison Kitchel, June 28, 1965, box 2, folder "Conservative Orgs. Other than FSA," FSA Records.

60. See Ronald Crawford to Denison Kitchel, February 18, 1966, box 1, folder "ACU," FSA Records.

61. There is no other evidence that the meeting took place. See Barry Goldwater, "Four Major Conservative Organizations to Cooperate and Coordinate," August 12, 1966, box 5, folder "Goldwater," FSA Records.

62. Walter Judd to Rudy Skogerboe, May 21, 1965, Walter Judd Papers, box 213, folder 4, HIA.

63. David Jones to the ACU Board of Directors, February 1966, box 132, folder 8, Rusher Papers. Jones's program considered what other groups were already in the midst of doing and then worked toward the three goals of making the GOP "representative of its membership," nominating a conservative for president in 1972, and the "creation of a Conservative Establishment which can mold public opinion."

64. "Get on Target with the ACU!" n.d., box 1, folder "ACU," FSA Records.

65. Mrs. R. B. Wenger to William Rusher, January 8, 1965, box 135, folder 7, Rusher Papers.

66. "Summary of Work Accomplished to Date," September 17, 1965, box 131, folder 8, Rusher Papers.

67. "American Conservative Union Proposal for Outline of 'Operation Insurrection,'" n.d., box 136, folder 7, Rusher Papers.

68. "Minutes of the Meeting of the Board of Directors," September 17, 1965, Stefan Possony Papers, box 215, HIA. It is not known whether the film was ever completed or distributed.

69. "ACU District Action Handbook," n.d., box 136, folder 1, Rusher Papers.

70. William Moomau to William Rusher, May 2, 1967, box 135, folder 9, Rusher Papers.

71. Rusher to Donald Hodel, January 7, 1969, ibid. In retrospect Rusher described the ACU's efforts at organizing local chapters as anything but successful: "A local live wire would typically be succeeded, in the chairmanship of his or her chapter, by a wire that was anything but live. Long spells of political inactivity were frequently enlivened in such chapters by factional disputes of inversely proportional intensity. There was always the temptation to drift away into other more immediately rewarding forms of political activity: local campaigns, other worthy causes, etc." Rusher, *Rise of the Right*, 133.

72. "Solution or Socialism?" January 1970, George Crocker Papers, box 2, HIA.

73. Neil McCaffrey to ACU Board of Directors, November 11, 1971, box 131, folder 14, Rusher Papers.

74. Ibid.

75. Rusher, *Rise of the Right*, 134.

76. Marvin Liebman to James P. McFadden, July 10, 1975, box 146, folder "ACU," Liebman Papers.

77. Mike Thompson to Phil Crane, March 17, 1978, Jameson Campaigne Papers, box 1, unlabeled folder, HIA.

78. Rusher, *Rise of the Right*, 224.

79. *National Review Bulletin*, September 3, 1960, 2.

80. Rusher, *Rise of the Right*, 63.

81. Prior to his work with the Loyalty Oath Committee, Caddy helped circulate petitions supporting Joseph McCarthy and later worked with Kent and Phoebe Courtney on their publication *Free Men Speak*. See John A. Andrew III, *The Other Side of the Sixties* (New Brunswick, N.J.: Rutgers University Press, 1997), 66.

82. M. Stanton Evans, "The First Fifteen Years Are the Hardest," *New Guard* 15 (September 1975): 6.

83. "The Sharon Statement," *National Review*, September 24, 1960, 173.

84. Evans, "First Fifteen Years Are the Hardest," 7.

85. Lawrence F. Schiff, "The Obedient Rebels: A Study of College Conversions to Conservatism," *Journal of Social Issues* 20, no. 4 (October 1964): 75. Even when YAF membership numbers, notorious for inflation, can be verified with non-YAF documents, the membership system guaranteed a far higher number of nonactive members than active members. One way in which YAF substantiated its claims to such high enrollment was by charging low prices for membership. Even in 1989 a

two-year membership was only $5 and a five-year membership $10. In this way YAF could not only cite impressive statistics, but the method made a plunge in "paper" membership numbers for any one year much less likely.

86. In 1971 the National Advisory Board included sixty-eight members of Congress, twenty-six academicians, and two governors, including Ronald Reagan. See *New Guard* 11 (October 1971): 10.

87. In 1964 YAF endorsed Barry Goldwater; in 1968, 1976, 1980, and 1984, Ronald Reagan; in 1972, Congressman John Ashbrook.

88. Schiff, "Obedient Rebels," 89.

89. Ibid., 94.

90. Ibid.

91. Ibid., 90.

92. Richard G. Braungart, "SDS and YAF: A Comparison of Two Student Radical Groups in the Mid-1960s," *Youth and Society* 2, no. 4 (June 1971): 447.

93. On parents, see ibid., 452; on religious backgrounds, see Richard G. Braungart, "Status Politics and Student Politics: An Analysis of Left- and Right-Wing Student Activists," *Youth and Society* 3, no. 2 (December 1971): 201; and on ethnic backgrounds, see Braungart, "SDS and YAF," 451–52.

94. Braungart, "Status Politics and Student Politics," 208.

95. Bernard Weinraub, "Unrest Spurs Growth of Conservative Student Groups," *New York Times*, October 12, 1969, 70.

96. *New Guard* 11 (April 1971): 19–21.

97. *New Guard* 6 (September 1966): 36.

98. See Peter Kihss, "18,000 Rightists Rally at Garden," *New York Times*, March 8, 1962, 1, 21; Noel E. Parmentel, Jr., "Gnostics at the Garden," *Commonweal*, March 30, 1962, 13–15; and "Convincing the Convinced," *Time*, March 16, 1962, 20–21.

99. Lawrence Goodwyn, *The Populist Moment* (Oxford: Oxford University Press, 1978), 34.

100. Form letter from Randy Goodwin, California YAF chairman, 1972, Social Protest Collection, box 23, folder 10, Bancroft Library, University of California, Berkeley.

101. George Fox, "Counter-Revolution," *Playboy*, n.d., 138, from *YAF in the News* 2, no. 6 (March 1970), Patrick Dowd Papers, box 3, folder "YAF/Newsletter," HIA.

102. Carol Bauman, "A Conservative View of Women's Liberation," *New Guard*, 12 (April 1972): 8.

103. Mrs. Kathy Teague, "A Rebuttal: The Most Admired Woman," *New Guard* 12 (June 1972): 13.

104. Fox, "Counter-Revolution," 178.

105. Confidential Memo from Randal Teague to National Board of Directors, October 5, 1969, Patrick Dowd Papers, box 2, folder "National Board Printed Matter and Reports," HIA.

106. As in many YAF events, the Stanford chapter's actions were more important for their symbolic than their actual physical resistance. YAF was far outnumbered by the radicals, and in the end the police were much more effective in breaking up or preventing sit-ins. Many of these same tactics were later adopted with greater effectiveness by both right- and left-wing groups. See Catherine S. Manegold,

"Abortion War, Buffalo Front: Top Guns Use Battle Tactics," *New York Times*, April 25, 1992, A1, A28.

107. The blue buttons originally denoted that the wearer was in solidarity with S. I. Hayakawa, the archconservative president of San Francisco State University. On the draft, see "Statement on the Draft," *New Guard* 9 (November 1969): 6.

108. Congressman Dana Rohrabacher, telephone interview by author, May 13, 1992.

109. A good summary of YAF's actions after 1970 can be found in Gregory L. Schneider, *Cadres for Conservatism* (New York: New York University Press, 1999), 167–76.

110. See Alan W. Bock, "Tripping on Freedom," *Rap*, Fall 1970, 4–9, in David Walter Collection, box 21, HIA. For Rohrabacher's life in the 1970s, see his correspondence with William F. Buckley, Jr., in box 233, folder 1956, Buckley Papers.

111. Stephen E. Ambrose, *Nixon* (New York: Simon and Schuster, 1989), 2:367–69.

112. For other alumni who made their conservative careers part of the public record, see Andrew, *Other Side of the Sixties*, 217–20; and Schneider, *Cadres for Conservatism*, 178–80.

113. In 1972 the population of 18–24-year-olds was almost 26 million out of a total voting population of approximately 140 million. U.S. Bureau of the Census, *Statistical Abstract of the United States: 1972* (Washington, D.C.: Government Printing Office, 1972), 377.

CONCLUSION

1. Although Republicans did not win either house in 1966, they did make impressive gains across the country, including capturing governorships in Florida, Nevada, Arizona, and California. Of the 153 candidates the ACU had endorsed, 133 won, while the moderate Ripon Society notched only 31 for its recommended 87. See Mary Brennan, *Turning Right in the Sixties* (Chapel Hill: University of North Carolina Press, 1995), 119.

2. Godfrey Hodgson, *America in Our Time* (New York: Vintage, 1976), 373.

3. Quoted in Terry H. Anderson, *The Movement and the Sixties* (New York: Oxford University Press, 1995), 212.

4. Memo from Fred Panzer to the President, September 16, 1968, WHCF PL, box 27, folder "PL/Wallace, George," LBJL. For poll results, see Memo from Fred Panzer to the President, July 12, 1968, ibid.

5. See Thomas Byrne Edsall with Mary D. Edsall, *Chain Reaction* (New York: Norton, 1992), 93–95.

6. Jerry Landauer, "GOP Cash Surprise: Small Donations Push Party's Fund Raisers into an Impressive Lead," *Wall Street Journal*, August 5, 1968, 1.

7. Ralph de Toledano, "Nixon vs. Wallace: How True Conservatives Stand," October 10, 1968, Ralph de Toledano Papers, box 2, folder "King Features Column, Sept.–Dec. 1968," HIA.

8. Stewart Alsop, "The Orange County Bug," *Newsweek*, June 30, 1969, 96.

9. "'Silent Majority' Speaks Out," *U.S. News and World Report*, June 8, 1970, 34.

10. "What's Going on inside America, Chapter 2," *U.S. News and World Report*, May 25, 1970, 18.

11. William Rusher to the Editors of NR, "Memo on the New Left," April 7, 1969, box 114, folder 2, Rusher Papers.

12. "Agnew Words Pay Off—in Funds," *U.S. News and World Report*, June 8, 1970, 38.

13. Quoted in Dan T. Carter, *The Politics of Rage* (New York: Simon and Schuster, 1995), 426. On San Francisco and the Bay Area, see George Crocker Papers, boxes 2 and 7, folders "Busing," HIA, and Lillian B. Rubin, *Busing and Backlash* (Berkeley: University of California Press, 1972); on Boston, the site of perhaps the most contentious fight over busing, see J. Anthony Lukas, *Common Ground* (New York: Knopf, 1986). See also Robert H. Bork, *The Constitutionality of the President's Busing Proposals* (Washington, D.C.: American Enterprise Institute, 1972).

14. *The Phyllis Schlafly Report*, June 1971, Elizabeth Churchill Brown Papers, box 39, folder 19, HIA.

15. See "A Declaration," *National Review*, August 10, 1971, 842.

16. See Rowland Evans and Robert Novak, "The Blast from Buckley," *Washington Post*, March 15, 1972, A20.

17. While space permits neither neoconservatives nor the religious Right to be discussed here fully, each faction went on to influence conservative and Republican politics well into the 1980s and 1990s. On neoconservatives, see Norman Podhoretz, *Breaking Ranks* (New York: Harper and Row, 1979); and Peter Steinfels, *The Neo-Conservatives: The Men Who Were Changing American Politics* (New York: Simon and Schuster, 1979). In the 1990s a new generation of conservatives emerged: the children of neoconservatives. See James Atlas, "The Counter Counterculture," *New York Times Magazine*, February 12, 1995, 33–38, 54, 61–65.

18. For more on the religious Right, see Dallas A. Blanchard, *The Anti-Abortion Movement and the Rise of the Religious Right* (New York: Twayne, 1994); Glenn H. Utter and John W. Storey, *The Religious Right: A Reference Handbook* (Santa Barbara, Calif.: ABC-CLIO, 1995); John C. Green et al., *Religion and the Culture Wars* (Lanham, Md: Rowman and Littlefield, 1996); and Clyde Wilcox, *Onward Christian Soldiers?* (Boulder, Colo.: Westview, 1996).

19. See Richard Viguerie, *The New Right: We're Ready to Lead* (Falls Church, Va.: Viguerie, 1981).

20. William Rusher, "Crossroads for the GOP," *National Review*, February 12, 1963, 110.

21. See Louis Uchitelle, "That Was Then and This Is the 90's," *New York Times*, June 18, 1997, C1, C6.

22. Members of MOTOREDE held letter-writing workshops to contact members of Congress as well as prospective members, showed filmstrips to prospective members, and canvassed friends for potential new members. See, for example, "The War on Life," "Sample Letters," "MOTOREDE Sharply Condemns Abortion," and "Movies Are Better than Ever!" all in box 3, folder "Motorede," JBS Records. In the late 1970s the JBS also established Tax Reform Immediately (TRIM) to join in the tax rebellion sweeping the nation, which culminated in California's Proposition 13.

23. MOTOREDE, "The War on Life," n.d., ibid.

24. Part of the reason behind the shrinkage of the JBS and other far-right groups, however, was the Republicans' ability to co-opt extremist issues and, in some cases, rhetoric.

25. Robert Welch and Medford Evans, "False Leadership: William F. Buckley, Jr., and the New World Order," 1979, 1, box 36, JBS Records. The "new world order" represented the foreign governments and the United Nations conspiring to strip the United States of its sovereignty when the UN took over. Such theories had circulated among far rightists for quite some time, but it was not until the late 1980s that they became part of the public discourse.

26. For example one of Evans's chapters tells the story of Edwin Walker's spurning by the rest of the movement in 1961 and includes an interview by William Rusher at the *National Review* offices in which Rusher tried to expose Walker's connections to the JBS, a tactic Evans expected from liberals but not from a conservative. See "False Leadership," 188.

27. For instance, Welch wondered why Buckley ran for mayor of New York City in 1965, since "if Mr. Buckley and his campaign contributed one iota to an understanding by the people of New York of the lawless horror which was being planned for them in the years ahead—or with which John Lindsay would try to engulf them in a much shorter period—than that contribution entirely escaped our attention." "False Leadership," 92.

28. Eric Westervelt, "Birch Society Teaches Right-Wing Values in Summer Camp," National Public Radio's "All Things Considered," July 24, 1994, transcript no. 1553–4.

29. The JBS, however, experienced tough times in the 1980s. In 1983 Congressman Lawrence McDonald of Georgia, who JBS leaders had recruited as the organization's new chairman, was killed in the downing of Korea Airlines flight KAL 007. Birchers immediately labeled the incident an assassination. Robert Welch's death in 1985 led to a shake-up in the JBS. The society moved from Belmont, Massachusetts, to Appleton, Wisconsin, and although it continued to espouse variations on its original themes, it did try new marketing methods. The society founded Robert Welch University and eventually entered the cyber era with a site on the Internet (www.jbs.org).

30. In many ways, Buchanan took the place of the JBS in the 1992 and 1996 elections, as he forced the GOP to respond to his 3 million supporters, which stretched the big tent to its limits. See Lynn Nofziger, "Victory First, Family Feud Later," *New York Times*, May 12, 1996, A13.

31. See Stephen Engelberg, "A New Breed of Hired Hands Cultivates Grass-Roots Anger," *New York Times*, March 17, 1993, A1, A11.

32. In 1974, however, Republicans as a whole favored Ford over all other possible candidates for president in 1976. A July 1974 Gallup Poll found 27% of Republicans thought that Ford would make the best candidate, followed by 16% each for Reagan and Goldwater. See George Gallup, *The Gallup Poll*, vol. 1: *1972–1975* (Wilmington, Del.: Scholarly Resources, 1978), 292.

33. William Rusher, *The Making of the New Majority Party* (New York: Sheed and Ward, 1975), xiii–xv.

34. Rusher also drew upon strategy he pioneered in his "Crossroads for the GOP" article, which was later expanded by Kevin Phillips in *The Emerging Republican*

Majority (New Rochelle, N.Y.: Arlington, 1969), which emphasized the growing importance of the Sunbelt and suburbs and the diminishing role of the urban voter. To make a third party viable, said Rusher, these new constituencies would need to play crucial roles as activists, rally their communities, and energize a new voting bloc. While Rusher's prediction did not come true in the 1970s, such voters did turn out in force for Ross Perot in 1992. In the meantime many of them declared a powerful allegiance to Ronald Reagan in the 1980s.

35. See "Notes for James L. Buckley on FBI," and James L. Buckley to Mr. Taliafero, January 6, 1978, both in box 124, folder "B," Liebman Papers.

36. The Republican party, flush from twelve years of Ronald Reagan and George Bush leadership, neglected movement culture in the 1992 campaign and paid a severe price. The Democrats, on the other hand, renewed their emphasis on rallies, showmanship, and inclusion and took advantage of Bill Clinton's enthusiasm for such campaigning.

37. In perhaps the most famous example, the 1988 Bush campaign aired a television advertisement featuring an African-American convict, in prison for murder, furloughed for a weekend under Massachusetts Governor Michael Dukakis's system, who then raped a white woman. The Willie Horton commercial was a landmark in political advertising; it featured a revolving-door prison where convicts shuffled in, entered a revolving door, and immediately returned to society as free men. Lee Atwater, Bush's campaign manager, knew the Horton ad would be controversial, but he also knew it would get results. It did. See Edsall with Edsall, *Chain Reaction*, 222–24.

38. See James Atlas, "The Counter Counterculture," *New York Times Sunday Magazine*, February 12, 1995, 33–38, 54, 61–65.

39. Lloyd Grove, "Barry Goldwater's Left Turn," *Washington Post*, July 28, 1994, C2. Goldwater's apparently liberal stances did not, however, preclude conservative candidates from making the pilgrimage to Phoenix in search of an endorsement. See Katharine Q. Seelye, "In Visit to Arizona, Senator [Bob Dole] Emphasizes Goldwater Roots," *New York Times*, February 26, 1996, C11.

40. Bob Herbert, "A Revolution Subsides," *New York Times*, October 23, 1997, A23.

41. William F. Buckley, "Notes towards an Empirical Definition of Conservatism," in *What Is Conservatism?* ed. Frank S. Meyer (New York: Holt, Rinehart and Winston, 1964), 211.

BIBLIOGRAPHY

MANUSCRIPT COLLECTIONS

Arizona Historical Foundation

Joseph Bastien Papers
Barry Goldwater Papers
Theodore Humes Papers

Brown University Library

John Birch Society Records

Federal Bureau of Investigation

FBI file no. 62-104401 Sec. 40

Hoover Institution Archives

American Subject Collection
Karl Baarslag Papers
Elizabeth Churchill Brown Papers
James Burnham Papers
Jameson G. Campaigne Papers
College Republican National Committee Records
George Crocker Papers
Ralph de Toledano Papers
Patrick Dowd Papers
Thomas Byrne Edsall Papers
Williamson Evers Papers
Raymond Feely Papers
Free Society Association Records
Devin Adair Garrity Papers
Kenneth Hall Papers
Walter Judd Papers
Denison Kitchel Papers
Alfred Kohlberg Papers
Thomas A. Lane Papers
Marvin Liebman Papers
Myers G. Lowman Papers
Raymond Moley Papers
National Republic Records
New Left Collection

Pacific Gas and Electric Company Records
Stefan Possony Papers
Frank L. Price Collection
Radical Right Collection
Ronald Reagan Papers
Ronald Reagan Subject Collection
Henry Regnery Papers
Republican National Committee Opposition Research Group Records
Kurt W. Ritter Collection
George Rochester Papers
United States Subversive Activities Control Board Records
Albert C. Wedemeyer Papers
Lloyd Wright Papers

Lyndon Baines Johnson Library

Confidential File
Democratic National Committee Papers
William Hunter McLean Papers
Frederick Panzer Papers
White House Central File

John F. Kennedy Library

John F. Kennedy Presidential Papers
Robert F. Kennedy Papers
President's Office Files
Arthur Schlesinger Papers
Lee White Papers
White House Central File
White House Name File

Library of Congress, Manuscripts and Archives Division

Bull Elephants Records
George Fielding Eliot Papers
William A. Rusher Papers
Lawrence Spivak Papers

Stanford University Libraries, Department of Special Collections

Margaret Meier Papers
Spyros Skouras Papers

University of California, Berkeley, Bancroft Library

Social Protest Collection

University of Oregon, Division of Special Collections and University Archives

Lee J. Adamson Papers
Tom Anderson Papers
T. Coleman Andrews Papers
Bryton Barron Papers
James W. Clise Papers
Lucille Cardin Crain Papers
Pedro A. del Valle Papers
A. G. Heinsohn Papers
James C. Ingebretsen Papers
Howard Kershner Papers
Granville Knight Papers
Archibald Roberts Papers
Willis Stone Papers
Lawrence Timbers Papers

University of Pittsburgh, Department of Special Collections

Archive of Industrial Society
Samuel P. Hays Post World War II Radical Movement Collection

Yale University Library, Manuscripts and Archives

William F. Buckley, Jr., Papers
John V. Lindsay Papers

BOOKS

Aho, James A. *The Politics of Righteousness*. Seattle: University of Washington Press, 1990.
Allitt, Patrick. *Catholic Intellectuals and Conservative Politics in America, 1950–1985*. Ithaca, N.Y.: Cornell University Press, 1993.
Ambrose, Stephen E. *Nixon*. 2 vols. New York: Simon and Schuster, 1989.
American Civil Liberties Union. *The Smith Act and the Supreme Court*. New York: American Civil Liberties Union, 1952.
American Friends Service Committee. *Anatomy of Anti-Communism*. New York: Hill and Wang, 1969.
Anderson, Terry H. *The Movement and the Sixties*. New York: Oxford University Press, 1995.
Andrew, John A., III. *The Other Side of the Sixties*. New Brunswick, N.J.: Rutgers University Press, 1997.
Belknap, Michael R. *Cold War Political Justice*. Westport, Conn.: Greenwood, 1977.
Bell, Daniel, ed. *The New American Right*. New York: Criterion, 1955.
———. *The Radical Right*. Freeport, N.Y.: Books for Libraries Press, 1963.
Berman, William C. *America's Right Turn: From Nixon to Bush*. Baltimore: Johns Hopkins University Press, 1994.

Bernstein, Barton J., ed. *Towards a New Past*. New York: Pantheon, 1968.

Biderman, Albert D. *March to Calumny*. New York: Macmillan, 1963.

Blanchard, Dallas A. *The Anti-Abortion Movement and the Rise of the Religious Right*. New York: Twayne, 1994.

Bork, Robert H. *The Constitutionality of the President's Busing Proposals*. Washington, D.C.: American Enterprise Institute, 1972.

Bouscaren, Anthony T. *A Guide to Anti-Communist Action*. Chicago: Regnery, 1958.

Boyarsky, Bill. *The Rise of Ronald Reagan*. New York: Random House, 1968.

———. *Ronald Reagan*. New York: Random House, 1981.

Branch, Taylor. *Parting the Waters*. New York: Simon and Schuster, 1988.

Brennan, Mary C. *Turning Right in the Sixties*. Chapel Hill: University of North Carolina Press, 1995.

Brinkley, Alan. *Voices of Protest*. New York: Vintage, 1982.

Broder, David S., and Stephen Hess. *The Republican Establishment*. New York: Harper and Row, 1967.

Brown, Edmund G. *Reagan and Reality*. New York: Praeger, 1970.

Broyles, J. Allen. *The John Birch Society: Anatomy of a Protest*. Boston: Beacon, 1961.

Buchanan, Patrick J. *Right from the Beginning*. Boston: Little, Brown, 1988.

Buckley, William F., Jr. *Cruising Speed*. New York: Putnam, 1971.

———. *Did You Ever See a Dream Walking?* Indianapolis: Bobbs-Merrill, 1970.

———. *Four Reforms*. New York: Putnam, 1973.

———. *God and Man at Yale*. Chicago: Regnery, 1951.

———. *On the Firing Line*. New York: Random House, 1989.

———. *Rumbles Left and Right*. New York: Putnam, 1963.

———. *The Unmaking of a Mayor*. New York: Viking, 1966.

———. *Up from Liberalism*. New Rochelle, N.Y.: Arlington, 1968.

Burkett, Elinor. *The Right Women*. New York: Scribner, 1998.

Burnham, James. *The Coming Defeat of Communism*. New York: John Day, 1950.

———. *The Web of Subversion*. New York: John Day, 1954.

Cain, Edward. *They'd Rather Be Right*. New York: Macmillan, 1963.

California Bureau of Criminal Identification and Investigation. *Para-Military Organizations in California*. Sacramento: California Bureau of Criminal Identification and Investigation, 1965.

Cannon, Lou. *Reagan*. New York: Putnam, 1982.

———. *Ronnie and Jesse: A Political Odyssey*. Garden City, N.Y.: Doubleday, 1969.

Carnes, Mark C., ed. *Past Imperfect: History according to the Movies*. New York: Henry Holt, 1995.

Carter, Dan T. *From George Wallace to Newt Gingrich: Race in the Conservative Counterrevolution, 1963–1994*. Baton Rouge: Louisiana State University Press, 1996.

———. *The Politics of Rage*. New York: Simon and Schuster, 1995.

Chambers, Whittaker. *Witness*. New York: Random House, 1952.

Chester, Lewis, Godfrey Hodgson, and Bruce Page. *An American Melodrama*. New York: Viking, 1969.

Christman, Henry M., ed. *The Public Papers of Chief Justice Earl Warren*. New York: Simon and Schuster, 1959.

Cohane, John Philip. *White Papers of an Outraged Conservative*. Indianapolis: Bobbs-Merrill, 1972.

Cohen, Lizabeth. *Making a New Deal*. Cambridge: Cambridge University Press, 1990.

Combs, James. *Film Propaganda and American Politics*. New York: Garland, 1994.

Combs, James, ed. *Movies and Politics: The Dynamic Relationship*. New York: Garland, 1993.

———. *Polpop 2: Politics and Popular Culture in America Today*. Bowling Green, Ohio: Bowling Green State University Popular Press, 1991.

Committee on Un-American Activities. "The American National Exhibition, Moscow, July 1959," *Hearings before the Committee on Un-American Activities*. Washington, D.C.: Government Printing Office, 1959.

———. *The American Negro in the Communist Party*. Washington, D.C.: Government Printing Office, 1954.

———. *The Communist Program for World Conquest: Consultation with Gen. Albert C. Wedemeyer*. Washington, D.C.: Government Printing Office, 1958.

———. *The House Committee on Un-American Activities: What It Is—What It Does*. Washington, D.C.: Government Printing Office, 1958.

———. *Internal Communism (The Communist Mind): Staff Consultation with Frederick Charles Schwarz*. Washington, D.C.: Government Printing Office, 1957.

———. *The Irrationality of Communism: Consultation with Dr. Gerhart Niemeyer*. Washington, D.C.: Government Printing Office, 1958.

———. *The Truth about the Film "Operation Abolition,"* pt. 1. Washington, D.C.: Government Printing Office, 1961.

Courtney, Kent, and Phoebe Courtney. *The Case of General Edwin A. Walker*. New Orleans, La.: Conservative Society of America, 1961.

———. *The Silencers*. New Orleans, La.: Conservative Society of America, 1965.

Crawford, Alan. *Thunder on the Right*. New York: Pantheon, 1980.

Cummings, Milton C., Jr., ed. *The National Election of 1964*. Washington, D.C.: Brookings Institution, 1966.

Dallek, Robert. *Ronald Reagan: The Politics of Symbolism*. Cambridge, Mass.: Harvard University Press, 1984.

Davis, Kathy Randall. *But What's He Really Like?* Menlo Park, Calif.: Pacific Coast, 1970.

DeKoster, Lester. *The Christian and the John Birch Society*. Grand Rapids, Mich.: William B. Eerdmans, 1965.

Diamond, Sara. *Facing the Wrath*. Monroe, Maine: Common Courage, 1996.

———. *Roads to Dominion*. New York: Guilford, 1995.

Diggins, John P. *Up from Communism*. New York: Columbia University Press, 1975.

Duffy, James P. *Who Is Destroying Our Military?* East Elmhurst, N.Y.: Torchlight, 1966.

Dunn, Charles W., and J. David Woodard. *American Conservatism from Burke to Bush*. New York: Madison, 1991.

———. *The Conservative Tradition in America*. Lanham, Md: Rowman and Littlefield, 1996.

Earl Warren Oral History Project. *Earl Warren: The Chief Justiceship*. Berkeley, Calif.: Bancroft Library Oral History Office, 1977.

Edsall, Thomas Byrne, with Mary D. Edsall. *Chain Reaction*. New York: Norton, 1992.

Edwards, Anne. *Early Reagan*. London: Hodder and Stoughton, 1987.

Edwards, Lee. *The Conservative Revolution*. New York: Free Press, 1999.

———. *Goldwater*. Washington, D.C.: Regnery, 1995.

———. *Reagan*. San Diego, Calif.: Viewpoint, 1967.

Eiler, Keith E., ed. *Wedemeyer on War and Peace*. Stanford, Calif.: Hoover Institution Press, 1987.

Ellsworth, Ralph E., and Sarah M. Harris. *The American Right Wing: A Report to the Fund for the Republic*. Washington, D.C.: Public Affairs Press, 1962.

Evans, M. Stanton. *The Future of Conservatism*. New York: Holt, Rinehart and Winston, 1968.

Faber, Harold, ed. *The Road to the White House*. New York: McGraw-Hill, 1965.

Fariello, Griffin. *Red Scare*. New York: Norton, 1995.

Faryna, Stan, Brad Stetson, and Joseph G. Conti, eds. *Black and Right*. Westport, Conn.: Praeger, 1997.

Felsenthal, Carol. *The Sweetheart of the Silent Majority: The Biography of Phyllis Schlafly*. Garden City, N.Y.: Doubleday, 1981.

Formisano, Ronald P. *The Transformation of Political Culture*. New York: Oxford University Press, 1983.

Forster, Arnold. *John Birch in Uniform*. New York: Anti-Defamation League, 1965.

Forster, Arnold, and Benjamin Epstein. *Danger on the Right*. New York: Random House, 1964.

———. *The Radical Right: Report on the John Birch Society and Its Allies*. New York: Random House, 1966.

———. *Report on the John Birch Society, 1966*. New York: Vintage, 1966.

Francis, Samuel. *Beautiful Losers: Essays on the Failure of American Conservatism*. Columbia: University of Missouri Press, 1993.

Frankel, Ernest. *Tongue of Fire*. New York: Dial, 1960.

Fried, Richard M. *Nightmare in Red*. New York: Oxford University Press, 1990.

Fryer, Russell G. *Recent Conservative Political Thought: American Perspectives*. Washington, D.C.: University Press of America, 1979.

Gaddis, John Lewis. *Strategies of Containment*. New York: Oxford University Press, 1982.

Gallup, George. *The Gallup Poll*, vol. 1: *1972–1975*. Wilmington, Del.: Scholarly Resources, 1978.

Gallup Poll Data. *Gallup Poll Reports, 1935–1968*. Princeton, N.J.: American Institute of Public Opinion, 1969.

Gellerman, William. *Martin Dies*. New York: John Day, 1944.

Gerstle, Gary, and Steve Fraser, eds. *The Rise and Fall of the New Deal Order, 1930–1980*. Princeton, N.J.: Princeton University Press, 1989.

Gilder, George F., and Bruce K. Chapman. *The Party That Lost Its Head*. New York: Knopf, 1966.

Gillon, Steven M. *Politics and Vision: The ADA and American Liberalism, 1947–1985*. New York: Oxford University Press, 1987.

Gitlin, Todd. *The Sixties: Years of Hope, Days of Rage*. New York: Bantam, 1987.

Gold, Howard J. *Hollow Mandates: American Public Opinion and the Conservative Shift*. Boulder, Colo.: Westview, 1992.

Goldberg, Robert Alan. *Barry Goldwater*. New Haven, Conn.: Yale University Press, 1995.

Goldwater, Barry. *The Conscience of a Conservative*. Washington, D.C.: Regnery Gateway, 1960.

———. *The Conscience of a Majority*. Englewoood Cliffs, N.J.: Prentice-Hall, 1970.

———. *Why Not Victory?* New York: McGraw-Hill, 1962.

———. *With No Apologies*. New York: William Morrow, 1979.

Goldwater, Barry M., with Jack Casserly. *Goldwater*. Garden City, N.Y.: Doubleday, 1988.

Goodman, Walter. *The Committee*. New York: Farrar, Straus and Giroux, 1968.

Goodwyn, Lawrence. *The Populist Moment*. Oxford: Oxford University Press, 1978.

Gordon, Rosalie M. *Nine Men against America*. New York: Devin-Adair, 1958.

Gottfried, Paul. *The Conservative Movement*, rev. ed. New York: Twayne, 1993.

Gottfried, Paul, and Thomas Fleming. *The Conservative Movement*. New York: Twayne, 1988.

Green, John C., et al. *Religion and the Culture Wars*. Lanham, Md.: Rowman and Littlefield, 1996.

Griffin, G. Edward. *The Great Prison Break: The Supreme Court Leads the Way*. Belmont, Mass.: Western Islands, 1970.

———. *The Life and Words of Robert Welch*. Thousand Oaks, Calif.: American Media, 1975.

Grove, Gene. *Inside the John Birch Society*. Greenwich, Conn.: Gold Medal, 1961.

Hamby, Alonzo. *Liberalism and Its Challenges*. New York: Oxford University Press, 1992.

Hardisty, Jean. *Mobilizing Resentment*. Boston: Beacon, 1999.

Hartz, Louis. *The Liberal Tradition in America*. New York: Harcourt Brace Jovanovich, 1955.

Heale, M. J. *American Anticommunism*. Baltimore: Johns Hopkins University Press, 1990.

Hero, Alfred O., Jr. *American Religious Groups View Foreign Policy: Trends in Rank-and-File Opinion, 1937–1969*. Durham, N.C.: Duke University Press, 1973.

Hicks, L. Edward. *"Sometimes in the Wrong, but Never in Doubt."* Knoxville: University of Tennessee Press, 1994.

Himmelstein, Jerome L. *To the Right: The Transformation of American Conservatism*. Berkeley: University of California Press, 1990.

Hixson, William B., Jr. *Search for the American Right Wing*. Princeton, N.J.: Princeton University Press, 1992.

Hochman, Stanley, and Eleanor Hochman. *The Penguin Dictionary of Contemporary American History*. New York: Penguin, 1997.

Hodgson, Godfrey. *America in Our Time*. New York: Vintage, 1976.

———. *The World Turned Right Side Up*. Boston: Houghton Mifflin, 1996.

Hofstadter, Richard. *The Age of Reform*. New York: Knopf, 1956.

Holmes, Joseph R., ed. *The Quotable Ronald Reagan*. San Diego, Calif.: JRH, 1975.

Hoover, J. Edgar. *Masters of Deceit*. New York: Henry Holt, 1958.

Horn, Stephen. *Memorandum to the California Newspapers, Radio, and Television*. n.p., 1964.

Hughes, H. Stuart. *Gentleman Rebel*. New York: Ticknor and Fields, 1990.

Hutchins, Lavern C. *The John Birch Society and United States Foreign Policy*. New York: Pageant, 1968.

Isserman, Maurice. *If I Had a Hammer: The Death of the Old Left and the Birth of the New Left*. New York: Basic, 1987.

Jackson, Felix. *So Help Me God*. New York: Viking, 1955.

Jones, J. Harry. *The Minutemen*. Garden City, N.Y.: Doubleday, 1968.

Judis, John B. *Grand Illusion*. New York: Farrar, Straus and Giroux, 1992.

———. *William F. Buckley, Jr., Patron Saint of the Conservatives*. New York: Simon and Schuster, 1988.

Katcher, Leo. *Earl Warren: A Political Biography*. New York: McGraw-Hill, 1967.

Katz, Richard N., comp. *The Legal Struggle to Abolish the House Committee on Un-American Activities: The Papers of Jeremiah Gutman*. Berkeley, Calif.: Meiklejohn Civil Liberties Institute, 1980.

Kessel, John H. *The Goldwater Coalition*. Indianapolis: Bobbs-Merrill, 1968.

Kirk, Russell. *The Conservative Mind*. Chicago: Regnery, 1953.

———. *The Wise Men Know What Wicked Things Are Written on the Sky*. Washington, D.C.: Regnery Gateway, 1987.

Klatch, Rebecca E. *A Generation Divided*. Berkeley: University of California Press, 1999.

Klehr, Harvey, John Earl Haynes, and Fridrikh Igorevich Firsov. *The Secret World of American Communism*. New Haven, Conn.: Yale University Press, 1995.

Kolkey, Jonathan Martin. *The New Right, 1960–1968: With Epilogue, 1969–1980*. Washington, D.C.: University Press of America, 1983.

Kominsky, Morris. *The Hoaxers*. Boston: Branden, 1970.

Knebel, Fletcher. *Seven Days in May*. New York: Bantam, 1962.

Kovel, Joel. *Red Hunting in the Promised Land*. New York: Basic, 1994.

Kuklick, Bruce. *The Good Ruler*. New Brunswick, N.J.: Rutgers University Press, 1988.

Lamb, Karl A., and Paul A. Smith. *Campaign Decision-Making: The Presidential Election of 1964*. Belmont, Calif.: Wadsworth, 1968.

Lesher, Stephan. *George Wallace: American Populist*. Reading, Mass.: Addison-Wesley, 1994.

Leuchtenberg, William. *Franklin D. Roosevelt and the New Deal*. New York: Harper and Row, 1963.

Levine, Lawrence. *Highbrow/Lowbrow*. Cambridge, Mass.: Harvard University Press, 1988.

———. *The Unpredictable Past*. New York: Oxford University Press, 1993.

Liebman, Marvin. *Coming Out Conservative*. San Francisco, Calif.: Chronicle, 1992.

Lively, Earl, Jr. *The Invasion of Mississippi*. Belmont, Mass.: American Opinion, 1963.

Lokos, Lionel. *Hysteria 1964*. New Rochelle, N.Y.: Arlington, 1967.

Lukas, J. Anthony. *Common Ground*. New York: Knopf, 1986.

Mahoney, J. Daniel. *Actions Speak Louder*. New Rochelle, N.Y.: Arlington, 1968.

Markmann, Charles Lam. *The Buckleys*. New York: William Morrow, 1973.

McAllister, Ted V. *Revolt against Modernity*. Lawrence: University Press of Kansas, 1996.

McEvoy, James, III. *Radicals or Conservatives?* Chicago: Rand McNally, 1971.

McNall, Scott G. *Career of a Radical Rightist*. Port Washington, N.Y.: National University Publications, 1975.

Meese, Edwin, III. *With Reagan*. Washington, D.C.: Regnery Gateway, 1992.

Meyer, Frank S., ed. *What Is Conservatism?* New York: Holt, Rinehart and Winston, 1964.

Miles, Michael W. *The Odyssey of the American Right*. New York: Oxford University Press, 1980.

Miller, James. *"Democracy Is in the Streets."* New York: Simon and Schuster, 1987.

Mintz, Frank P. *The Liberty Lobby and the American Right*. Westport, Conn.: Greenwood, 1985.

Moley, Raymond. *How to Keep Our Liberty*. New York: Knopf, 1952.

———. *The Republican Opportunity*. New York: Duell, Sloan and Pearce, 1962.

Morreale, Joanne. *A New Beginning*. Albany: State University of New York Press, 1991.

Morris, Edmund. *Dutch*. New York: Random House, 1999.

Murray, Charles. *Losing Ground*. New York: Basic, 1984.

Nash, George H. *The Conservative Intellectual Movement in America since 1945*. New York: Basic, 1976.

O'Connor, John J., ed. *Image as Artifact: The Historical Analysis of Film and Television*. Malabar, Fl.: Robert E. Krieger, 1990.

O'Reilly, Kenneth. *Hoover and the Un-Americans*. Philadelphia, Pa.: Temple University Press, 1983.

Oshinsky, David. *A Conspiracy So Immense*. New York: Free Press, 1983.

Patterson, James T. *Grand Expectations*. New York: Oxford University Press, 1996.

———. *Mr. Republican: A Biography of Robert Taft*. Boston: Houghton Mifflin, 1972.

Perkus, Cathy, ed. *COINTELPRO: The FBI's Secret War on Political Freedom*. New York: Monad, 1975.

Petro, Sylvester. *The Kohler Strike*. Chicago: Regnery, 1961.

Philbrick, Herbert A. *I Led 3 Lives*. New York: Grosset and Dunlap, 1952.

Phillips, Kevin. *The Emerging Republican Majority*. New Rochelle, N.Y.: Arlington, 1969.

Piper, J. Richard. *Ideologies and Institutions*. Lanham, Md.: Rowman and Littlefield, 1997.

Podhoretz, Norman. *Breaking Ranks*. New York: Harper and Row, 1979.

Pollack, Jack Harrison. *Earl Warren: The Judge Who Changed America*. Englewood Cliffs, N.J.: Prentice-Hall, 1979.

Powers, Richard Gid. *G-Men: Hoover's FBI in American Popular Culture*. Carbondale: Southern Illinois University Press, 1983.

———. *Not without Honor*. New York: Free Press, 1995.

———. *Secrecy and Power: The Life of J. Edgar Hoover*. New York: Free Press, 1987.

Rae, Nicol C. *The Decline and Fall of the Liberal Republicans from 1952 to the Present*. Oxford: Oxford University Press, 1989.

Reagan, Ronald. *An American Life*. New York: Simon and Schuster, 1990.

————. *The Creative Society*. New York: Devin-Adair, 1968.

Reagan, Ronald, with Richard G. Hubler. *Where's the Rest of Me?* New York: Duell, Sloan and Pearce, 1965.

Redekop, John Harold. *The American Far Right: A Case Study of Billy James Hargis and the Christian Crusade*. Grand Rapids, Mich.: William B. Eerdmans, 1968.

Reinhard, David W. *The Republican Right since 1945*. Lexington: University Press of Kentucky, 1983.

Reuther, Victor G. *The Brothers Reuther and the Story of the UAW*. Boston: Houghton Mifflin, 1976.

Riesman, David. *The Lonely Crowd*. New Haven, Conn.: Yale University Press, 1958.

Roback, Thomas. *Recruitment and Incentive Patterns among Grassroots Republican Officials: Continuity and Change in Two States*. Beverly Hills, Calif.: Sage, 1974.

Rogin, Michael Paul. *Ronald Reagan: The Movie*. Berkeley: University of California Press, 1987.

Rovere, Richard H. *The Goldwater Caper*. New York: Harcourt, Brace and World, 1965.

Rubin, Lillian B. *Busing and Backlash*. Berkeley: University of California Press, 1972.

Rusher, William A. *The Making of the New Majority Party*. New York: Sheed and Ward, 1975.

————. *The Rise of the Right*. New York: National Review Books, 1993.

Schechter, Harvey B. *How to Listen to a John Birch Society Speaker*. New York: Anti-Defamation League of B'nai B'rith, n.d.

Schneider, Gregory L. *Cadres for Conservatism*. New York: New York University Press, 1999.

Schoenberger, Robert A., ed. *The American Right Wing*. New York: Holt, Rinehart and Winston, 1969.

Schomp, Gerald. *Birchism Was My Business*. New York: Macmillan, 1970.

Schuparra, Kurt. *Triumph of the Right*. Armonk, N.Y.: M. E. Sharpe, 1999.

Shadegg, Stephen. *What Happened to Goldwater?* New York: Holt, Rinehart and Winston, 1965.

Silk, Mark. *Spiritual Politics*. New York: Simon and Schuster, 1988.

Simmons, Jerold. *Operation Abolition*. New York: Garland, 1986.

Skousen, W. Cleon. *The Naked Communist*. Salt Lake City, Utah: Ensign, 1958.

Smith, John, as told to Stanhope T. McReady. *Birch Putsch Plans for 1964*. Domino, 1963.

Sorman, Guy. *The Conservative Revolution in America*. Chicago: Regnery, 1985.

Staebler, Neil, and Douglas Ross. *How to Argue with a Conservative*. New York: Grossman, 1965.

Steinfels, Peter. *The Neo-Conservatives: The Men Who Were Changing American Politics*. New York: Simon and Schuster, 1979.

Stockman, David A. *The Triumph of Politics*. New York: Harper and Row, 1986.

Stouffer, Samuel A. *Communism, Conformity, and Civil Liberties*. Gloucester, Mass.: Peter Smith, 1963.

Sugrue, Thomas J. *The Origins of the Urban Crisis*. Princeton, N.J.: Princeton University Press, 1996.

Taft, Robert A. *A Foreign Policy for Americans*. Garden City, N.Y.: Doubleday, 1951.

Tanenhaus, Sam. *Whittaker Chambers: A Biography*. New York: Random House, 1997.

Thimmesch, Nick. *The Condition of Republicanism*. New York: Norton, 1968.

Thorne, Melvin J. *American Conservative Thought since World War II: The Core Ideas*. New York: Greenwood, 1990.

Trilling, Lionel. *The Liberal Imagination*. New York: Viking, 1950.

U.S. Bureau of the Census. *Historical Statistics of the United States: Colonial Times to 1970*. Pts. 1 and 2. Washington, D.C.: Government Printing Office, 1975.

————. *Statistical Abstract of the United States: 1972*. Washington, D.C.: Government Printing Office, 1972.

U.S. Senate. *Hearings before the Special Preparedness Subcommittee of the Committee on Armed Services*, "Military Cold War Education and Speech Review Policies," pts. 3 and 4. Washington, D.C.: Government Printing Office, 1962.

————. *Report by Special Preparedness Subcommittee of the Committee on Armed Forces*, "The Use of Military Personnel and Facilities to Arouse the Public to the Menace of the Cold War and to Inform and Educate Armed Services Personnel on the Nature and Menace of the Cold War." Washington, D.C.: Government Printing Office, 1962.

Utter, Glenn H., and John W. Storey. *The Religious Right: A Reference Handbook*. Santa Barbara, Calif.: ABC-CLIO, 1995.

Vahan, Richard. *The Truth about the John Birch Society*. New York: Macfadden, 1962.

Viguerie, Richard. *The New Right: We're Ready to Lead*. Falls Church, Va.: Viguerie, 1981.

Waldor, Milton A. *Peddlers of Fear*. Newark, N.J.: Lynnross, 1966.

Weaver, John D. *Warren: The Man, the Court, the Era*. Boston: Little, Brown, 1967.

Weeks, William Rawle. *Knock and Wait a While*. Boston: Houghton Mifflin, 1957.

Welch, Robert. *The Blue Book*. Belmont, Mass.: Western Islands, 1959.

————. *The Life of John Birch*. Chicago: Regnery, 1954.

————. *The Neutralizers*. Belmont, Mass.: John Birch Society, 1963.

————. *The New Americanism*. Boston: Western Islands, 1966.

————. *The Politician*. Belmont, Mass.: John Birch Society, 1963.

————. *The Road to Salesmanship*. New York: Ronald Press, 1941.

Wesbrook, Stephen D. *Political Training in the United States Army: A Reconsideration*. Columbus, Ohio: Mershon Center of Ohio State University, 1979.

West, Cornel. *Race Matters*. Boston: Beacon, 1993.

Whitaker, Robert, ed. *The New Right Papers*. New York: St. Martin's, 1982.

White, F. Clifton, with William J. Gill. *Suite 3505*. New Rochelle, N.Y.: Arlington, 1967.

————. *Why Reagan Won*. Chicago: Regnery Gateway, 1981.

White, G. Edward. *Earl Warren: A Public Life*. New York: Oxford University Press, 1982.

White, John Kenneth. *Still Seeing Red*. Boulder, Colo.: Westview, 1997.

White, Theodore H. *The Making of the President—1964*. New York: Athenaeum, 1965.

————. *The Making of the President—1968*. New York: Athenaeum, 1969.

Whitfield, Stephen J. *The Culture of the Cold War*. Baltimore: Johns Hopkins University Press, 1991.

Whyte, William H., Jr. *The Organization Man*. New York: Simon and Schuster, 1956.

Wilcox, Clyde. *Onward Christian Soldiers?* Boulder, Colo.: Westview, 1996.

Williams, William Appleman. *The Tragedy of American Diplomacy*. New York: Norton, 1959.

Wills, Garry. *Reagan's America*. New York: Penguin, 1988.

Wolfe, Gregory. *Right Minds: A Sourcebook of American Conservative Thought*. Chicago: Regnery, 1987.

Woodward, C. Vann. *Thinking Back: The Perils of Writing History*. Baton Rouge: Louisiana State University Press, 1986.

Wyman, Carolyn. *I'm a Spam Fan*. Stamford, Conn.: Longmeadow, 1993.

Young, Fred Douglas. *Richard M. Weaver, 1910–1963: A Life of the Mind*. Columbia: University of Missouri Press, 1995.

INDEX